J. S. FORBES

HALLMARK

A History of the London Assay Office

J. S. FORBES

HALLMARK

A History of the London Assay Office

With a foreword by
PHILIPPA GLANVILLE

THE GOLDSMITHS' COMPANY

UNICORN PRESS

LONDON

UNICORN PRESS
21 Afghan Road
London SW I I OQD

Published by Unicorn Press 1999 in conjunction with
the Goldsmiths' Company
Copyright © John Forbes 1998

The moral right of John Forbes to be identified as the
author of this work has been asserted in accordance
with the Copyright, Designs and Patents Acts of 1988

A catalogue record for this book is available
from the British Library

ISBN 0 906290 26 0

Set in Bembo
Designed and produced by
Pardoe Blacker Publishing Limited
Lingfield · Surrey

Printed in Hong Kong
by Midas Printing Limited

Contents

GOLDSMITHS' HALL

WHEN JOHN FORBES retired as Deputy Warden of the London Assay Office in 1983, after some thirty years' service, the Wardens little realised that he would devote another seven years to research the history of the place from which he had just retired. We are indebted to him for the care and attention which he has brought to this task, and the Goldsmiths' Company is delighted to publish his research so that a wider readership may benefit from his knowledge which is founded on a lifetime's experience of assaying and hallmarking. Seven centuries of hallmarking is a remarkable story to relate and deserves this excellent book.

PRIME WARDEN

19 May 1999

Acknowledgements

I WOULD LIKE to express my sincere gratitude to David Beasley, Librarian, and Susan Hare, former Librarian of the Goldsmiths' Company. Their encyclopaedic knowledge of the history of the Company and their expert advice on many aspects of it have been invaluable. They have both given freely of their time to checking my manuscript and have suggested a number of improvements. David's help in the selection of illustrations is especially appreciated. May I additionally thank them and Jenny Prentice for producing on countless occasions heavy minute books, each one of which had to be carried to the library from their place of safety in a remote part of Goldsmiths' Hall. I would also wish to thank Robin Buchanan-Dunlop, Clerk of the Company, David Evans, Deputy Warden, Frank Bennett, former Deputy Warden and Paul Johnson, Superintendent Assayer, for their assistance with the final chapter of the book.

I am indebted to Christopher Challis of the School of History, University of Leeds, for much useful information concerning Tudor coinage and the Royal Mint, and to Mrs H. Bradley, Archivist of the Haberdashers' Company, Mrs P. Benedikz, Librarian of the Birmingham Assay Office, Mrs J. Richardson, Librarian of the Sheffield Assay Office, Ronald Le Bas, former Assay Master of the Dublin Assay Office, Graham Dyer, Librarian and Curator of the Royal Mint and Ian Pickford for their kindness in supplying answers to my queries. I would further like to thank the Guardians of the Standard of Wrought Plate in Birmingham for permission to quote from their early minute books.

Foreword

Consumer protection in the precious metals has a long history. The emperor Anastasius is given the credit for introducing the first systematic control and marking system; Byzantine governors in the late fifth and early sixth century were stamping official marks on plate. Although this is taken as the earliest evidence for the formal testing and marking of gold and silver objects, the Old Testament is rich in references to weighing out precious metal, and both ingots and coinage had a precious content to be recorded and protected in the interests of good government.

The story of how these controls evolved in London, from the earliest references to protecting 'sterling' and the King's mark of the *teste de leoparde* to the present-day complexities of laser marking and atomic absorption, is the theme of this fascinating study

Phrases from this apparently narrow and esoteric world have enriched our daily language. To have 'gone through the fire', to be 'tried and tested', to refer to a sure test as a 'touchstone', to praise something as of 'sterling standard', or, adopting the jargon of the advertising world, to describe something as 'hallmark quality' is to exploit the specialised language long in use in assay office procedures. The procedures were driven by a real need for certainty and the system had to be utterly dependable; indeed, it had the force of law.

In his loving and painstaking study, the fruit of many years' labour, John Forbes constantly refers to the human element, to the characters – goldsmiths, chancellors and kings, workmen – whose acts are documented in the Minute and Committee books of the Company and the specialised records of the Assay Office itself. This is the first time that these sources, principally but not solely the rich seven hundred-year old archive of the Goldsmiths' Company, have been explored from this perspective.

Great names from the history of English silver people the pages – De Lamerie in trouble with the Customs for exporting unmarked plate to the Tsarina of Russia, and Henry VIII's goldsmith, Robert Amadas, pocketing the official mark punches and disappearing from the City.

Potentially these records could make a unique contribution to the history of the goldsmiths' craft and so to the larger story of the economic history of Britain. From the prosperity of the late 1630s, a sudden drop in the total weight of plate passing through the Assay Office reflects the political turmoil of the Civil War. From 1773 the daily weights of all large and small work passing through the Office is recorded in surviving ledgers. Much later, in the early twentieth century, the First World War had the curious effect of increasing the demand for smallwares, especially silver watch cases.

The technical information which John Forbes lays bare has never been available before and is far removed from the traditional concerns of collectors and curators who rely on the evidence of hallmarks with the utmost trust. The minutiae of the Assay Office can bring unexpected rewards for the study of decorative art. A splendid Elizabethan ewer and basin, richly engraved with English monarchs and scenes from the Bible with a birthright theme bears the date letter *k with a difference* in use for part only of the year 1567/8. Thanks to a quirk of institutional history – the arrival of Thomas Keeling as Assayer after Christmas 1567 – we can date the testing and marking of this magnificent set between January and July 1568, just when Elizabeth was facing political criticism from the nobility over her failure to marry and growing support for her rival Mary Queen of Scots. The ewer and basin, which was a special commission, is a subtle expression of the prevailing tension at court. Although its original patron is still unidentified, the hallmark's precision will one day be a vital clue to its purpose.

For metallurgists the methods of assaying have become more and more scientific and precise over the last century, a far cry from the touchstone and cupel of the early Tudor assay wardens. But alongside this increasing precision runs an alternative history of increasingly clever frauds and their detection, a theme which John Forbes handles with discretion. This inevitable consequence of the burgeoning nineteenth century market in antique plate found an immediate response in the Assay Office. As early as 1849 'spurious wares' with transposed marks were being offered for sale in Bath, as the Minute books ruefully note. The rediscovery of the meaning of marks and date letters, a code always understood by the Assay Office staff, was rapidly exploited by connoisseurs and dealers from the 1850s. It has been the foundation for 150 years of silver scholarship but the creativity of fraudulent and inventive operators still gives work to the Antique Plate Committee today.

This study is a model of dedicated scholarship made accessible and its discoveries will reflect new light into many areas of silver study.

PHILIPPA GLANVILLE
Richmond, February 1999

Introduction

TESTING ARTICLES made of precious metal and stamping them with special marks – hallmarks – to indicate that they are of a minimum standard of purity has been carried out by the Worshipful Company of Goldsmiths for nearly seven centuries. Thus the Goldsmiths' Company, one of the oldest of the craft guilds or City livery companies, has an unrivalled record of public service in the field of consumer protection. Moreover, it has always considered this duty to be of the utmost importance, and throughout the whole period has spared no effort to ensure an effective and efficient service.

There are currently four authorized assay offices in the United Kingdom where articles are tested (assayed) and hallmarked. The London Assay Office is administered by the Goldsmiths' Company but other independent governing bodies are responsible for the offices at Birmingham, Sheffield and Edinburgh. Under the present British law, any article which is offered for sale in the course of trade and described as gold, silver or platinum must be hallmarked, unless it falls within one of the few specifically exempted categories. The four assay offices therefore provide modern purchasers with a unique protection.

We shall be concerned here only with the London Assay Office, tracing its history and development from early times. It is the story of an establishment that was originally charged with the task of testing and marking a relatively small number of articles but has grown into one which handles more than five million items each year. The process of assaying and hallmarking is one of the earliest applications of chemical analysis and we shall note the influence of advancing scientific knowledge in this field during the last two centuries. It will also be of interest to see how the work of the Office has been affected, not only by the increasing population of the country, but also by changing fashions, fluctuating economic climates and various measures imposed by governments of the day. Problems – human and otherwise – were encountered from time to time and we shall see how they were dealt with, but we should not forget that it is these which tend to be highlighted rather than the long periods of trouble-free routine that went unrecorded.

The prime purpose of a hallmark is to guarantee that the metal of which an article is made contains a certain minimum proportion of gold, silver or (since 1975) platinum. However, the various symbols comprising a complete hallmark convey other information, such as the name of the maker or sponsor of the article, the date of marking and the assay office concerned. These additional details are naturally of particular significance in the case of antique silver – so much so that some knowledge of hallmarks is almost essential for a collector or anyone with more than a passing interest in old silver.

On countless occasions the Goldsmiths' Company has taken action against offenders who have disregarded the hallmarking statutes for personal gain – in times past by fining or imprisonment on the wardens' own authority and in later years by prosecution in the courts. It has always been a function of the Assay Office to provide the necessary evidence and its detailed records provide an insight into the way in which the Company has discharged the responsibilities it shares with the other hallmarking authorities for protecting the marks and discouraging fraud.

Another aspect of the work of the Assay Office is the Trial of the Pyx. This periodic testing of samples of newly minted coins of the realm has been the responsibility of the Goldsmiths' Company for many centuries. Although entirely separate from its hallmarking function and requiring the attention of the staff for short periods only, it is nevertheless one of the principal events in the calendar.

A medieval craft guild was composed of members of a single trade and its essential features were common worship, mutual help (including relief for the poor), social gatherings and the encouragement of good and honest commercial practice. Thus the membership of the goldsmiths' guild was initially restricted to craftsmen working in gold and silver and refiners who supplied the metal. Later, because the freedom of the Company could be claimed by patrimony, an increasing proportion of its members were from other occupations. However, the importance of retaining close association with the craft has always been acknowledged and the proportion of 'trade' members has not been allowed to fall below about a quarter of the total.

The main sources for this book have been the records of the Goldsmiths' Company but other relevant material has been found in the Public Record Office, the British Museum and Guildhall Libraries. The Company's minute books are remarkable not only for having survived almost intact, but for the scrupulous care with which they have been compiled over the centuries. The earliest book of 'Wardens' and Court Minutes' dates from 1334. There is unfortunately one volume missing, namely for the period 1579 to 1592; otherwise the series is complete and provides an amazing storehouse of information concerning the diverse activities of the Company. The entries are somewhat fragmentary for the early years but gradually they become longer and from the sixteenth century onwards records of meetings are usually written in considerable detail.

The fourteenth-century minute books are in Norman French and accordingly difficult to read; however, they contain relatively few references to assaying. The researches of the late Professor T.F. Reddaway and Miss L.E.M. Walker published in *The Early History of the Goldsmiths' Company* have been largely relied upon for this period and for part of the fifteenth century. *The Tudor Coinage* by Dr C.E. Challis should also be mentioned as an invaluable source of information concerning the relationship between the Company and the Mint during the sixteenth century.

In addition to the eighty-one bound volumes containing the minutes of Wardens' and Court meetings covering the period 1334 to 1942, there is much other archival material such as account books, apprenticeship and freedom books and miscellaneous loose documents. There are also more than one hundred and fifty books relating solely to the Assay Office, dating from 1727 to 1978, and containing statistics of work received for hallmarking, assayers' records, cash receipts etc. Furthermore, there are forty-one books in which details of the registrations of makers' marks from 1697 to 1975 are recorded.

To have given a reference for every use of material from the Company's records would have produced a confusing text as there would have been so many. Therefore no references are given if such was the source, but dates are liberally cited and it should not be difficult to locate an original entry if anyone so wishes.

Modern spelling has been used throughout and all dates are in accordance with the New Style Calendar, i.e. the new year commencing on 1 January. Where a twelve-month period extends over two calendar years – for example the term of office of the Prime Warden or Lord Mayor – it will be referred to by a single date, that of the year in which it commences. Similarly a 'date letter' will be denoted by a single year, namely the one in which it was first used. Weights are recorded according to the troy system (1 oz troy is equivalent to 1.097 oz avoirdupois).

CHAPTER ONE

THE EARLY YEARS

L ITTLE IS KNOWN of craftsmen working in gold or silver in Britain before the Norman conquest, although undoubtedly they did exist. The first positive evidence of a regular trade in articles made from precious metals is a reference in the royal records to a guild of goldsmiths which was heavily fined in 1180 for being established without leave from the Crown.[1] Seventeen other guilds were mentioned, but as their fines were smaller, we can assume that the goldsmiths – whose number included those we now call silversmiths – were members of a flourishing craft. Gold would have been mainly confined to rings, bangles, brooches and similar items; silver, however, would have been used not only for articles of personal adornment but also for many domestic wares such as spoons, dishes and cups – albeit for the custom of well-to-do members of society. Silver was also the principal metal for the coinage of the realm.

In its pure state silver is too soft for the manufacture of articles that have to stand up to constant wear; it is necessary to add another metal in order to produce an alloy of sufficient hardness. The one that has been most frequently used for this purpose from ancient times is copper, a base metal. Gold is similarly hardened with copper or silver or a mixture of both. Obviously, the cost of the resultant precious metal alloy is in inverse proportion to the amount of hardening agent. Hence it was realized at an early date that a standard was necessary to ensure that an unscrupulous craftsman or moneyer was not using too much of the cheaper metal. The sterling standard for silver coinage is thought to have been first adopted in Saxon times.[2] As the responsibility for ensuring an adequate supply of money lay with the King, he was naturally concerned to see that this standard (11 oz 2 dwt in the pound troy) was maintained by those entrusted with the prerogative of minting. For this reason arrangements for periodic independent testing of the coinage were instituted at least as early as the thirteenth century, under a procedure which became known as the Trial of the Pyx.

In those days, and indeed throughout several successive centuries, the silver coinage and silver articles were in a sense complementary, since their worth was largely the intrinsic value of the metal itself. Silver articles would frequently be sold by owners in need of cash; a stock of plate was a convenient form of savings for a rainy day. Unlike a hoard of money it had a practical use, but if necessary it could be consigned to the melting pot and converted into currency. It was clearly desirable, therefore, that there should be a standard for silver articles in line with that of the coinage. The benefit of a standard for gold wares was also apparent, because of their exceptional value and the use of the metal as a medium of exchange.

Thus in 1238 an Ordinance of Henry III, directed at workers in gold or silver and entitled 'De auro fabricando in Civitate Londonarium', decreed that no gold should be used 'of which the mark was not worth at least one hundred shillings' nor any silver 'worse than the King's money'.[3] The Mayor and aldermen were ordered to appoint six faithful and discreet goldsmiths of the City of London who were to have the responsibility of ensuring adherence to these requirements. It was the first of many measures designed to protect members of the public from the fraudulent practices of dishonest craftsmen. It is perhaps as well to make the point once again that the term 'goldsmiths' includes workers in silver; the word 'silversmith' was not in common usage at that date.

STATUTE OF EDWARD I

It is, however, in 1300 that our story really begins. Edward I, having in the previous year passed a statute designed to protect the coinage and to conserve the nation's silver, now turned his attention to the closely related problem of the standard of gold and silver wares. By a further statute he provided the rudiments of a hallmarking system which has continued without interruption down to the present day.[4] Silver articles were to be up to the sterling standard, the same as the coinage, and no vessel of silver was to leave the hands of the maker until it had been assayed (tested) by the 'guardians of the craft' and marked with a leopard's head, a symbol probably taken from the Royal Arms. As already mentioned, sterling was 11 oz 2 dwt of pure silver in the pound troy, which in the modern notation is 925 parts of silver in 1000 parts of the alloy, or a purity of 92.5 per cent.

Gold articles were not required to be marked but they had to be no worse than the 'touch of Paris'; and the appointed guardians were instructed to go round the goldsmiths'

THE LEOPARD'S HEAD MARK; *an early example struck on the bowl of a fifteenth-century diamond point spoon.*

Gold and silver assays

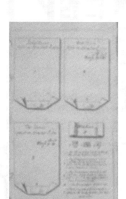

To appreciate the significance of certain parts of the early chapters it is necessary to understand the ways in which the fineness of gold and silver alloys were formerly expressed – the millesimal system and percentages are relatively modern concepts.

TROY WEIGHTS AND SILVER ASSAYS

The troy system was formerly used not only for weighing precious metals but also in the case of silver alloys for denoting their fineness (purity). In this system:

> 24 grains (gr) = 1 pennyweight (dwt)
> 20 dwt = 1 troy ounce (oz)
> 12 oz = one pound troy (lb)

The fineness was expressed as the number of ounces and pennyweights in the pound troy (ie the weight of pure silver in one pound troy of the alloy). The words 'in the pound troy' were often omitted – typical results of assays might be reported as '11 oz ½dwt' or '11oz 3dwt'. Assayers sometimes used another notation, reporting their results as the number of ounces and pennyweights 'better' or 'worse' than the sterling standard (11 oz 2 dwt in the lb troy). Thus

> 11 oz ½dwt would be written as 1½dwt worse
> 11 oz 3 dwt would be written as 1 dwt better.

The troy pound and pennyweight are no longer legal weights – but the prices of precious metals are still quoted as so much per troy ounce.

GOLD ASSAYS

A different method based on the carat system was used for denoting the fineness of gold. 24 carats represented pure gold and each carat was divided into 4 grains.

Between 1575 and 1798 the only legal standard for gold was 22 carats and assay reports were usually given with reference to this standard – for example, '1 carat 2 grains worse'. Even after the introduction of lower legal stands, the results were still reported with reference to the 22 carat standard.

shops to check their wares accordingly. The word 'touch' in this context refers to the standard, but it could also mean a mark, as 'to touch' meant to strike an official mark on an article. The standard for gold, the 'touch of Paris', was 19⅕ carats, or 800 parts per thousand. One carat is equivalent to one twenty–fourth part; pure gold is therefore 24 carats. Provincial England was not forgotten; these same standards for gold and silver were to apply not only in London but also in other towns of the kingdom.

It is clear that purchasers were being defrauded by makers who were selling articles of gold or silver of inferior purity and it was recognized that they were in need of protection. By this enactment the King placed the onus of ensuring compliance with the standards firmly on the senior members of the craft or guild.

THE FIRST CHARTER OF THE GOLDSMITHS' COMPANY

In 1327 the goldsmiths' guild was granted its first Royal Charter by Edward III.[5] The members were given the right to choose 'good, true and competent men' with fairly wide powers by which to exercise a close control of the trade. Four such men, called wardens, were elected each year, the changeover taking place on 19 May, the day of the goldsmiths' patron saint, St Dunstan. The first or Upper Warden later became known as the Prime Warden. He will be referred to by the latter title in the following pages. After some years a Court of Assistants was established, consisting at first of present and past wardens, but later of other senior members as well. The Court became the governing body of the Company, responsible for all major decisions but the wardens met more frequently and attended to routine matters. The other members were divided into two classes; those with special privileges were called liverymen and the rest were known as 'the generality' or later as freemen. Two respected senior members were elected 'renters' for one year, their duties being the admini- stration of the properties in the City which the Company began to acquire from the end of the fourteenth century. Increasing activities soon necessitated the appointment of two permanent officials, the Clerk and the Beadle, but we do not know the precise dates on which they first took office. The Clerk came to have considerable influence on the policies of the Company and his advice was frequently sought by the wardens and Court. At a later period he took over the duties of the renters. He was usually a practising lawyer and acted as the Company's solicitor, responsible for negotiating new charters and instituting prosecutions for offences against the hallmarking statutes.

Eight years after the granting of the charter, a statute was passed which well illustrates the close relationship between silverware and the coinage of the realm. The statute of 1335 forbade goldsmiths to melt coins as a source of raw material and prohibited the export not only of coinage but also silver or gold in the form of plate.[6] The official searchers at the ports would have had the benefit of the statute of 1300 – at least in theory – in that they would have been able to distinguish articles of silver from base metal by the presence of the mark of the leopard's head. Indeed it may have been partly with this in mind that the mark was prescribed.

Another statute in 1363 strengthened the existing regulations by introducing a compulsory maker's mark.[7] Every master goldsmith was required to have his own symbol, known to those whom the King appointed to oversee his work; and he was to 'set' it on all articles of his making after they had been assayed by the overseers and struck with the 'King's mark'. In the absence of any evidence of royal overseers in London at this time we must presume that the Company continued to exercise the powers already bestowed on it. The maker's mark, however, became an established symbol. Originally it took the form of a device, such as a bird, a star or a cross – probably in many cases the same as the sign by which the maker's shop was known – but later the use of the maker's initials became the more usual practice.

Before long the Company was in serious danger of losing the prerogative which it had been granted under the statute of 1300 and the subsequent Royal Charter. Goldsmiths were suspected of selling substandard wares and in 1379 the Commons petitioned the King to put assaying under municipal control in cities and boroughs with the aid of the Master of the Mint. In reply the King decided that he would appoint assayers in London and other places and that his own officers would be responsible for the marking. But it was expressly stated that the Ordinance was experimental and that it was to last only until the next Parliament.[8] Probably nothing was done as there is no record of any royal appointments. In the meantime the Company was actively pressing its own case. It achieved its objective when Richard II granted a second charter in 1393: the Company's status and responsibilities not only remained intact but its powers were thereby considerably strengthened.[9]

EARLY TESTS FOR SUBSTANDARD WARES

In the fourteenth century London was by far the largest town in the kingdom, with a population which has been estimated at 40,000. There existed a thriving trade in gold and silver wares and the Goldsmiths' Company was one of the most prestigious of the guilds. In common with the other guilds, it was only too anxious to exercise control over its craft – in the interests of honest dealing and to protect its members against unfair competition from workers who used substandard metal, a malpractice which could be extremely lucrative. Unfortunately, the records of the Company's activities in the fourteenth and early fifteenth centuries do not give a completely clear picture of the manner in which the wardens carried out their duty of assaying and marking. A number of surviving silver spoons of this period which bear the stamp of a leopard's head in the bowl are proof that the Company's wardens were marking articles; we also know that they carried out assays, and had more than one method of testing available to them.

One method was of great antiquity – the touchstone test.[10] The gold or silver article was rubbed on a smooth black stone to produce a narrow streak of the metal. Then a similar streak was made alongside, using an alloy of known purity, called a touch-needle. The colours of the two streaks were compared. Quite small differences could be detected and in this way it was possible to determine whether the article was up to the standard of the touch-needle. Although less accurate than other methods the touchstone test had the advantage that it could be carried out in a goldsmith's shop or on the premises of a maker. As a means of testing gold it was later improved by introducing an additional operation – treating the streaks with either nitric acid or dilute aqua regia and noting any difference in the reactions. With this modification it still has a use owing to its speed and convenience; in the hands of an experienced assayer it is capable of providing fairly reliable results for gold alloys above the 14 carat standard.

ASSAY BY FIRE

A more accurate method was the cupellation assay, sometimes called the fire assay. This was based on the same principle as that used in the commerical refining of silver, and provided the main method by which the purity of silver articles was determined until comparatively recent times.[11]

TOUCHSTONE, *late seventh century* AD, *excavated in an Anglo-Saxon cemetery at Lord of the Manor near Ramsgate in 1977. Gold streaks can be clearly seen in the centre.*

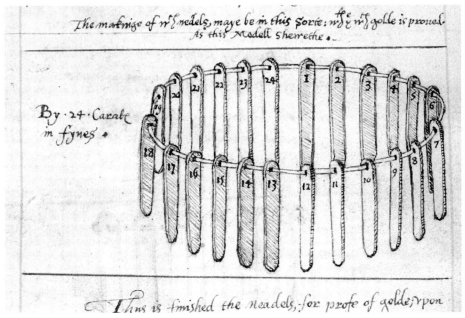

The makinge of n[?] nedels, maye be in this Sorte: n[?] n[?] golle is proued. As this Modell shewethe.

By ·24· Carate in fynes ·

This is finished the neadels, for profe of golde; vpon

TOUCHNEEDLES. *Illustration from* A Goldsmith's Storehouse, *1604.*

In order to test an article a sample of the metal had first to be removed from it. This could sometimes be accomplished by cutting off a small piece but more usually it involved the taking of scrapings, an operation usually referred to as 'drawing'. A portion of the scrapings or cuttings was carefully weighed on a sensitive balance made specially for assaying. In the sixteenth century the nominal weight of sample favoured was either 15 or 30 grains. After wrapping in a sheet of pure lead foil the weighed sample was transferred to a cupel, a small cup made of bone ash, which had previously been positioned in a charcoal-fired muffle furnace maintained at red heat with a through draught of air. Under these conditions the lead and all the base metals in the sample were converted into their molten oxides and absorbed into the cupel. The precious metal, being neither oxidized nor absorbed, remained on the surface. When the lead and base metals were judged to be completely separated from the precious metals the cupel was allowed to cool and the solidified bead removed and accurately weighed. The fineness was then calculated by comparing the weight of the bead with the weight of the original sample. Several samples could be cupelled at the same time. As the bead also contained any gold which might have been present (for example as an impurity), the final result actually represented the silver plus gold content. However, since the value of gold was much higher than that of silver, this was considered to be of little consequence.

An essential requirement for an assayer was an accurate set of weights. This was based on a single weight called an 'assay pound' or 'pound subtil' which

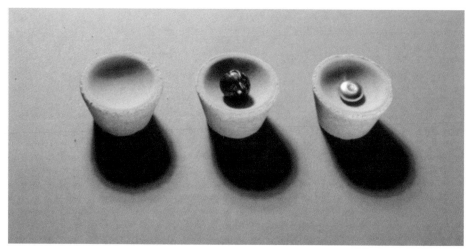

CUPELLATION ASSAY FOR SILVER, *showing (left) empty cupel, (centre) cupel with sample wrapped in lead foil and (right) cupel with silver bead after furnace treatment.*

was commonly 30 grains. The assay pound did not have to be exactly 30 grains provided the lesser weights were true fractions of it. It was not too difficult for the assayer to make a set of weights and to check one against another in order to ensure a correct relationship.

In the sixteenth century, and possibly earlier, the cupellation method was also used for the assay of gold. It is in fact still employed for this metal since no modern technique has comparable accuracy. The procedure is similar to the silver assay but more lengthy. After weighing the sample a quantity of pure silver is added so that the total silver content (including any already present in the sample) is equal to about two and a half times the weight of gold. The additional silver is necessary for complete separation of the gold. The sample and the added silver are cupelled with lead as already described. The silver has now to be removed from the precious metal bead. This is effected by flattening the bead into a thin strip, coiling it and then immersing in boiling nitric acid (formerly called aqua fortis), an operation known as 'parting'. After some minutes a 'cornet' of practically pure gold remains; this is annealed at red heat and then weighed. By comparing its weight with that of the original sample the gold content of the latter can be calculated. An alternative, but less accurate method for assaying gold, called cementation, was in use before nitric acid was known. No extra silver was added but after cupellation any already present was removed by heating the bead of gold and silver in a crucible with a mixture of brick dust, salt and sulphates of iron and copper. The silver chloride thus formed was absorbed into the brick dust and the gold recovered.

Although eminently satisfactory for the assay of gold, the cupellation method suffered from certain disadvantages when used for silver – inconsistent assay results sometimes led to controversies and complaints which are recorded by the Company. Considerable skill and experience were required on the part of the assayer. He had to be competent in the use of the balance, in judging by eye the temperature of the furnace and in determining the precise point at which cupellation was complete. Many references in old books and

THE ASSAY OFFICE *in the seventeenth century, showing the Assayer at the balance. Detail from the frontispiece of* A New Touchstone for Gold and Silver Wares, *1677.*

manuscripts refer to the necessary qualities. One of the earliest is in a tract of 1507 which says:

> ... there is no man that can do this by the teaching of any man but only by experience of proof and of exercise, notwithstanding he may fail sometimes in this reckoning that doth make him full expert and cunning therein; but with good taking heed thereunto, the very truth shall be known to him ... [12]

And another, written a hundred years later, gives a list of the various essentials the assayer should attend to, such as the furnace, cupels, lead and weights, and then goes on to say:

> In all of which the premises if any defect be made the assay is uncertain and unreportable; which asketh a good judgement, gotten by years and experience than by speculation and dispute ... that besides his grounded experience in this science or mystery should have a perfect eye to view and as steady a hand to weigh; for other men's senses cannot serve him ... [13]

If accurate results were to be obtained the assayer needed proper equipment, in particular a sensitive balance, accurate weights and a well-constructed muffle furnace. Given all these requisites and despite certain underlying weaknesses when used for the assay of silver, the method was capable of giving remarkably good results. It was by far the earliest example of chemical analysis: centuries were to elapse before satisfactory methods were devised for determining the purity of other metals, such as copper or tin.

SEARCHES

During the fourteenth century and most of the fifteenth the assaying and marking, or 'assay and touch' – the term used at that time – were undertaken by the wardens, either by themselves or, if lacking the necessary skill, probably assisted by another member of the Company. In common with the practice of other City livery companies, such as the Girdlers, Skinners and Cutlers, the wardens carried out regular searches of shops and workplaces during which they kept a sharp lookout for substandard wares. They also made special searches at the great annual fair of St Bartholomew in the City of London and at Our Lady Fair in Southwark. Bartholomew Fair took place annually in Smithfield (originally in the churchyard of the Priory of St Bartholomew) from 23 to 25 August. It was first held in the reign of Henry II in response to the growing cloth trade. All kinds of wares and trinkets were offered for sale and there were many side shows, the latter gradually taking over from serious trading. The fair eventually fell into disrepute owing to incidents of riotous behaviour and it was closed in 1855. In most years between the fifteenth and eighteenth centuries the wardens conducted a search at the fair, dressed in their ceremonial gowns and hoods. The right to hold a fair in Southwark was

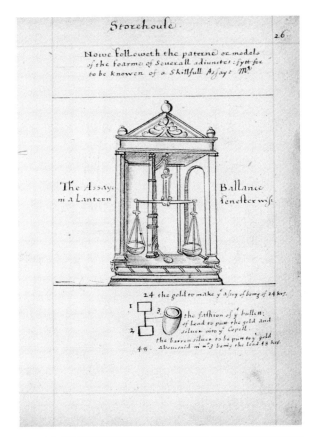

ASSAYER'S BALANCE AND
OTHER APPARATUS *used in
the assaying of gold and silver.
From* A Goldsmith's
Storehouse, *1604.*

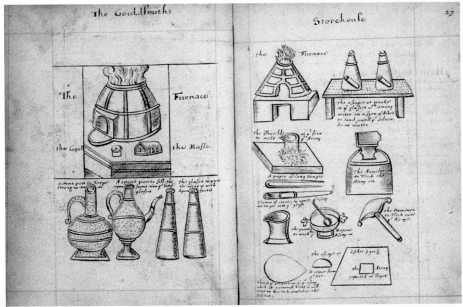

granted to the Corporation of London in 1402 and was withdrawn in 1765. In the latter part of the fourteenth century the wardens extended their periodical searches to other parts of the kingdom.

As in the case of many other London trades, the goldsmiths were grouped in certain fairly small and well defined areas. They were located in two principal sites in the City, one in Lombard Street and the adjacent lanes, the other at the western end of Cheapside, including the streets leading northwards from it – Foster Lane, Gutter Lane and Wood Street. Those with premises outside these districts, either in the City itself or in neighbouring places such as Southwark or Westminster, were few in comparison, although Southwark was of some significance as an area in which there were a number of foreigners working. Some goldsmiths, mainly foreign, were practising in precincts immune from the City's jurisdiction, such as St Martin-le-Grand. A great influx of gold-smiths from Germany and the Low Countries took place during the fifteenth and sixteenth centuries, and the Company was much concerned to see that they obeyed its regulations.

Cheapside – or Cheap as it was then called – was the main street of London. The goldsmiths' shops, known as Goldsmiths' Row, situated on its southern side to the west of the Church of St Mary-le-Bow, were to become a special feature of the City. They prompted an Italian visitor writing in about 1500 to say: 'In one single street named Cheapside leading to St Paul's there are fifty-two goldsmiths' shops, so rich and full of silver vessels, great and small, that in all the shops in Milan, Rome, Venice and Florence put together I do not think there would found so many of the magnificence that are to be seen in London'. And we know that in this same street there existed a thriving goldsmiths' quarter at least two centuries earlier.[14]

In the course of their visitations to goldsmiths' workshops the wardens made touchstone tests of the gold and silver wares they found on the premises. By the end of the fourteenth century, and probably earlier, they were also taking samples from silver articles for the purpose of carrying out cupellation assays. The accumulated residues of these samples, called 'diets', are referred to in the minute books on a number of occasions, the first specific mention being in 1387. The weights of the diets are recorded for each of the years 1468, 1469 and 1472 to 1475 and they are substantial, averaging about 6½lb troy, thus indicating that a large number of samples must have been taken. In each of the above years there is also a diet of about 1 oz of gold. In one case this is described as 'assays of gold' and in another as 'broken gold fined' (meaning refined) – it seems therefore that some gold assays were also carried out by a method other than the touchstone, either by cupellation or cementation.

We do not know for certain where the cupellation assays were carried out, but the likelihood is that from the second half of the fourteenth century they would have been at the Company's own Hall. In 1339 a site and building had

GOLDSMITHS' ROW *in Cheapside, from a watercolour of the 1547 coronation procession of Edward VI by S.H. Grimm. Grimm's work, owned by the Society of Antiquaries of London, is a copy of a wall painting, no longer extant, at Cowdray House.*

been acquired in Foster Lane, slightly to the north of the goldsmiths' quarter or 'goldsmithry' in Cheapside.[15] The building was subsequently used as a common meeting place. It is therefore reasonable to suppose that the Assay Office dates from about that time, although, it is not mentioned in the rather fragmentary early records of the Company's activities. The exact date on which the first assay was carried out in Goldsmiths' Hall must therefore remain unknown, but six and a half centuries after the acquisition of the original building the Assay Office is still housed on the same site, although the Hall has been twice rebuilt.

Exactly how the assaying was carried out before the Company had its own headquarters can only be conjectured: maybe reliance was placed entirely on touchstone testing. And as regards the 'touching' of articles with the mark of the leopard's head, again there is no direct evidence of where this took place, but it is possible that, even after the Hall was available, it was done on the premises of the maker during the wardens' searches. This would have been quite feasible, as only simple equipment was required – an anvil, hammer and punch. It is also possible, however, that once the Company had its own premises workers may sometimes have brought their wares to the Hall to be assayed and touched; it would have been inconvenient if they had always had to await the next visit of the wardens to their own workshop before offering their wares for sale.

The efficiency of the system must have varied considerably in the early years in view of the unsettled conditions that existed throughout much of the fourteenth century. Disasters such as the Black Death would in all probability have resulted in a virtual cessation of the goldsmiths' trade, and in consequence the need for assaying. Since the plague at its height claimed the lives of all four wardens in one year (1348) it would indeed have been extremely difficult to maintain any continuity, even had it been required, and a gap of two years in the Company's records at this time is an indication that its activities were temporarily halted. There were to be further pestilences in 1361 and 1368, and the decrease in population alone following these catastrophes would have adversely affected the demand for silver to a considerable degree.

Furthermore, the accuracy of assaying must have suffered to some extent due to the frequent change of wardens. Their terms of office expired after one year, although they were often re-elected at a future date; it was only later that they served for four consecutive years. Some of them would have been trained as assayers but certainly not all. If they had no prior experience they would either have had to learn the technique or more probably would have called upon the services of a member of the Company who possessed the necessary skill. There appears to have been a shortage of such members in 1446 because the Prime Warden, an ex-warden and a senior liveryman were 'deputed to learn the craft and assay of all manner of gold and silver both in the cupel and cement [cementation]'.

Whilst in office the wardens had to devote a considerable amount of their time to the Company, but they did not undertake their duties entirely without reward. Among their perquisites were the accumulated residues of assay samples, the 'diets'. By 1469, however, some members had become dissatisfied that the wardens should be entitled to keep the diets, feeling that they ought to be made available for the benefit of the Company as a whole. A general assembly decided that in future the wardens should undertake their searches at least once a quarter, or more frequently if necessary and that all diets of spoons, cups, salt-cellars and other wares taken by them should be kept for making standing cups and 'other jewels' for the use of the Company.

In addition to the samples taken for the purpose of testing finished articles for compliance with the standard, there may have been some arrangement for the assaying of the ingots or raw materials used by the workers. We know that this was the practice after 1478 and it is possible that it was already in operation before that date. Unfortunately the records are insufficiently detailed for us to be absolutely sure of the procedures adopted, but those described above are the most likely. What is certain is that the wardens were kept actively employed in dealing with the affairs of the Company, not least when concerned with assaying and marking.

TRIAL OF THE PYX

As early as 1248 goldsmiths had been called upon to carry out an independent test of recently minted coins. In that year the mayor and citizens of London were entrusted by the King 'to elect twelve discreet and lawful men of our city of London and join with them twelve skilful goldsmiths of the same city ... who shall go before our Barons of the Exchequer at Westminster and examine upon oath, both the old and the new money of our land, that it be made of good silver ... ' [16] A record also survives of a trial of coins, which became known as the Trial of the Pyx, in 1475, which was entrusted to a jury consisting of five goldsmiths, all senior members of the Company, who were sworn before the Lord Chancellor at Westminster. [17] They were Humphrey Hayford, who was serving as Prime Warden and who was to become Lord Mayor of London two years later; Robert Hill, who had been Second Warden in 1472 and became Prime Warden in 1481 and 1482; William Elger, who was six times elected a warden; John Kirkeby and David Panter who also served as wardens.

Members of the Company were also called upon from time to time to provide the official 'trial plates' which were used as controls when testing the coins. Much expertise and care were devoted to making these plates to ensure that their composition was in accordance with the prescribed standard of the coinage. Portions of many of them have survived, including two made in 1477

The Royal Mint

The Tower of London in the sixteenth century.

From the thirteenth century until 1810 the Royal Mint was housed in the Tower of London. In that year it moved to new premises outside the perimeter of the Tower and in 1975 moved to its present home in Llantrisant, South Wales.

There has always been a close association between the Goldsmiths' Company and the Mint. For more than two hundred years, from the early fifteenth century, the principal officers of the Mint were often goldsmiths, either deputizing for an absent favourite of the Crown or appointed in their own right. The wealthy Hugh Bryce, Bartholomew Read, Martin Bowes and Richard Martin were all senior officers of the Mint who also served as Prime Warden of the Goldsmiths' Company; they also all became Lord Mayor and received knighthoods.

Several of the Company's assayers held positions at the Mint during part of their careers and members of the Company have served on the jury at the Trial of the Pyx (the periodic testing of the coinage of the realm, see page 29) since the thirteenth century.

(one of sterling silver and the other gold of a standard of 23 carats 3½ grains). Each has a certificate stating that Robert Hill, William Wodeward, John Kirkeby and Miles Adys were sworn in the Star Chamber before the Chancellor of England, Treasurer and Privy Seal and many other noble lords of the King's Council to make the plates.[18] Hill and Kirkeby had served on the Pyx jury two years before; Woodward had been a warden on five separate occasions and Adys was Fourth Warden at the time.

The plates were made in the form of a sheet which was cut into several portions. They are now generally referred to as 'trial plates' but in former times they were known as 'trial pieces'. After about 1560 the current official standard was also frequently called 'the indented piece' because the several portions were cut with serrated edges. For the sake of uniformity, however, the description 'trial plate' will be used here throughout for the plates used in testing the coinage. (This will additionally serve to distinguish them from the standards used by the Company in connection with hallmarking, which were also called 'trial pieces'.)

GOLDSMITHS' WEIGHTS AND SUBSTANDARD WARES

A further important responsibility of the Company was the checking of balances and weights used in the goldsmiths' workplaces and shops. Obviously substantial ill-gotten profits could be made by the use of faulty balances or weights. Checking was normally carried out by the wardens during their searches and any offenders subsequently fined. But occasionally, as in 1360, the Company ordered a general sizing of all weights used by London goldsmiths. In 1417 a new standard pile (set of weights) was provided and kept at the Hall for this purpose. Goldsmiths – as well as assayers – used the troy system (see page 17).

In those days the price of a gold or silver article was apportioned between the cost of manufacture (the fashion) and the value of the precious metal. The latter accounted for the major part of the total sum. Every goldsmith's shop would have had a balance and set of weights, and each article purchased would have been weighed – probably in front of the customer. The total cost would then have been calculated according to the current price of the precious metal plus the charge for the fashion.[19] This is still the practice in most countries of the Middle East. In fact, if one can imagine entering one of the fifteenth century shops in Cheapside, the impression gained would probably be not dissimilar to the experience of visiting a typical modern counterpart in the goldsmiths' quarter of an Arab market – except that there would generally have been more silver than gold in the London shop. Both might afford a glimpse of two or three craftsmen working in a back room with hammers, anvils and other tools.

During their searches the wardens frequently found articles that appeared to be below standard when tested by touchstone, including many that were too small to bear the Company's mark. Their normal practice was to seize the suspect wares and bring them back to the Hall for further testing. If the articles were silver they were assayed by cupellation and the precious metal content precisely determined. Should their suspicions be confirmed, the wardens, sitting as a court, summoned the culprits to appear before them and meted out appropriate punishment. In the first instance it would be a fine, for a second offence a larger fine, and if the vendor or worker continued to offend he might be fined an even greater sum or be imprisoned.[20] To ensure that the substandard articles were not put to sale they were usually broken by the wardens before they were returned to their owners. The second page of the Company's first minute book records that in the year 1334 Walter de Algate and Thomas Bamme were fined 3s 4d for making a buckle of substandard gold. There are countless entries relating to such offenders in this and the subsequent minute books and details of their punishments are usually recorded.

An example of a flagrant offender was Thomas Wood who had four shops in Cheapside, the tenure of three of which he held for a period of sixty years.

During a search of his premises in 1470 the wardens found two substandard silver cups for which he was fined 13s 4d. He was also fined for a similar offence in respect of two silver-gilt salt cellars and yet again for a girdle harness. Finally, on a later search the wardens took various articles to the Hall and ordered him to send others for confirmatory assays. These proved to be greatly below standard and he was fined £10, a considerable sum in those days. After this he was a reformed character, becoming a warden in 1475 and eight times Prime Warden as well as an alderman. Wood died a wealthy man. The Company eventually inherited his Cheapside property.

The Company's charters gave the wardens the right to search not only in London but also in other parts of the country. Accordingly, from time to time they set out and rode to distant places in England and often included on their itinerary important fairs such as those at Stourbridge in Cambridgeshire, Winchester, Bristol or Salisbury. Suspect wares were seized and taken to the Hall. Often they had been made by London craftsmen, as in the case of some spoons found in 1468 on the premises of one John Fabian of Coggeshall in Essex. These articles were not only substandard but, more seriously, bore imitation marks of the leopard's head. The actual makers – Deryk Knyff, an alien working in Southwark and Thomas Gomercy – were imprisoned for five days and each fined 20 shillings, a surprisingly mild punishment in the circumstances.

But the standard of wares made outside London could hardly be controlled adequately by infrequent searches. Moreover, the arrangements for the assay and marking of plate in London, which relied on periodic visits by the wardens, gave ample scope for less scrupulous members of the trade to circumvent the law. An ordinance of 1379 stated that gold and silver wrought by goldsmiths was often less fine than it ought to be and the same was again noted in a statute of 1423, which made any warden who marked a substandard article liable to a penalty.[21] No doubt the wardens were doing their best, but nevertheless many wares were being sold which were below the minimum legal standard. With the object of further strengthening the law, another statute was enacted in 1478[22]. However, the earlier statute, which also designated York, Newcastle, Lincoln, Norwich, Bristol, Salisbury and Coventry as assay towns, was not repealed and for many years it remained one of the integral parts of hallmarking legislation. It forbade the sale of wrought silver unless it was as fine as sterling and required that no harness of silver be sold unless marked with the leopard's head.[23]

CHAPTER TWO

THE FIRST PERMANENT ASSAYER

THE STATUTE OF 1478 was an important one for the Company. As in the case of some of the earlier statutes its object was partly to safeguard the coinage – from melting or exportation, for example – but it was more especially concerned with regulating the craft of goldsmiths. Many of the existing provisions were restated and given new emphasis. One change, however, was that the minimum legal standard for gold articles was now fixed at 18 carats (750 parts per thousand). The standard for silver wares was unaltered – they were to be 'as fine as the sterling; except such thing as required solder in the making of the same, which shall be allowed according to the solder necessary ... ' The Act also stated that no 'harness of silver plate, or jewel of silver' wrought in the City of London or within two miles of it was to be set to sale before it had been touched with the mark of the leopard's head crowned, providing it would bear the same, and with the worker's own mark or sign. The workers had to make known their marks to the wardens. Foreigners ('strangers') had to work in the 'open streets' and the wardens were given explicit powers to search their workshops.

The statute also stated that the 'keeper of the touch' (one of the wardens) had been putting the mark of the leopard's head on substandard wares, and if this could be proved in regard to any particular article, he would be liable to forfeit double its value. One half was payable to the King and the other to the party 'grieved or hurt'. Moreover, any person was entitled to sue for the same – thus significantly extending the legislation. Naturally the wardens were worried that they might be taken to court if a substandard ware bearing the Company's mark were offered for sale, and it was almost certainly this clause in the statute which led them to take a close look at the manner in which the assaying and marking was conducted.

It was realized that the wardens' periodic inspections were insufficient in themselves to ensure that all articles had been assayed and marked as required by law, nor did the arrangements provide an adequate safeguard against substandard plate being inadvertently struck with the leopard's head. The system was not working satisfactorily, principally because of the intermittent nature of the assaying and the fact that not all wardens had the necessary skill. But there was another reason why the wardens themselves might have wished to alter the procedure. By a decision of the whole Company taken nine years earlier they had been deprived of their perquisites – the residues of samples or diet. Consequently there was little incentive for them personally to carry out large numbers of assays, entailing much time and inconvenience.

The wardens, with the approval of the whole membership of the Company, decided therefore to make a fundamental change in the system. In December 1478 a full-time salaried assayer was appointed to carry out all the routine assaying on their behalf. In future workers would be obliged to bring their newly made wares to the Hall; if these were found by the Assayer to be up to standard, they would be duly stamped with the Company's marks. This is the origin of 'hallmark' – the mark of Goldsmiths' Hall – although the word was not in common usage until much later; the expression then current was still 'the touch'. The Assayer's duties were precisely defined and he was required to swear on oath to make true assays 'without favour, affection, hate or evil will showing to any party' (see Appendix I). The wardens had made an eminently sensible decision and it resulted in a system which has remained unaltered in principle to the present day.

CHRISTOPHER ELYOT, THE FIRST ASSAYER

It was of paramount importance that the holder of the newly created position should have impeccable qualifications and that his integrity should be beyond question. The Company appointed Christopher Elyot to the new post at a salary of £20 per annum. Although not specifically recorded, it is possible that he and his family were given living quarters within the Hall, as were his successors. Aged about thirty, Elyot, a liveryman, had been apprenticed to Hugh Bryce, a distinguished member of the Company, who was Prime Warden at the time of the new appointment. Bryce had held various senior offices at the Royal Mint, besides running a lucrative business as a goldsmith in Cheapside which brought a number of royal commissions. He also had other commercial interests. In short he was a rich and influential man, becoming Lord Mayor of London in 1485 and receiving a knighthood in the same year. It is probable that Elyot had learned to assay at the Mint during his apprenticeship with Hugh Bryce and there is no doubt that he was highly skilled in the art. In 1480 he was elected Renter, combining the duties with his normal work.

It was fortunate for the Goldsmiths' Company that at the time the statute of 1478 was enacted its affairs were in the capable hands of four distinguished wardens (see page 49). Hugh Bryce, the Prime Warden, was supported by Henry Coote, Miles Adys and William Palmer.[1] Coote was later elected an alderman

THE ORDER FOR QUARTERAGE *and the appointment of Christopher Elyot, the first Assayer. (Goldsmiths' Company Minute Book A, 1478.)*

and sheriff and served as Prime Warden no less than seven times between 1483 and 1506. He was a notable benefactor to the Company, leaving it a number of properties under his will. Miles Adys became City Chamberlain, an important civic post, from 1479 to 1484 and had been one of the four members of the Company responsible for making the trial plates in 1477 (see page 30). Palmer was a successful goldsmith and supplier of jewels to the royal court. The decision to reform the old system of assaying and marking which had been in operation for nearly two hundred years was undoubtedly due to the foresight of these four men and to their grasp of the principles involved. Three months earlier they had ordered the compilation of the Company's first volume of ordinances and statutes. This book, which is still preserved in its

THE OATH OF THE ASSAYER. *(Goldsmiths' Company Book of Ordinances, 1478–83.)*

original binding, contains the ordinances or rules which regulated the trade practices and other duties of the Company's members. They cover such matters as working to the true standards of fineness of gold and silver and the enrolling of apprentices. The book also records the oaths which had to be taken by the wardens, the Clerk, the Assayer and the Beadle, and by new freemen on completion of their apprenticeship. Members were expected to comply rigidly with the ordinances, which for several centuries were read out at least once every year at a general assembly of the whole Company or sometimes to the livery only.

As first holder of the post of Assayer (usually referred to as the Common Assayer, but also sometimes called the Assay Master and sometimes the Deputy Assayer or just the Assayer), Christopher Elyot's duties were clearly defined in the solemn oath he was required to take on his annual election to the office (see Appendix I). He had to receive goods daily between six and ten o'clock each weekday morning, to take samples, normally in the form of scrapings, from all articles and to make assays using the fire assay (cupellation) method. He also had to ensure that every article carried the appropriate maker's mark; if it did not he was to return it unassayed.[2] If he found an article to be substandard and it was new, he had to report to the wardens, who would normally break it and fine the maker. If, on the other hand, it had been made before 1478, he could return it to the owner intact, with the proviso that if the same article were submitted a second time he had to tell the wardens so that punitive action could be taken against the offender.

Elyot would certainly have been a competent craftsman as well as a skilled assayer; the makers would not have been happy if someone without a background and knowledge of the making of silverware were subjecting their costly products to an operation which could be potentially damaging. The quantity of articles he had to deal with is not known but it was obviously small in comparison with the workload in later centuries. There were approximately two hundred members of the Company at the end of the fifteenth century, but by no means all of them would have been engaged in actual manufacture. Some may have been exclusively retailers and others, such as finers (refiners), engaged in peripheral trades. Also, no doubt, some who had completed their apprenticeships were employed as journeymen by other members.

The vast majority of the articles sent for marking were silver – no express requirement existed in any of the statutes for the leopard's head mark to be struck on gold wares. It is extremely unlikely therefore that many of these would have been sent for marking; one must suppose that the control of their standard was still by means of the wardens' searches, during which articles would be tested by touchstone and, if suspect, brought back to the Hall for cupellation assays. That the wardens were not neglecting this aspect of their duties is evident from the records of fines for making or selling substandard gold wares.

ASSAYER'S OTHER DUTIES

Besides dealing with newly made wares, the Assayer also had the duty of assaying the members' raw material – the silver or gold in ingot form before it was fashioned. This was a further safeguard, not only for the Company but also for the maker, since preliminary testing at this stage went a long way to ensuring that the final products would not be rejected when eventually sent for assay and marking. The workers may have sometimes brought the actual ingots, but more probably they would have removed and submitted a small sample in the form of a cutting. Dealing with these samples – later known as by-assays – was time-consuming and added significantly to the Assayer's main work. According to his oath, if the Assayer found any of the members' ingots deficient in standard he was required to adjust them by melting and adding fine gold or silver, on the understanding that the necessary quantity was provided by the member concerned. There is, however, no evidence that he was actually called upon to perform this particular task.

There were, however, other duties which fell on the Assayer. Any articles which the wardens seized during their searches were brought back to the Hall for him to assay. After one of their more thorough sorties the number might be large – putting an extra burden on him, since he would incur the wrath of the

St Dunstan's Day

St Dunstan's Day, 19 May, was the anniversary of the patron saint of goldsmiths and an important date in the calendar of the Goldsmiths' Company. It was the day when the new wardens were installed and the occasion of a special service in St Paul's Cathedral, followed by a grand feast in Goldsmiths' Hall. From 1478 it was also the day on which the date letter was changed. After the Reformation the wardens' installation took place at irregular dates until 1696, when the ceremony was usually held on 29 May. More recently it has moved back to St Dunstan's Day (or near to it), although the date letter is now changed on 1 January each year.

makers if he neglected the routine work: a rapid service was expected and there would soon be complaints if this were not achieved. Sometimes the Assayer would be required to accompany the wardens on their searches, especially if they themselves were not skilled in the art of touchstone testing. His temporary absence from the Office under such circumstances must have caused some difficulties. The checking of goldsmiths' weights also came within his province. Edicts were issued by the Company from time to time, compelling members of the trade to send their weights to the Hall for verification or correction and to be stamped with the mark of the leopard's head.

In the year of his appointment Elyot took an apprentice; others who had been indentured to him in 1471 and 1472 may still have been working for him. He had to pay the wages of his 'servants' out of his own salary. As regards other expenses: the assay balance and furnace may have been provided by the Company but he would have had to pay for the materials – charcoal, cupels and lead. Charcoal in particular was an expensive item. Cupels would have been made either by himself or by one of his servants, a process that involved dampening and compressing bone ash (or 'slow ashes', as the substance was then called) in a special mould and then drying the resulting cupel thoroughly before use. In addition the furnace required constant attention as the lining tended to disintegrate with the action of the lead fumes. There is no mention of a weigher at this early date, but almost certainly the articles were weighed in bulk on receipt and again before delivery to the makers. This would have required a large balance and a set of troy weights.

Elyot was instructed not to charge for his services. But in order to cover at least a part of the cost of assaying it was decided that every man who was a 'brother' (member) should pay the Company eight pence quarterly, as was the practice in the Companies of other crafts in the City. This levy was known as quarterage. There was also the diet – the excess scrapings which were retained by the Company; these also helped to meet the costs. The contemporary records are silent about the pure silver beads which resulted from the assays (assay bits or assay pieces) but the Assayer was probably allowed to retain them – we know this was so at a later date. There is no doubt that he was able to supplement his salary of £20 per annum by virtue of certain perquisites.

INTRODUCTION OF THE DATE LETTER

The appointment of a permanent Assayer had not entirely relieved the wardens of their active part in the process of hallmarking. One of them had to attend regularly in the Assay Office to strike the mark of the leopard's head on all articles passed by the Assayer.

The piece was supported on a suitably shaped anvil and the marks applied by hand using a hammer and puncheon (punch). The design of the mark had been modified by the statute passed in 1478 – the leopard's head was now surmounted by a crown in order to differentiate between plate marked before and after that date. It was also clearly desirable to be able to identify both the Assayer and the warden concerned, in case any hallmarked article should subsequently prove to be substandard. For this purpose another mark was introduced, in the form of a letter of the alphabet in a distinctive shield. The

EXTRACT FROM MINUTE BOOK *of the Goldsmiths' Company showing the names of the wardens at the time of the appointment of Christopher Elyot in 1478. The date letter (A) is illustrated in the margin.*

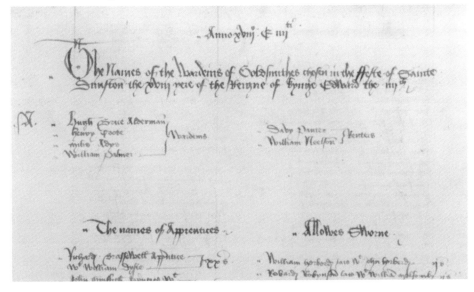

letter was changed each year on the same day as the new wardens took office, which at that time was on St Dunstan's Day, 19 May. The sequence ran from A to U omitting J. On the completion of an alphabet, either the style of letters or the shape of the surrounding shield or both were altered. The precise twelve-month period in which an article was assayed and marked could thus be easily ascertained.

This new symbol, now known as the date letter, was originally called the 'assayer's mark'. It was struck by him on all articles that he had passed, the warden subsequently adding the leopard's head alongside. A drawing of the first letter, a Lombardic 'A', appears in the margin of the minute book against the names of the wardens. There are no known surviving articles bearing this letter but the 'B' for 1479 can be clearly identified on a chalice and paten belonging to the Church of St Mary the Virgin, Nettlecombe, Somerset.

It cannot be claimed that the concept of a date letter originated with the Company, because it was already in use in France. It had been first adopted by the Montpellier guild of goldsmiths in 1427 and gradually taken up by the guilds in other towns, for instance Paris in 1461.[3] In the course of time the date letter proved to be an invaluable guide, in fact an almost infallible one, in dating old silver. This benefit is of course quite incidental to its original purpose, which was to ensure accountability.

THE TRIAL OF THE DIET

Some twenty years after the introduction of the new system the junior warden was given further duties. After marking the articles which had been passed, he was required to put the excess scrapings (the diets) in a box, and once a month to assay the contents as a check on the accuracy of the Assayer's work. The frequency with which the diet was tested was eventually reduced to once or twice per year, the procedure being entrusted to a committee of members of the Court of Assistants. The Trial of the Diet, as it became known, was a major event in the schedule of the Company's activities. Although the results of the early trials are not recorded, those dating from the mid-sixteenth century onwards were meticulously entered in the minute books, showing that this check was considered to be of great importance. At the trials, the diet was weighed, melted and cast into an ingot. Then, after the ingot itself had been weighed, one or more samples were cut from it and assayed. Of course, if these assays were satisfactory this merely confirmed that the diet as a whole was up to standard. It was no proof that individual samples were correct, but it nevertheless provided a most useful assurance that the Assayer was not consistently passing substandard silver.

In the mid-sixteenth century it was laid down that diet should be retained for the trial at the rate of two grains from every one pound troy of plate hallmarked. The recorded results of the trials invariably show the weight of diet

CHALICE AND PATEN *belonging to the Church of St Mary the Virgin Nettlecombe, Somerset. The hallmark consists of the maker's mark (a jug?), the leopard's head crowned (inverted) and the date letter B for 1479, the year after the appointment of Christopher Elyot, the Company's first Assayer.*

before and after melting. After 1620 the total weights of all articles hallmarked during the relevant periods are shown alongside the diet figures. The diet was a valuable source of income for the Company which helped to balance the cost of the Assayer's salary; the ingots were normally sold in exchange for items of plate which could be used by the Company.

The date of Elyot's resignation as Assayer is not known, but it was some time before 1495 – it may have been when he was elected Third Warden in 1492. In 1500 he became deputy to Sir Henry Wyatt at the Mint, a position he held for nine years until his death. Wyatt's title was Controller and Assayer but as senior positions at the Mint were often sinecures, it is probable that Elyot had full responsibility for the assaying. Elyot again became a warden in 1500 and 1508, finally Prime Warden in 1509, the year in which he died. (His successor at the Mint was Thomas Aunsham, whose description of the cupellation assay of gold and silver, handwritten in 1507, has survived.[4]) He had married Philippa, sister of Lady Read, the wife of the wealthy Sir Bartholomew Read, one of the Company's great benefactors, who had been Lord Mayor of London in 1502.[5] In 1511 Lady Read, then a widow, gave £6 13s 4d for an obit for the souls of Elyot and his wife to be held annually in the Church of St John Zachary where they were buried. The church was at the east corner of Noble Street and Maiden Lane (now Gresham Street); it was destroyed in the Great Fire in 1666 and not rebuilt. Since 1945 the former churchyard and an adjacent plot of land has been set out and maintained by the Goldsmiths' Company as a garden for the public.

ELYOT'S SUCCESSORS

There is little known about Elyot's successor, William Preston, except that he had been apprenticed in 1471 to his father Richard, who had twice been a warden, and that he had more than one quarrel with the Beadle, John Hede. He was a cousin of William Wodeward, a former 'graver of coins' at the Mint, who had been five times a warden and who had served on the jury for making the new trial plates in 1477. This relationship may well have helped Preston to obtain the post of Assayer; it is significant that both he and his father were named as executors of Wodeward's will.[6] There is no record of Preston's appointment, but in April 1495 the wardens ordered him to 'make his fire' every day from 8 until 12 noon. It seems he was not attending regularly at the Assay Office and after further warnings he was given three months' notice of dismissal in December 1497 for 'divers great faults'.

Five days before Preston's dismissal took effect, a special committee, consisting of the four wardens together with Elyot and three others, interviewed three applicants for the vacant post. John Jonys was appointed at the same salary as his predecessor (£16 per annum).[7]

Jonys had been indentured in 1466 to Robert Botiller who died in 1471. After this he was 'turned over' to Thomas Wood who was Prime Warden eight times between 1485 and 1503. Jonys no doubt had his own premises some time after receiving his freedom, maybe combining the making of silverware with some private assaying. As he did not take up his new appointment until December 1498, the wardens presumably took responsibility for the assaying during the intervening nine months.

John Jonys was Assayer at the opening of the sixteenth century. He appears to have carried out his duties to the satisfaction of the wardens and the members of the trade, except for a slight lapse in the year 1512 when he was ordered to attend to his office in person. In the same year he took an apprentice named Lewis, paying the accustomed fee of 20 shillings and promising the wardens that he would 'set him to school to learn to read and write'.[8] A number of other apprentices were indentured to him both before and after his appointment as Assayer and he also employed several 'strangers' (foreigners). In February 1520 he was granted leave of absence to ride into Cornwall and to stay there until midsummer. Perhaps his health was failing for he died in 1525 at the age of about seventy-two, having served for twenty-seven years. His bequests to the Church of St Mary Staining in Wood Street where he was buried show that he was a deeply religious man.[9]

WINE CUP, 1493. *The hallmark consists of the date letter Q, the crowned leopard's head (inverted) and the maker's mark. One of the earliest surviving pieces of fully hallmarked secular plate.*

lyues Rulers. Constal
and other his faythfu
they be wythume lib

CHAPTER THREE

EARLY SIXTEENTH CENTURY

S UPPLEMENTING the routine work of the Assayer, the wardens continued to make regular searches, not only in London but also in other parts of the country. However, they sometimes encountered a lack of co-operation which occasionally amounted to open hostility. They felt that their authority needed strengthening. Fortunately, in 1505 a new charter was obtained from Henry VII – though not without considerable expense. It was renewed by Henry VIII shortly after his accession to the throne in 1509. These charters gave the wardens the clear right to order wares found when searching within three miles of London to be sent to the Hall. Furthermore it empowered them to fine or commit to prison anyone offending against the Company's ordinances and to seize and break substandard articles found anywhere in England.

It so happened that in the very next year the Company faced a strong challenge from the goldsmiths of Norwich following a search by the wardens, during the course of which a quantity of substandard silver had been seized.[1] Representatives from this flourishing centre of the trade came to London to argue their objections before the King's Council sitting at Greenwich. But the Company won the day; the Council decided that its ordinances were as valid within the city of Norwich as in the City of London. It was a most useful precedent. Backed by this ruling, similar country searches were carried out by the wardens at intervals during the next two hundred years. Suspect wares were seized, balances and weights checked and fees taken for administering the oath prescribed for provincial workers.[2] In the seventeenth century cupellation assays were sometimes carried out during the course of the search and offenders fined on the spot, but before this the suspect articles themselves were always brought back to the Hall for assay. Offenders were then summoned to London to appear before the wardens.

Although the minimum standards for gold and silver wares applied throughout the country, the legal provisions with respect to the *marking* of articles made or

FIGURE OF HENRY VIII: *detail from a document containing extracts from the 1505 Charter recorded in the Company's* Book of Ordinances, *c.1513*.

sold outside London were less precise than those which applied in the capital. The Company's original charter of 1327 contained the following passage:

> And in all cities and towns of England where there are goldsmiths and to which merchants come they shall make and keep the same ordinances as they of London do. And one or two men from every such city or town shall come to London on behalf of their craft to fetch their certain touch of gold and silver, also the punch with the leopard's head with which to mark their work as was ordained in time past ...

The statute of 1300 contains a similar clause except that the words 'punch ... times past' are omitted. It may be significant that a system of hallmarking was introduced in France in 1275 whereby articles of silver had to bear a mark guaranteeing the standard (*poinçon des communautés*), the form of mark being different for each town. The fact that the statute of 1300 was enacted just twenty-five years later suggests that it may have been based on the French ordinance and that it intended to make marking compulsory elsewhere than in London. It is certainly possible that punches were supplied to the civic authorities in other towns.

There are in existence five spoons each of which has the leopard's head mark in the bowl, the tongue of the leopard appearing in the form of a letter. It has been suggested that the letters were to identify the town in which the spoon was marked. The clearest are E, B and N, which could represent Ebor (York), Bristol and Norwich – all mentioned as assay towns in the Act of 1423. However, this seems to be disproved by the fact that the spoons with the letters B and N have the same maker's mark. An alternative theory is that there was a date letter system in operation prior to 1478.[3] Yet another possibility is that the purpose of the letters was to identify the punch maker (engraver).

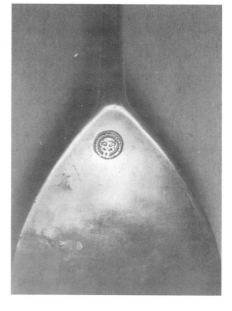

The statute of 1363 and the ordinance of 1379 stated that royal commissioners would be responsible for assaying and marking in cities throughout the realm, but there is no evidence that any such appointments were made. Certain cities were, however, designated 'to have divers touches' under the Act of 1423 and it is

LEOPARD'S HEAD MARK *in bowl of fifteenth-century spoon, one of a group where the tongue of the leopard appears to be in the form of a letter, in this case an 'N'.*

known that later in the century assay offices were in operation in Norwich and York.[4] However, in spite of these measures, it is unlikely that much provincial plate was hallmarked at this early date. It was not until two centuries later – in 1697 – that the law unequivocally made hallmarking of silver compulsory throughout the country.

NEW ORDINANCE

The new system adopted in 1478, with its daily facilities for assaying and marking at the Hall, was undoubtedly a great improvement on past practice, but it seems that not all members of the Company were regularly submitting their newly manufactured silverware. It was therefore decided to issue a strongly worded ordinance which read:

> It is ordained by the assent of the whole Fellowship of Goldsmiths that no goldsmith put to sale no manner of plate nor other stuff of silver until he hath set thereon his own mark, and then the same stuff so marked to be brought to the assay house at Goldsmiths' Hall there to be assayed and abled good, then the assayer to set thereon his mark and after[wards] the wardens to set thereon the leopard's head crowned.[5]

THE TOUCHWARDEN *striking the mark of the leopard's head. Detail from the frontispiece of* A New Touchstone for Gold and Silver Wares, *1677.*

Although the ordinance mentioned wardens, the duty of striking the leopard's head mark was subsequently made the responsibility of one warden only – the most junior or Fourth Warden, known also as the Touchwarden.

The Company could compel the submission of silver wares only, since hallmarking of gold was not required by statute. However, the wording of the ordinance presupposed that some gold wares would be submitted, because it goes on to say:

> ... and that no goldsmith presume to bring or send no manner of work of gold nor silver to Goldsmiths' Hall to be touched but it be truly made without default [deception] to the wardens in the assay taking ...

The ordinance incidentally shows that the Company was still worried that a substandard article might be inadvertently marked with the leopard's head. It says that anyone who sent such deceptive work to the Hall would be required to provide a surety or to enter into an obligation to discharge the wardens should they be prosecuted for unwittingly marking any of his pieces which were later proved to be below standard.

The seriousness with which the Company took its responsibility for assaying and marking is exemplified in an incident which occurred in 1511. The Touchwarden in that year was Robert Amadas, who had established a thriving business as a goldsmith. He was later to become one of the richest men in the City, due largely to royal patronage as goldsmith to Henry VIII, a lucrative position at the Mint as deputy to the master-worker and marriage to a wealthy heiress, the granddaughter of Sir Hugh Bryce (see page 34).[6] In fact Amadas was one of the most powerful men to hold the office of Prime Warden during the century. However, while Touchwarden he neglected his duty in that he gave the leopard's head punch to the Beadle, Edward Frodestam, asking him to do the marking in the Assay Office because he himself had a dinner engagement. He later confessed that it was not an isolated instance. Not only that, but on another occasion he had taken the punch to his house in a bag with certain keys and had departed out of town unknown to any of his fellow wardens. One of them had discovered the punch when he went to Amadas' house to fetch the bag. A fortnight later the other wardens reported the irregularities of their colleague to the Court of Assistants (described in this instance as 'an assembly of them that have been wardens'). The Court, numbering thirteen persons, agreed that Frodestam should be dismissed and that Amadas should pay a fine of £5 or give a gilt cup to the Company. It was expected of the Touchwarden, as of the Assayer, that he should faithfully and conscientiously carry out the duties entrusted to him, irrespective of status.

The Company's minute books of the early sixteenth century contain many references to offences committed by members of the trade and the ensuing punishments. Some of the offenders were discovered by the Assayer in the course of his daily work, some by the wardens during their searches in London or in the country, and others as the result of complaints received. The scale of fines as laid down by an ordinance of the Company was 2s for a first offence, 6s 8d for a second and 20s for a third. For a fourth offence the member was committed to prison until such time as he would 'agree' with the wardens or else be denied 'the assay and touch' and all other benefits of the Company.

We find examples of all the main types of offence which have continued to come to light from time to time down to the present day. The most frequently mentioned is the making or selling of substandard wares. For instance, in 1513 Robert Cowper was fined 2s for making silver wedding rings 4oz 2dwt worse than sterling.[7] In the same year a more serious misdemeanour was that of Thomas Agland, who spent fifteen days in the compter (prison) and was then put in the stocks at Goldsmiths' Hall in the sight of the whole Company. His offence was making hooks, catches and rings which he had filled with copper. After obtaining the new charter in 1505 the Company had its own compter in Bread Street and the offender would be escorted there by the Beadle; only exceptionally was it necessary to refer cases to the City authorities and jurisdiction of the mayoral court.

There are also records of substandard gold wares such as a ring made by William Skelly in 1513; he was denied the assay and touch but later forgiven. And as illustrations of offences discovered during country searches there are the cases of Peter Streech of Exeter who was fined 6s 8d in 1517 for making spoons 32dwt worse than sterling and Richard Basset of the same city who was fined 3s 4d for a similar offence in the following year. Peter Streech offended again in 1530 and was fined 15s in respect of six spoons found to be 17dwt worse. Four months earlier John Tallon of Coventry was fined 2s for making substandard wares including a spoon 30dwt worse. And there were many others.

An offence, which eventually became known as transposing, is mentioned in 1533: one John Harte was ordered to be committed to the compter for cutting out the mark from one article and soldering it into another one – the cover of a salt. The wardens may have relented in this instance because the decision to imprison him, having been entered in the minute book, was subsequently crossed out. Mixing good and substandard silver in the same article was an offence that was frequently discovered by the Assayer. In 1535, for instance, Thomas Whytlocke was sent to the compter for making pots, the bodies of which were 9dwt worse than sterling but the covers 2dwt better. This was 'thought to be done to deceive the assayer'.

Sometimes workers were found to have substandard raw material on their premises, which usually resulted in a fine. Furthermore it was agreed by a general assembly of the Company in 1528 that not only should the maker of a low standard article be fined but also the supplier of the faulty metal. Another offence was the use of an excessive amount of solder when making an article. This was considered to be especially serious if done deliberately to add weight – as in the case of John Chandler who filled a silver cross with too much solder in 1523 and was fined 6s 8d. In order to achieve a sufficiently low melting point, solder must necessarily have a lower fineness than the parts on which it is used. For sterling silver wares the usual composition of the solder is two-thirds silver to one-third base metal.

The above are just a few examples typical of the numerous recorded misdemeanours that were dealt with by the wardens. Shortly after returning from a search, the wardens, armed with the Assayer's reports on the articles they had seized, would interview a succession of offenders. Sometimes the culprits would be summoned from remote parts of the country, which in itself must have occasioned them considerable hardship, in addition to the fines and the breaking of their work. But possibly for those working in London the stigma of being called before the wardens caused a greater distress than the imposition of a fine or the loss of the fashion of the articles involved; the whole of the craft would soon know of their misdeeds. For more serious offences the punishment of being put in the stocks in the Hall on an assembly day in full view of the members of the Company was a particular disgrace. However, not all offenders reformed after appearing before the wardens; some were repeatedly fined or imprisoned. The same Thomas Agland mentioned above transgressed again in April 1522. He was ordered to be set on a stool in the Hall with all his hooks and other wares 'hanged upon him in the sight of all men and afterwards to be warned to avoid London forever'. If he were to be found again in the City he was to be set in the pillory. There is no record of a reprieve.

The ultimate sanction, to be dismissed from membership of the Company and denied the facility of sending goods for hallmarking, in effect prohibited transgressors from following their trade as master goldsmiths, at least in London. This final punishment was sometimes prescribed, but usually after a short period, the offender – provided he sufficiently repented and undertook to obey the wardens in future – was reinstated. We have already noted the case of Thomas Wood who attained high office in the Company after earlier misdemeanours. Others included Henry Averell, a London goldsmith, who was fined for selling substandard wares at Stourbridge Fair in September 1522. In November of the same year he was elected Renter and in 1528

SILVER-GILT FONT CUP AND COVER. *The hallmark shows the date letter F for 1503, the crowned leopard's head and maker's mark (a crossbow). This piece would have been assayed by John Jonys..*

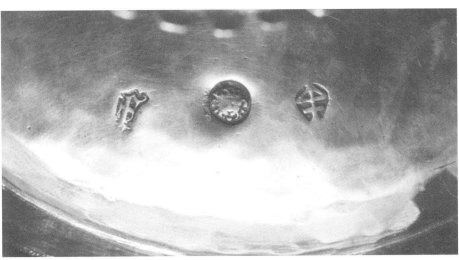

Touchwarden. He subsequently served as Third Warden in 1531, Second Warden in the following year and Prime Warden in 1538. Robert Hartop, a goldsmith in Cheapside, fined for similar offences at the same time as Averell, later served as Touchwarden, rising to Second Warden in 1550. It is slightly ironic that during this time he carried out a series of searches in various parts of the country which resulted in many fines. Even John Chandler and Thomas Whytlocke must have become reformed characters; Chandler was Touchwarden in 1539 and Whytlocke was appointed Beadle in 1546.

STANDARD TROY WEIGHTS

The use of faulty weights or balances was a recurring problem. Even the royal goldsmith, Morgan Wolff, was fined 20s in 1530 for having two piles of weights – one too light and the other too heavy! He did not risk offending again and ten years later he was elected Touchwarden, advancing to Third Warden in the following year.

A search by the wardens in 1495 had resulted in the discovery of no less than twenty such offences and in 1516 many complaints were received by the Company that 'goldsmiths gravely offend in using their balances and weights in so much that in four or five shops scarce one shall agree with another, contrary to the good laws of God and man and to the great abusing of the King's subjects'. As a corrective the Company ordered all goldsmiths within two miles of London to bring their weights to be certified at the Assay Office and then stamped with the leopard's head and date letter. For this purpose a new box of standard weights was to be kept at the Hall. It was inscribed:

> This is the right standard of troy wt belonging to the Goldsmiths' Hall marked with the letter of the Hall and leopard's head being in weight 42 lb 8 oz, sized by M. Fenrother, Ald. Ashley, M. Wastel, M. Read being Wardens a 8 Regi H 8 for all goldsmiths to resort unto.

It was decided at the same time that all balances and weights would be checked during a quarterly search. Since there are many references to fines for untouched weights, one can assume that the wardens enforced the order to the best of their ability. It certainly involved much extra work for the Assayer, but it was also a means of augmenting his income.

The Company's new order for certifying weights was followed by a regulation setting minimum prices for new wares. This also specified maximum prices which goldsmiths were permitted to pay for old articles sold to them as scrap. Distinction was made between untouched silver articles, plate of the old touch (ie pre-1478) and plate of the new touch. The prices per ounce were not to exceed 3s, 3s 2d and 3s 4d respectively. Broken silver-gilt plate could be sold at a higher price – not more than 3s 7d – since the gold could be separated on refining. The differential between plate of the old and new touches clearly shows that hallmarks applied after the appointment of a permanent assayer in 1478 were regarded to be of greater benefit as a guarantee of the standard than those of an earlier date. There can be no doubt that the new system was working well.

Another matter to which the Company had repeatedly to give attention was the registration of makers' marks. All workers were required by law to make their marks known to the wardens, who for their part had to ensure that the records were kept up to date. Reminders were sent out periodically, as in 1528 when every worker was ordered to bring in his puncheon (punch) 'to be set in the table in the Say House'. It was necessary to issue identical orders on many occasions in succeeding centuries.

Before 1526 the standard of English gold coins – sovereigns, angels and nobles – stood at 23 carats 3½ grains, but in that year a new coin, called a crown, was minted in 22 carat gold. Thereafter coins of both standards were issued. For the trial plate of the new standard (known as crown gold) a special jury was appointed and sworn in the Star Chamber. Two silver plates were also made, one of sterling and the other of a lower standard for a coin called a double plakke. A copy of the report of their proceedings, dated 30 October 1526, still exists, as does a portion of the trial plate for crown gold.[8] There also survives a silver plate with a fineness of 885 parts per thousand which is probably the plate of the lower standard.

The jury had now taken on a new format, consisting of thirteen members of the Company with four City aldermen. Similarly constituted juries were responsible for testing newly minted coins at Trials of the Pyx in 1527, 1530 and 1533. The members were sworn in the Star Chamber before the Lord Chancellor in office – Cardinal Wolsey, Sir Thomas More and Sir Thomas Audley, respectively.[9] A much enlarged jury (sixteen goldsmiths, one goldfiner and twelve members of other City Companies) was appointed for a further Trial in 1534.[10] It is not known who undertook the actual assaying, but on the last three of the above occasions it is probable that it was Edmund Lee, the Company's Assayer, since his name appears on each of the lists of jurymen. However, William Knight, a Mercer and a future Assay Master of the Mint, was also included in 1534. We shall shortly be meeting him again in another connection.

A special Trial was held in December 1537 at the direction of Thomas Cromwell, Keeper of the Privy Seal. It was unusual in that it was held at Goldsmiths' Hall not the Star Chamber and that the coins were minted at Canterbury, where the Archbishop, by custom, held the prerogative of minting. The Archbishop at this time was Thomas Cranmer. The assays were carried out – certainly this time by Edmund Lee – in the presence of ten members of the Company and five others. It is the first Trial to be documented in the Company's own records.

The apprenticeship system

This system was firmly established in the goldsmiths' craft in London by the middle of the fourteenth century and, like many other medieval crafts, was the usual means by which successive generations were trained. The length of service was originally ten years, but in 1400 it was reduced to seven. In addition to housing, clothing and feeding an apprentice, a master had to pay the Goldsmiths' Company 20s at the 'binding' (reduced to 2s 6d by statute in 1531). Sometimes the apprentice had to submit a 'masterpiece' to the wardens to prove his ability and he had to show that he had been taught to read and write. On completion of his service he was entitled to the freedom of the Company on payment of 2s and swearing an oath of obedience to the wardens. He could then set up in business on his own. Apprentices were normally indentured at about the age of thirteen. If a master died the apprentice was usually 'turned over' to another member of the Company.

Apprentices are still bound through the Company and many craftsmen, including some present members of the Assay Office staff, have learned their skills in this way.

After the accession of Elizabeth I in 1558 the Company was given the entire responsibility for Trials of the Pyx. Henceforth all the jurymen were nominated from its members and sworn before the Lords of the Privy Council at the Star Chamber where the proceedings continued to be held. The Company's own Assayer was chosen as a matter of course, as it was primarily his duty to assay the coins. Since that time all Trials of the Pyx down to the present day have been undertaken by juries of similar constitution although the venue for the trial has changed more than once.

EDMUND LEE

Edmund Lee succeeded John Jonys as Assayer in 1525. Aged about fifty, he was already in the senior hierarchy of the Company, having served as Renter in 1510, Fourth Warden in 1514 and Third Warden in 1520. As Fourth Warden or Touchwarden he would have had useful experience of the procedure in the Assay Office. Before his appointment he was dwelling in Cheapside, where he presumably practised as a working goldsmith and possibly undertook private assaying as well. He was obviously a skilled assayer since he was able to take over the duties immediately. We know that he had acted as arbitrator in a controversy between John Jonys and a certain John Bushell in 1519, which almost certainly involved testing articles rejected by his predecessor. His name appears on a list of members of the Company showing their contributions towards a sum of money paid to Henry VIII in 1522; his was £6, indicating that he was reasonably well-to-do at that time. Four years earlier he had donated towards the rebuilding of the burnt-out Minories. His salary as Assayer was £20 per annum but in addition he and his family had free accommodation in the precincts of the Hall and there were always the perquisites. He would have had to pay his assistants himself and supply his own materials such as cupels and charcoal. He earned a little extra for sizing weights; at that time every freeman of the Company was entitled to have one set checked without charge but for extra weights had to pay the Assayer at the rate of one penny for every one pound troy.

Six apprentices were bound to Lee between 1498 and 1514; another, John Craswell, was indentured in 1520 and was presumably still serving when Lee was appointed Assayer in 1525. He took a further apprentice, John Foxe, in 1529, and then Owen Draper who received his freedom in 1537.[11] We do not know whether any of them continued to work in the Assay Office after completing their service. Since John Foxe stole silver from Lee to the value of £11 he was unlikely to have been kept on. Craswell apparently set up in business on his own, because a John Craswell, probably the same man, was in serious trouble in 1529 for incorporating substandard parts in a number of salts. He was set in the stocks at the Hall but after confessing that he had made a dozen similar articles, he said he had not the wherewithal to recompense his customers. As a result he was sent to Newgate prison where he died. However, not all of Lee's apprentices behaved so discreditably – Thomas Tuttie (Totyll), who was indentured in about 1540, later became deputy to three of his successors.

Lee had a son, Richard, who was not apprenticed to his father but served under another master and received the freedom in 1532. In 1540 Richard was promised the position of Assayer on the death of his father on the condition that he practised the making of assays of gold and silver. In the event he declined the post (probably because of the unusual situation shortly to be recounted) but in the meantime he had taken advantage of learning the skill of assaying from his father and subsequently held appointments as Assay Master at the London and York Mints.

Unconnected with his office as Common Assayer, Edmund Lee was one of three commissioners for the parish of St John Zachary for collecting the lay subsidies granted by Parliament to Henry VIII in 1534. It was to these commissioners that the Company in the following year made a return of the annual income from rents received from its properties (£190) and the value of its plate and other possessions (£500 4s). Lee himself was rated in 1541 on goods valued at £20 for which the tax was ten shillings – a modest figure showing that he had not prospered financially like some contemporary goldsmiths, such as Morgan Wolff, the Royal Goldsmith, whose assessment was £1000.

Edmund Lee died in 1546 having been Assayer for about twenty years. No complaints about his work are recorded during the whole of this time; he obviously worked efficiently and apparently avoided incurring the hostility of the makers. The Assayer did not have an easy role, especially when obliged to have substandard articles broken or a maker fined; this was by no means an infrequent occurrence and tempers were apt to flare up in such circumstances and enmities to ensue, as we shall see in the case of some of Lee's successors.

In his will Lee left a blue gown, his best doublet, a jacket and a gold ring to his son Richard, 20s each to Richard's two sons and his daughter's son, 20s to his servant Alice Kent, 6s to the priest of St John Zachary where he was buried, 13s 4d to the livery of the Company for a 'potation' and the residue of his goods and property to his wife Joanne.[12] The Company granted the lease of apartments adjoining the Hall to his widow and son.

Edmund Lee's successor was Oswald Lye (sometimes spelt Lee, but there is no evidence that he was related).[13] His appointment is not actually recorded, the probable reason being that at the time the Company was facing a grave crisis – Henry VIII had temporarily appointed his own two nominees as joint Assay Masters. Oswald Lye could not therefore be officially appointed to the post.

This turn of events calls for some explanation. By 1542 the proceeds from the dissolution of the monasteries were dwindling and the King was much in debt due to the war with France. In order to alleviate the situation he had decided to engage on the disastrous experiment of debasing the coinage.[14] In this connection it seems that he may have wished to obtain inside information about the gold and silver workers and their trade. He no doubt felt that it would be to his advantage to have his own appointees in the Assay Office. He had to produce an excuse for this intrusion, so he accordingly accused the Company, or rather its members, of great faults in the manufacture of gold and silver, hinting that they were not adhering to the standard – a hypocritical move if ever there was one, considering his own conduct with regard to the coinage. But in this way he also had in mind to exact some money from the Company in return for a royal pardon.

SIR MARTIN BOWES

At this crucial time the Company was fortunate in having as one of its senior members Sir Martin Bowes, a man of many parts, who had considerable influence in court circles as well as in the City. He was an alderman, a future Lord Mayor (1545) and Member of Parliament, and had been Prime Warden

SIR MARTIN BOWES *c.1500–1566. The portrait was presented to the Goldsmiths' Company by W. Faithorne in 1679 to avoid serving as Touchwarden; he was not a practising goldsmith.*

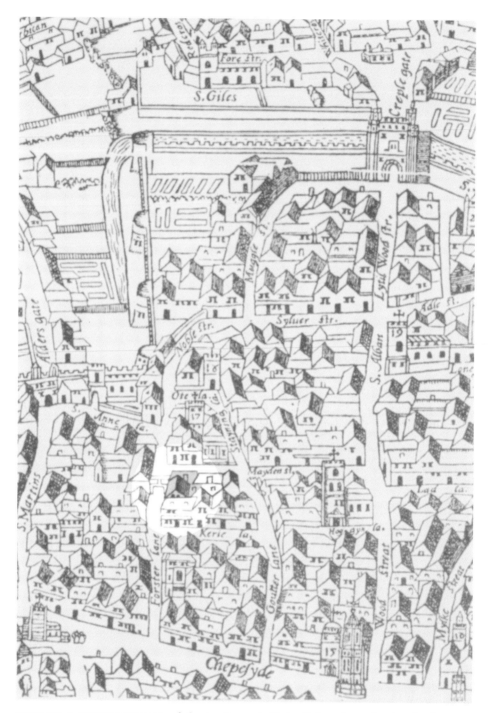

PART OF A WOODCUT MAP *of about 1562, probably by Robert Agas, showing the first Goldsmiths' Hall in 'Forster Lane'.*

for the past two years. Since he had been Touchwarden in 1532 and had taken part in trade searches he was well versed in Assay Office matters. Not only was he a rich and successful trading goldsmith, but more importantly in the present context he was Master-Worker of the Mint and in this capacity responsible for putting the programme for the debasement of the coinage into operation. He therefore probably knew what was afoot before the crisis arrived at the Company's door. He must have foreseen that it would be in its best interests for the Company to strengthen its control of the trade so as to forestall criticism from any quarter. Whilst he was Prime Warden (in 1536), a regulation was issued relating specifically to gold wares. These were not normally submitted for hallmarking, but in an attempt to strengthen its control, the company ordered that all gold workers should have a maker's mark which they should strike on articles weighing in excess of ½oz.

We find Bowes making certain further proposals at a meeting of the Court of Assistants in November 1542. These included an order to compel all makers of small silver wares under 1oz in weight to have a new maker's mark registered at the Hall, and to strike it on all their work. He also suggested that all articles marked with the 'old touch' should be broken and none offered for sale; and further, that no one should deliver to any workman making either large or small wares any silver that was not as good as sterling, preferably silver from ingots that had been assayed at the Hall. His proposals were adopted. Thorough country searches were carried out at this time, probably again at Bowes' suggestion: in March and April 1543 Richard Hartop the Third Warden, visited Coventry, Lichfield, Derby, Nottingham and Worcester, returning with many substandard wares.

These precautionary measures did not, however, prevent the King from proceeding with his plan to intervene in the Company's affairs. It was forced to surrender its charter to the Lord Chancellor, Thomas Wriothesley (later first Earl of Southampton), and the possession of the Assay Office was handed over to Matthew Dale (Haberdasher) and William Knight (Mercer) on 21 July 1544. These two had arrived at the Hall two days earlier with a commission from the Lord Chancellor and other members of the King's Council 'to be admitted say masters/makers of assays & touch for the Company'. Moreover, the Company was obliged to pay an exorbitant annual fee for the two officers. We do not know whether Dale or Knight themselves ever did any of the actual assaying at the Hall, although Knight was suitably qualified, since he became Assay Master at the Southwark Mint in 1547, 1548 and 1550 and at the Tower Mint in 1551 and 1556.[15] It is much more likely that Edmund Lee (or Oswald Lye after Lee's death) continued with his routine duties as the Company's Assayer although nominally responsible to the King's appointees. (Neither Knight nor Dale are named again in the Company's records after July 1544 when they took possession of the Assay Office. Oswald Lye, however, is mentioned on a number of occasions in the years immediately following, which strongly suggests that it was he who was carrying out the work and not the King's nominees.)

Without delay the Company petitioned the Lord Chancellor to intercede with the King on its behalf, promising to pay the sum of 3000 marks (£2000) in return for a royal pardon and confirmation of its ancient privileges. The petition specifically referred to the King's nominees in the Assay Office in these terms:

> Your said supplicants were and yet be burdened and charged with great annual sums of money to certain new officers late appointed by the King's Majesty for the touching and assaying of gold and silver amounting yearly £103 6s 8d, which offices may be as well furnished and served yearly with the sum of £20. ... It may therefore please the King's Majesty that your said supplicants may have the keeping of the touch and making of the assays as they have had in times past at their own charge ... that all such good order shall be kept as shall be thought reasonable and in consideration thereof that all the said new officers late appointed may be thereof discharged and removed.

Faced with an uncertain future the Company was kept in suspense for three years, but fulfilled its various obligations as usual. The wardens made searches in London and in the country, including for example, one in 1546 when they visited Bristol, Gloucester, Birmingham and Lichfield. Offenders were made to come to London from these towns to answer to the wardens. A culprit from Birmingham was sent to the compter for 3 days for 'misworking of hooks, pins and catches worse 14 dwt with casts worse 3 oz 1 dwt'. As regards London, an edict was issued in November 1546 that there was to be no buying or selling of silverware by candlelight, a frequently repeated order aimed at preventing deception. Amongst other offenders, William Walton was sent to the compter for working silver that was 9 dwt worse than standard and John Bevercot also for adding substandard feet to five round salts after they had been touched. George Webb was fined 10s because his weights were too light. A hollow gold ring filled with lead which which had been discovered by the wardens was taken to the Lord Chancellor to be shown to the King's Council. The Company was clearly at pains to demonstrate to the Council that it was conscientiously carrying out its duties.

It may be surmised that it was in part due to the influence of Sir Martin Bowes behind the scenes that the Company was permitted to continue its normal activities. It may also have been through his intercession that, to its great relief, it received the royal pardon and confirmation of its charter in May 1547. There must have been a more conciliatory mood at the summit of affairs of state under the government of the Protector Somerset following the death

THE MARK OF THE LION PASSANT. *A crowned lion passant guardant was first used in 1544. The crown was omitted after 1550. A lion passant (not guardant) was used after 1820. This 3.3 cm-high model was used for making the punches subsequent to 1916.*

of Henry VIII in the preceding January. From this time forward the responsibility for the Assay Office was firmly back in the hands of the Company. Never again was there any similar interference by the sovereign. The records show that in May 1548 Oswald Lye took the oath for the due execution of his office of Common Assayer at the same time as the wardens were sworn.

THE LION PASSANT GUARDANT

In the very same year (1544) as the King foisted his nominees on the Company to act as Assay Masters a new symbol was first struck in addition to the leopard's head and date letter. This symbol was the lion passant guardant. It may be that the use of a royal emblem was intended to show that the Crown was now involved with the Assay Office – in theory, if not in fact. It is perhaps significant that the head of the lion depicted in this new symbol was at first

surmounted by a crown which was removed in 1549, two years after the Company had received the royal pardon and the restoration of its rights. Whatever its original purpose, either a lion passant guardant or a lion passant was used on all silver wares of the sterling standard hallmarked in England before 1st January 1999 (see page 314). It was also used on gold wares up to 1844, excepting those of the 18 carat standard marked after 1798. It is perhaps the best known of all the hallmark symbols. It may also be significant that two versions of the shield surrounding the date letter for the year 1544/5 have been noted, but as with the introduction of the lion passant symbol itself, this is not referred to in the Company's records.

OSWALD LYE

In contrast to his predecessor, the new Assayer – Oswald Lye – comes over as a difficult character with a quick temper. He was involved in several altercations with craftsmen. In 1547, for example, William Ledham complained that his plate had been unjustly broken. When appearing before the wardens both he and Lye each agreed to choose two honest men to settle the controversy – a frequently used procedure. But coming out of the meeting Lye gave vent to his feelings and delivered Ledham a blow on the head – for which he was fined 20s. At a subsequent meeting Lye named Thomas Stanley, Assay Master at the Tower Mint, and Robert Browne, a skilled assayer, as his chosen men.[16] Stanley, however, would 'not meddle with the matter' so Lye chose John Langley instead. Ledham chose Lawrence Warren, Assay Master at the Canterbury Mint, and John Harryson. The plate in question was delivered to the four arbitrators for assay. The outcome is not specifically minuted, but a later entry mentions a basin of William Ledham's being 1dwt worse than standard and a ewer 1½dwt better, which were probably the selfsame pieces. This incident

A SILVER-GILT STANDING CUP *bearing a hallmark for 1545, including the lion passant guardant (inverted), first used in the previous year.*

serves to illustrate the compactness of the goldsmiths' community in those days – Browne, Warren, Harryson and Langley had all been near neighbours of Oswald Lye when he was working in Goldsmiths' Row; Ledham later had a shop there and a dwelling house in nearby Gutter Lane.[17]

On another occasion Lye incurred the animosity of John Hycks, a spoon-maker and a frequent offender in respect of substandard wares. Hycks got the worst of it: he was committed to prison for three days for 'very slanderous words'. In 1552 Lye quarrelled with others nearer home – Thomas Whytlocke (the Beadle) and John Bromborough (the former Clerk). The first disagreement was patched up and the two 'drank to each other'. But the wardens with two members of the Court of Assistants considered the matter between Lye and the former Clerk and his wife, and decided that 'because the said Oswald Lee [Lye] is so stiffnecked, unruly and forward, they have licenced the said John to attempt what law he will against the said Oswald and they have promised to further him therein.' Lye's excitable nature apparently did not mellow with either age or experience because two years later the wardens agreed that 'next time that Oswald Lee doth revile any of the Company of Goldsmiths he shall pay for a fine 20s'. In spite of his faults he was presumably a competent assayer – there were many instances of rejections that were not queried, even though the assay reports were frequently only one pennyweight below standard.

Several apprentices had been indentured to Oswald Lye. Two deserve mention. Thomas Tuttie, whom he had taken over from Edmund Lee on the latter's death, completed his service in 1547. He was subsequently appointed deputy to Lye and to his two successors, continuing in the Assay Office until his death in 1575. In 1559 Lye was paying him £6 13s per annum in wages – a fair proportion of his own salary. Ralph Barton, another apprentice, was 'set over' to Lye in 1555 with six years to serve, but his master died before he completed his term. Twenty-two years later Barton was appointed Assayer of Gold and Weigher of Plate and continued working in the Assay Office until the year of his death in 1603. After 1576 he had subsidiary employment as assistant to the Assay Master at the Tower Mint. His father who had been a blancher at the Mint was appointed Beadle to the Company in 1557.

Oswald Lye died in 1559. The post of Assayer had been promised to Richard Rogers, a working goldsmith with two shops in Goldsmiths' Row and a liveryman of one year's standing.[18] However, Richard Lee had some claim in view of the Company's earlier undertaking to offer him the position on the death of his father Edmund Lee, which he had not accepted when it became vacant. The Company received letters supporting Richard Lee from the Earl of Bedford and from Lord Strange writing on behalf of Queen Elizabeth. The dilemma was resolved when Lee voluntarily relinquished all right, title and interest in the post. Richard Rogers was then appointed Common Assayer in November 1559 at a salary of 50 marks (£33 6s 8d).[19]

CHAPTER FOUR

THE ELIZABETHAN ERA

T HE DEBASEMENT of the coinage had resulted in high inflation causing
untold hardship to many: a change in direction was clearly required.
Thus an indenture of 5 October 1551 between Edward VI and the
Mint officers for the supply of new silver coins expressly required the standard
to be '11 ounces 1 pennyweight of fine silver out of the fire and 19 pennyweight of allay in the pound troy'. Further indentures in Mary's reign, dated
1553, 1557 (two) and 1558, required it to be '11 ounces fine silver out of the
fire and 1 ounce of allay in the pound troy'.[1] The words *out of the fire* are
important. This phraseology was clearly meant to signify that when the coins
were assayed the fine silver remaining on the cupel should be weighed without
any allowance for loss in the fire (cupellation). It also meant that this weight
should indicate a fineness of 11 oz 1 dwt (or 11 oz for Mary's indentures) in the
pound troy. Since there was a loss of silver during cupellation of about 2 dwt in
the pound, this effectively meant that the sterling standard had been fully
restored for Mary's coins and an even higher standard specified for those of
Edward VI.

A trial plate of the new standard was made in 1553. It may have been the
work of members of the Company, although there is no surviving record to
prove it. A portion of this plate, which is inscribed '11 ounces fyne', still exists
and according to a modern assay the true silver plus gold content is almost
exactly 925 parts per 1000 or 11 oz 2 dwt in the pound troy (equivalent to 11 oz
out of the fire), showing that the plate had been accurately made according to
the standard specified in the indenture of the same year. Results of sixteenth-
century assays would of course have included the small amount of gold present
in the plate.

In 1560 Elizabeth I wisely decided to replace the whole of the debased
coinage, a difficult but entirely successful operation. A new indenture dated 8
November of that year stated: 'In every pound weight of silver of these
moneys shall be 11 oz 2 dwt fine silver and 18 dwt allay. Which 11 oz 2 dwt fine
silver and 18 dwt allay is the old right standard of sterling of England. ... '[2]
The words 'out of the fire', which had been included in the four earlier

indentures, were omitted, thus reverting to a form of wording used before the debasement. The Company was requested by the Privy Council to appoint a jury for making a new trial plate for use at future Trials of the Pyx. The list of sixteen jurors was headed by Sir Martin Bowes, who no longer held office at the Mint. Richard Rogers, the Company's Assayer, was naturally on the list as it was his responsibility to assay the new trial plate to confirm it was of the correct fineness. A portion of this plate still exists; a modern assay shows its silver plus gold content to be 933 parts per 1000 or 11 oz 4 dwt, which would correspond to a figure of 11 oz 2 dwt out of the fire. The jury evidently assumed that this was what was intended by the indenture.[3] We shall see that the lack of a more precise wording of the indenture would result in much controversy in following years.

THE TWO VERSIONS OF THE DATE LETTER FOR 1560. *The one on the right was used after the 6 January 1561, when the Company decided that no plate in future would be touched which assayed under 11oz 2dwt (ie a fineness of 11oz 4dwt after allowing for the loss of silver in the cupellation assay).*

The plate (in common with the one made in 1553 and all subsequent plates) was cut into several portions with a fine saw in such a manner that the edges were tooth-shaped (indented). The separate portions – kept at the Treasury and the Mint – could thus be authenticated at any time by fitting them together. The 1560 indented trial plate was used at the Trial of the Pyx for testing the coinage during the next forty years. The same jury appointed in 1560 was responsible for making two gold trial plates, one of 'fine gold' (23 carats 3½ grains or 994.8 parts per 1000) and one of 'crown' gold (22 carat or 916.6 parts per 1000). Portions of both these plates have survived.

There had been no change in the standard as regards silverware. During the period of the debasement the Company had continued to keep to the standard to which it had been accustomed (11 oz out of the fire or 11 oz 2 dwt actual – ie 925 parts per 1000). However, in December 1560 it was decided that since the coinage 'contained in fineness 11 oz and upward', after 6 January 1561 no plate would be hallmarked under the fineness of 11 oz 2 dwt; and to distinguish plate marked before and after the operative date 'the letter of the year' would be 'graven around for a difference', that is, surrounded by a distinctive shield. Knowing there was a loss of 2 dwt in the cupellation assay, one can say with confidence that the real standard adopted by the Company from that date – after allowing for the loss – was 11 oz 4 dwt (933 parts per 1000). Confirmatory evidence in support of this assertion is to be found in the results of the trial of the diet taken from silver articles hallmarked between June 1560 and June 1561. Two separate diets were assayed at the trial – 'the last diet of the old standard of

11 oz fine', the assay report for which was 11 oz dwt and 'the first diet of the new standard of 11 oz 2 dwt fine', which assayed at 11 oz 2 dwt 'just'. Assay results were always reported as they were found without any allowance for the loss of silver in the cupellation process. Thus the true figure for the diet of the new standard – as we would now express it – after due correction for the loss would have been about 11 oz 4 dwt or 933 parts per 1000.

The Prime Warden at the time it was decided to adopt a higher standard for silverware was Sir Martin Bowes, the former Master-Worker of the Mint, and the Second Warden was Thomas Stanley, the Controller of the Mint. We shall see, however, that future officers of the Mint did not accept that the Company's interpretation of the standard should apply to the coinage. Indeed, the scene was set for a bitter controversy in twenty years' time between the Company's Assayer and the Master-Worker of the Mint. But as far as silverware was concerned, the Company tenaciously adhered to its decision concerning the standard for nearly seventy years. It was not until 1629 that, as a result of a lawsuit, it was forced to revert to the 'old standard'.

RICHARD ROGERS

After Elizabeth's great recoinage the Company was frequently called upon to carry out the duty of the Trial of the Pyx. Records show there were trials in 1561, 1567, 1571, 1572 and 1573. An established procedure was followed. The wardens were required by warrant from the Lords of the Treasury to nominate a jury of members of the Company who were then summoned to appear before their Lordships and other members of the Privy Council in the Star Chamber at Westminster.[4] On the appointed day the jurymen were sworn by the Remembrancer of the Exchequer. They then proceeded to make their tests to ascertain whether or not the pyx coins (representative of those minted since the last trial) were in conformity with the tolerances for weight and fineness as laid down in the indentures between the Sovereign and the senior officers of the Mint. Sufficient coins of each denomination and each mint mark were selected to make up approximately 1 lb troy in the case of silver or a smaller weight for gold. The lots were separately weighed and the total face value of each was checked to establish whether the coins were within the specified tolerance for weight. Each lot was then melted into an ingot, a sample of which was assayed alongside a sample taken from the standard trial plate kept in the Treasury.

An account of the Trial of the Pyx held in 1600 (written by a member of the jury) mentions that a furnace was permanently installed in the Star Chamber but that all the other necessary equipment was taken there by the Company on each occasion.[5] At that Trial the jury numbered fifteen and the Prime Warden was elected foreman. After the oath had been administered the Lords of the Council went to dinner and the jury set to work with the object of completing their task before their Lordships had finished their repast! However, finding that the assays of the coins were below those of the trial plate, the jury expressed themselves dissatisfied with the furnace and asked their Lordships if they could carry out further tests at the Hall. Their request was granted but Goldsmiths' Hall did not become the permanent venue for assaying the coinage for another two and a half centuries.

Following the appointment of Richard Rogers as Assayer in 1559 the routine of the Assay Office at first ran smoothly. But it soon became apparent that he had no intention of giving up his business in Cheapside, nor of moving his residence to the house provided in the Hall, although repeatedly instructed to do so. It was naturally considered a conflict of interests for the Assayer to continue working in the trade. The question of his future was discussed at length by the Court of Assistants in December 1564 but no decision was reached. There is no doubt that the Court considered Rogers to be extremely able and there was great reluctance to discharge him, in spite of the irregularity. Rogers himself continued to adopt delaying tactics. Then, in 1566 his situation was further compromised when he was appointed Assay Master at the Tower Mint under Thomas Stanley, now the Under-treasurer, who was also a member of the Court of Assistants.[6] Rogers' employment at the Mint was clearly incompatible with his position as the Company's Assayer since in the latter capacity he was responsible for the assay of the coinage at the Trial of the Pyx. As the minutes state: '… if any occasion of any such trial should now arise, for that he being Assay Master in both offices, should in executing the said trial, of necessity be his own judge, not without suspicion of partiality.' In July 1566 the members turned for advice to Sir Martin Bowes, but he died on 4 August before he had had an opportunity of giving his opinion.

The matter had not been resolved before a Trial of the Pyx was due to be held in February 1567. As it was obviously undesirable that Rogers should be responsible for the assaying, two other skilled assayers were selected to sit on the jury – Robert Browne and Richard Lee. Although this solution temporarily removed the dilemma the Company was not at all happy; the Lord Treasurer was consulted and as a result a commission of enquiry was set up. In the meantime Thomas Stanley was approached by his fellow members of the Court of Assistants. As Under-treasurer he was virtually in control of the Mint but he would not release Rogers from his post, although he was eventually forced to do so when the commission reported. The parallel debate concerning Rogers' refusal to give up his business in Cheapside dragged on for another ten months, until on Christmas Eve 1567, after an offer of an addition of £10 per annum to his salary if he would conform had met with no response, the Court agreed that he should be forthwith discharged. Rogers was obliged to accept this decision but he cleverly started to bargain for compensation for loss of office. He eventually agreed to accept £40.

Rogers was elected Renter in 1570, at the same time agreeing to submit himself to the judgement and order of the Company for matters between them. His expertise was still put to good use as he was called upon from time to time to assay articles which had been the subject of controversy between his successor and certain makers. In 1574 he was convicted of usury – a practice undoubtedly indulged in by others of his profession – but this does not seem to have affected his career, nor indeed his standing within the Company, as he was elected Fourth Warden in 1577.[7] He died in July of the following year. A number of apprentices had been indentured to him, including Humfrey Scott who received the freedom in 1575 and who was to become Assayer himself in due course. Rogers' nephew, also Richard, who was originally apprenticed to Thomas Stanley, was 'set over' (transferred) to his uncle on the death of his master in 1576.

Rogers died a rich man, owning a number of houses and land in the City as well as in Middlesex and Shropshire. It would seem that the acumen he showed in his dealings with the wardens whilst Common Assayer must have extended to his other business activities; but his Shropshire property was inherited – he originally came to London from that county to learn his trade. His first wife Katherin died in 1571. He remarried but his widow, Elizabeth, did not benefit under his will – he bequeathed his goods and chattels to Richard, his nephew and former apprentice, expressing a hope that the Company would grant him the lease of the dwelling house and shop in

The Goldsmiths' community

Between the fourteenth and eighteenth centuries the goldsmiths were a close-knit community, attending at Goldsmiths' Hall when summoned, mostly living and working in a small area around Cheapside or in Lombard Street. Their workshop, retail shop and living quarters were usually on the same premises. Many held their leases from the Company and the wardens often had to adjudicate when neighbours quarrelled, a not uncommon occurrence in the congested housing conditions. Families, extended to include live-in apprentices (see page 54), often intermarried. Thomas Keeling, the Assayer, for instance, was married to the daughter of another goldsmith, Robert Wygge, in 1555; their daughter married William Dymock, who was indentured to Keeling and succeeded him as Assayer.

Cheapside.[8] But in November 1578 Rogers' widow applied for the lease herself. The Company at first upheld her claim, but ultimately the lease did go to the younger Richard Rogers who later became Controller of the Mint. He became Prime Warden of the Company in 1601 and we shall have occasion to mention him again later.

THOMAS KEELING

The next holder of the post of Common Assayer was Thomas Keeling. A liveryman since 1552, he had served as Renter in 1559 and was about forty-six years old at the time of his appointment in January 1568. He had been active in the trade in Lombard Street, presumably with some success as he was assessed at £50 in goods for the subsidy granted to the sovereign by parliament in that year.[9] Already thirteen apprentices had been indentured to Keeling. In 1571 he took a further apprentice, Robert Flynte, who was to serve in the Assay Office for a number of years; and in 1577 yet another, William Dymock, who in due course became Common Assayer himself.

THE TWO VERSIONS OF THE DATE LETTER FOR 1567. *The one on the right was used after the appointment of Thomas Keeling, who succeeded Richard Rogers as Assayer in that year.*

It is on record that Keeling was a churchwarden of the parish church of St Mary Woolnoth in 1560/61. He had a large family – five children by his first wife, Alice, who died in 1554, and ten by his second wife, Thomasin, whom he married in 1555.[10] At least one son and a daughter died in early childhood, but even so, the house which was provided for him at the Hall must have been somewhat crowded. Thomasin was the daughter of Robert Wygge, a successful goldsmith with a lease of 'The Greyhound' in Goldsmiths' Row in Cheapside.[11] It is perhaps no coincidence that Wygge was a warden in the year (1566) that Keeling was promised the post of Assayer at such time as it became vacant.

Because of Rogers' mid-term departure there are two versions of the date letter mark for 1567–8, in order that plate which Keeling had passed could be distinguished from any for which his predecessor was responsible. From early January to 13 July 1568 the date letter, 'K', has the addition of a small pellet below it.

Although an experienced man had been appointed Assayer, the Court of Assistants was seemingly concerned at the shortage of other members of the Company who were skilled in the art. In 1570 John Gardener, a liveryman, was granted an increase in 'relief' on the condition that 'he forthwith set up the practice of assays making for the instruction of the Company'.[12] The

Court relied on such of its members who possessed the necessary skill to carry out assays on any articles rejected by the Assayer which became the subject of controversy. There were soon to be a number of occasions on which their assistance was required. In 1572 Ralph Barton, the former apprentice of Oswald Lye, was offered a yearly fee of £4 for attendance on the wardens when they made their searches and at other times when they needed his services in making assays. This arrangement was to lead to a bitter quarrel with Keeling in a few years time.

CHECKING OF WEIGHTS

The wardens had to deal with many offences at this period; most were for making or selling substandard wares but others included the use of inaccurate weights – an ever-present problem. In the course of a search in the West Country by two of the wardens in 1571, which included visits to Bristol, Wells, Bridgwater, Taunton, Barnstaple, Exeter, Ilminister, Sherborne, Shaftesbury and Winchester, no fewer than fifteen persons were found using weights which had not been sized and stamped by the Company. In the following year a search at the time of Bartholomew Fair resulted in the discovery of seven similar offences. In all cases the weights were either brought back to the Assay Office for checking or the owners were required to send them.

A PILE OF TROY WEIGHTS *provided for the Goldsmiths' Company in 1588, one of fifty-eight sets which were copies of a new standard set legalized by Royal Proclamation and distributed to various towns throughout the country.*

In 1573 some attention was given to the Company's own standard set of weights. It was agreed that it should be sized and made perfect and then should remain in the custody of the wardens, only to be used in 'cases of great necessity'. A second set or pile was to be checked against this primary standard and used for the routine sizing in the Assay Office. Each year, or more frequently if thought necessary, it was to be compared the first set and so 'kept perfect, upright and just'.

In 1574 action was taken by the Privy Council to establish new official standards of both avoirdupois and troy weights. A jury of nine merchants and twelve goldsmiths was appointed for this purpose. Regrettably the set of standard troy weights produced by the jury, although supposedly based on the Company's 'great pile', was soon discovered to be inaccurate. On several occasions during the next eight years the Company asked the Privy Council to authorize the provision of a new one. In the meantime routine sizing of troy weights was temporarily discontinued. Finally, in 1582 another jury of eighteen merchants and eleven goldsmiths was empanelled to produce avoirdupois and troy standards.[13] The resulting set of troy weights, known as the Exchequer set, which was again based on the Company's weights, was legalized and acted as the primary standard until as late as 1824. Under a Royal Proclamation a number of copies were made in 1588 and sets were sent to cities and towns throughout the country.[14] Fifty-eight sets altogether were distributed, including one which was provided for the Company and which is still in its possession. It consists of thirteen separate weights ranging from 2 dwt to 256 oz.

According to the 1588 Proclamation all troy weights used throughout the kingdom had to be stamped with the letters EL and a crown after they had been checked against the new standard sets by locally appointed officers. The Company immediately submitted a petition to the Lord Treasurer (Lord Burghley) drawing attention to its own ordinance, which required its members only to use troy weights that had been sized by the wardens and stamped with the mark of the leopard's head.[15] The Company requested that its ordinance might be permitted to remain in force and that all such weights might continue to be checked by the wardens and marked with the leopard's head in addition to Her Majesty's mark – a request that was apparently granted.

Coinciding with its involvement in the preparation of the new official troy weights, the Company was forced to review its policy in regard to the standard for gold wares. Although the statute of 1478 stipulated a minimum of 18 carats the Company had for many years insisted – rightly or wrongly – on a minimum of 20 carats, and this ruling was confirmed at a meeting of the Court of Assistants in 1564. The statute, although originally enacted for a period of seven years only, had been twice re-enacted, but it finally expired in

1572. During a single search in March 1573 the wardens seized gold articles from over forty traders; all except three proved to be below 20 carats on subsequent assay. The wardens now had serious doubts as to whether they were in order in insisting on a minimum standard of 20 carats. It was accordingly agreed in June of the same year that there would be a fine of ten shillings in respect any article found to be below 18 carats, but the opinion of counsel would be taken on the legality of imposing a fine if the assay report were between 18 and 20 carats. Before the matter had been finally resolved, however, legislation was passed in 1575 setting a new minimum standard of 22 carats.[16] This may seem surprising, but it was probably in order to bring the standard for gold wares into line with a coinage standard called crown gold, which had been introduced as an alternative to 'angel gold' (23 carats 3½ grains) fifty years earlier (see page 53). This was to remain the minimum standard for gold wares for the next 223 years.

The new statute also laid down the standard for silver wares; it stated that 'no goldsmith may ... sell or exchange any plate or goldsmiths' wares of silver less in fineness than that of 11 oz 2 dwt.' This was the first time that the standard had been expressed in figures as opposed to just 'sterling'. The Company interpreted the new statute as meaning that silver articles should assay at 11 oz 2 dwt out of the fire, in line with the decision it had taken in 1561 – although we do not know if such was the intention of the legislators. Strangely enough, the statute made no reference to the marks of the leopard's head or lion passant. Some writers on old silver have attributed the absence of hallmarks on many pieces made during the next hundred years to this omission. However, the earlier statutes of Edward I (1300) and Henry VI (1423), which required silver vessels and harness of silver to be marked with the leopard's head, were still in force.

That the expertise and standing of the Company's Assayers was recognized by the State is evidenced by the appointment in 1575 of Richard Rogers (the former Assayer) and Thomas Keeling (the present Assayer) as members of a sub-committee of four which was given the task of resolving a dispute at the Mint.[17] Richard Martin, the Warden of the Mint, had accused John Lonyson, the Master-Worker, of not adhering to the standard laid down in the coinage indenture. Lonyson contended that he was entitled to

RICHARD MARTIN, *aged 28; from a portrait medal by Stephen of Holland. British Museum.*

work to the limit of the permitted tolerance (2dwt in the lb troy), whereas Martin considered that the tolerance was meant to cover accidental variations only. There was a further difference of opinion between them as to whether the Warden of the Mint had a right to be present when silver was melted and alloyed. The committee reported in favour of Martin,[18] although we shall see that Keeling later became his bitter opponent while remaining a close friend of Lonyson.

DISPUTES

The period during which Thomas Keeling held the position of Assayer is of more than passing interest for several reasons and deserves to be considered in some detail. Firstly, because Keeling himself was undoubtedly an unusual and controversial character; secondly, because it illustrates how attempts to solve technical problems were hampered in an age in which scientific knowledge was lacking; and thirdly, because the incidents which took place underline the close relations that existed between the Company, the Mint and the highest officers of the State.

The first eight years of Keeling's term as Assayer were unexceptional; presumably the work was carried out to everyone's satisfaction. Then in May 1575 his deputy Thomas Tuttie died and Robert Flynte, who had been apprenticed to Keeling, was appointed to succeed him. In November, a complaint was received by the wardens. It came from the same Richard Martin (later Sir Richard), an extremely powerful figure within the Company and outside it. He was a successful goldsmith in Cheapside and at the same time Warden of the Mint. Some indication of his character can be gained from the fact that at this very juncture he had quarrelled not only with Lonyson at the Mint but also with his fellow members on the Court of Assistants, reviling them with 'sharp and unseemly words' which had so taken everyone aback that the wardens felt they should be fully recorded in the minute book. The cause of the dissent is not clear but there was some suspicion that Martin was in league with one William Sutton, who claimed to have obtained a commission from the Queen authorizing him to search for defective wares. The wardens were put to much trouble to prevent this intrusion on their prerogative.

Martin's complaint against Keeling was that some plate he had submitted had been damaged in sampling. It may well have been sampled by Flynte, but Keeling would have had to accept responsibility. However, after inspecting the vessel in question, the wardens decided that the complaint was unwarranted. Martin was not a forgiving man and there ensued an unfortunate hostile relationship between him and Keeling, which was to continue for many years, much to the latter's disadvantage.

Then, in March 1576 came a complaint from a Robert Marshall, who alleged that Keeling had made 'untrue' assays of some candlesticks which had been rejected and broken. Marshall had melted the articles and brought the ingot to the wardens with an assay report of 11 oz 3 dwt. The wardens were unconvinced because 'it was molten silver which in melting ever groweth fine, besides that in melting divers helps may be used to make the silver more fine'. Keeling had so far been on the winning side, but he had other worries – his house and that of the Beadle were visited by 'the contagious sickness of the plague'. In view of his large family this must have caused Keeling much anxiety. The wardens were taking no risks and until the danger was over they held their meetings away from Goldsmiths' Hall; one in August 1576 at Armourers' Hall and three in September at nearby Waxchandlers' Hall.

Six months later, in February 1577, a number of craftsmen – 'workers' or 'workmen' as they were called – complained that Keeling was taking too much sample from their plate; that his reports of by-assays – the assays of their ingots or raw material – were inaccurate; that he had caused their plate to be broken when it was in fact up to standard; and that he had marked silverware – six salts and three dozen spoons – which was below standard. Some of the workers also said that by-assays of their ingots had been reported standard by Keeling but that he had subsequently rejected articles made from the same material. Endeavours to settle these and later disputes were to occupy the wardens and Court of Assistants on and off for the next eight years.

On receipt of the first complaints Keeling asked if an independent person could be appointed to re-assay the articles in question. The wardens chose Richard Rogers, the former Assayer, to carry out the assays in the presence of the four wardens together with six members of the Court – including Richard Martin. The salts and spoons were found to be below standard. To add to Keeling's difficulties, he quarrelled with his colleague Ralph Barton.

The wardens decided that the workers' grievances were sufficiently serious to warrant a committee of enquiry. Three men from the livery were nominated by the wardens and Court of Assistants, and another three liverymen were chosen by the 'yeomanry' (freemen). The six men were asked to make recommendations. A month later on 15 May 1577 the wardens and assistants studied the report of the committee and made certain orders which were read out at a general assembly of the Company fifteen days afterwards. Essentially these were that any complaints about the Assayer should be made to the Court and that if they were considered warranted he would be required to make recompense for any loss sustained. Two complainants in particular – Henry Cowley and Garrett Richards – maintained that their work had been rejected through malice of the Assayer. The committee disagreed, being of the opinion that it was due to his or his servant's negligence.[19] Cowley was then in the process of taking Keeling to law but when pressed by the wardens he agreed to drop the suit and abide by the findings of four arbiters, two chosen by him and two by Keeling. Garrett Richards likewise agreed.

In the meantime, in July 1577 Richard Martin, who was now a warden, made a significant recommendation which was acted upon immediately. He proposed that two ingots of silver, found by assay to be 11 oz 2 dwt, should be kept at the Hall, one in the custody of the Assayer and the other with the wardens. They were to be assayed by Keeling and a 'skilful man' with him, and by William Williams, the Assay Master at the Mint, also with a 'skilful man'. These ingots, or trial pieces, were then to be used as controls. The principle was that a sample from the trial piece would be assayed at the same time as any article which was the subject of controversy. This was henceforth to become normal practice; it is surprising that it had not been adopted earlier, since trial plates had long been used in similar fashion as standards for the coinage.

The new trial piece was soon put to use in an attempt to settle the dispute concerning Cowley's and Richards' silver. The wardens had already ordered Cowley's pieces (five platters) to be assayed in their presence by William Humphrey, a former Assay Master at the Mint, but the results are not recorded. These articles and Garret Richards' silver (a salt, tankard and ewer) were assayed again in the presence of three wardens, including Richard Martin. The results (meticulously detailed in the minute book) show the average figure for all the assays to be exactly equal to the standard, but some individual results are slightly below. The dispute was still not settled, nor had it been a year later.

In the following month the three dozen spoons which had been hallmarked although allegedly below standard were assayed again in the presence of the same wardens. This time assays of the knops as well as the bodies were carried out and a comparison was made between 'lymell' (ie scraping) samples and hard (cutting) samples. The knops were found to be standard but the lymell assays of the bodies were 1 dwt below standard. An interesting conclusion is recorded, namely that the results of lymell assays were ½ dwt lower than those of 'hard' assays. This difference possibly accounted for some of the disputes, since the by-assays of ingots were probably carried out on hard or cutting samples whereas the plate made from them would normally be sampled by scraping.

Further assays of differing weights were taken from a single piece of silver, presumably to ascertain the repeatability of the method and its reliability with varying sample weight. The maximum difference between the highest and lowest result is 1 dwt for the quarter-assays; results for the four whole-assays (30 grains) are almost identical. There is no doubt that these trials were carried out very carefully. They must be one of the earliest recorded investigations into the accuracy of a method of chemical analysis. But of course, since the scientific principles of the process were not understood, the investigators were working under considerable difficulty.

The second bone of contention between the workmen and Keeling now came to a head – they accused him of retaining too much of the samples. The matter was considered by the Court of Assistants on a number of occasions. One or two members, including notably Lonyson, had some sympathy with Keeling, but all agreed that it was against his oath to retain any scrapings or residues except for the diet. They decided that according to custom the total diet should not exceed 4 grains in the pound troy, consisting of 2 grains for the diet box and 2 grains in respect of the 'waste in the assays and spillings'. Keeling was ordered to return to the workers all scrapings in excess of the diet and all residues from the by-assays. What he retained – referred to as 'the waste in the assays' (ie the 'assay bits') – were still a substantial perquisite. However, Keeling was determined not to give up what he considered to be his right without a struggle. He was repeatedly called before the Court of Assistants and asked whether he would abide by their order. At one such meeting in January 1578 he indulged in a verbal confrontation with Richard Martin which certainly did not help his cause. 'You are a parlous man Mr Warden Martin,' he exclaimed in a a great passion, 'and use me horribly and you have set a rabblement of naughty men against me. I have been fysted this five year by you, and you take the advantage of me so horribly, you ought to stand at the bar, as I do, and not to sit as my judge'. Such behaviour was obviously not acceptable and the meeting was adjourned to the following day for a decision on whether he was deserving of punishment. When sent for, he at first refused to appear, but eventually came; and on being asked if he would obey their order he said he would agree against his will to return the excess scrapings from plate after allowing for the diet, but definitely not as regards the residues from by-assays, unless he had due recompense in return. The wardens lost patience and called for the Beadle to escort him to the compter. The Beadle tried to do as ordered but 'as soon as he was in the yard, by reason of an outcry which was made by the Assayer's children, he brake from the said Beadle and went into his house'.

A week later Martin addressed a general assembly of the Company saying that he had been charged with acting out of malice to the Assayer and protested that this was not true. He asked anyone who thought he had so acted to speak out in front of them all. As might be expected, no one spoke – it would have required much courage to have done so.

Before long the old complaints against Keeling started coming in once more. A petition was received in February 1578, signed by twelve workmen, including Cowley and Richards. The wardens decided to appoint yet another small committee to consider the matters in contention. This time it was to be four liverymen, two to be chosen by the 'yeomanry' (freemen) and two by the liverymen themselves. But before the new committee had a chance to deliberate, the wardens had referred the matter of Keeling's indiscipline to the jurisdiction of the Lord Mayor, the ultimate course when their authority had been directly challenged by one of the Company's own members.

As a result of his appearance before the Lord Mayor (Sir Thomas Ramsey), Keeling was forthwith committed to prison for disobedience to the wardens. The length of his imprisonment is not recorded, but he was called before the Court of Assistants on 10 April 1578, three months after his unfortunate outburst, and the draft of a submission, the wording of which had been approved by the mayoral court, was read out to him:

> First, whereas you have disobediently broken the decrees and ordinances of your Wardens and Company in the execution of your office and have also disobediently rescued yourself from their correction which they had lawfully adjudged you unto. So they for execution thereof were driven to pray aid of my Lord Mayor. How say you, are you heartily sorry before God that you have thus offended us your Wardens and Company, and never intend to do the like again hereafter, and specially will you hereafter in all lawful things and matters be obedient to your Wardens and make true delivery of all such stuff of gold and silver that shall be brought unto you by any brother of this Company for making of assays – the accustomed diet of the house only except, according to the late order – and will you from henceforth deal uprightly with all the bretheren of this Company in the office of Common Assayer whilst you shall use the same without malice or partial favour towards any according to your oath and ordinance of this Company?

At last Keeling repented and signed the submission. He was informed that at the next meeting his salary would be reviewed. He refused several offers of an increase and it was not for another three months that agreement was reached; his new salary was to be £40 per annum plus a relief 'in respect of his great charge of children' of £33 6s 8d per annum. Out of this he had to pay for all coals (charcoal), cupels and lead and his 'servants' wages. He was to have no other 'avail' in money, silver or anything else except the 2 grains per pound troy of plate for the waste and spillings (assay bits). The one Warden who might have helped him to get a more favourable deal, his predecessor Richard Rogers, had been ill and had just died. An undated and unsigned memorandum, listing the expenses of the Assay Office, survives in the Public Record Office. It was undoubtedly written by Keeling at this time in support of his appeal for a higher salary. The document (see opposite) is of interest as it provides authentic details of the Assayer's budget in the sixteenth century.[20]

NEW REGULATIONS

The foregoing disputes prompted further consideration of the management of the Assay Office. In August of the same year (1578) regulations drafted by the three remaining wardens (Richard Martin, John Mabbe the elder and Thomas Nicholls) were approved by the whole Company. They were the most comprehensive yet recorded.

The Charges of the Say House Yearly

	per annum
For 2 men servants 3 meals every day at 2d a meal each	£18. 4. 0
2 coats each, one winter, one summer	1. 12. 0
1 cloak each every other year	13. 4
1 cap each	2. 8
2 pairs of hose & 2 of nether-stocks	13. 4
2 shirts & 2 bands	10. 0
2 doublets each	12. 0
2 pairs shoes each	4. 0
My own diet 6d the meal (and so hath the basest serving man that serveth any man yearly)	18. 4. 0
14000 coppels	4. 13. 4
10 loads of coals used in the say house	11. 5. 0
Lead used in the say house	1. 6. 8
12 mufflers for the furnace	1. 4. 0
Pot earth for mending & repairing the furnace	2. 0
2 books for entering the plate and says	4. 0
20 lbs candles used in the say house	5.10
Paper & ink	2. 6
For gressix, fire tongs, coppel moulds & other tools in the say house	3. 4
Sum total	£60. 4. 0

I have no more left out of my fee of £80 yearly but £19.16s to find my wife and children their meat, drink, apparel, coals and other things, and my maidservant's wages and her food. Besides all this my own apparel not reckoned. . . . Trusting your worships will have further consideration. . . .

Keeling's duties were to be the drawing (sampling) and assaying of all silver plate and the assaying of unwrought silver (by-assays). He was to keep a record of all assays and weights of parcels received. If he found any plate to be under standard or doubtful he was to give notice to the wardens, who were to arrange to have the plate re-assayed with the trial piece in the presence of at least one of them and two members of the Court of Assistants 'so as the truth may best appear without any favour or malice to any party whatsoever'. Keeling's successors were not only to be sworn yearly but to be required to provide sureties 'for the true executing of their office and redelivery of such plate as they shall receive.'

Ralph Barton was appointed Common Assayer for gold, Weigher of plate 'to and fro', Keeper of the weigh house and Sizer of weights. It was also his duty to assay all items which the Assayer had found to be under standard or doubtful. In addition he was to take in the money for charges and train someone to deputize for him as necessary. He was to have an annual salary of £33 6s 8d and to put in sureties for the true re-delivery of all plate left in his custody.

The new regulations also entitled all members of the Company paying quarterage to have silver by-assays free of charge if brought in before 9 o'clock in the morning (later in the day there was to be a charge of one penny). Likewise, plate brought before 9 o'clock would be assayed and marked free of charge but after that time there was a charge depending on the type of article and the number submitted. For every gold by-assay brought before 9 o'clock by any member paying quarterage there was to be a charge of fourpence, or sixpence if brought later. Silver by-assays submitted by anyone not paying quarterage were to be charged twopence and gold by-assays twelve pence. All parcels of silver articles were to be re-delivered weight for weight except for four grains in every pound weight – two grains for the diet box and two grains to the assayer for his waste and spillings in drawing and making the assay. The regulations also laid down a charge of fourpence for entering a maker's mark, and included a scale of charges for sizing of weights. Finally there was a clause to the effect that any member of the Company who was found guilty of 'colouring' would be fined ten shillings. Colouring was the term used to denote the submission of work on behalf of another maker who was not entitled to the 'assay and touch'.

In spite of the contentions centred on Keeling, the wardens were anxious that his family should not suffer; they therefore agreed that his wife's allowance should be increased by five marks (£3 6s 8d) a year. Keeling seems

SILVER-GILT TAZZA *bearing the hallmark for 1584. This was two years before Thomas Keeling, the Assayer, was discharged, so he would have been responsible for assaying the piece.*

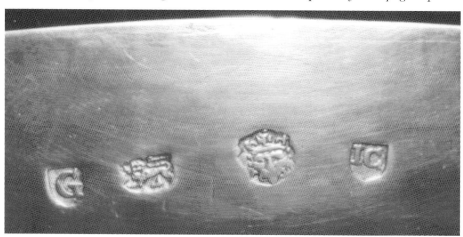

to have been concerned about accommodation for his family if he should die or lose his position, because in November 1578 we find him a suitor for a house owned by the Company which had become vacant in Foster Lane. His application was unsuccessful but the wardens agreed that if Mrs Keeling should survive her husband she should have 'some mete tenement for her dwelling'. The wardens also appeared to recognize that Keeling might relinquish his position, and it was agreed that in such an event he should have £50 a year during his lifetime, providing he conducted himself honestly 'like a good member and brother of the Company'.

THE STERLING STANDARD

The minute book for the remainder of the period of Keeling's tenure of office as Assayer is missing, but we do have the benefit of a number of manuscripts from other sources, notably the papers of Lord Burghley, the Lord Treasurer, Elizabeth I's principal adviser. From them we learn that certain workers were still not satisfied and continued to complain. The various documents also provide evidence of further hostility between Keeling and Richard Martin, this time concerning another matter, which taken together with the workers' complaints eventually resulted in the ending of his career.

The new controversy was spread over the years 1583 to 1586 and under a welter of complex arguments was basically concerned with two opposing views of what constituted the sterling standard. Keeling maintained that, according to the current legislation and Mint indentures, true sterling silver should assay at 11oz 2dwt in the lb troy *out of the fire*, and therefore to make it the correct proportions of the constituent metals were 11oz 4dwt of pure silver and 16dwt of copper. Martin argued that sterling silver was produced by co-mixing 11oz 2dwt of pure silver and 18dwt of copper,[21]. The conflict had implications for the coinage as well as for plate, and as Martin had, since 1582 been Master-Worker in addition to Warden of the Mint, he was now the recipient of the profits accruing from coining: Keeling's interpretation was clearly not in his interest.

Keeling admitted that the sterling standard before the year 1560 was indeed as Martin now interpreted it. However, he insisted that it had been raised by 2dwt in the lb troy in that year under the Mint indenture for new coinage. This had certainly been the Company's view at the time (see page 65). The Company's own trial piece made on Martin's suggestion in 1577 also assayed at 11oz 2dwt *out of the fire*. The statute of 1575 had not clarified the issue; it expressed the standard for silverware in terms of ounces and pennyweights for the first time, but with no reference as to whether this meant 'out of the fire'. The Company had, nevertheless, always taken the view that this was the intention.

Martin had great influence and rallied much support within the Company, which is not surprising as he was Prime Warden during part of the time, not to mention his aldermanic status. Some members, for example John Brode, who was Melter at the Mint, owed their living to him. William Williams, the Mint Assay Master, who was also a member of the Company, and his son Walter Williams who succeeded him in 1586, were naturally on Martin's side; and so was Barton who had been working part-time at the Mint. But Keeling was not without his supporters; one in particular was Christopher Wase, a future Prime Warden. As no agreement could be reached the matter was referred to the highest authority – Lord Burghley, the Lord Treasurer.

Lord Burghley acted without delay – it brought into question the standard for coinage of the realm – but he may well have had difficulty following the argument: his response was to elicit the opinions of Martin, Keeling and Ware[22] and to order a Trial of the Pyx. The Trial was duly held in November 1583[23], and proved satisfactory in itself, but of course failed to resolve the conflicting opinions of Martin and Keeling concerning which was the true standard.

Whilst this dispute was in progress certain craftsmen were still complaining that their work was being unfairly rejected. Keeling was in no doubt that most of his problems could be traced to Martin and in November 1583 he sent a detailed list of his various grievances to Lord Burghley.[24] He said that Martin had 'tied the whole company of workmen to the weakening of the standard, where heretofore they found themselves no way grieved but contented to obey the authority of the Hall'. His submission also included the following passage: '... touching the proceeding in speech between Mr Alderman (Martin) and my wife, that she should persuade me to yield to his comixture and then he would stand my good friend and do for me what he was able to do ...'. Keeling intimated that he was not to be influenced in this manner.[25]

In an endeavour to resolve the question of the standard for silverware, Burghley arranged for a meeting to be held at Goldsmiths' Hall in April 1584.[26] It was attended by Sir Walter Mildmay, Chancellor of the Exchequer, Thomas Fanshawe, Queen's Remembrancer, and George Peter Osborne, the Lord Treasurer's Remembrancer, with the wardens and other members of the Company. The record of the meeting begins:

> ... divers questions have been stirred and moved between the wardens and assistants of the Goldsmiths on the one party and Thomas Keeling their Common Assayer, Christopher Wase and Lawrence Johnson joining in opinion with the said Assayer, on the other party ...

Opposed to Keeling and his supporters were Richard Martin, now Prime Warden, the three other wardens and eight members of the Court of Assistants. It was at first agreed that the trial piece which had recently been made by the Company and delivered to the Lord Treasurer should be used to try all doubtful silverware. However, not everyone present was satisfied, so it

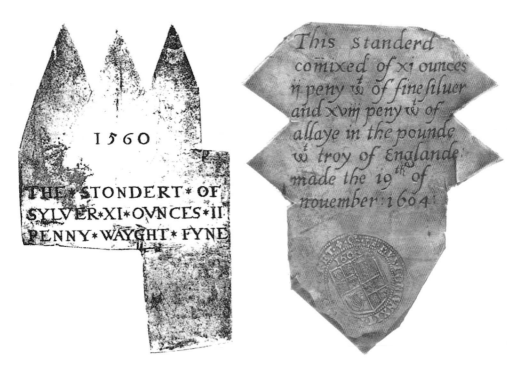

Left plate: 1560 / THE * STONDERT * OF / SYLVER * XI * OVNCES * II / PENNY * WAYGHT * FYNE

Right plate: This standerd comixed of xi ounces ij peny w' of fine siluer and xviij peny w' of allaye in the pounde w' troy of Englande made the 19th of nouember 1604

SURVIVING PORTIONS *of the silver trial plates of 1560 and 1604, held at the Royal Mint, showing the significant difference in the wording of the engraved legend.*

was finally decided that a new one should be made by mixing copper with some silver which had been found to be 11 oz 18¼ dwt fine. A subsequent letter from Sir Walter Mildmay to the Company, dated 17 June 1584, clarified this decision to some extent by stating that the new trial piece was to be made by calculating the weights of the two metals which would be required to make it exactly standard on the assumption that there would be no change in their proportions on co-mixing and melting.

We do not know if a new trial piece was made in accordance with these instructions. What we do know is that the Company continued to adhere to the interpretation it had adopted since 1561. Nor was there any immediate order for replacing the existing indented trial plate for the silver coinage. It was seventeen years before the Treasury issued a warrant for a replacement, directing the Company to provide it. The jury at this later date produced two ingots, one in the proportion of 11 oz 2 dwt of silver and 18 dwt alloy (the standard postulated by Martin) and the other 11 oz 4 dwt and 16 dwt alloy (as

A PLAN OF THE 1604 SILVER TRIAL PLATE *showing how it was to be cut (indented). The plan is taken from a book recording the Trials of the Pyx and new trial plates 1604–49, in the possession of the Goldsmiths' Company.*

The true model of the standerd of Siluer.

supported by Keeling and others) which were delivered to the Lords of the Council for them to choose which of these co-mixtures should be used.[27] A portion of the final plate as approved by the jury is still in existence, as is another made in 1604. The 1601 plate is inscribed with the legend:

> eleven ounces two peny weight of fyne silver comixed with eighteene peny weight of allay in the pound weight Troy

and similar wording is used on the 1604 one, indicating that they were made by exact mixing of the pure constituent metals in these proportions. In contrast to these plates, the one made in 1560 bears the legend:

> The Stondert of sylver XI ounces II penny wayght fyne

and the earlier 1553 plate merely has the words 'XI ounces fyne'[28] (see page 84).

The surviving record of the procedure adopted for making the 1601 and 1604 plates suggests that the fine silver used was assumed to be fully pure and that the theoretically correct weights of the two metals were mixed together, and this is confirmed by modern assays. Sir Richard Martin, still Master-Worker at the Mint, had at last achieved his objective.

KEELING/MARTIN DISPUTE

But even after providing the new indented trial plates for the Treasury in 1601 and 1604 (see page 100) the Company still stood firm as regards the standard for silverware. It considered it was bound by the statute of 1575 and not by any subsequent coinage indentures or the warrants for new indented trial plates. Anxious lest it should be prosecuted for marking silver which might be held to be below standard, the Company continued to adhere to its own interpretation for the next twenty-eight years. It was not until 1629 that a judicial decision forced it to accept that the latest coinage trial plate represented the true standard for silverware as well as the coinage.

However this is looking ahead. To return to the controversy between Martin and Keeling and to the meeting held at the Hall in 1584, the record contained an ominous paragraph about Keeling himself. This stated: 'Also the complaints and controversies betwixt the workmen and the assayer are committed to the order and judgement of the Wardens and Assistants as a matter of their judgement of right belonging. And if the assayer will not be obedient to their order and judgement then he is to be removed from his office and a more conformable man to be placed in his room'. For the time being, no action was taken against him, but the writing was on the wall.

The meeting at the Hall was primarily concerned with the standard for silverware, not the coinage and Martin had by no means convinced the authorities of the justness of his cause. Keeling had sent another memorandum (undated) to Burghley entitled 'Observations to be thought upon at the taking of the pyx at the Star Chamber'.[28] In it he made some sensible and pertinent suggestions: (a) that 'Alderman Martin should not be the nominator of such as are on their oaths to try the pyx seeing he is a party belonging to the making of the money'; (b) that no officer of the Mint should be a party to the trial, such as Williams, Brode or Barton; (c) that the coins should be tried by the indented trial plate or the trial pieces made in 1577 or 1583[29] and (d) that 'greater considerations ought to be had in the melting of the pound weight of moneys that they be not fired with saltpetre or suchlike … ' Possibly as a result of this memorandum another Trial of the Pyx was held on Burghley's orders in February 1584; a satisfactory verdict was returned, but Martin was nevertheless still accused of issuing substandard coins.[30] Further trials were carried out at his own request at Goldsmiths' Hall in July and August 1584.[31] This time the results were unfavourable to him, the assays of the coins coming out below those of the trial plate – which significantly was still the old indented trial plate of 1560. But the most acrimonious imputations concerning his coins came two years later from Robert Flynte, Keeling's former deputy, who had left the service of the Company some years previously to work for Lonyson, Martin's predecessor as Master-Worker.[32]

Flynte was no longer at the Mint nor active in the trade but in view of his charges (and possibly others) Lord Burghley ordered a special trial of Martin's coins by a jury of seventeen senior members of the Company, including Keeling, Richard Rogers (the younger) and William Dymock. It was held in the Star Chamber on 13 May 1586.[33] They followed the same procedure as was normally adopted at the Trial of the Pyx, with one significant difference – in spite of objections by Keeling, Rogers and another member of the jury, Henry Sutton, no trial plate was used as a control. Martin had strongly opposed its use and was able to obtain the support of the majority.[34] The assays by Keeling and Dymock were satisfactory but Sutton, who had been a member of the jury responsible for making the indented trial plate in 1560, afterwards wrote to Burghley saying: '… also how uncertain assays made by the judgement of the eye at several times hath been reported; I cannot be satisfied without the moneys had been tried and fired with the foresaid indented piece to know whether they truly reported …'[35]

Lord Burghley had taken pains to ensure fairness. The informer Flynte was invited to witness the proceedings at the trial and was asked to comment on anything he did not like. He was even given the opportunity of assaying the ingots himself, an offer he refused. At the time Flynte seemed to be satisfied but later wrote to Burghley saying that a trial plate should have been used; also that the assays should not have been carried out on coins that had been melted, since their composition was liable to be altered in the process.[36] He sent a report of assays he himself had made on individual coins he had selected at random.[37] Some of them were slightly below 11 oz 2 dwt, although within the tolerance permitted in the indentures.

GRANT OF ARMS *to the Goldsmiths' Company in 1571. The Company's role in hallmarking is illustrated by the coat of arms with the leopard's heads in the shield, and in the crest which is in the form of a demi virgin holding a balance in one hand and a touchstone in the other.*

In June of the same year, no doubt as a result of receiving Flynte's report, Burghley instructed Keeling and Richard Rogers (the nephew of the former Assayer) to carry out further tests on a number of Martin's coins, assaying each one separately. They too found some to be slightly below 11 oz 2 dwt.[38]

An attempt to discredit Flynte, who was causing so much trouble, is revealed in another unsigned document among Burghley's papers.[39] In it Flynte is accused of illicitly appropriating drawings (scrapings) when employed at the Assay Office; pawning a gilt bowl belonging to Henry Cowley; being 'a haunter of evil women' and enticing apprentices to abscond after stealing from their masters. It is probable that the source of at least some of these assertions was William Dymock, Flynte's former colleague in the Assay Office. Dymock was in line for Keeling's position and would have been anxious to ingratiate himself with Martin, although he must have felt he owed some allegiance to his former master (Keeling), especially since he was married to his daughter.

There the matter was allowed to rest. The controversy that had caused so much acrimony died a natural death without causing any further trouble for Martin, which is perhaps only fair, as his coins were well up to the standard as we would now interpret it.

DISCHARGE OF KEELING

In June 1586 the Company at last decided that Keeling should be discharged. There is amongst the State Papers at the Public Record Office an undated petition from Keeling addressed to Queen Elizabeth, in which he says:

> I have been turned out of my office by Alderman Martin's procurement because I would not consent to a new comixture whereby utterly to overthrow your majesty's standard and indented piece and ... do therefore most humbly appeal to be protected in my true and faithful service.[40]

In July 1586 the wardens and assistants wrote to Lord Burghley stating that it was untrue that Keeling had been dismissed because of his disagreement with Martin on the definition of the standard – on the contrary it was because of his inaccurate assaying.[41] They enclosed some rather unconvincing evidence of their contention, saying also that if Keeling had been willing to put in sufficient sureties for the due and true execution of his office he would not have been dismissed – apparently he had not been prepared to do so.[42] In August of the same year Lord Burghley received a testimonial signed by forty goldsmiths supporting Keeling.[43] They said that they had never found or known him to have dealt fraudulently or deceitfully but always honestly and uprightly – and 'for ought we know or can learn (he) hath borne and behaved himself as every honest Christian man ought to do.' But Keeling was not reinstated; nor did he receive a favourable reply to his petition to the Queen. In the meantime the wardens themselves supervised the Assay Office.

One must have considerable sympathy for Keeling. He was obviously a man of high principles who was conscientiously carrying out his duty to the best of his ability. He was determined to stick to opinions he considered to be right, even to the extent of suffering a term of imprisonment and eventual loss of occupation. His misfortune was really twofold. First, he was faced with extremely powerful opposition in the person of Sir Richard Martin and had less support than he deserved from other members of the Court of Assistants. Secondly, he was hampered by the fact that the cupellation assay as then practised had limited accuracy. He was rejecting articles which assayed at only ½ dwt below standard, whereas the method was hardly reliable to this degree.

It should, nevertheless, be recognized that the wardens and Court of Assistants were also in some difficulty, as on one hand they had to consider the interests of the members of the Company, but on the other hand they were concerned that no silver should be passed and hallmarked which might at a later date be found to be below standard. It is clear that they spared no effort to resolve the controversies. However, the evidence of inaccurate assaying by Keeling was slim and on the matter of the retention of the scrapings, it would appear that his salary was inadequate without this perquisite; he had to stand firm for as long as he could. As regards the definition of the standard, Martin's view is of course the one we would accept today, but Keeling was only upholding the decision which the Company had adopted for some years and indeed, as far as silverware was concerned, continued to observe for another forty-three years after his dismissal. It is easy for us to see how sterling silver should be alloyed and assayed, but we should remember that in those days there was no fund of scientific knowledge on which to draw. There was, for instance, no means of determining the purity of fine silver except by cupellation assay, with its inherent inaccuracy.

Keeling died in 1590, aged about sixty–nine. He left what little he had to his wife Thomasin, whom he refers to in his will as a loving and 'careful' mother to his children.[44] He had been in financial difficulties more than once during his lifetime. In 1568 he had borrowed £60 from the Company. And his well-to-do father-in-law, Robert Wygge, who died in 1570, referred in his will to debts that Keeling owed him.[45]

As for Sir Richard Martin, he continued as Master-Worker at the Mint until his death in 1617 at the age of eighty–three, having served there for nearly sixty years. After 1599 he held the position jointly with his son, also Richard, who predeceased him by one year.[46] Sir Richard was Lord Mayor for part of each of the years 1589 and 1594, and Prime Warden of the Company in 1579, 1583, 1587 and 1592. He was a tenant of the Company in a large property ('The Harp') in Cheapside, at the corner of Bread Street, where for many years he carried on his lucrative business as a goldsmith, later moving to Tottenham for his private residence whilst holding a number of other properties.[47] In

addition to the great wealth he amassed from money-lending and his operations at the Mint he derived considerable income as the Queen's goldsmith.
There is also some evidence, but not conclusive, to suggest that he or his son
may have been connected with the Grasshopper in Lombard Street, the
goldsmithing/finance business which originated with Sir Thomas Gresham
and eventually became Martins Bank.[48]

Sir Richard's fortunes changed dramatically, however, towards the end of his
life – he ran into financial difficulties after he and his son became involved in
overseas trading ventures, and in 1597 he was accused of misusing money
deposited in his care at the Mint. In 1599, while remaining Master-Worker, he
was persuaded to surrender his other post of Warden of the Mint to Sir
Thomas Knyvett, a member of Elizabeth's court, who contrived to ruin him
financially.[49] This led a short period of imprisonment for debt in 1602 at the
instigation of none other than a fellow member of the Court of Assistants,
John Brode, his one-time supporter and colleague at the Mint. Two months
earlier Brode himself had been in Marshalsea prison for a short spell,
presumably for debt and possibly on account of Martin. Brode was a warden at
the time and having requested Martin's presence at the Hall arranged for his
arrest as soon as he arrived. Later in the year Martin was struck off the Court
of Aldermen on account of his prison sentence. Meanwhile, his adversary
Knyvett continued to prosper and was raised to the peerage in 1607.

A successor to Keeling was probably appointed soon after his discharge but
as the relevant minute book is missing we do not know the exact date. Several
years previously the Company had – not without difficulty – turned down a
suitor for the reversion of the post. In 1579 the Company had received a letter
under the Queen's signature from Mr Wooley, Her Majesty's Secretary for the
Latin Tongue, recommending a certain Robert Sharpe for the position of
Assayer to succeed Keeling in due course. Sharpe, a tenant of the Company in
Goldsmiths' Row, was a liveryman and had been Renter in the previous year;
he was also one of the 'six men' who had been elected to review the
complaints against the Assayer in 1577. On receipt of the letter the Court of
Assistants interviewed him but he was clearly unsuitable for the post as he
admitted he had no knowledge of assaying – although he said he would
quickly learn from those who were then in office. It was a delicate situation,
but Sharpe was persuaded not to press his application. Although not securing
him the position of Assayer, Robert Sharpe's seemingly powerful connections
assisted him in another matter. At the special request of Robert Dudley (later
Earl of Leicester) and Thomas Parry, Treasurer of the Queen's Household, he
had been granted – ahead of other applicants – the lease of a property in St
Matthew's Alley leading out of Goldsmiths' Row.

CHAPTER FIVE

ASSAYERS IN ADVERSITY
1592 to 1642

W HEN THE SURVIVING RECORDS of the Goldsmiths' Company resume in July 1592, we find (from comparison of the relevant diet figures) that the total weight of articles submitted annually for assay and hallmarking had risen from about 100,000 to 150,000 oz during the thirteen years of the missing records. This was due in part no doubt to the increase in the population of London, which had certainly doubled in the previous fifty years and would double again in the next fifty. It was probably also due to the generally sound economic circumstances of the wealthier classes; there had been a growing divergence between the living standards of the rich and the poor. Moreover, although the country was still at war with Spain, the defeat of the Spanish Armada four years earlier must have resulted in relatively settled conditions in London and elsewhere and have contributed to the healthy state of the trade.

There were now two Assayers in office – Humfrey Scott and William Dymock, who had been trained in the Assay Office as apprentices of Richard Rogers and Thomas Keeling respectively. Ralph Barton's role (see page 79) was now mainly confined to that of Weigher.

In 1593 the wardens, accompanied by William Dymock, made an extensive country search in the eastern counties, starting at Stourbridge Fair near Cambridge. It had been normal practice on country searches to test articles by touchstone and to seize any that appeared to be much below standard and bring them back to the Hall for cupellation assays. On this occasion, however, suspect articles were assayed by cupellation during

THE DEMI-VIRGIN *from the parchment scroll in the Rogers Salt (see page 96), holding a gold-streaked touchstone and balance.*

the course of the search, so the equipment (furnace and balance) and materials (charcoal and cupels) must have been carried by accompanying servants, but the records give no clue as to whose premises were used for the assaying. The search at Stourbridge Fair took place on 27 August, after which the party proceeded to King's Lynn, Norwich, Yarmouth, Beccles and Ipswich. About two hundred articles from the premises of thirteen different traders were found to be sub-standard. Each offender was fined on the spot between 2s 6d and 20s and the articles broken. A full written report with the names of the offenders, together with the results of the assays and the fines imposed was later submitted to the Court of Assistants.[1] Many large wares are mentioned, such as beakers, bowls and salts, some of them made by London goldsmiths. On earlier country searches the wardens had usually restricted their seizures to small articles, probably for ease of transport.

Arising from this latest search the Company's authority was challenged by a goldsmith in Ipswich, which calls to mind the protest by the city of Norwich nearly a century before (see page 45). In consequence, the Company decided

A DETAIL *of London from the south bank of the Thames by C.J. Visscher, published in 1616.*

there would be no country search in the following year but the advice of counsel would be taken on the extent of the Company's powers. The Ipswich case, which was referred to the Court of the Star Chamber, dragged on for two years. The result is not recorded but one can assume it was settled to the Company's satisfaction, because regular country searches were resumed. In 1599 it was agreed that a search should be made in the West Country by two of the wardens, with a proviso that charges for livery, horse hire and other necessities were not to exceed a 'reasonable proportion' and that only Dymock and two almsmen of the Company should accompany them apart from their own servants. They found many substandard wares at the Bristol and Marlborough fairs, as a result of which fourteen persons were fined between 2s and 20s each. Again the assaying was carried out locally.

Provincial searches were continued for the next few years, but in 1604 it was decided to forgo the usual visit to places away from London as it would be likely to be very dangerous 'in respect to the present contagion, spread already in most places of the country' – there had been a serious outbreak of the

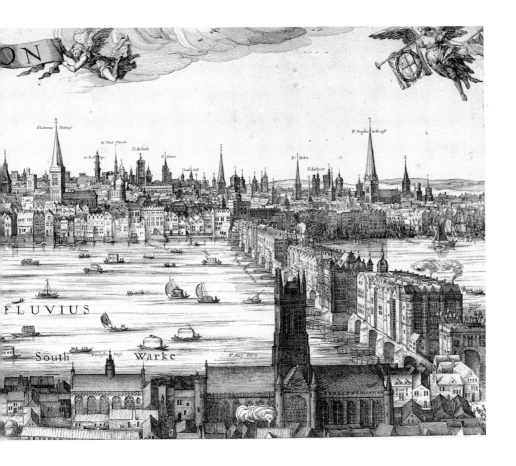

plague in London in the previous year. To this was added a stipulation that in the year following 'if it shall please God that the sickness may then cease, the wardens then to perform their search as accustomed'. In the event no country search was undertaken until 1607. On that occasion it was agreed it should be carried out by two wardens with the Beadle and an almsman in attendance and the 'assayer's man or ... some such skilful man of the Company in the stead and place of the assayer for the assaying of defective plate ...' A country search must have been quite a hazardous venture; apart from the risk of sickness and the discomforts of travel, the wardens were never certain they might not meet with a hostile reception by local traders. By carrying out the assaying *in situ* and avoiding the transport of valuable articles, the wardens at least avoided yet another danger – the possibility of robbery.

COUNTERFEITING HER MAJESTY'S TOUCH

Towards the close of the sixteenth century an outbreak of counterfeiting occurred which is well documented. Alexander Marshall and John More, both working goldsmiths, had already offended in 1595 by using excessive solder of a low standard in the manufacture of salts, for which they were fined 20s. Two years later they, together with one Robert Thomas, were discovered to have supplied a number of articles bearing counterfeit hallmarks to 'sundry goldsmiths and others'. The items in question included substandard beakers, salts, bowls and pepper boxes. In view of the seriousness of the offence the Company referred the matter to the Lord Treasurer. All three were found guilty of counterfeiting by the Court of the Star Chamber but it was believed that Marshall had fled the country. Their sentence was:

> that they shall be taken to Her Majesty's prison of the Fleet and thence conveyed and set in the pillory at Westminster with their ears nailed thereto and with a paper on their heads inscribed with these words, 'For making false plate and counterfeiting Her Majesty's touch'; and they shall afterwards be again set in the pillory in Cheapside with the like paper on their heads, there to have each an ear cut off, afterwards to be led through Foster Lane (where they dwell and where they made the said false and fraudulent plate), and again to the prison of the Fleet, there to remain until they shall have each paid unto Her Majesty a fine of 100 marks.

This well illustrates that counterfeiting hallmarks was a grave crime; indeed it is still so considered at the present day, although the nature of the punishment has now been modified!

Five years later another offender, named Kooper, cut the hallmark out of a

THE ROGERS SALT, *hallmarked 1601. It was given in 1632 to the Goldsmiths' Company by Richard Rogers (the nephew of Richard Rogers the Assayer) who was Prime Warden and Controller of the Mint at the time.*

silver bowl and 'lewdly and cunningly' soldered it into a copper bowl which was subsequently silvered. Not only this, he also confessed to removing the finials of six hallmarked spoons and substituting base metal ones which were then gilded. This time the Company itself dealt with the culprit. He was put in the stocks in full view of the whole membership with the offending bowl in his hand and then sent to prison until he had found sufficient sureties for working to the proper standard. After acknowledging his fault, he was later released and expressed his sorrow on his knees before the wardens. He was lucky not to have been taken to the Star Chamber!

FAILURE AT TRIAL OF THE DIET

Up to this time the trial of the diet had never revealed evidence of any irregularity on the part of the assayers. However, on 2 August 1599 the diet – in spite of being tried several times with the trial piece in the presence of three wardens and ten assistants – proved to be under standard. The Clerk was ordered to forbear entering the assay report in the minutes, so we do not know how far it fell short, but whatever the result, it must have caused much consternation, especially to the two assayers. Without knowing all the facts it is impossible for us to pass judgement, but the Court of Assistants took an exceedingly serious view of the affair. Scott and Dymock had not been required to keep separate diets, so they stood or fell together. Even if the failure had been due to the negligence or incompetence of one of their servants, they would still be held responsible.

The matter was considered at great length by the wardens and by the Court of Assistants. At first they were inclined to suspect some corrupt practice on the part of one or both of the assayers, such as favouring certain workmen for reasons of friendship or financial gain, but nothing of this nature could be proved. Each assayer tried to shift the blame on to the other, but neither would admit to any irregular practice.

In an attempt to discover any substandard wares which had been passed and marked, the wardens immediately made search, concentrating particularly on shops which stocked spoons made by one William Cawdwell, whom they suspected of connivance with the assayers.[2] Cawdwell was a specialist spoon maker with a substantial business; many of his products have survived. A great number of spoons were taken from eighteen different shops and many assays were carried out. The average of all the reports was 11 oz ½dwt. As this was *out of the fire*, ie not corrected for cupellation loss, the spoons were in all probability up to the standard as we would now define it, but they were slightly under standard according to the interpretation then adopted. All of them were broken and the owners compensated by the Company. Cawdwell was fined £10 and dismissed from the 'assay and touch', although the second part of the sentence was later rescinded.

It was decided that the two assayers should be dismissed, but fortunately for them, the wardens were unable to find any other officer with sufficient skill to replace them. They were henceforth not sworn as 'common assayers', but continued to work under the strict supervision of the wardens. After eight months of this uncertainty, the Court of Assistants, after long debate, decided that it would 'be likely that more abuses would abound in deceitful workmanship' if a new 'unskilful man' were appointed, and that in the meantime Scott and Dymock should be retained, but as hired persons, not as officers of the Company. At this juncture Humfrey Scott died. It was then agreed that there should be only one assayer in future, but that arrangements should be made to ensure the appointment of able persons under him to ensure continuity. In spite of Humfrey Scott's supposed misdoings, the wardens did not forget his widow; she was allowed 40s towards her husband's funeral expenses and a weekly pension of 18d.

In their deliberations the wardens took into consideration not only two letters from the Rt. Hon. Sir John Fortescue, Chancellor of the Exchequer, writing on behalf of Dymock, but also that the latter had 'very diligently applied the business of the assay office and carried himself very even between the workmen ...' since the failure of the diet.[3] It was thought that there ought not to be an unsworn Assayer but there was still no other suitable candidate. Dymock was accordingly called, and humbly confessing his former negligence and promising to amend his ways, was sworn sole Common Assayer. Sir John Fortescue had asked the Company to give a reasonable allowance for the proper maintenance of the office and in deference to this request Dymock's salary was increased to £60 per annum. At the same time he was ordered to take an apprentice who was to be taught the business of the Assay Office, so that there would be 'sufficient and able persons for succeeding times'. Dymock continued in his post for another seventeen years.

Three months before Humfrey Scott died further troubles caused some disruption of the work of the Assay Office. He and Dymock had been in dispute with Ralph Barton, the Weigher. Nine years earlier they had privately agreed to pay Barton £20 per annum in return for taking over from him the sizing of weights and the gold assaying with the attendant perquisites. Payments had become overdue. Barton's son-in-law was also involved, since he tried to secure from Scott and Dymock the discharge of a debt he was owed by Barton. On being refused he threatened to bring an action against them in the Star Chamber for passing substandard spoons. The wardens were asked to adjudicate. Such disputes were always taken seriously; all parties were questioned and the case reviewed at several meetings. Barton had said some uncomplimentary things about the wardens, who were particularly aggrieved that he should have rashly 'acquainted strangers with the secrets of this house' (telling his son-in-law about the spoons) and that he had 'set over' some of his duties without their permission. However, they took into consideration the 'infirmity of old age, especially when possessed by a man naturally contentious'. It was finally agreed that the assayers should keep the duties in question, as Barton was too aged to perform them anyway, and that instead of the £20 annuity they should pay him £6 13s 4d annually in addition to paying off the £5 debt due to his son-in-law. Thus the dispute was settled.

Three years later, in January 1603, Barton finally resigned and died within two months. Dymock took over the weighing of plate as a temporary expedient and at the same time petitioned for an increase in salary. He was granted an additional £10 per annum, on the understanding he kept his recently indentured apprentice, Walter Barkesby, and did not put him out of his service without the consent of the wardens. They were obviously concerned that there should be someone in the Assay Office who was competent in assaying besides Dymock himself. To this end it was stipulated that there should be a trial of Barkesby's ability on every quarter day should the Court so desire it. Barkesby was the only one of Dymock's seven apprentices to receive the freedom by completion of service. Thomas Dymock, who succeeded his father as Assayer, was granted the freedom by patrimony.

NEW TRIAL PLATES

In 1600 the Company was requested to make a trial plate of a standard 3 oz in the lb troy (250 parts per thousand) for the coinage of Ireland. Then in 1601 and again in 1604, as we have already mentioned, it was asked to provide new sterling silver plates. Furthermore it was required to make a plate of crown gold (22 carat) in 1604 and one of 'fine gold' (23 carats 3 ½ grains) in the following year. As customary, a jury of members of the Company was sworn in the Star Chamber on each occasion. According to the warrants issued in 1600 and 1601 there were six members described as 'being men known to be of skill, knowledge and experience'; they included William Dymock and two refiners, Edward Green and Humphrey Westwood.[4] The same persons were appointed in 1604 with the addition of seven other senior members of the Company. Dymock received a special payment for his charges for 'coals, mufflers, coppels (cupels), lead, melting pots and other necessaries and for his servant's pains.'

Portions of all of these plates survive. As we have seen (page 84) they were made by exact co-mixing of the theoretical weights of copper and the purest silver (or gold) available. In adopting this method it was obviously important that the gold and silver should be of the highest possible purity and the jury took appropriate measures. The itemized costs for making the 1604 plates show that payment was made to the refiners for their 'extraordinary pains and care in the business'. Their skill in refining has been confirmed by modern analysis of a surviving portion of the silver plate, which shows a remarkably low level of impurities.[5]

One portion of each plate was kept at the Mint and another at the Treasury. The 1601 trial plate was first used at a Trial of the Pyx in 1603, from which date, except for a few breaks, the Trial was held annually for the next forty-five years. The Company retained portions of the crown gold plate (22 carat) and the second of the sterling silver plates. The instructions for making them stated that they were to be used as standards not only for the coinage but also for gold and silver wares; but as we have noted, the Company in fact continued for the time being to use its own silver trial piece for the latter purpose.

LINKS WITH THE MINT

After the death of Sir Richard Martin in 1617 the most senior positions at the Mint were granted to Royal favourites with no technical experience.[6] Much of the real running of the establishment was contracted to members of the goldsmiths' trade: the close connection between the Company and the Mint thus continued. For example, the refiner Sir John Wollaston was Melter at the Mint – an extremely lucrative post – for over thirty years, and for much of this time he was also an influential member of the Company, becoming Touchwarden in 1633 and Prime Warden in 1639. He also achieved high civic office, serving as Lord Mayor in 1643.

Another link with the Mint was the common employment of an engraver. The Company's demands on his time were not great, however, as only a small number of punches probably no more than ten, were in use at any time. At the start of the seventeenth century the Engraver was Charles Anthony, a member of the Company who also held the same office at the Mint in succession to his father Deric Anthony. Charles Anthony had to be called before the wardens on several occasions for exceeding his authority. At one point he alleged that he held a patent giving him the sole right of making all stamps and punches. It so happened that he was a suitor for a lease of one of the Company's properties and the wardens were only prepared to put his claim forward to the Court of Assistants if he would acknowledge that he made the punches as a servant of the Company, not as a right under his patent. This he willingly did, serving to emphasize the hold the Company had over many of its members, who often relied on it for their working and living accommodation. Anthony was subsequently granted the lease and was excused the usual fine on the condition that instead of his annual fee of 10s he made the punches free of charge during his lifetime.

In 1614 he was again summoned before the wardens. The reason on this occasion was that he had been sizing goldsmiths' weights, for which he said he had been granted the prerogative by the Warden of the Mint. The Company considered this to be an infringement of its own rights. The matter was not settled before Charles Anthony's son Thomas succeeded his father as Engraver in the following year. He too claimed the prerogative of sizing troy weights.

However, he wilted when confronted by the wardens and agreed to discontinue this activity in deference to their orders. In fact they were able to force his hand, for he had recently been caught committing an offence which was a serious one in the eyes of the Company. The wardens, presumably acting on a tip-off, had found on his premises four wine bowls on which he had overstamped an old date letter with the current letter 'T'. His excuse was rather lame – that the punch at the Hall was defective and that when it had been brought to him to be repaired he had tried it out on the articles in question.

NUREMBERG SILVER

In 1607 the wardens had had to deal with a complaint from six working goldsmiths accusing certain members of the Company of selling silverware imported from Nuremberg in Germany. The quality of workmanship of this plate was exceptionally good but the silver was some 7 dwt in the pound troy below the English standard; the complainants felt that this was unfair competition. The Company took appropriate action. In February 1607 a Mr Hampton was fined 20 nobles for selling four items of Nuremberg silver to another goldsmith. He refused to pay and was promptly sent to prison, which soon brought him to heel; the plate was broken and part of the fine was awarded to Henry Chesshire to whom he had sold the articles. For his part in the affair Chesshire was denied the 'assay and touch' except for spoons. Other substandard wares from Nuremberg were found by the wardens during their searches and were broken. One of the offenders, William Ward, actually resoldered the pieces of a Nuremberg cup after it had been cut by the wardens and returned to him. For this further misdemeanour he was fined 10s.[7]

Eleven years later the Company became involved in a contentious issue concerning a Nuremberg ewer and basin which had been sold to the Dean of Westminster by John Williams, the King's goldsmith. The Dean sent them to the Company to enquire whether they were 'sufficient and lawful plate'. After receiving the assay reports, which confirmed that they were well below the English standard, the Court of Assistants decided that Williams should be fined 50s and that the ewer and basin should be broken. Williams was instructed to recompense the Dean accordingly, but he refused to do so, nor would he pay the fine, insisting that the sale was legal and threatening to take the Company to law if necessary, even if it should cost him £1000. The Company uncharacteristically retreated, perhaps fearing the possible displeasure of Williams' royal patrons, and was itself forced to compensate the Dean for the loss of his ewer and basin.

In 1623, when searching in Cheapside, the wardens seized more Nuremberg plate from a Thomas Wakefield. But before taking further action they decided to seek legal advice as to whether the Company's powers extended to

CUP AND COVER,
Nuremberg c.1600, by
Hans Petzolt, in the
Victoria and Albert
Museum.

foreign silverware and thus to settle the matter once and for all. They consulted Mr Noye of Lincolns Inn (later to become Attorney General to Charles I). He confirmed that all goldsmiths were bound, not only by the law but also by the Company's ordinances, not to sell any silver article below the sterling standard. No Nuremberg plate was up to that standard.

JOHN REYNOLDS

Other offences continued to come to light and many substandard wares were broken. Country searches had now reverted to the old format whereby suspect articles were brought back to the Hall; long lists of wares taken on searches in London and elsewhere are recorded in the minute books. In 1614, in an endeavour to curb workers from adding to articles after hallmarking, the Assayer was instructed to stamp the feet of bowls and similar articles with the mark of the lion – provided this could be done without damage (see pages 116–117). By this time Dymock was nearing the end of his forty years of service in the Assay Office. He died in 1617 aged about 53. The minute book records 'that on Monday the 8th day of September Anno Dni. 1617 being Our Lady Day about 7 of the clock in the evening, William Dymock, Common Assayer to this Society, departed this transitory life'. His widow was granted a pension of £5 per annum, later increased to £6 13s 4d, and the lease of a tenement adjoining the Hall.

Dymock's son, Thomas, who had been promised the position of Assayer on his father's death, was now duly appointed and sworn. He was not a success and received many admonitions from the wardens. In February 1619 they threatened to discharge him if he did not reform. He probably suffered from ill-health because he died in the following September at the age of twenty-five.[8]

Because of Thomas Dymock's failings the Court agreed that the office of Assayer was 'a place of great trust to be supplied by men of skill and integrity and doth much concern the safety of the Company.' They decided that 'for the better performance thereof, such as shall hereafter be chosen to that place shall from henceforth be yearly chosen by the wardens and assistants'. There were four applicants for the vacant post: John Reynolds, Thomas Masters, Henry Williams and Thomas Lawrence. Each was subjected to a practical examination under the surveillance of the refiner Humphrey Westwood – now a warden – and three members of the Court of Assistants. Samples of silver were specially provided and two days were allotted for testing each candidate. The Court duly received a report on the trials in October 1619 and proceeded to vote on the candidates. On the first ballot Williams and Lawrence were eliminated and on the second Reynolds was elected by fifteen votes to twelve.[9] He had the advantage that he had been deputizing for Thomas Dymock during the latter's illness, but it may also be significant that he had been apprenticed in 1599 to Richard Rogers, Controller of the Mint, an influential member of the Company who had been Prime Warden in 1601.

It is of interest to note that Reynolds had been forced out of a promising career at the Mint. Three years after receiving his freedom in 1606 the senior officers had recommended him to the Earl of Salisbury, the Lord Treasurer, for the post of Master-Worker in succession to Sir Richard Martin. They stated:

> John Reynolds has been trained ten years in the service of the Mint, and is become expert in making assays of gold and silver, trial of mines and ores, melting, rating and co-mixing gold and silver to any kind of standard, so that he is sufficiently informed in any service that concerns the master-worker's place ... [10]

It seems he was granted the reversion of the post but Martin hung on to it until he died in 1617 at the age of eighty-three. In the meantime Reynolds was granted an annuity of £40 for assisting the Mint Assay Master. After Martin's death the duties of the Master-Worker were taken over by the other senior Mint officers or sub-contracted to refiners in the goldsmiths' trade. Reynolds accordingly decided to look elsewhere for employment – hence his application for the post of Assayer at Goldsmiths' Hall.

It was not long before Reynolds made a number of requests to the wardens. He wished first to be granted the prerogative of sizing weights as had his predecessor; secondly, to be given a daily list in writing from the Weigher of the silver submitted for assay and marking; thirdly, to have the Assayer's house repaired. All these requests were granted. On completion of the house repairs at a cost of £61 14s 7d he was ordered to take up residence with his family. The wardens also provided him with an assay balance for which they paid £3 6s but insisted that it remained their property.

It was about four months after Reynolds was appointed that a special committee was set up by the Court of Assistants to review the Company's ordinances and other regulations. One of its recommendations read as follows:

> It is also thought necessary that hereafter all gold plate to be made be touched with the leopard's head according to the Statute of 18 E:1 and to that purpose the Statute to be read to the Company on the next quarter-day and oftener as the occasion shall require. [11]

This was probably not put into effect; there was in fact no Statute 18 E:1. The powers of the Company in regard to the hallmarking of gold articles had never been as well defined as they were for silver. Gold wares had regularly featured in the wardens' searches and certainly gold articles were received for hallmarking from time to time but no statute had referred to the marking of gold articles with the leopard's head. Even forty-four years later in 1664, when asked by the Government to provide figures for the quantity of silver and gold hallmarked, the Company was unable to do so in the case of gold plate, because (as it said) so seldom was any made that it was not the custom to make any entry in the books. The earliest surviving pieces of hallmarked gold plate are a chalice and paten bearing the date letter for 1507.[12]

THE WIRE-DRAWERS

Besides their use in coinage, plate and jewellery, considerable amounts of the precious metals were required for the manufacture of gold and silver thread, which together with associated materials, such as spangles and purl, were commodities much in demand. They were used in embroidery, especially of expensive clothes, ceremonial robes and badges, and for making gold braid or lace. The fine wire was manufactured by wire-drawers, whose trade was peripheral to that of a goldsmith. Of course the thread was too thin to bear a hallmark but the Company tried to maintain some control over the standard – with varying success. Samples were periodically taken by the wardens during their searches and given to the Assayer for report. In 1622 the wardens discovered several large consignments of silver thread that had been imported from Dordrecht in Holland. Assays of this so-called 'Dort silver' showed that it was well below the English standard, consisting of about one-third copper. The Company found that it was not easy to take effective action but after the wardens had made a number of representations to the Privy Council the importers were ordered to return the whole of the consignments to the country of origin.

For some time the London gold and silver wire-drawers had been intent on forming their own Company and in 1623 they succeeded.[13] However, the charter of incorporation granted by James I in June of that year had a short life; its terms ran contrary to the constitutional powers of the City as vested in other livery Companies, since a 'Governor' was to be appointed directly by the King. The charter was revoked by James in July 1624 after a Bill for its ratification had been rejected by Parliament. It is nevertheless of interest to us because of its reference to the Assayer of the Goldsmiths' Company. The charter stipulated that either he or the Assay Master of the Mint was required to assay all gold and silver used by wire-drawers, but whether they were ever called upon for this purpose during the twelve months in which the charter was in operation is not known. Closely associated with the wire-drawers were the refiners who supplied them with their raw material. The twenty-two members of the Court of Assistants of the new Company during its brief existence included the refiners Robert Jenner, Simon Owen and John Wollaston, all of whom rendered distinguished service to the Goldsmiths' Company.

Many complaints of abuses in the manufacture of gold and silver thread were voiced in the years following the revocation of the wire-drawers' charter and there were several contenders for a role in regulating their trade. Lady Roxburgh petitioned for a licence to assay 'in the bar' all the gold and silver used for the manufacture of thread and the Earl of Holland similarly applied for authority to assay the thread after it was made.[14] However, the successful candidate was Thomas Violet, a member of the Goldsmiths' Company. In the late 1630s Charles I granted him the prerogative of searching for, seizing and defacing substandard gold or silver thread and prosecuting offenders. Assays were to be undertaken by the Assayer of the Goldsmiths' Company under Violet's direction. Violet undertook his task with great vigour, incurring the enmity of many and putting several offenders in the pillory on the strength of the Assayer's reports. He even prosecuted the Queen's silkman and seized 50lb of silver lace in the possession of the Lord Mayor.

Violet also turned his attention to what he considered to be abuses by some refiners. He accused Sir John Wollaston of making excessive profits as Melter at the Mint, maintaining that he received £30,000 in the decade 1630–40 and that he had cheated the King of nearly £3000 yearly.[15] As a result the King appointed Violet as Master of the Mint at a fee of £500 per annum and also Melter in Wollaston's place. But Wollaston soon had his revenge. The opportunity occurred when he was Lord Mayor during the Civil War. In January 1644 Violet was indiscreet enough to bring a letter of peace from King Charles at Oxford to the City of London. He was forthwith committed to the Tower, where he remained in close confinement for four years and his estate was sequestered. But this was by no means the end of Violet: he recommenced his campaign after his release and indefatigably petitioned first Cromwell and then Charles II for a return of his former commission as overseer of the wire-drawers' trade. However, the granting of monopolies had been severely criticized by Parliament and he was not successful. The wire-drawers, meanwhile, continued in their campaign for separate recognition in the face of prolonged opposition by the Goldsmiths' Company. They were ultimately granted a charter of incorporation in 1693 and the Worshipful Company of Gold and Silver Wyre Drawers is still today an active City Livery Company.[16]

At the time of the discovery of the substandard silver thread from Holland three of the wardens were undertaking a further search when they were involved in an incident which is of interest because it shows how the Company dealt with members who obstinately refused to obey its rules. William Ward, who had offended some fourteen years earlier by selling Nuremberg silverware, had achieved some seniority in the Company and early in the year 1622 had been elected Renter. He had chosen to pay the customary fine of £50 instead of serving, but he still owed £30. The wardens suspected he was again selling substandard wares and for this reason decided to carry out a search. On 6 August of the same year, accompanied by the Assayer, they proceeded to his premises in Cheapside. There they were not only resisted by his servants but were also met with 'threatening speeches' and were shut out of the house in a small yard. Ward's servants then went into the chamber where his silver was on sale and having drawn the curtains removed 'such of his plate as they thought fit'. Meanwhile the unfortunate Reynolds was locked in another room. After many hours the wardens were forced to admit defeat and had to return empty-handed although they were confident that Ward was in his house the whole time and that the servants were acting under his directions.

Such behaviour was not to be tolerated, but the wardens had some difficulty in getting Ward to appear before the Court of Assistants. At first he made excuses and sent his servants instead, so the Court decided that the wardens should take a 'distress' (distraint) from him in order to ensure his attendance. The wardens accordingly went a second time to his premises and although they succeeded in bringing away a silver-gilt standing-cup and cover his servant would not open the door to the inner room. At the next meeting of the Court, on 16 August, Ward himself appeared and was told he owed £30 – the balance of the fine in lieu of serving as Renter – and a further fine of five marks (£3 6s 8d) for resisting the wardens' search. He said he would pay on the condition that he was excused all offices and attendances in the Company, but the Court considered this unreasonable. He appeared again four days later but after much arguing he now refused to pay anything. The Court decided the time had come to seek the help of the Lord Mayor, who forthwith made an order that Ward should pay the two sums of £30 and £3 6s 8d within one month. Three months later Ward had still not paid and was summoned to appear before the new Lord Mayor on the afternoon of the 24 November. This had the desired effect; 'being better advised' Ward came to the Hall and paid the fines in full. In 1628 he was elected Fourth Warden but was excused on payment of another fine – one suspects that it was realized he would hardly make a suitable Touchwarden! Three years later he again refused to allow the wardens and Assayer to search his premises but the outcome is not recorded. It may be significant that Thomas Sympson, one of the wardens involved in the earlier search, was now Prime Warden and it may well be that it was at his instigation that Ward's activities were again investigated.

OUTBREAK OF THE PLAGUE

A serious outbreak of the plague in 1625 resulted in a disastrous drop in the silver trade; the weight of articles marked between 14 June and 25 November was only 34,812 oz, about one third of the figure for a similar period in the previous year. It has been estimated that there were some 20,000 deaths during an eleven-week period. An indication of how seriously it affected the Company can be gathered from the fact that there were no wardens' meetings for four months after 12 July. When they were resumed the Prime Warden reported that 'in this time of the visitation of this City with that contagious sickness of the plague' he had received many requests for assistance from poor members of the Company in poverty and distress, and 'in pity thereof' had on his own initiative disbursed charity money on the Company's behalf. Fortunately the trade recovered within a few months and after another seven years submissions to the Assay Office had more than doubled. In November 1625 Reynolds told the wardens that he was receiving at least three times as many by-assays as any of his predecessors and requested some allowance. To ease the burden he had engaged two of the Company's almsmen whom he entrusted with drawing (sampling) and making assays – William Clarke and Richard Wooton. The Court considered this arrangement to be undesirable and that instead he should take an apprentice. Reynolds failed to comply and two years later the matter was raised again. He said that he had employed Clarke for six years and that he was fully satisfied with his performance. Clarke was allowed to continue but not to make assays; Wooton was to be dismissed. Seven weeks later a spoonmaker named Edward Holle complained that Clarke had spoiled some spoons in drawing. This was acknowledged and Clarke was ordered to compensate him.

For some time the Court had considered it unsatisfactory that Reynolds should be 'party and judge in his own cause', for example in repeating assays which were the subject of controversy. It had accordingly been decided in 1625 to engage a re-assayer who would do any special assaying required by the wardens. Alexander Jackson had been appointed in this capacity. In view of the shortage of skilled assayers in the Company, he was also required to instruct any members or their children or servants who wished to learn the technique. Although this appointment relieved Reynolds of some of his work, he persisted in his demands for a higher remuneration, which the Court resolutely refused to entertain. In 1629 he produced figures to show that his expenses were not far short of his salary. He said that he was making 15,000 assays each year, for which the cost of cupels was at least £10 and that this, together with the price of candles and the wages he paid to his two journeymen, left him with only £17 10s out of his salary of £70 per annum. He maintained this was a meagre allowance considering he attended daily, and that the value of the plate which he handled was worth on average about £70,000 per annum. But the wardens were still reluctant to grant any increase.

Meanwhile disagreements arose with some of the silver workers. They queried the trial piece that was used when checking articles in doubt (those which failed on the first assay), claiming that some which had been rejected at the Hall had passed when assayed at the Mint. Such discrepancies were occurring, of course, because the standard adopted at the Mint was in accordance with the 1604 indented trial plate, while the Company was adhering to its own trial piece which was of a higher purity (see page 76).

The Court of Assistants debated at length whether the Company's own piece should be used when assaying doubtful articles or whether the indented

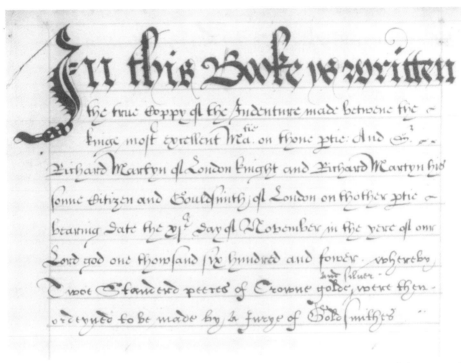

FIRST PAGE OF A BOOK *kept by the Goldsmiths' Company in which Trials of the Pyx and new trial plates were recorded from 1604 to 1649.*

trial plate should replace it. The majority felt that it would be safer to continue with the Company's piece as this would ensure without question that no articles would be passed unless they were in conformity with the statute of 1575. This was notwithstanding that the Treasury instructions for making the 1604 indented trial plate had stipulated that one portion was to remain with the Company for use in the assay of silverware. Getting no satisfaction from the Company, the aggrieved workers took their case to the Lord Mayor and Aldermen, who ordered that further assays should be carried out in the presence of some of the Aldermen, the wardens and the workers. Accordingly on 5 February 1629 a number of recently rejected spoons submitted by Edward Holle and Benjamin Yates, specialist spoonmakers,[17] and a cup of Thomas Francis were re-assayed; they were found to be slightly below the standard of the Company's own trial piece but better than the King's indented trial plate.

Matters were soon brought to a head. Holle took legal action against Reynolds, Clarke, his assistant, and Edmund Rolfe (the Touchwarden) for rejecting and subsequently breaking nineteen dozen spoons which he maintained were fully up to standard. The case was heard before the Chief Baron of the Court of Exchequer, Sir John Walter, at the Guildhall on 14 February 1629.

The defence was that the spoons were only 10 oz 19 dwt in fineness and that the King's indented trial plate was not the true standard for silver wares. In referring to the Treasury instructions for making this trial plate, the Company's counsel maintained that the paragraph authorizing its use as the standard for silver wares had not the force of law and could not alter the terms of the statute of 1575 to which the Company was strictly bound. However, the jury found for Holle and against the defendants. Damages with costs were assessed at £31 10s but these were not immediately paid and on 5 May Clarke was committed to prison. On 4 June Edmund Rolfe was also arrested and compelled to pay the £31 10s to secure his own release. Clarke was finally freed on 22 June. It seems the Company at first proposed to deduct the amount of the damages from the Assayer's salary in order to reimburse Rolfe – a further cause of complaint from Reynolds.

After the Guildhall hearing, Reynolds told the wardens that he had in fact always assumed that the King's indented trial plate was the correct standard and that he had never caused any silver to be broken if it was up to that standard.[18] This would be in line with his early training and experience at the Mint, but hardly consistent with some of his rejections. Anyway, he was severely rebuked. Now, however, as a result of the verdict at the Guildhall, the Company had no option but to accept the King's indented trial plate as the true standard for silver wares in future.

Since the Company's portion of the indented plate would be rapidly exhausted if it were in regular use, it was essential to have another working trial piece of corresponding fineness. Much time was spent in formulating directions for making it. The historic meeting at the Hall in 1584 had been convened (see page 83) to determine the true standard but it had also been concerned with the procedure for making a new trial piece. It had been followed by a letter from Sir Walter Mildmay, Chancellor of the Exchequer, giving more detailed instructions, and it was resolved that the new trial piece should be made in accordance his instructions.

Such was the importance attached to this matter that on 19 March 1629, only a month after the Holle case, members of the Court of Assistants gathered in the Assay Office for making the new working trial piece. Sir Hugh Myddelton, now aged sixty-nine and the most respected member of the Company – best known for his New River Company, which provided London with the first good supply of clean water – was particularly requested to attend.[19]

Three refiners, John Wollaston, William Gibbs and Simon Owen,[20] supplied four ingots of pure refined silver which were assayed by Reynolds. Each ingot was assayed four times, the average of all the results being approximately 11 oz 19 dwt. Mildmay's instructions, which were to calculate the required weights of the two constituent metals according to the assay report of the refined silver,

Refiners

Refiners, or finers as they were formerly called, were specialists who supplied the craftsmen with their gold or silver, the necessary skills being normally acquired through apprenticeship. Refining could be a lucrative occupation, especially if it extended to operations at the Mint. In the seventeenth century, for instance, Sir John Wollaston, Sir Peter Floyer and Williams Gibbs and his brother Richard, all based close to Goldsmiths' Hall, amassed considerable fortunes in their undertakings. All gave distinguished service both to the City and the Goldsmiths' Company. The Company relied on the services of one or more refiners when required to provide new trial plates as standards for the coinage.

were not in fact followed. In spite of Reynolds' assay results it was assumed that the refined silver ingots were fully pure – a justified conclusion since there would have been some cupellation loss when assaying them; the same assumption had been made when the 1604 plate was made.

Four portions of pure copper each weighing 18 dwt were put into the bottom of the pot, followed by four portions of the refined silver, each portion weighing 11 oz 2 dwt and taken from the separate ingots. The whole was then melted down twice, but the assayer was not satisfied and decided it should be melted down once more, which was done on the following day. It was then cast into an ingot and forged. Reynolds made duplicate assays of both the new piece and the King's indented plate in two separate fires. In the first fire three of the four assays were 'all alike and one of the assays of the new piece was less than the other by a quarter dwt'. In the second fire the four assays were all equal to the King's indented plate. Twelve days later arrangements were made for further independent assays. Wollaston, Gibbs, Owen,

EWER AND BASIN *with hallmark for 1611 and maker's mark SO, which has been attributed to Simon Owen. He was primarily a refiner but presumably also dealt in the supply of plate. According to the Company's minutes a ewer and basin together with a quantity of diet silver was delivered to Simon Owen in 1611 for melting. It was accompanied by an order for a new ewer and basin, in all probability these pieces. They were subsequently sold by the Company in 1637 and have only recently been rediscovered.*

Thomas Francis and Henry Williams each assayed the new piece and found it agreed with the indented plate.

The provision of the new trial piece by no means signalled the end of the workers' complaints. Within two months thirteen of them (including, as might be expected, Edward Holle) presented formal protests and all appeared in person before the Court of Assistants.[21] Eight separate reasons were given why neither the Assayer nor his servants were fit to 'judge or censure the plate'. The petition was unsigned. On being asked why, they said that not all of them could justify every one of the complaints. Accordingly each of the eight paragraphs was then signed by those supporting it.

The complaints were damaging. Even allowing for exaggeration, it is clear that Reynolds had made enemies of a certain section of the trade. One suspects that it was his character and overbearing approach that were largely to blame. The petition contained the following passages:

> Because he having set aside all fear of God hath violated his annual oath by favour, affection, hate and evil wills … Because he is partial in his office, allowing plate of the fineness of the standard to be touched for them he favoureth and causing the wardens to break some far better of the workmen disapproved by him …

And again:

> Because of his fury or rather madness, who in his rage hath misused many, as sometimes he hath broken plate when he hath passed it for good, writing thereon 'have a care' or 'take warning' … Because of his other employments he cannot attend his office as he ought but leaveth the sole managing thereof to his servants … Because he does abet and maintain his servants to abuse men, compelling them to pay money, despising any order given by the wardens but suffering them to detain men's silver both in assays and drawings.

And the final paragraph:

> Presumes he has sufficient protection as king's servant, daring any man he hath wronged to touch him.

The appointment of a re-assayer had not alleviated the tension. Alexander Jackson, who held the position, actually signed three of the paragraphs himself – maybe he already had his eye on Reynolds' post.

Reynolds submitted a long counter-petition in defence, in which he put his side of the controversy. He pointed out that it was the ancient custom for plate found to be below standard to be broken with due ceremony and solemnity by the wardens at one of their meetings in the presence of the maker. He said that this procedure had a very salutary effect, but that it had lately been changed and plate was now broken in the Assay Office by one of the wardens without ceremony. Reynolds maintained that because of this innovation

> Edmund Holle, a younger man of the Company, who having a quantity of spoons to be touched, the same being assayed and found defective and thereupon by his own consent broken, this man, being not seasoned by that true obedience as by his oath is required to his wardens, out of his turbulent spirit, did afterwards cause some of the spoons to be assayed by Mr Symon Owen, a finer but no sworn officer from whose report any assurance may be taken, and others of them to be assayed and made into moneys at the Mint. Both which trials the property of the spoons being altered in the melting, and so tried contrary to the manner of the trials of the spoons made by your petitioner, whose manner in making the assays (is) to draw every particular spoon and to mingle the drawings together, whereas in the meltings they may force it and so make the silver finer for the assay ... This affront of his to his wardens and to your petitioner their Deputy ... to be without precedent in former times and an action full of presumption and most dangerous in the consequences thereof for the preserving of government both in the City and country ... will grow into an open contempt of the Company's ordinances and become a pattern to other factious persons on like occasions.

Reynolds also pointed out that Holle had had defective spoons broken in the Assay Office on three occasions since the hearing at the Guildhall. He then mentioned his 'mean allowance' and requested an additional payment for making fires every day and for 100 assays of gold articles taken on searches and, quite reasonably, one would have thought, a remittance for the charges he had borne for joiner's work in the Assay Office. Finally, he asked for some action to be taken for the relief of his servant, William Clarke, who was still in prison. Perhaps unwisely, he hinted that he had powerful friends who would be helpful to him, but added that it was far from his thoughts to call on them – until obliged to do so.

The wardens were getting impatient with Reynolds' continual requests for an increase in salary. They called him to attend a meeting of the Court of Assistants at which his petition and the list of his expenses were read out. He was then asked to leave the meeting, whereupon Edmund Rolfe related many affronts that Reynolds had given to the wardens during the past year and more particularly to him as Touchwarden. The question was moved whether Reynolds was fit to continue as Common Assayer. It was then agreed by the ballot box – by nineteen votes to five – that some other candidates besides Reynolds should be put into the next election of Assayer. The election took place in the following month of June 1629 and Alexander Jackson (then the Re-assayer), Thomas Masters, Henry Williams and Thomas Francis were nominated along with Reynolds. Alexander Jackson was elected, Thomas Masters being appointed Re-assayer in his place.

The Company had not heard the last of Reynolds. He put in an appeal to be re-instated, which was not accepted. He also refused to vacate his house in the Hall unless compelled to do so by law and the Company was forced to set in motion legal steps to evict him. In the meantime he had sent a petition to the King alleging wrongful dismissal and in response the Company delivered a counter-petition to the Privy Council. A special Court of Assistants was called on 18 January 1630 to consider the case, which was to be heard before the Council on the following day. The wardens were detailed to instruct the Company's legal adviser, as well as the Recorder of London. The Council – represented by the Lord Keeper (Thomas Lord Coventry), the Lord President and the Vice-Chamberlain – ruled that 'the wardens were the officers for the assays and that Reynolds was but their deputy to be placed and displaced by them at their pleasure according to his demerits'; and that 'it pleased their lordships to reprehend Reynolds for his miscarriage towards the wardens'. Their Lordships nevertheless recommended that as Reynolds 'had been a servant to the Company divers years', he should be reinstated or, if not, that he should receive some monetary compensation.

The Court of Assistants decided that Reynolds should have some amends for loss of office, with the proviso that he agreed to the recall and suppression of a publication 'whereby he doth scandal the former deputy officers of assays and all workmasters of the Company and in particular one of the late wardens'. Further,

> that he may as a brother of the Company not attempt anything directly or indirectly to the disturbance of the Company or any of the said wardens, and to deliver up to the Company the quiet possession of their house and such things within the house as he detaineth from them. And the puncheon of the lion be delivered to the wardens to whom the same doth belong.

This did not settle the matter. Reynolds again petitioned the King, as a result of which the wardens were informed that 'His Majesty being well informed of the petitioner's abilities … commanded another full hearing of the cause before the Lord Keeper, the Lord President and Mr Vice-Chamberlain.' It was held at Whitehall on 31 March 1630. The wardens declared that they were willing to give Reynolds £100 besides £24 which was due to him. Their Lordships concurred but with the stipulation that Reynolds should deliver the house and the punches in his possession. They also ordered the recall and suppression of the book and directed Reynolds to 'carry himself hereafter respectfully towards the said Company in general and in all peaceable and

COMMUNION CUP AND PATEN *from St Mary, Fetcham, in Middlesex, with hallmark for 1636, and an additional lion passant mark struck on the foot to prevent fraud.*

quiet manner towards the particular members thereof as becometh a brother of the same society'.[22]

The wardens paid the £24 owing to Reynolds; (for gold assays and joiner's work in the Assay Office – at least a year overdue) and in return Reynolds handed over two punches, the lion and the letter 'L' (for the year 1628). Then, on the morning of 18 June 1630, he came to the wardens saying he would deliver possession of the house and demanded the sum of £100 according to the order of the Privy Council. It was agreed this would be paid to him in the afternoon. According to the relevant minute, '... he was well satisfied and being requested by the wardens to dine with them, he thereunto condescended and after dinner the said sum of £100 was paid unto him for which he gave a receipt and departed in a friendly manner'. The wardens were no doubt thankful the matter had at last been resolved without further bitterness. Reynolds was nothing if not persistent; some thirteen years later he approached the Company asking for some further consideration to supplement the £100 awarded to him on his dismissal. Not surprisingly he was unsuccessful.

Looking back on Reynolds' service with the Company it is evident that many of his misfortunes, like those of Keeling sixty years earlier, stemmed from the fact that the technical processes with which he was concerned were not fully understood, although his knowledge of them was undoubtedly superior to that of most of his contemporaries. He was correct, for instance, in saying that differing assay results might be expected for a batch of silver spoons, depending on whether the sample was taken from the articles themselves or from the ingot obtained after melting them. The conditions under which the melting was carried out could well affect the result. Also it is now known, although not so in Reynolds' time, that some segregation of the main constituents is inevitable in sterling silver unless special precautions are taken to prevent it. Furthermore, Reynolds certainly cannot be blamed for the dispute over the trial piece. And as regards the workers' accusations of impartiality, the employment of a re-assayer should, one would have thought, have removed much of the vexation they felt, although clearly it did not do so. It is significant that Holle continued to have spoons rejected long after the court case; on his fifth offence the Court of Assistants considered committing him to prison, but eventually on his promise not to offend again settled for another fine.

Probably Reynolds' main fault, apart from his attitude towards some members of the trade, was that he left too much of the daily work to his servants. The petition from the thirteen workmen refers to his other employments and to his being the 'King's man' – did he perhaps continue to work at the Mint in some capacity during his time with the Company? What is again apparent is that the position of Assayer required someone with more than just technical competence. It was necessary that he should be seen to be fair and not unreasonable in dealing with members of the trade, a small number of whom, perhaps owing to their cantankerous natures, needed to be approached in a tactful manner.

After his discharge Reynolds returned to the Mint, his former place of employment – if indeed he had ever completely left it. We know that he was still working there as Under-Assayer in 1649.[23] During this time he compiled tables for adjusting the fineness of gold and silver alloys, which were first published in 1651.[24] In 1633 he spent seventeen weeks in the Fleet prison for debt. The cause of this further misfortune – according to one of his petitions – was that he was owed £900 by Sir Thomas Aylesbury for making sets of weights.[25] The date of his death has not been traced.

The above events may give the impression that the Assay Office was never free from disputes and permanently in a state of turmoil, but such was certainly not the case. The complaining craftsmen did not necessarily represent the majority of those submitting work for assay and marking, and in between the incidents described here the daily routine continued without interruption, many thousands of articles being received, the vast majority passed and hallmarked. There had recently been a substantial growth in the receipts of silverware. In the first quarter of the century the amounts had remained fairly steady at around 200,000 oz per annum but then they rapidly increased, reaching a peak of more than 500,000 oz by 1637. On average, about one per cent of all wares were found to be below standard and were broken. This figure rose to between 1½ and 2 per cent towards the end of the century but dropped again after 1700.

FURTHER DISPUTES

On 26 June 1630, the Assay Office received an item for marking of sufficient interest to warrant a special entry in the minute book. This was a gold standing-cup and cover weighing 296 oz made by Thomas Francis for Thomas Vyner, a goldsmith in Lombard Street, and sold by him to the civic authorities 'to be given as a free gift from the City of London by the Lord Mayor and Aldermen tomorrow 27 June at the Court of St James's at the baptism of the young Prince'. The young Prince was the future Charles II, who in due course became a close friend of Thomas Vyner's nephew, Robert.

The appointment of the new Assayer – Alexander Jackson – in 1630 did not entirely pacify the whole of the trade. In February 1631 nine workers petitioned the Lord Mayor and Aldermen, accusing Jackson not only of wrongfully rejecting some of their wares but also of detaining others for several weeks. Jackson, hitherto a complainant, was now on the receiving end. The petitioners asserted that the wardens although not skilled in assaying had nevertheless supported the Assayer. The petition was duly considered by the wardens, who were no doubt greatly incensed that the signatories should have gone over their heads to complain to the Lord Mayor. Jackson said that he had made many tests of the articles in question and had found them to be worse than standard. The wardens ordered more assays of the items belonging to one of the petitioners, Robert Snowe, a liveryman of nine years' standing. The thirty-six trencher plates and dishes were found to be ½dwt worse than standard and were forthwith broken. All the petitioners were summoned and after the relevant ordinances had been read out to them they were each ordered to pay a fine of £2 for their affront to the wardens.

A month later Snowe was asked to pay the fine imposed for 'exhibiting and publishing a slanderous petition against his wardens'. He utterly refused and justified himself by saying 'he had been much wronged by some in this assembly' and that he would appeal again to the Lord Mayor and Aldermen. Only one of the petitioners paid his fine and the Court accordingly directed the wardens to take distresses from the others in the form of pieces of silverware. A constable and one of the Lord Mayor's officers accompanied the wardens to the petitioners' premises where various articles were seized, including a ewer weighing 30oz 7dwt from Robert Snowe, a salt weighing 10oz 11dwt from Clement Carter, a sugar box and cover from William Cooke, a bowl from Richard Carter, a round salt weighing 16oz 15dwt from John Adderton and eight thimbles, ten bodkins and a small 'currall' (child's toy) from Thomas Duffield. The next day Duffield came to apologize to the wardens, saying that he had been persuaded to sign the petition by Clement Carter, who had asked to meet him at the Flying Horse tavern, where were Robert Snowe, Thomas Francis and (of course) Edward Holle. Ten days later the distresses were sold; the differences between the receipts from the sales and the amounts of the fines were offered to the respective petitioners, all of whom refused to accept the money – they were out for blood.

In April Robert Snowe took out subpoenas in the Court of Exchequer against Mr Warden Manning, Alexander Jackson (the Assayer), Thomas Masters (the Re-assayer) and Ralph Robinson (the Beadle), charging them with wrongful breaking of his plate. He also laid information against the Company in the Star Chamber 'for the discovery of the indirect practices and combinations amongst themselves'. In reply the Company decided it should itself take proceedings against Snowe and his associates in the Star Chamber and lost no time in petitioning the Privy Council for assistance and protection 'against the clamours and unbridled courses of some unruly members of their Company whose aim is only to work deceitfully without control'.

After due consideration in June 1631, the Council referred the matter to the Attorney General for report, ordering him to move a stay of the proceedings in the Court of Exchequer. At the same time, in view of Snowe's

SIR THOMAS VYNER (1588–1665), *the wealthy goldsmith-banker, and uncle of Sir Robert Vyner, was Touchwarden in 1634, Prime Warden in 1645 and Lord Mayor 1653. This portrait, by Gerard Soest, was presented to the Goldsmiths' Company in 1671.*

'disobedience and refractory carriage, tending to contempt and opposing of all order and government ... ', the Council encouraged the Company to hasten their proceedings against him.[26]

After questioning both sides, the Attorney General – William Noye – issued his report which was considered by the Council on 6 April 1632.[27] The case hinged on whether the assay should be carried out on a 'sad' (solid) sample or on drawings (scrapings). The Company stated that Snowe's plate had been found by the Assayer and Re-assayer to be below standard, and that it had also been found 'wanting' after further tests by both assayers in the presence of Wollaston and other members of the Court of Assistants. This was not contested by Snowe, but he said that if the assays had been made with 'sad' samples and not drawings his plate would have 'held good'. The Company maintained that it was the normal practice in the Assay Office to use drawings since it would be impossible to take solid samples from every piece of plate. In his report the Attorney General said he could not discern that there was any malice against Snowe, either by the Assayer, Re-Assayer or any other person, and he upheld the right of the Company to take samples by drawing. The Council accepted the report; it was an important and satisfactory decision for the Company.

The Council additionally ordered that Snowe should be required 'to submit himself to the Company and its government'. Nearly two years later he had still not done so. In December 1632 he went some way towards apologizing to the Court of Assistants, but his submission was not accepted as it was considered he was not sufficiently contrite. As there is no further mention of the Company's action against Snowe and others in the Star Chamber, it is probable that it was decided to drop it.

To emphasize the seriousness of submitting substandard silver for assay it was decided that in future no such plate would be broken in the Assay Office but only in the parlour (of the Hall) in the presence of the wardens – a return to former practice. During the next twelve months both Snowe and Holle had substantial quantities of plate broken – sixteen basins, six dishes, two trenchers, twelve saucers and twelve salts submitted by Snowe, and 198 spoons by Holle.

John Wollaston was elected Touchwarden in 1633 and Thomas Vyner in the year following. They were both destined to have distinguished careers, amassing considerable wealth – Wollaston as Melter at the Mint and Vyner as a successful goldsmith banker. Thomas Vyner tried to avoid serving as Touchwarden by offering to pay a fine but this was refused; being classed as a working goldsmith he was expected to do his stint of duty. Whilst serving he reported to the Court of Assistants in February 1635 that Thomas Duffield had brought to the Assay Office two silver kettles and three large candlesticks which the Assayer found to be 'deceitfully made'. Duffield, it will be remembered, was the petitioner who had apologized to the Court some months earlier, but on this occasion when informed of the Assayer's findings he had come to the Hall and 'in a violent and outrageous manner did so misbehave himself towards Mr Jackson, the assayer, that he (Jackson) affirmed he was in fear of his life, because he thrust him out of the office and he brake a great part of the glass window belonging thereto, and giving many vile and reviling speeches ... ' Jackson quoted Duffield as saying 'he would put his guts out about his heels'. Duffield was summoned before the Court and Jackson read his reports of the assays. The bodies of the kettles and candlesticks and the plate of the nozzles were up to standard but the handles of the kettles and the swages of the nozzles were 20 dwt worse. Submitting parcels containing articles of differing fineness was always considered a serious offence as it was assumed it was done fraudulently. Duffield was committed to the compter and not released until he apologized twelve days later. He was also ordered to pay Jackson 3s 6d for new window glass.

Country searches were not neglected at this time, in fact they were very thorough in some years, carrying out silver and sometimes gold assays by both touchstone and cupellation. Following a detailed report by the Assayer and two wardens of a West Country search in the summer of 1633 (their thorough report takes up eighteen pages of the minute book), the Court decided that two wardens should ride into some part of the kingdom once every year.

In July 1635 wardens Richard Taylor and Francis Chapman, with the Clerk and the Assayer in attendance, set out on a search to the north. After a week's riding they reached Newcastle on 4 August. There they searched in the shops and at the fair that was in progress, carrying out touchstone and cupellation assays and imposing fines where appropriate. They then retraced their steps as far as York, and from there to Lincoln, King's Lynn, Norwich, Ipswich, Colchester and Chelmsford, searches being made in each of these towns. Included among the articles tested were silver beakers, bowls, porringers, spoons, bodkins, thimbles and various kinds of gold rings. The whole exercise took about one month and is another good illustration of the importance the Company attached to country searches. This one was not particularly rewarding from a financial standpoint; the total fines amounted to £119, but after deducting charges for the journey only £23 remained. Those who took part were thanked profusely for 'their great pains, care and diligence for the credit of the Company and the good of the Commonwealth in undertaking so tedious a journey ... wherein also appeareth that the endeavours of the Clerk and Assayer in this journey was not wanting.' It was also confirmed that searches were to continue 'until a general reformation be had throughout the kingdom'. It must be said, however, that these occasional searches had little permanent effect on the quality of provincial wares, which we know from surviving examples were frequently below the minimum legal standard.

In November 1635 yet more spoons submitted by Edward Holle were broken. He said that six of them were made by a Nathaniel Giles in Lombard

LIST OF SUBSTANDARD WARES, *seized by the wardens at a search in Norwich in 1635. From the contemporary Goldsmiths' Company Minute Book.*

Street but marked with his (Holle's) maker's punch. This was known as 'colouring' and the wardens considered it to be a greater offence than using substandard silver. However, on his promise never to mark another man's work with his own punch in future, he was fined only two shillings.

At this period the Company had to deal with a further source of irritation. Certain pewterers were marking their products with a leopard's head, a lion and a date letter similar to the letter 'S' used by the Company for the year 1635. One culprit was successfully prosecuted. At the Company's instigation

GOLDSMITHS' HALL *rebuilt in 1636, as shown by John Ward, the Company's surveyor in 1692. The Assay Office was in the area to the left of Fleur de Luce Court.*

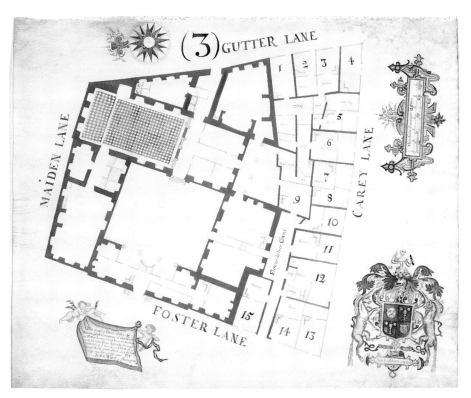

the Privy Council bade the Lord Mayor and Aldermen to require the Master and wardens of the Pewterers' Company to restrain their members from such practices and to punish offenders. The Lord Mayor subsequently ordered that the members of the Pewterers' Company should in future strike only one mark 'as anciently accustomed' in addition to the maker's own mark and that any articles bearing impressions similar to hallmarks on silver were to be called in and the marks defaced.

In November 1637 Robert Snowe, who had still not apologized, now found himself in serious trouble. He had to answer charges in the Star Chamber for illegally exporting gold and silver, melting current coins and buying bullion at higher prices than allowed at the Mint. This turn in his fortunes produced a change of heart. He appeared before the Court of Assistants asking for the Company's help, at the same time submitting to its authority in accordance with the order of the Privy Council. As a result he was restored to favour after paying a £50 fine in order to be excused from holding the office of Renter and shortly afterwards he was elected to the Court of Assistants. We do not hear of him again.

REBUILDING OF GOLDSMITHS' HALL

In 1634 the Company decided that the Hall was in such a state of disrepair that rebuilding could no longer be delayed. The old building, together with some of the adjacent tenements, was demolished and for the next few years meetings were held in Scriveners' Hall in Noble Street. It is not recorded whether the Assay Office was also accommodated there. Jackson lost his house and was given £50 in compensation, approximately equivalent to five years' rent; he resided for some years in nearby Mugwell Street.

It was not the best time for the Company to embark on such an expensive venture, especially as it was soon obliged to raise large amounts of cash for various taxes such as 'ship money' and for its share of loans forced on the City by the King or Parliament. In 1638 the Company was required to lend the King £560, its contribution out of a total of £12,000 for all City Companies; and two years later it had to find a further £3500 to meet another demand on the City, on this occasion amounting to £50,000. Then in June 1642, £7000 had to be raised as part of a loan of £100,000 requested by Parliament for relief in Ireland. Thirty-four items from the Company's collection of silver were sold in 1637 and the annual diet, which hitherto had been turned into plate, was exchanged for much needed cash. Considerable sums had to be borrowed from members and others, including £100 at 7 per cent interest from Alexander Jackson and a larger sum from the Clerk, William Haselfoote. It was not until another eighty years or so had passed that a satisfactory financial position was restored, the Company being forced to raise money on interest during most of the intervening period.

The rebuilding of the Hall to the design of Nicholas Stone and with the advice of Inigo Jones, Surveyor to the Crown, was completed by 1638. Considerably larger than the old Hall, the new structure took in additional land to the south on which formerly stood a number of houses. Richard Cooke, the Weigher, had expected a dwelling in the Hall, but as his hopes were frustrated he asked if the lease of his house in Wood Street could be extended to twenty-one years. His request was granted in view of the care and pains he had taken in his work; and when two years later he was an unsuccessful suitor for one of the new houses by the Hall, he was given a yearly gratuity of £10 – this time in consideration of his advanced age.[28] The pressing need for economy is exemplified by an entry in the minutes dated 1637, which notes that the auditors had taken exception to a bill for fifteen shillings brought in by Cooke for cleaning the balance and other expenses disbursed by him. Only after some debate did the Court sanction payment 'in respect of his extraordinary pains and daily attendance', but added that his reimbursement was not to be taken as a precedent.

In the ten years prior to the rebuilding of the Hall the trade in silverware had increased spectacularly. More than 500,000 oz of silver were marked in the twelve months from May 1635 to May 1636, but a further outbreak of the plague caused a substantial drop during the following six months. In August the wardens instructed the Assayer 'to make fire but two days in a week, on Wednesdays and Saturdays, in regard of the present visitation in London with sickness … ' Within months, however, trade recovered, the weight of silver received at the Assay Office reaching a total of 577,000 oz between June 1637 and May 1638, the highest ever recorded up to that date. The figures were more than double those of twenty years earlier, which was probably due not only to the increase in the population of the capital but also to the flourishing state of the economy as a whole, especially during the years 1629 to 1635.

Owing to the greater workload the 'by-assays', which had always been part of the Assayer's duties, was being neglected. The workers were keen to have Thomas Francis, who was skilled in assaying as well as in his trade as a silver craftsman, officially appointed to test their raw material. As one of those involved in the controversy eight years earlier, Francis had caused the Company much aggravation. Nevertheless it was agreed in November 1640 that he should undertake this work in his own house for a trial period of one month. At the end of this time thirty workers subscribed to a paper, saying they were very satisfied with his assaying and they 'prayed that he may continue, so that they may be enabled to make their work according to standard and thereby avoid the great damage and loss formerly sustained for want of such help.' It was therefore decided that the arrangement should remain and after some haggling Francis's fee was fixed at £40 per annum. He soon expressed dissatisfaction with this, saying '… It hath been my daily and whole employment this year'. The concession was in any case short-lived; after running for approximately two years it was terminated in October 1642. The amount of work submitted for hallmarking had now dropped dramatically and Jackson could easily resume responsibility for the by-assays. This time the reason for the sudden decline was the onset of the Civil War.

THE COAT OF ARMS OF SIR JOHN WOLLASTON, *displayed in Goldsmiths' Hall.*

CHAPTER SIX

THE CIVIL WAR TO 1697

B Y THE END of 1642 the Civil War had entered its first phase. It was to have dire consequences for the Company and the trade, as indeed for the country in general. Besides lending money for the defence of the City against possible Royalist attack, the Company agreed to provide a fire engine, ladders, hooks, pickaxes, spades and three dozen leather fire buckets, also muskets, swords, and pikes for the Parliamentary army under the Earl of Essex. A part of the Hall was converted into a granary. The manufacture of silverware almost ceased; in the three years November 1642 to November 1645 only 26,300 oz were hallmarked, compared with well over a million ounces in the previous three. The diet taken from articles marked between 21 June and 8 November 1643 was only just over 4 dwt but it was nevertheless tried as usual. In January 1643, the Beadle reported that it was impossible to obtain quarterage payments as so many shops were shut and members 'gone for soldiers'. In November, John Wollaston, the refiner – now Sir John – was elected Lord Mayor, which involved the Company in some further expense, as did the election of William Gibbs as Sheriff in the following year and Thomas Vyner in 1648. Wollaston received a gift of £100, Gibbs and Vyner £50 each – less than was formerly donated in view of the Company's financial position. According to custom they were also lent a substantial quantity of the Company's plate during their terms of office.

Notwithstanding the war, it was decided in 1644 to resume local searches. In August the wardens visited Lombard Street, Aldgate, Tower Hill, London Bridge, Fleet Street, the Strand, Farringdon Street, Holborn and Westminster. The list of wares brought back to the Hall to be assayed consisted mainly of rings and commemorative medals. First signs of a recovery in the trade occurred in 1646 but in the succeeding difficult years activity was still low. There was certainly a slow steady increase in the weight of silver coming into the Assay Office after that date but even by 1656 it had not equalled the pre-war figures.

There was no cessation of the Trials of the Pyx during the Civil War. Orders were issued by Parliament and trials were held in 1643, 1644, 1645

This standerd commixed
of xxij carrects of fine
gold and ij carrects of
assaye in the pound wt.
troy of England made
the xxij of Nouember
1649

SURVIVING PORTION *of the 1649 gold trial plate, in the possession of the Royal Mint.*

(twice) and 1647 before the Commissioners of the Great Seal and members of the Committee of Revenue appointed by the House of Commons. By the time of the Commonwealth the indented trial plates made in 1604 and 1605 were running short and in November 1649 the Company was issued with a warrant from the Council of State to provide new ones. The wardens were required to appoint a jury of the most experienced and able men to appear before the Council to take the usual oath before proceeding. The fourteen jurymen included Sir John Wollaston, who together with his former apprentice, Alderman Thomas Noell, supplied the pure metals. Among other members were Sir Thomas Vyner, a refiner named Matthew Mason, and of course, the Assayer, Alexander Jackson, who was responsible for much of the work involved. The final cost to the State was £128 3s 6d which included a payment of £2 to Thomas Simon, the Mint Engraver, who indented (cut) the plates and engraved them. Simon, one of the greatest of the Mint engravers, also acted as the Company's engraver, and as such was responsible for making the hallmarking punches.

The only occasion on which these new plates were used at a Trial of the Pyx was in 1657, no trials being held between 1649 and that date. Due no doubt to this lapse of time and consequent lack of experience of the Treasury officials, the trial in 1657 started badly. By order of the Lord Protector, Oliver Cromwell, the jury duly appeared at Westminster before the Lords Commissioners of the Great Seal, the Commissioners of the Treasury, two judges and the Barons of the Exchequer.[1], but what followed was a fiasco. The trial plates provided by the Company and delivered to the Council of State in 1649 had apparently not found their way into the Treasury of the Exchequer! The jury had to be dismissed and the trial postponed for a fortnight.

ASSAYER'S SALARY

In 1655 Alexander Jackson made one of his regular requests for a rise in salary. He presented two papers, one giving the cost of running the office a hundred years earlier (apparently a copy of Thomas Keeling's submission see pages 78–9) and the other his current outlay. The first showed the expenses to have been £60 4s per annum, which the Assayer paid out of his yearly fee of £80, so that he had £19 16s for his own 'pains and attendance'. The second showed the present expenses to be £104 and as Jackson's salary was only £70, he thus had to find an additional £34 per annum. Ten years earlier he had taken his son Abraham as an apprentice and had instructed him in the 'mistery of an assayer'. Abraham Jackson had been made free in 1652 and had since continued to work in the Assay Office without any salary from the Company. The Court decided that instead of increasing the Assayer's salary his son should be given £20 per annum to encourage him, and hoping thereby that he would continue to work for his father. Apart from his son and the Weigher – his former apprentice John Aynge – any other staff would have been paid by Jackson himself; clearly his salary by itself was still insufficient to meet all his expenses. We know he was receiving regular interest payments on the money he had lent the Company and he had been paid for assaying silver wire and thread seized by Thomas Violet under a special commission from the King. In 1639, for instance, Violet had seized 112 parcels of wire for assaying which Jackson had charged £5. But this particular source of income had ceased since the Civil War. He did, however, have the substantial perquisite of the 'assay bits'.

THE RESTORATION OF THE MONARCHY

Although the Company felt it could not increase the Assayer's salary, and in spite of its weak financial position, it managed to raise £840 towards a gift of £12,000 by the City of London to Charles II on his Restoration, but again only by dint of borrowing. On 29 May 1660, the day of Charles' famous entry into the City, twenty-seven members of the Company rode behind the King on his progress to Whitehall and deputizing for one of those originally chosen was a Mr Jackson. Alexander Jackson was then fairly advanced in age, so it may have been his son Abraham who took part. The Lord Mayor's precept had required the participants to be 'of the most grave, comely and tall persons' of the Company and to be 'well horsed and apparelled in their best array and furniture of velvet plush or satin and chains of gold and to wear their swords' and each of 'the said persons to have one footman with a truncheon ...'

These displays of loyalty were costly. In February 1661 the Company had to pay £420, its proportion of a total of £6000 for the expenses of receiving the King on the day before his Coronation when he passed through the City from the Tower of London to the Palace of Westminster. This sum proved inadequate and the Company had to find another £210. Another great spectacle was the procession on the River Thames on the occasion of the journey of the

TRIUMPHAL PROCESSION *of Charles II and Catherine of Braganza from Hampton Court to Whitehall in 1662. In the central foreground is the Goldsmiths' Company's float, which would have been followed in the procession by the Company's barge, here shown in the middle distance. This etching by R. Stoop is in the Guildhall Library.*

King and Queen from Hampton Court to Whitehall in August of the following year. The Company's contribution was a floating tableau comprising the Figure of Justice holding a balance in one hand and a touchstone in the other – a representation of the Company's arms – and several persons working at the goldsmiths' craft. Following immediately behind this boat was the Company's barge with members of the Court of Assistants and liverymen on board. The Assay Office would certainly have been closed on that day and the Assayer in his place in the procession. The occasion is described in the diaries of both Pepys and Evelyn, the latter wrote:

> I was a spectator of the most magnificent triumph that ever floated on the Thames ... all the thrones, arches, pageants, and other representations, stately barges of the Lord Mayor and Companies, with various inventions, musiq and peales of ordnance both from the vessels and the shore, going to meete and conduct the Queene from Hampton Court to Whitehall, at the first time of her coming to towne ... His Majesty and the Queene in an antiq-shap'd open vessell, cover'd with a state or canopy of cloth of gold, made in the form of a cupola, supported with high Corinthian pillars, wreath'd with flowers, festoons and garlands.

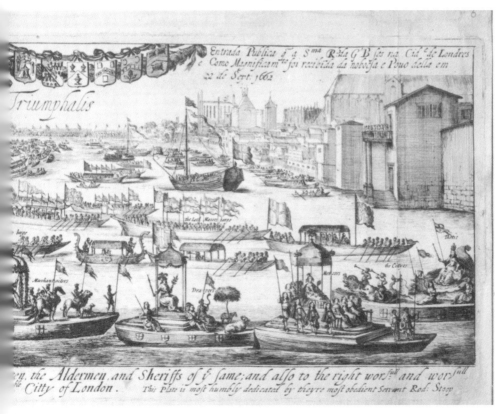

The wardens were mindful of the needs of the members who were taking part:

> because it was uncertain how long the Company may be upon the water there should be provided for breakfast 4 fore-ribs of beef to be eaten at the Hall before the Company take barge, and that they likewise carry with them in their barge 12 neats' tongues, 5 dozen bottles of Canary wine, 3 dozen bottles of claret and white, 4 dozen bottles of ale and 12 dozen penny rolls.

Three years later a precept was received from the Lord Mayor demanding £2000 as a contribution towards a loan from the City to the King. Charles II was proving to be as demanding on the City as his father. It was agreed it should be paid and the money borrowed. An additional but comparatively small drain on the Company's resources was the hearth tax which had been revived in 1662; the assessment for the Hall was based on thirty-three hearths.

With the Restoration of the monarchy in 1660 it was considered necessary to have three new trial plates to replace those made during the Commonwealth, although they had been used only once at a Trial of the Pyx. On this occasion Sir Thomas Vyner headed the list of jurymen and the refiner Matthew Mason supplied the pure metals. The normal procedure was followed.

For some years the Company had been eager to promote a Parliamentary Bill in order to strengthen its powers for controlling the trade – its authority had rested mainly on the statutes of 1300, 1423 and 1575 together with the terms of its charter. But Charles I had ruled for eleven years since 1629 without Parliament, so no opportunity had arisen to introduce legislation. In 1640, however, encouraged by the imminent recall of Parliament, a committee of eighteen representing all grades of membership of the Company, was appointed by the Court of Assistants and it met repeatedly over the next two years to formulate new proposals. No copy of the resulting draft Bill has been traced but it must have been comprehensive as it is recorded that it ran to 29 sheets. It was finally approved by the Court of Assistants and was ready to be introduced in the House of Lords when the Civil War intervened. Another committee was appointed in 1650 following receipt of a petition from members of the Company. It met on a number of occasions during the next few years to discuss reform of the law, but frustratingly nothing was achieved. A further petition in 1653 referred to strangers (foreigners) who were ruining the trade. This was of course nothing new; similar complaints had been voiced periodically during the past three hundred years, but they were now more persistent and they feature prominently in the Company's records for the following half century, especially after the influx of Huguenot refugees which followed the Revocation of the Edict of Nantes in 1685.

Goldsmith-bankers

Edward Backwell

In the second half of the seventeenth century, in addition to their dealings in plate, goldsmiths often accepted cash deposits from their customers and issued notes, thus becoming the forerunners of the modern banking system. Some, like Sir Thomas Vyner and his nephew Robert, amassed great fortunes by lending to the State or Crown. Thomas Vyner, who was Prime Warden of the Company in 1645, served as Lord Mayor in 1653 and was knighted in the following year. Sir Robert Vyner was knighted in 1665 and became Prime Warden in 1666, at the time of the Great Fire (he also followed in his uncle's footsteps and became Lord Mayor in 1674). Sir Robert was on close terms with Charles II but was owed more than £400,000 when in 1672 the King stopped payments from the Exchequer. He survived in business for a time but due to loss of interest on the loan became bankrupt in 1684, dying four years later.

Another goldsmith-banker, Edward Backwell (Prime Warden in 1660), who had been appreniced to Thomas Vyner, suffered a similar fate. His business partnership with his own former apprentice, Sir Charles Duncombe (Prime Warden in 1684, Lord Mayor in 1708) at the Grasshopper in Lombard Street was the precursor of Martins Bank. Similarly, Sir Thomas Hallifax (Prime Warden in 1768) was one of the original partners in Glyns Bank, later Glyn Mills & Co. All these influential men gave valuable assistance and advice to the Goldsmiths' Company in regard to its hallmarking responsibilities.

In 1660 the Court of Assistants appointed yet another committee to prepare a Parliamentary Bill with the purpose of curbing 'abuses' in the trade and at the same time to consider the possibility of an amendment to the charter to strengthen the wardens' powers so that they would not be obstructed in their searches. It seemed an opportune time to approach the King, since he owed much to the City for the vital role it had played in securing his Restoration. The committee was a large one, chaired by Sir Thomas Vyner and consisting of six assistants, six liverymen and six members of the 'commonalty'. After many meetings and much deliberation over the next fifteen months a draft Bill was agreed and ready for presentation to Parliament in February 1662. Included were the following proposals:

(a) no person who was neither a freeman of the Company nor had served a seven years' apprenticeship to a goldsmith to be allowed to practise in the trade;

(b) the wardens to be granted the power to search (with the assistance of other specially chosen members of the Company), to impose penalties for offences and to break substandard wares;

(c) mayors, sheriffs, bailiffs and constables to assist the wardens where necessary in their searches;

(d) to make an addition or alteration to an article after it had been hallmarked to be an offence;

(e) goldsmiths to be permitted to use only troy weights certified by the Company;

(f) the number of apprentices which a goldsmith could take at any one time to be limited.

Thus the Bill was an attempt to give statutory authority to powers the Company had hitherto exercised under its charter or its own ordinances.

It so happened that a parliamentary committee was simultaneously considering a Bill for regulating the wire-drawers' trade. The Company wanted control over the wire-drawers to be within its province and its own draft Bill was amended accordingly. It included clauses not only specifying the minimum standard of silver wire but also stipulating that all bars of precious metal used by wire-drawers were to be assayed by the Company and marked with the leopard's head. Sir Thomas Vyner, Alderman Meynell, Edward Backwell and several others were elected to attend Parliament in order to carry through the Bill which was to be presented by Captain Jones, one of the Members of Parliament for London.[2] But the considerable effort in preparing the Bill proved fruitless. Another attempt was made in 1664 to obtain a simpler Act with greater powers of search as the main objective; Meynell, Backwell and others presented a draft Bill with an accompanying petition to the King, but again without success.

In the meantime the Company received a setback in its struggle to prevent foreigners from working in the trade. In 1664 Charles II acceded to a petition by two goldsmiths, Wolfgang Howzer and Jacob Bodendike, who had settled in England and had asked if he would grant them the right of 'assay and touch'. In rejecting a counter-petition from the Company the King did say, however, that the two goldsmiths were not to employ foreign workmen and that he would 'be very sparing in recommending foreigners to any like privileges properly belonging to the natives of this kingdom'. Howzer came from a family of goldsmiths in Zurich, where he was a freeman of the local guild. Bodendike was from Limburg in Germany. He worked in the liberty of St Martin-le-Grand having been granted denizenship in 1661. He was admitted to the freedom of the Company by redemption in 1673 on the condition that he presented a piece of silver worth not less than £10.

There followed further entreaties to the Company from its trade members, who maintained that other foreigners were getting the favour of nobility by persuading them that no Englishmen could produce workmanship comparable to their own. The Company's answer was that, being a corporation, it was precluded from taking legal action, but that it was open to any of its members to do so. This was in line with advice it had received from counsel in 1661.

At this time the Assay Office was entrusted with an unusual assignment. The Company's attention had been drawn to the fact that spoons made in recent years had not been 'wrought for length and wideness of the bowl as they ought to be, but much shorter in the handle, and lesser in the bowl than heretofore.' In July 1663 it was directed that a sample spoon should be hung up in the Assay Office to serve as a pattern and that if any spoons were received which were not made in accordance with its dimensions, the Assayer should return them to be refashioned. How long this order was in force is not recorded.

JACKSON'S DISMISSAL

In 1661 the Company had received yet another petition from certain craftsmen with three requests: that the Assay Office should be open every day (instead of four days a week); that there should be an assistant assayer; and that no diet should be retained. When asked by the Court of Assistants for his comments Jackson agreed to the first request, provided work was brought in before nine o'clock – as indeed it should have been according to an existing order. As regards the second request, after a debate it was decided that Abraham Jackson should take the Assayer's oath along with his father, as he already did much of the work. Not unexpectedly the third request for return of the diet was declined.

When consulted about the above petition, Jackson took the opportunity of saying that he had been greatly abused by ill-language from some makers for endeavouring to have them observe the accustomed orders of the Court of Assistants. He asked if regulations could be reissued, clarifying the procedure to be adopted if a controversy arose. He referred to an earlier custom which had lapsed, whereby two wardens were always present at the retrial in cases of dispute and at the breaking of substandard plate. A few months later one John Neave queried the results of assay of two candlesticks, and in accordance with Jackson's request they were re-assayed in the presence of the wardens. The bodies were found to be agreeable to the standard but the bases and feet were 11 dwt and 15 dwt worse respectively. Neave then accepted the reports; the candlesticks were broken and he was fined thirty shillings.

But other makers were not so easily placated. A further petition was delivered in January 1664. Separate statements were signed by plateworkers Thomas Harris, Francis Crompton, Edward Hand, Daniel Rutty and Hugh Bollen, and a spoonmaker John Cox, objecting to the delay in the return of work that had been put 'in doubt' but had eventually passed.[3] They also questioned the accuracy of Jackson's reports of by-assays. But there was one far more serious allegation. Three of the signatories affirmed that Jackson's two servants were marking plate that had failed on assay and were receiving payment from the owners in return; furthermore, that they were not only doing this at the Assay Office but were even visiting certain makers' workshops, taking with them the date letter and lion punches and striking the marks on substandard tankards and wine cups. Francis Crompton, alleged that he had paid one of the servants, 12d for marking plate in this way, and that since the punch of the leopard's head was not available – it being in the custody of the Touchwarden – the servant had struck the lion punch crosswise so as to resemble the leopard. Edward Hands said that he had given 12d to another servant, to mark ten trencher plates that had been in doubt at the Assay Office for a week. John Cox added that he had had half a dozen spoons similarly marked on paying Jackson's man sixpence. The two servants concerned, John Field and Thomas Franklin, were aged about seventeen and both were serving as apprentices to Jackson's son Abraham.

The signatories of the petition were called before a special committee of the Court of Assistants. Three days later the committee met again to consider an answer made in writing by Jackson and his son. This was probably the same undated document signed by Jackson which is still in the Company's archives. In it he gives reasons for the delay in dealing with work 'in doubt'. He also says that such articles were sometimes returned to the owners for 'boiling' in order to remove dirt but were often not re-submitted to the Assay Office. But he does not satisfactorily explain how the substandard articles came to be marked by the two servants. His submission ends with the following rather pitiful appeal:

> ... it is too long a work for me to declare all troubles and dangers that belong to this place – it hath brought me many a mighty cost and if the lord did not uphold me they would make me mad. I pray be not angry with me for I have served long and done you justice with care and a good conscience and I still remain your poor servant to serve you faithfully a little longer.

He was at that time aged about seventy-two.

On 15 February 1664 the Court approved the committee's recommendations; Jackson was instructed to discharge Field and Franklin forthwith and to keep the punches locked up, with the key in his own care. He was also to 'make fire' daily whilst plate in doubt was to be tried the following day. If any workman required a further trial his signed request was to be kept in a special book 'to prevent his future clamour and complaints against the said Assay Master'. Where plate consisted of several components soldered together, the Assayer was directed to draw or cut a sample from each and, if found standard, to strike the lion mark on all parts that were capable of receiving it. The workmen were requested to leave 'getts' (gates or sprues) on such pieces that could not be drawn, and if any parts of articles were found to be below standard the whole was to be broken by the wardens. It appears that candlesticks of a new pattern were being made deceitfully, with some parts up to standard and others below. One case has already been mentioned.

Jackson discharged Field as directed but foolishly allowed Franklin to remain. Eight months later further information was received by the wardens that plate belonging to one Joseph Fabian had been marked by Franklin, although it had never been assayed. A special meeting of the Court was called; Jackson and his son were summoned and the order of the previous February was read to them. Jackson acknowledged its receipt, but his son denied having seen it. They said they could not tell how the miscarriage had happened, the father adding that if it appeared they had not performed their duty he would make satisfaction, and for his part would relinquish the office if they so pleased.

Selected members of the Court of Assistants met to consider what should be done. They decided that the Assayer had been remiss and negligent in not observing the order made in February – that although he had discharged Field, he was still employing Franklin; that he was not 'making fire' every day; that he had received plate which had not been weighed; that he had detained plate in doubt for several days; and that had made untrue reports of by-assays. They recommended that Jackson and all others in the Assay Office should be discharged and that the regulations should be restated. The proposals were accepted by the Court and immediate action was taken to implement them. The Prime Warden (Alderman and Sheriff Charles Doe), had in fact fore-stalled the Court in one respect. He reported that he had already caused Jackson, his son and the servants to vacate the Assay Office, and that he had then locked it and brought away the key.

It was a sad ending to the careers of the Jacksons. There was no suggestion that they were directly implicated in the frauds but it seems Alexander Jackson had become too old for the work and had let things slide; he had served four years as Re-assayer and thirty-five as Assayer. During that time he had taken no less than sixteen apprentices; they included his son Abraham, who had served for nineteen years, and John Aynge, who was later reinstated as Weigher and held the position for a total of forty years altogether. Jackson was undoubtedly respected in the City community. He was elected a member of the Common Council for Aldersgate ward in 1652 and again in 1659. He died in 1670.

Jackson expressed a wish to be buried near his late wife in the churchyard of St John Zachary. Like many goldsmiths he had close connections with this church which was destroyed in the Great Fire four years before his death. He was churchwarden in 1637–8. The Church of St Anne & St Agnes, whose parish included that of St John Zachary after the Fire, still has in its possession two patens made in 1706 from a dish which according to their inscriptions was 'the gift of Alexander Jackson, saymaster of Goldsmiths' Hall to the parish church of St John Zachary, London 1638'. Although losing their positions in the Assay Office the Jacksons were comfortable financially. Abraham inherited his father's houses in Charterhouse Yard and Charterhouse Lane with rents of £100 per annum, of which £20 was to be paid to Alexander's other son Isaac.[4] Abraham, who had been granted an 80-year tenancy of the house in Mugwell Street formerly leased by the Company to his father, died in 1700, leaving £20 to the poor children of Christ's Hospital and £10 to the poor of the parish of St John Zachary. Five houses in Snow Hill, four in Seacole Lane and one in Foster Lane went to his wife Sarah.[5]

The real culprits of the sudden and unforeseen upheaval in the Assay Office did not escape retribution. Joseph Fabian, the workman whose plate had been fraudulently marked, was imprisoned in Newgate on a warrant from the Lord Chief Justice. Franklin, who confessed to conspiracy with Fabian, was committed to the Wood Street Compter. Both were charged and prosecuted at the Old Bailey. Plate made by Fabian for other goldsmiths was called in – John

St John Zachary

The parish church of the Goldsmiths' Company, St John Zachary, stood at the corner of Maiden Lane (now Gresham Street) and Noble Street. Many members of the Company worshipped and were buried there, including the first Assayer, Christopher Elyot (see page 41) and several of his successors – Edmund Lee, William Dymock and Alexander Jackson – and their wives. The church was destroyed in the Great Fire of 1666 and not rebuilt. The churchyard, however, remained and, after bomb damage during the Second World War, it was transformed into a garden by Assay Office staff and other workers at the Hall. It is open to the public and still maintained by the Company.

Colville sending twelve tankards weighing 258 oz 13 dwt, and John Haslin three salvers, a cup and cover, two tankards and five plates weighing 249 oz 16 dwt. They were compensated at the rate of 5s 6d per oz for all these pieces, some of which were found to be as much as 15 dwt worse than standard. Field is not heard of again but Thomas Franklin claimed the freedom of the Company ten years later. It is recorded that during a search at Southwark Fair in 1682, the wardens seized various articles from a Thomas Franklin, a lottery man – possibly the same Franklin.

JOHN BRATTLE

As a result of these unfortunate events the Assay Office had to be rapidly re-staffed. Nominations for the vacant post of Assayer included John Brattle and Samuel Bartlett. Bartlett had been apprenticed to Thomas Vyner and had been a member of the jury responsible for making the 1660 trial plates. As in the case of Reynolds, Jackson's predecessor, the early backgrounds of both Brattle and Bartlett were at the Mint. Brattle had probably started his career in the engraver's department where his father was employed, but he had also learned the skill of assaying. In 1649 the Mint Assay Master, Thomas Wood-ward, was dismissed for refusing obedience to the new Council of State and had emigrated to a plantation on the York River in Virginia, declaring he would not see England again till the monarchy had been restored.[6] During the Commonwealth years, Brattle and Bartlett were each employed at different times in place of Woodward. Brattle in particular was highly commended by the Warden and Master of the Mint for his skill, and at the Restoration in 1660 he was given the position until Thomas Woodward returned.[7] But the patent for the post of Assay Master of the Mint had been granted to Woodward as a family interest and Brattle was later forced to relinquish the title in favour of Woodward's son John, who applied in 1661 to hold it until his father's return or, if his father were dead, to have it himself.[8]

Thus Brattle and Bartlett were looking for other employment when the vacancy occurred at the Hall. Brattle was duly elected and moved with his wife and family into the accommodation provided in the Hall as soon as it had been vacated by Jackson. Eight months later John Woodward fell victim to the plague and died on 7 June 1665. Brattle was anxious to regain the position at the Mint and it was granted to him pending the return of Thomas Woodward on the understanding that he should be allowed also to work for the Goldsmiths' Company.[9] Now he was responsible for the assaying at the Mint as well as at the Hall. Since it had been decided that the Assay Office should be open every day, it is probable that one of his two servants undertook the assaying at the Hall on the days he was working at the Mint.[10]

Soon after his appointment by the Company Brattle submitted a paper in which he said that Jackson had made all his assays using a furnace fired by coal, whereas he (Brattle) now used charcoal at considerably greater personal expense. It was agreed that the use of coal gave rise to uncertain reports and ought not to be permitted. In view of the extra cost Brattle was awarded a gratuity of £15.

A further problem was encountered at this time – a number of punches had broken during use, possibly because of faulty hardening. Thomas Simon the Engraver may have lost some of his skill; in any case a successor had soon to be found as he died in August 1665, no doubt another victim of the plague. Martin Johnson was appointed. Simon had been Head Engraver of the Mint since 1645 and was one of its greatest artists[11] (see page 130).

THE GREAT FIRE

There is no mention in the Company's minute books of the Great Plague and the effect it had on the Assay Office, but the statistics for the amount of work received during that terrible year of 1665 speak for themselves. The weight of silver hallmarked in the months of July to October dropped to 15,498 oz, compared with nearly 100,000 oz in the same period of the previous year – most of those who could afford to leave London had departed to a safer part of the country. Yet, as happened after earlier outbreaks of the dreaded plague, the trade recovered to a large extent within a few months. But then London was struck by a second great catastrophe.

The Great Fire started in Pudding Lane in the early hours of Sunday morning, 2 September. By daybreak on the following Tuesday it had reached the eastern end of Cheapside and was also spreading towards Goldsmiths' Row from the south. Soon the flames were in range of Foster Lane.

Most people were busy trying to save their own goods and chattels, but just before the Hall was engulfed by the fire, Alderman Sir Charles Doe, a gold-smith in Cheapside,[12] who had been Prime Warden two years earlier (see page 139), arrived on the scene, and asked for the keys of the strong room. He commandeered a cart which had been jointly hired by Brattle and the Beadle to take their own personal belongings to safety, and used it instead to carry away all the Company's plate and records. They were taken to Edmonton to the house of a Mr Broadbank, a friend of Brattle. Mr Broadbank was paid £8 10s for his services and the cart owner received £5. The Hall was gutted, but the outer walls remained intact: all around was devastation. If it had not been for the timely action of Sir Charles Doe this history of the Assay Office could never have been written.

The unfortunate Brattle was deprived of the chance of saving his own property but the Company, grateful for his co-operative attitude, gave him £40 in compensation. Although the interior of the Hall was almost entirely destroyed it was nevertheless possible to find a corner of the building as provisional accommodation for the Assay Office, which was thus able to remain open. No doubt the arrangements were far from ideal, but continuity was maintained even during this calamitous time. As a further temporary measure meetings were held in a rented house in Grub Street.

Restoration of the interior of the Hall took place in a somewhat piecemeal fashion as and when the Company could afford to pay for the work in progress. Members were asked to subscribe and Sir Robert Vyner, who was Prime Warden at the time of the fire, donated the generous sum of £300. Much of the Company's plate was sold to provide further funds.

Remarkably, although most of the City lay in ruins, the silver trade revived much more rapidly than one would have expected. The weight of wares hallmarked in the nine months following the fire was only a quarter less than the average for the same months in the years 1660 to 1665.

But although the trade had fully recovered by October 1668 some working goldsmiths were dissatisfied and by-passed the Company by directly petitioning the Privy Council. Their main concern was the number of aliens (foreigners) competing for custom but they complained also about delays in the return of their work from the Assay Office. Furthermore they maintained that many shopkeepers were putting to sale unhallmarked plate as well as substandard small wares and that the wardens were not carrying out enough searches. In its counter petition to the Privy Council the Company said:

> It is confessed that for some years the wardens have not searched all over England but only in London and not so frequently as formerly in regard to the late visitation of the plague and the fire, and by the opposition they have met by persons refusing to let the wardens search. Nevertheless they have and do endeavour as much as in them lieth a performance, and in order thereunto did formerly present their humble petition to his majesty with a Bill to be passed into an Act of Parliament.

They also said that they now had in their service 'so honest and able a person ... namely Mr John Brattle' that since he had been employed no complaints had been received about the Assay Office.

As a further measure a committee was appointed to formulate proposals for correcting abuses in the trade, and a few weeks later the Company sent the Privy Council the following list of remedies which it intended to adopt:

(1) the wardens would make search in the City and Westminster once a month and in the country once a year;

(2) goldsmiths would be required to bring all their untouched plate to be assayed and touched;

(3) all working goldsmiths in and around the City and Westminster would be required to bring their marks to the Hall to be struck on a table to be kept there;

(4) all works of gold would be required to be up to the legal standard or otherwise to be defaced;

(5) the Company would employ a number of working goldsmiths to inquire into abuses and give notice to the wardens;

(6) all freemen of the Company would be forbidden to employ aliens.

At the same time the Company entreated His Majesty to issue a Proclamation for suppressing aliens working in the goldsmiths' trade and to command that all sheriffs, mayors and their officers and justices of the peace should assist the wardens in their searches in all places. The Privy Council appears to have been satisfied with the Company's proposals and let the matter drop, but no royal proclamation which might have assisted the Company was forthcoming.

Even though Brattle was at the Mint during part of the week, the Company was most satisfied with its choice of Assayer. In 1668 the Court made him a gift of £40 in consideration of the 'care and diligence in the management of the affairs of the Assay Office, which for the space of three years last past he hath carried on with much quietness and content both unto the Company and workmen'. It was hoped this would be an inducement for him to remain in the Company's service. But Brattle's reaction was to submit another paper, this time setting out his personal expenses in running the Office. They were as follows:

Cupels 600 a week	£16 0s 0d per annum
Lead for assays	£2 0s 0d
Charcoal	£20 0s 0d
Mufflers (muffles)	£2 0s 0d
For 2 servants wages and diet	£32 0s 0d
Total	£72 0s 0d

Sir Robert Vyner and Edward Backwell were included amongst those appointed to consider the matter. As Brattle's salary was only £70 per annum they could hardly have reached any other conclusion than that he deserved an increase, especially bearing in mind that the reputation of the Company stood so much higher since his appointment. Also some allowance was due for the rent of a house which he had been forced to occupy since the loss in the fire of his free accommodation in the Hall. But rather than raise his salary, it was decided to grant him a gratuity of £50 a year.

However, Brattle did not in fact wish to continue working at both the Mint and the Hall and when in January 1669 he was offered the post of King's Assay Master on a permanent basis he accepted it.[13] The Company received a letter from the Lords Commissioners of the Treasury confirming that the King had appointed Brattle his Assay Master at the Mint, and that he had commanded him to relinquish his place as Assayer at the Hall, 'since the pyx could not be tried while the two posts were in one hand'. Sir Robert Vyner and two of the wardens were detailed to intercede with the Lords Commissioners to try to persuade them that it would be in order for Brattle to continue in his present position as well as in the new one, but if the Commissioners would not agree, to give the Company reasonable time to find a replacement. But notwithstanding the great influence of Vyner they were unsuccessful. The Company had no alternative – they had to release him. It is indeed surprising that the possibility of his continuing in both posts should even have been considered. It was a repetition of the situation that had arisen almost exactly one hundred years earlier when Richard Rogers had held the two appointments simultaneously.

Brattle subsequently had a successful career at the Mint and in 1682 he received a knighthood. The award may have been due less to his position at the Mint than to recognition by Charles II for his part as a young man in conjunction with his father in editing the *Eikon Basilike*. This treatise was alleged to have been written by Charles I as his last message to his people.[14] In 1686, as Sir John Brattle, he was appointed to a commission for 'inquiring of concealed lands' in certain counties, one of the other fifteen commissioners being Samuel Pepys.[15]

THE FIRE OF LONDON, *1666, artist unknown.*

Sir Isaac Newton
1642–1727

Sir Isaac Newton, best known for his scientific achievements while an academic at Cambridge, spent the last thirty years of his life first as Warden (1696–99) and then (1699–1727) as Master-Worker at the Royal Mint, positions in which he served with distinction, paying great attention to detail in regard to both administrative and technical aspects of the coining operations.

He had a brief and acrimonious encounter with the Goldsmiths' Company, eventually settled in his favour, following an adverse verdict at the Trial of the Pyx in 1710 (see page 166). He maintained that the new gold trial plate which was used for the first time on that occasion had been purified beyond the normally accepted level.

In 1703 Newton was elected President of the Royal Society, a position, along with his Mint office, he held until he died at the age of eighty-four.

Earlier in his career Brattle was probably responsible for one of the earliest papers to be read before the Royal Society, on 23 February 1661, the year before its incorporation. The paper, which was brought in by Lord Brounker (the first President) was concerned with the assay of silver and in particular with the increase in weight of the lead during cupellation. It shows the results of experiments carried out at the Mint at the time Brattle was acting Assay Master there.[16]

John Brattle died in 1692 whilst still at the Mint and was succeeded by his elder son Daniel, who was followed in 1712 by his other son Charles. Daniel was Assay Master at the Mint during the great recoinage of 1696 and both brothers served during the Mastership of Sir Isaac Newton.[17] Newton had a high regard for their capabilities and when the position of Mint Assay Master became vacant on the death of Daniel Brattle he strongly supported Charles Brattle in preference to another contender, Catesby Oadham. At Newton's request a special trial was arranged in which both were asked to assay some samples of gold. Charles Brattle's results were far better than Oadham's – he had evidently been well taught by his father, for whom he had worked without salary for twenty years before acting as assistant to his brother for another twelve.[18]

WILLIAM BADCOCK

Two refiners – Peter Trovell and Robert Gregory – and a Henry Bloomer were nominated for the position of Assayer at the Hall following John Brattle's resignation in January 1669. Peter Trovell was elected. He had been indentured to a refiner, John Noell, and had taken over the Noell refining business in Noble Street. He soon made a good impression as Assayer and the Court agreed he should have an annual gratuity of £50 as had earlier been granted to Brattle.

Following the discovery of a number of serious offences the wardens decided in 1672 to consult the King's Attorney. He advised them to acquaint the King. This they did with the help of Sir Robert Vyner who had considerable influence with Charles II. The King immediately granted the Company a Royal Warrant with authority not only to search for and seize any counterfeit plate but also to arrest offenders – a much more powerful instrument than the charter.

In an attempt to eradicate less serious offences the Company had earlier required all makers to register new marks. Then, in 1676, a notice was issued stating that all wares of gold or silver, large or small, had to be assayed and hallmarked before they were put to sale, unless they could not 'conveniently bear' the marks. However, two years later it would seem that the Company must have been advised that under the existing law only certain specified articles were required to be hallmarked. Accordingly a revised notice was issued which confirmed that all articles had to bear a maker's mark but confined compulsory hallmarking to 'all manner of silver vessels, hilts for swords, silver buckles for belts, girdles amd other harness of silver'.[19] It appears the Company was not too sure of its powers; interpretation of the law was undoubtedly a problem. It was heartened, however, by the receipt of an address signed by forty-five smallworkers and dealers who declared their readiness not to make or put to sale any small wares that were not up to standard, and promising to make known to the wardens all persons who worked deceitfully.

Following the issue of the first of the above notices the Company received a petition from a number of its members requesting greater efforts to stop foreigners from working in the goldsmiths' trade and to prevent the sale of substandard wares. To meet the second of these requests it was decided that some 'honest and understanding persons' would be employed to buy suspect gold and silver wares and to bring them to the wardens for assay, so that the vendors could be fined if appropriate. It was felt that this procedure was generally preferable to legal proceedings, and from time to time during the next forty years the Company employed a number of such agents to purchase articles, both in London and in the rest of the country.

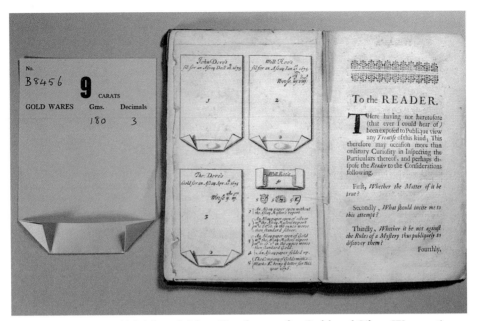

AN ILLUSTRATION *(right) from* A New Touchstone for Gold and Silver Wares, *1677, showing how a sample should be submitted to the Assay Office for a private assay. The same method of wrapping a sample (left) is still used at the Assay Office.*

One of the agents who helped the Company in this way was William Badcock, a maker of sword hilts and mounts and author of an informative book on hallmarking and the law entitled *A Touchstone for Gold and Silver Wares.*[20] Badcock was an efficient spy. In 1677, the year in which the first edition of his book was published, he produced two pairs of cuff buttons, three pairs of shoe buckles and a wedding ring, all of them bought from one Wilson in Fleet Street who had refused to allow the wardens to enter his premises. In the previous year Badcock had brought to the wardens a parcel of substandard silver belt buckles purchased from a Ralph Crowther of Covent Garden at a cost of £10 7s 9d. As it was not Crowther's first offence the decision was taken in his case to prosecute by indictment and advice was taken of counsel (Mr Sanders) and Mr Jeffreys, the Common Serjeant of the City. This was the same infamous Judge Jeffreys who is chiefly remembered for his brutal sentences at the Bloody Assizes after Monmouth's rebellion in July 1685. Jeffreys was later to become Lord Chief Justice and Lord Chancellor.[21]

Mr Jeffreys' advice to the wardens is not recorded but Crowther retaliated by appearing before them and producing evidence to show that members of the Court of Assistants had themselves been selling substandard small wares. It seems the wardens thought it prudent to drop this prosecution and instead Crowther was persuaded to confess his faults and was then fined.

In his book Badcock draws attention to the widespread sale of substandard small wares and recommends how members of the public could seek redress under the law if they were defrauded. He suggests that if anyone purchased a suspect article not bearing a hallmark, they should remove a sample and send it to the Assay Office for a private assay. He even illustrates how the sample should be wrapped in an assay paper bearing the relevant particulars. A pamphlet by William Tovey, a fellow goldsmith, published at about the same time provides further proof of the difficulty the Company faced in controlling the standard of articles that were not required by law to be assayed and hallmarked.[22] It was Tovey who, together with one Edward Robinson, had presented the address signed by forty-five smallworkers and other dealers (see page 147).

In April 1677 the indefatigable Badcock submitted detailed proposals for a new Act of Parliament, probably containing similar suggestions to those he was to set out in *A New Touchstone for Gold and Silver Wares* (1679). Badcock also refers in his book to foreign workers not paying taxes, 'living in holes and corners' and he comments: '... 'tis no marvel that these aliens flourish and

SIR ROBERT VYNER AND HIS FAMILY *by John Michael Wright, 1673; in the National Portrait Gallery.*

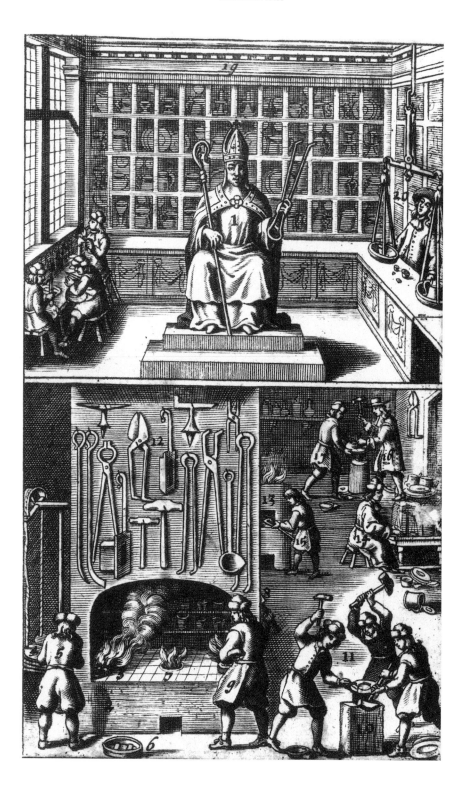

grow rich, and the natural English artificers become beggars and thieves'. How to prevent aliens from working as goldsmiths in London was a matter that had been debated at length by the Company. In the previous year, following receipt of the petition from its members, it had resolved that notwithstanding counsel's opinion – taken fifteen years earlier – it should itself take legal action. Mr Jeffreys, the Common Serjeant, was consulted but he advised waiting for the judgement in an action against an alien clockmaker in which he was appearing for the Clockmakers' Company. That case was probably unsuccessful since it was not followed by any similar prosecution by the Goldsmiths' Company. It seems it was impossible to take effective action against aliens working in the trade, except to exclude them from the assay and touch. But the Company had eight years earlier voted £30 to its trade members for the prosecution of aliens and in 1678 joined with other City Companies in opposing a Bill which was before Parliament in that year to permit Protestant aliens to exercise manual occupations. However, by this time public opinion was generally in sympathy with the foreign refugees.

Although it must have been clear that the Company was endeavouring to track down offenders, some members still felt that the wardens were not making enough searches and in March 1678 they submitted another formal complaint to the Privy Council. The wardens and their legal adviser, accompanied by Sir John Shorter – Prime Warden in the previous year and a future Lord Mayor – and several members of the Court of Assistants appeared before the Council to answer the charges.[23] As a result the King's Attorney was asked to prepare a draft document for Charles II to consider with a view to strengthening the wardens' powers of search. With hopes raised the wardens forthwith proceeded to the King's Attorney and left copies of the Parliamentary Bill and the petition which had been presented to the Council fourteen years earlier (see page 136). Disappointingly, nothing was achieved – the reason given being that it was not convenient to introduce a Bill in the House of Lords owing to pressure of other business.

The wardens had certainly not abandoned their searches: many are recorded, mainly local but some also in the country – including, for example, in 1683, visits to Salisbury, Winchester, Frome, Marlborough and Bristol, followed by areas nearer home in Southwark, Westminster, St Martins in the Fields, Holborn and Cheapside. The Company was still relying on its charter for the necessary authority, except that when making their usual search at Bartholomew Fair and the surrounding district in 1682 the wardens took the precaution of first obtaining warrants from the Lord Chief Justice authorizing them to seize substandard wares from certain specified dealers. The wardens were now frequently resisted, a sign of the steady erosion of their powers.

FRONTISPIECE *of* A New Touchstone for Gold and Silver Wares, *1677, depicting a goldsmith's shop with a statue of St Dunstan, a silversmith's workshop and the Assay Office.*

Another offence, less common but more serious than the sale of substandard wares, namely transposing, came to light in the year 1680. The Touchwarden at the time was Thomas Loveday, a refiner with a business close to the
Hall.[24] He reported to the Court of Assistants that he and the Assayer had
made trials of a two-eared cup, soldered to the base of which was a piece of
silver bearing the Company's marks, obviously removed from another article.
The body of the cup was 7 oz 18 dwt worse – grossly below standard. Loveday
said that he and the Assayer had searched the premises of certain goldsmiths

DETAIL FROM THE PLATE *of 1682, shown opposite. The mark usually referred to as 'a*
goose in a dotted circle', shown in the left-hand column, is attributed to John Duck, who
became Assayer in 1695.

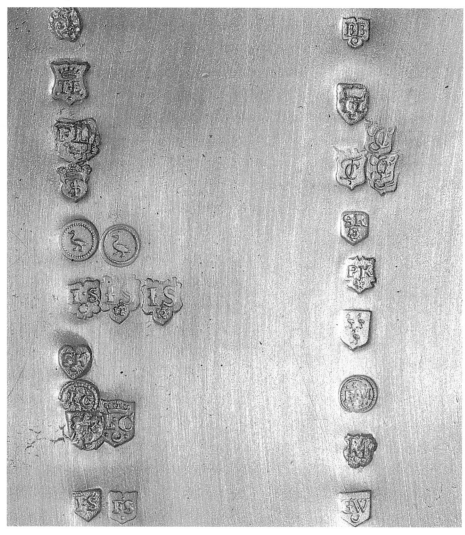

GILDED COPPER PLATE *bearing impressions of makers' marks dating from 1682.*

and had seized several similar cups also bearing transposed hallmarks. Prosecutions followed and two offenders were convicted, one of whom was sentenced to the pillory.

Not all touchwardens were as conscientious as Thomas Loveday. John Gilbert, who followed him in 1681, had the dubious distinction of being the only holder of the office to be discharged for neglect of duty.

FIRE IN THE ASSAY OFFICE

But 1681 turned out to be a year of disaster for another reason: in November the Assay Office was totally destroyed by fire, as were the adjoining Assayer's and Clerk's quarters. The Court was convinced that it was caused by the carelessness – if not the wilfulness – of Thomas Stratton, the Assayer's servant, who lodged in the Hall. He was forthwith dismissed. The rewards for helping to extinguish the fire show that it was no trivial affair; they were given to eight Phoenix men, five chimney sweepers, several officers of the Thames Water, the engineer of the fire-engine for Christchurch and six others who assisted. Later, others were rewarded, including 'several who wrought one of the engines which came from the Guildhall'. The provision of fire-fighting appliances had been made the responsibility of the City parishes after the great conflagration of fifteen years earlier. The equipment was, however, still primitive and never adequate for the purpose, but on this occasion the Hall was at least preserved from being totally gutted a second time.

For us today, the most serious loss in the fire of 1681 was the register of makers' marks. The method of recording the registrations at that time is described by William Badcock:

> In this office [the Assay Office] is kept for publick view, a Table, or Tables, artificially made in Columns, that is to say one Column of hardened Lead, another of parchment or Vellum, and several of the same sorts: In the Lead Columns are struck or entered the Workers Marks, which are generally the first two Letters of their Christian and Surnames, and right against them in the Parchment or Vellum Columns are written and entered the Owners Names.[25]

Shortly after the fire Badcock presented a paper to the Company stressing the need for a new table and a book in which to enter the workers' names and addresses. These were duly provided and the table survives – a copper plate measuring 24 by 18 inches bearing the impressions of 323 makers' marks. The book unfortunately has not come down to us, the earliest suriving book of this type dating from 1697 (see page 163).

Very little remained in the Assay Office after the fire. Three lots of molten metal were, however, recovered from the debris. On assay they were found to be equivalent to 23 lb 3 oz 8 dwt of sterling silver, then worth about £72. At first the Court advised Trovell the Assayer that it would be his responsibility to make good the damage to the Hall, but happily for him he was not held to this. He did, however, have to pay £7 11s 0d for the diet lost; it was estimated to be 29 oz according to the weight of wares received between 28 September and 23 November 1681 (the day of the fire). Records do not show where the Assay Office was accommodated for the next few years, but it is probable that another part of the Hall was made available. We do know that the new Office as well as the Assayer's and Clerk's quarters had been rebuilt and were in occupation by the end of 1686.

It must have been a worrying time for Peter Trovell and his health suffered. He contracted 'palsicall distemper' and the Court considered him 'somewhat incapable to execute the office as it ought to be'. Although he was re-elected Assayer for a few more years he was succeeded in 1686 by his assistant Nathaniel Bowles, who had no doubt been doing most of the work. Bowles had been apprenticed to Thomas Loveday, the refiner, and had received his freedom in 1668.

SURRENDER OF COMPANY'S CHARTER

The problem of raising funds for the rebuilding of the Assay Office was not readily solved in the wake of debts that had been incurred in meeting the demands of the Stuart kings. The City had played a major role in the events leading up to the restoration of Charles II, but later in his reign it was at logger-heads with him. His continuing demands for money were followed by his freezing of payments from the Exchequer in 1672, which severely hit some members of the Company, such as Robert Vyner and Edward Backwell. Now, nine years later, the King was in further conflict with the City. He was trying to gain control of the verdicts of its judicial courts. For the rest of the country this was by no means impossible as the juries were appointed by the sheriffs who were themselves appointed by the Crown, but according to its charter the sheriffs of the City of London were elected by the liverymen of the City Companies. In desperation, in 1683 Charles demanded the surrender of the City's charter. In the following year the Livery Companies were forced to follow suit, his intention being to issue new charters whereby he could obtain control over the constitution of their governing bodies. The charters of towns and boroughs throughout the kingdom were also amended in such a way that the members of their corporations were his supporters, who would ensure that candidates favourable to him would be returned at the next Parliamentary elections. However, Charles died in February 1685 before these had been held.

Three months later the Company succeeded in obtaining a new charter from James II. It was brought to the Hall by Alderman Charles Duncombe, who was Prime Warden at the time. (Duncombe was a successful goldsmith-banker, originally apprenticed to and later in partnership with Edward Back-well at the Grasshopper in Lombard Street. He subsequently continued the business – which later became Martins Bank – with great success in partnership with Richard Kent. He was a member of the deputation to William of Orange requesting him to come forthwith to the City in 1688. He became an MP in 1695, was knighted in 1699 and served as Lord Mayor in 1708. At the time of his death in 1711, he was reputedly the richest commoner in England.)

SURVIVING PORTION *of the 1688 silver trial plate.*

The Lord Chancellor – the notorious Judge Jeffreys – had been helpful in securing the new charter for the Company. But nothing of course could be achieved without its price; a bill of charges had to be met and it was decided that it would be prudent to give a present of silverware costing £150 to the Lord Chancellor – for many favours received, as the relevant minute truthfully records. Duncombe was profusely thanked for his efforts on the Company's behalf. But the Company would in future be forced to rely less and less on its charter for exercising the duty of controlling the trade. Although its responsibility for hallmarking was secure under statute, many of its powers, in common with those of other City Livery Companies, were dwindling at a time when Parliament was progressively assuming much of the authority that was formerly the prerogative of the Crown.

During his short reign James II proved as troublesome to the City as had his predecessors. As part of his nationwide campaign to place his nominees in key positions he succeeded in excluding many eminent London citizens from holding civic office. With this in mind he had made it a condition when re-storing or granting new charters to the City Companies that he could displace any of their members at will. As regards the Goldsmiths' Company, the Clerk, Charles Sprackling, was the first casualty in May 1687 and then in September the King ordered the removal of certain assistants and liverymen: three of the wardens, fifteen members of the Court of Assistants and seventy-four liverymen were on his list. New wardens were elected for the remainder of the

Company's year and another Court of Assistants numbering nineteen was appointed. Again in February 1688 the King ordered the removal of a further eight assistants and liverymen. They included John Loveday, a refiner and nephew of Thomas Loveday.

Then in October 1688, only two months before he fled abroad and less than one month before William of Orange landed in England, James, realizing he had gone too far, restored all privileges, liberties and franchises to the City and the Livery Companies – the cost to the Goldsmiths' Company being a further £18! This meant that displaced members were restored to their former status.

ONE OF A PAIR OF TANKARDS, *1686, by John Duck. The duck floating serenely under the bridge may be an allusion to his name.*

The day-to-day work of the Assay Office continued as usual during the momentous events preceding the Great Revolution of 1688. The Company's portions of the trial plates had apparently survived the fire in the Assay Office – probably they were kept in the strong room which fortunately was not destroyed. But in May 1688 the Court of Assistants was informed that the standard piece made in 1660 was depleted. The Lords Commissioners of the Treasury were approached and they duly issued a warrant to the Company on 26 June for making new plates of both gold and silver. A jury was appointed, of which the key members were the refiners Peter Floyer and John Loveday, and Nathaniel Bowles, now the Company's Assayer. Floyer supplied the pure metals and the melting and casting were carried out at his premises in Foster Lane. The ingots were assayed, forged, planished, indented and engraved as usual, but the whole operation was rather prolonged; it was not until 15 November 1688 that the plates, together with the jury's verdict, were finally delivered at the Treasury Chambers in Whitehall. Until shortly before delivery of the verdict Floyer and Loveday had, by order of the King, been displaced as assistant and liveryman respectively, but the Company presumably considered that their expertise was nevertheless indispensable. They were still on the roll of freemen and therefore eligible to act as members of the jury. Floyer was subsequently reinstated and went on to become Prime Warden.[26]

In December 1693 Nathaniel Bowles acquired a new assistant, a working goldsmith called John Duck, who had already helped the Company by purchasing substandard wares. Eighteen months later Bowles himself submitted his resignation as Assayer in order to take up a position he had been offered at the newly established Bank of England.[27] Duck was elected in his place.

Duck, the new Assayer, had been apprenticed to Roger Stevens who died in 1673. After this he had continued to work with Stevens' widow Katherine at her premises in one of the Company's houses adjoining the Hall, receiving the freedom in 1677. In 1678 he had married his master's daughter, also named Katherine. The mother died in 1691 or 1692 and as her daughter – Duck's wife – had predeceased her she left the remainder of her lease and her estate to Duck and his three daughters. He presumably wound up the business soon afterwards when he was appointed assistant to Bowles. The maker's mark 'a goose in a dotted circle' (so-called) has been attributed to John Duck[28] (see page 152). There are still in existence several high quality silver pieces bearing this mark.

Within two years of Duck's appointment as Assayer the passing of a statute, designed primarily to protect the coinage, heralded a new chapter in the history of hallmarking.

CHAPTER SEVEN

THE BRITANNIA STANDARD
1697 to 1720

OWARDS THE END of the seventeenth century Parliament became greatly concerned about the scarcity and deplorable state of the silver coinage. Most of the coins in circulation had been minted before the introduction of edge milling and had suffered badly from clipping. The clippers had the advantage not only of an inviting export potential but also of a ready market nearer home; the heavy demand for new silverware and the consequent shortage of the metal were such that there was a great temptation for refiners and silversmiths to purchase raw material derived from clippings or even melted coins. Clipping and 'diminishing' the coinage were classed as treason and therefore punishable by death, but they were nevertheless extremely lucrative pursuits. Although some of the culprits were caught and executed, others eluded prosecution and continued to prosper.

There were lengthy debates on the matter in both Houses as a result of which a number of different measures were suggested as remedies. A Bill introduced in 1694, if passed, would have made it an offence for anyone – including goldsmiths – to buy or sell silver bullion that was not of foreign origin. It was dropped after strong objections by the Company, but a year later another, more acceptable to goldsmiths, passed to the Statute Book.[1] Under this Act, the buying or selling of clippings carried a penalty of £500, and to emphasize the seriousness of the offence any person convicted was to be branded with a hot iron on the right cheek with the letter R. Also, no one except a trading goldsmith or refiner was to buy or sell bullion. Furthermore no silver bullion was to be exported unless stamped by the wardens of the Goldsmiths' Company on the strength of an oath sworn by the owner and by a credible witness to the effect that no part of it was from current coin, clippings or plate wrought within this country. The Company was required to make an entry of all ingots so stamped in a book kept for the purpose (such a book, unfortunately has not survived). The wardens with two or more members of the Court of Assistants were empowered to enter the home or workshop of any person suspected of contravening the Act and to make seizures.

Mr John Sutton
in Lombardstreete
Present Touchwarden
Aprill ye 15th 1697
Dead

John Snelling in
Holbourn
Dead

John Spackman at Charring
Cross Left of

John: Smithson in the
Minories free Haberdasher

Wm Scarlett in foster Lane
free Imbroyder — Dead
June ye 29 1720 Old Star

John Shepherd
in Gutter Lane Dead

Joseph Stokes in St Olave's
Street Southwark
Dead

Alice Sheene in Ball
Alley in Lombard Street
Aprill: 29: 1700 Dead

ffrancis Singleton
in fosterlane dead
Dead

Tho: Spackman in foster Lane
May 25th: 1700
Dead

Richard Syngin Gray Land

Saml Smith
in Sweethings Lane Sep: 27: 1700

John Martin Stockar
in ye Strand
July: 1 1710 Dead

Thomas Sadler
in foster Lane Aug: 25 1701
Dead
Thomas Sadler des Sta—

John Smith in
Holbourn
Dead
2

Wm Spring
in the Strand near Charring
Cross Aug 30: 1701
2

Joseph Shepard in Ball
Alley in Lombard Street
Dead

Daniell Sleamaker
in Northings Lane
Aug: 15: 1704 Dead

A PAGE *of the new register of makers' marks commencing in 1697, showing the mark of the Touchwarden.*

THE GREAT RECOINAGE OF 1696

Parliament then decided that there should be a complete recoinage of the hammered (unmilled) money, and to ensure a high rate of production mints were established at Bristol, Chester, Exeter, Norwich and York to supplement the output of the London Mint. In order to obtain sufficient silver for this major operation it was necessary, not only to collect in the old coins, but also to encourage people to bring silver wares to the mints for melting. To this end a further Act passed in March 1696 forbade the use of any silver articles except spoons in the public rooms of inns or taverns.[2] And under the same measure no bullion was to be exported without a certificate – this time from the Court of the Lord Mayor and Aldermen – showing that it was of foreign origin.

As a possible further means of attracting silver to the mints, advantage was taken of a Bill that was put before Parliament in January 1697. Its primary purpose was to levy taxes on paper and vellum but an additional clause was inserted to impose a duty on all existing silver articles which had not been sent for melting and coining by a certain date and to require them to be stamped with a special mark. If the Bill had passed in this form the collection of the duty would have presented enormous administrative difficulties and there would inevitably have been much evasion. The Company predictably raised objections and the clause was deleted. However, the main purpose of the Bill was to raise revenue for the cost of the recoinage operation and it was passed without the controversial clause.[3] A tax on windows of houses provided additional revenue for the undertaking.[4]

Also early in 1697 another Bill was introduced and it quickly received Royal Assent in March of that year. It was entitled 'An Act for encouraging the bringing in of wrought plate to be coined'.[5] Since it incorporated important changes in the hallmarking law, the Company must have been consulted, but its records are strangely silent on the matter; no objections or even comments are mentioned. The Act not only contained measures in line with its title but also others to prevent the melting of coins for making silverware. To achieve the first of the objectives, any hallmarked silver wares brought to one of the mints was to be accepted and paid for at the rate of 5s 4d per ounce. To achieve the second objective the old sterling standard for silverware – 11 oz 2 dwt in the pound troy (or in the modern notation 925 parts per thousand) – was abolished and a new standard of 11 oz 10 dwt (958.4 parts per thousand) substituted. New hallmarks were prescribed: a lion's head erased in place of the leopard's head and a figure of Britannia instead of the lion passant. The new compulsory standard became known as Britannia, but at the Assay Office it was always referred to as 'New Sterling', a description still occasionally used.

The government hoped that the introduction of the Britannia standard would discourage melting of coins. The metal derived from this practice, being of the old sterling standard, would need to be enriched by alloying with fine silver before it could be used for the manufacture of silverware – an additional operation which would be relatively costly. The new Act was concerned only with silver; it did not alter the standard for gold articles – they still had to be 22 carat and if submitted for hallmarking, they were struck with the marks of the lion passant and leopard's head as before.

To coincide with the commencement of the Britannia standard the Assay Office not only changed the marks as required under the Act, but also started a new cycle of date letters. This left the letter 'U' of the then current cycle unused. The court hand alphabet was adopted, the letter 'A' being used only during the short period from 27 March to 28 May 1697.

The new Act had far-reaching consequences for the future of hallmarking, although this does not seem to have been fully appreciated at the time. It was the first new law on the subject for 120 years and it cast its net much wider than had any earlier legislation. The provisions were not restricted to London; the law stated unequivocally that silver articles made and sold anywhere in England had to be hallmarked. Not only was the standard raised but other aspects of the law were also changed. For example, the only articles exempted from hallmarking under the Act were 'silver wire and such things as in respect of their smallness are not capable of receiving a mark'. Earlier statutes had

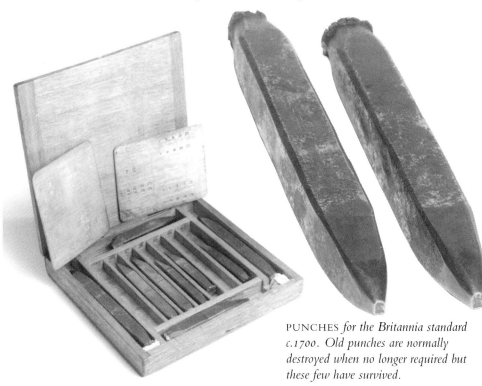

PUNCHES *for the Britannia standard c.1700. Old punches are normally destroyed when no longer required but these few have survived.*

been far less explicit. But the new law made no mention of searches; the wardens still had to rely on the charter for the necessary authority.

The Act required all makers to have a new design of mark. Early makers' marks had been in the form of a symbol but by this time it had become almost universal practice to use the initial letters of the Christian and surname of the maker. Sometimes these were combined in the same punch with an additional symbol such as a fleur-de-lys or star – the letters (or letters and symbol) usually being enclosed in a shield. The new Act stipulated that makers' marks now had to consist of the first two letters of the surname. All makers had to register their new marks at the Assay Office, together with their names and addresses. Books were provided for this purpose and fortunately all but two of the continuous series of registers from that date to the present day have survived. They contain inked impressions taken from the actual punches and provide the principal basis for the identification of makers – a matter of particular interest to collectors and students of antique silver.[6] The use of symbols in conjunction with the letters in a maker's mark was still permitted for a short time after the new legislation, but eventually symbols were disallowed altogether, as is the case today. Some 20,000 individual makers or firms registered marks at the London Assay Office between 1697 and 1975.

The Company was at pains to ensure that all articles, even those that were too small to be hallmarked, at least bore a maker's mark which could be identified if necessary. An order was accordingly printed and circulated throughout the trade in August 1698. It read as follows:

> Whereas several ringmakers and other workers in small wares of gold and silver do live privately in obscure places and work and make such wares worse than standard, to the great abuse of his Majesty's subjects; and whereas the said wares ought to be marked with the mark of the maker thereof, which is now very much neglected … it is this day ordered that all such ringmakers and other workers in small wares … do forthwith enter their respective marks and places of abode at the assay office at Goldsmiths' Hall in a book there kept for that purpose … and all shopkeepers … are required henceforwards not to employ any smallworkers or buy any small works of gold or silver of any such smallworkers until they have marked all such small works as will not bear the touch at the Hall with their own marks.

It would seem that not all smallworkers obeyed this order because in 1716 a further one was issued, obliging makers of wares which were too small to be hallmarked 'to alter their present marks and use the first two letters of their surnames in old English characters, to enter their marks at the Assay Office, and to work in the new (Britannia) standard. An inspection of the relevant register shows that there was some response to the order but not as great as one would have expected.

In the haste in which the Act of 1697 was passed the provincial centres of the trade had been completely forgotten and their craftsmen found themselves in great difficulties. The new legislation required articles to be hallmarked at the Assay Office in London and made no reference to any other office. York, for instance, already had an assay office which was now unable to operate. After receiving a number of petitions from the provinces, Parliament responded promptly and an Act of 1700 provided for the establishment of Companies of Goldsmiths and assay offices in the towns in which mints had recently been set up.[7] Even then the legislators had forgotten Newcastle, which was not a town designated for a mint but had a number of working goldsmiths who found it hard to comply with the new law. A petition to the House of Commons from the local traders resulted in a further Act in 1702 for establishing a Newcastle Goldsmiths' Company and an assay office in that town.[8]

As we shall see, the Act of 1700 was relevant not only to the provincial offices but also to the London Goldsmiths' Company, since by implication it gave any craftsman, no matter where he was working, the right to register a maker's mark at an assay office – at least that was the interpretation of the Company's legal advisers some twenty years later.[9] Thus, although it was not immediately realized at the time it was passed, the Act effectively put an end to the Company's power to refuse the right of the 'assay and touch' to non-freemen or to those who had repeatedly offended against its ordinances.

Because of the raising of the legal standard of silver, a new trial piece was urgently required. Following the receipt of a warrant from the Treasury to nominate a jury, twenty members of the Company were duly sworn and assembled at the premises of Peter Floyer in Foster Lane, where the plate was made and sawn into six pieces. The Company retained the largest piece, a portion of which still remains at Goldsmiths' Hall, and portions were also sent to the recently constituted provincial assay offices. It was of course only for use in assaying silver wares: the sterling trial plate of 1688 was used for assaying the coinage at Trials of the Pyx held in 1697, 1701 and 1707.

According to the Acts of 1700 and 1702 the provincial offices had to send their diets to the Mint for testing, but only if ordered to do so by the Lord Chancellor or Keeper of the Great Seal. It was not until 1707 that such an order was issued. In that year the London Goldsmiths' Company was asked to try the diets of the York, Chester, Exeter and Newcastle Assay Offices. This was done on the same day as the Trial of the Pyx after adjournment from the Exchequer to the Hall. All were found to be up to the Britannia standard. However, the Chester Office was rebuked for having a hole in the lid of the diet box 'through which the diet might be put in or taken out at pleasure without inlocking of the box'. On opening the box the jury was 'much dissatisfied, believing that the true diet had been taken out and in lieu thereof other pieces of standard plate put in'.[10] This was to be the only occasion on

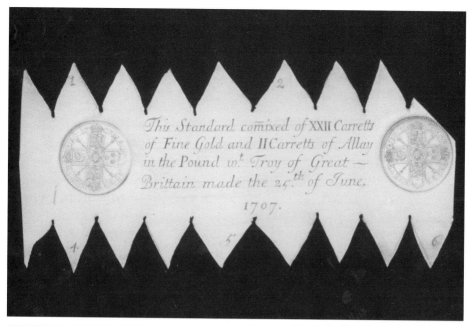

SURVIVING PORTION OF THE GOLD TRIAL PLATE *of 1707, held at the Royal Mint, showing the original indentations at the top and bottom. The plate was used at the Trial of the Pyx in 1710 when the jury rejected the coins as being below standard.*

which the above offices were required to submit their diets. Fourteen years later the Company debated whether it should apply to the Treasury for authority to carry out further trials of the diets of the provincial offices, but it was decided that it would not be proper to take the initiative.[11]

Trials of the Pyx were now held about once every three years. Most of them ran smoothly but a disaster occurred at the Trial in 1707 – the furnace got out of hand and set fire to the roof of the Exchequer building. Happily the conflagration was extinguished without doing any great damage and the Lord Chancellor was pleased to adjourn the proceedings to Goldsmiths' Hall for completion of the task.

In the same year of 1707 England and Scotland were united under the Act of Union. This called for the continuance of the Mint in Edinburgh and for bringing it into line with the Tower Mint in London. It also meant that new trial plates (sterling silver and 22 carat gold) were required for a recoinage of the Scottish money; they were made between the 11 and 21 June at the premises of John Cartlitch, a refiner in Oat Lane.[12] Cartlitch, who was a member of the jury appointed by the Company for the purpose, and incidentally serving as Touchwarden, supplied the precious metals. His skill was undoubted: the gold was of such exceptional purity that the resulting trial plate, as we now know from a recent assay, was very close to the true standard.

Using the Treasury portion of the 1707 gold plate for the first time at a Trial of the Pyx in 1710, the jury found the coins to be one part per thousand below standard, to the intense annoyance of Sir Isaac Newton, the Master of the Mint, and other officials, who all protested vociferously. Newton maintained that the gold used in the manufacture of the new trial plate had been over-purified. He considered it unfair that trial plates should be made from gold or silver that had been purified beyond the normally accepted level. Newton himself assayed the new gold plate alongside those made in 1688 and 1660. He found it to be better than standard by five-twelfths of a grain (921.0 parts per 1000), the 1688 plate one sixth of a grain better (918.4) and the 1660 plate exactly standard (916.6). We now know from recent assays of surviving portions that the new plate was in fact 916.9, ie only very slightly above, whereas the two earlier ones were appreciably below standard – the 1688 plate being 914.4 parts per 1000, and the 1660 plate 912.8.[172] Newton stressed the great cost to the Treasury if gold coins had to be made of a standard corresponding to the new plate. He must have argued his case well as he had the last word – at the next trial in 1713 the coins were tried against all three plates (1660, 1688 and 1707) but after that the 1707 plate was not used again. The 1688 plate was adopted as the recognized standard in all subsequent trials until the early nineteenth century.

The Trials of the Pyx ensured a continuing association between the Company and the Mint but there was another reason for their close relationship – the ready convertibility of plate into coinage. Wrought silver was still considered by most people to be a form of savings which they could readily turn into cash in time of necessity or if they were tempted by a high silver price. This is well illustrated by the result of a proclamation by Queen Anne in 1711 to encourage owners to bring their silverware to the Mint for coining. They were offered attractive rates: hallmarked plate of the sterling standard at 5s 6d per troy oz and plate of the Britannia standard at 5s 8d. In the three days 11, 12 and 14 May the Mint received 101,137 oz in the first category and 54,504 oz in the second; then from 15 May to 19 June a further 55,328 oz in the first category and 24,123 oz in the second – altogether totalling more than a third of an average year's production of silverware by the London trade. The mint also accepted 38,954 oz of unhallmarked plate but the price was not fixed until it had been assayed.[13]

The amount of work submitted to the Assay Office had dropped appreciably in the months preceding the introduction of the Britannia standard. This was possibly due to the uncertainty caused by impending legislation, bearing in mind that at one stage a retrospective duty was envisaged. Also contributing to the decline was the Treasury's policy of encouraging the sale of silver to the mints and thus diverting it from use in the manufacture of new articles. But the lull in activity in the trade was only temporary; within twelve months of the introduction of the new standard receipts for hallmarking were equalling the figures of three years earlier. After 1703 they rose even higher, averaging about 600,000oz per annum. There was clearly a continuing demand for new silverware in spite of the increased cost of the metal.

FINANCIAL DIFFICULTIES

The staff in the Assay Office at this time must have been under considerable strain. Apart from the Assayer and the Weigher, there were probably not more than three other workers; considering the quantity of silver received, they did well to maintain the rapid turnround that was expected by the trade. Additional members of staff could only be engaged if the Assayer were able to afford their wages. However, his salary had been kept to a minimum because of the prevailing state of the Company's finances which, as we have seen, had been the cause of much concern ever since the reign of James I. The Stuart kings had drained the reserves by their frequent demands and money had to be borrowed at high interest rates. The decision to rebuild the Hall in 1634 had entailed more expense and then the Company had to contribute its share of the cost of defending the City during the Civil War. The damage to the Hall in the Great Fire and the subsequent fire in the Assay Office brought further burdens on the already stretched finances. It is not surprising, therefore, that the Company continued in debt in the years following. Much of its own collection of plate had already been sold and in 1711 the Court made an uncharacteristically rash decision – to sell most of the residue and to buy tickets in the Classis lottery which was promoted by the Government in that year.[14] The proceeds of the sale amounted to £482 17s 10d, with which twenty tickets were bought. Alas, no prize was forthcoming.

Such was the poor state of the finances that in 1705 John Duck, the Assayer, was owed £300 in arrears of salary. Considering that his annual salary was only £70 this surely must have meant considerable hardship for him. It seems he was of necessity long suffering. He was subjected to the inconvenience of having to move out of his house in the Hall for eighteen months to make way for Sir Charles Duncombe and then Sir Peter Floyer during their shrievalties in 1699 and 1701. And he was forced to move again in 1704, this time so that the Lord Mayor, Sir Owen Buckingham, could be accommodated. Sir Owen was not a member but the Company was no doubt eager to obtain the rent. Nine years later Duck asked for compensation, saying it had cost him £25 to rent a house for the twelve months. It was agreed this should be allowed and he was given a bond for £220 which included the £25 as well as outstanding salary! In 1714 the river barge and bargehouse together with plate and other goods in the Hall were mortgaged to him as security for a debt of £426 8s. In

June 1715 the Company's stock of pewter was sold to pay his arrears of salary but he was still owed £170 in the following May.

The Weigher's salary was also the Company's responsibility. In 1706, George Garthorne, who had recently succeeded William Ryland as Weigher, had been awarded a gratuity of £5 to supplement his annual salary of £20 in consideration of his care and diligence together with 'his present mean circumstances'. But other workers in the Office were still employed by the Assayer and paid by him out of his salary – when he could get it. There are frequent small reminders of the need for reducing expenditure; in 1719 for example, Garthorne, on presenting a bill for £5 8s 7d for candles, oil and washing of the sweep, was told to be more economical.

The unfortunate Duck was allowed to retire in 1716 on the grounds of ill health at the age of sixty-three, before the Company's fortunes turned. He did not, however, escape being elected Renter in the same year and was only excused on payment of £30. He had served in the Assay Office for twenty-three years and in his early seventies he was invited to become a member of the Court of Assistants on payment of £5. It is not recorded if he accepted; perhaps he felt he was too old, but as he lived to the age of ninety-two it is more likely that he had become disenchanted with the Company. Soon after his retirement he was admonished for accepting £70 from Nathaniel Bowles in return for supporting the latter's election as his successor. In view of the delays in the payments of his salary and considering the morals of the age, his acceptance of the money does not seem too unreasonable. One cannot help having some sympathy for him; he would certainly appear to have been underpaid in view of the responsibilities of his office. On the other hand one should not forget the hidden extras – the perquisites. These included payments for assaying articles purchased by agents from suspected offenders or seized by the wardens on their searches, and he was also, of course, entitled to the 'assay bits', the value of which could have been as much as £70 a year.

In spite of the precarious state of the Company's finances, it was nevertheless decided in 1708 that £200 should be spent on a pageant on the occasion of the accession of Sir Charles Duncombe to the Mayoralty. Three floats, each drawn by six horses, were provided to represent the Mystery of Goldsmiths, the Chariot of Justice and the Temple of Apollo. Duck took part in person on the first float, appearing in his natural role as Assay Master. He was accompanied by Garthorne (the Weigher) and Thomas Cooke (the Drawer) with others representing a planisher, a raiser, a chaser, three forgemen and a bellows man.

THE EARLIEST SURVIVING SILVER COFFEE POT, *in the Victoria and Albert Museum and hallmarked 1681. It is attributed to George Garthorne, who served as Weigher at the Assay Office from 1706 to 1731. Also shown is the registration of Garthorne's Britannia standard maker's mark in 1697.*

Much thought had been given by the Court as to how the Company's financial difficulties could be eased. In 1711, the year of the unfortunate decision to gamble in the Classis lottery, a special committee was convened to consider ways of reducing expenses. Any deficit on the working of the Assay Office had always to be borne by the Company out of its other revenues and one of the committee's main recommendations – apart from economies in the cost of dinners – was that means should be found for the Office to 'bear its own charges', in other words to break even. This was to prove far from easy to achieve and the Standing Committee, as it was later called, met many times. In fact it continued in being long after the financial circumstances had improved, when it became primarily concerned with matters appertaining to the Assay Office. All important resolutions were subject to approval by the Court of Assistants.

One not inconsiderable source of income was derived from the fines recovered from makers or sellers of substandard wares. Many of the offences were discovered by the wardens on their searches in London and elsewhere and latterly agents had been commissioned to look for suspicious articles and to purchase them where appropriate. Between 24 May and 9 June 1699, for example, offenders from thirty-three different towns were summoned to appear before the wardens and were fined. In 1706, one of the agents, Mr Wells, was paid £227 for buying 'coarse' wares. In the following year he received £85 17s. As a result of his and other purchases, fines were imposed on dealers in Aylesbury, Bristol, Chard, Cirencester, Oxford, Bath, Gloucester, Exeter, Portsmouth, Dorchester, Bishops Stortford, Northampton and other places. It was probably the result of one or more such purchases that prompted Duck to write to the recently constituted Newcastle Goldsmiths' Company to draw its attention to substandard buckles and snuff-boxes on sale in that area – an early example of exchange of correspondence between the assay offices, which was uncommon at that date. Two London searches in 1715 resulted in the seizure of 120 articles and sixty persons being called to the Hall and fined. In August of the same year the wardens exacted fines from thirty different traders during their annual search at Bartholomew Fair and the neighbouring area. These are just typical examples; there were many others.

With increasing frequency, however, the wardens found themselves challenged during their searches. On one occasion it was reported that even some fellow members had reviled the wardens 'in a rude and indecent manner'. Repeated attempts had been made by the Company to obtain legislation in order to confirm and strengthen its powers, but they had been unsuccessful. It reluctantly began to accept that it could no longer act on the authority of a royal charter unless the terms were backed by Act of Parliament. Other City Companies had been experiencing similar difficulties and they too were gradually forced to abandon their searches. Unlike the Goldsmiths' Company, however, most of them had no alternative means of controlling their crafts – they had no counterparts to the hallmarking statutes.

The wardens were naturally concerned to know exactly where they stood in law and in 1716 they took counsel's opinion. The advice received was that their right to search did not extend beyond the three-mile limit of London, nor did they have the authority to enter the premises of non-members against their wills: although the Company's own members were obliged to obey its by-laws, to submit to search and to pay fines where imposed, other workers or dealers were not. Counsel also advised that the only way in which penalties could be recovered legally from offenders who were not freemen was by action in the courts. Any article sold or exposed for sale which contravened the Act of 1697 was liable to be forfeited – in the words of the Act: 'the one half to the King and the other half thereof to such person or persons that will seize or sue for the same, to be recovered by action, bill, suit or information in any Court of Record ... '

This advice was a grave setback as having to sue for penalties in the courts was time-consuming and by no means always financially lucrative. In spite of the legal opinion the Company continued to exact arbitrary fines from some country dealers, but after a few years this practice was stopped, no doubt the wardens fearing they might be taken to court for exceeding their powers. In future, offences by non-freemen would have to be dealt with by due legal process.

A valuable source of income down the centuries had been the diet, but this by itself was now far from sufficient to cover the expense of running the Assay Office. From the time the 1697 Act came into force an increasing number of small wares had been received. Although these were assayed in the same manner as large wares the amount of diet retained was inevitably small in proportion to the work involved in assaying and marking. The Assayer himself disliked dealing with small wares, because although he was entitled to the 'assay bits' he had to recompense the sender for any sample drawings taken in excess of the diet entitlement. He maintained that this resulted in an inadequate return for his labours.

Hitherto, apart from the quarterage, there had been no standard monetary charge for hallmarking – except for a small fee for marking gold articles which resulted in an income of about £15 per annum. A charge of 3d per item was levied on the sender, out of which the Assayer was allowed 6d per parcel. It now seemed reasonable to make a charge for assaying and marking small silver wares. It so happened that in December 1715 a petition was received from a number of snuff-box makers who complained about the widespread trade in substandard articles of certain types. They requested the Company to take steps to ensure that all small wares were submitted for assay and marking. Their real motive may have been to endeavour to exclude foreign workers from practising their craft. The petitioners intimated that they would be prepared to pay a fee for marking. Representatives from the trades of snuff-box maker, buckle maker, sword-hilt maker and watchcase maker were forthwith consulted. After inevitable opposition from some of them and then much haggling over the amounts to be paid, agreement was obtained for charging 6d each for marking sword-hilts and watchcases, 3d for snuff boxes, 2d for a pair of spurs, ½d for a pair of buckles and 1d for knife hafts and 'suchlike small things'.

As a further means of improving the financial position consideration was given to the possibility of differential charges. In earlier days the Company had always restricted the privilege of the 'assay and touch' to its own members, with rare exceptions. Latterly, however, it had granted the facility to freemen of other City Companies.[15] Thus we find in the registers of makers' marks dating from 1697 names of both gold and silver workers who were freemen of the Haberdashers, Grocers, Merchant Taylors and other Companies and there were no doubt similar entries in the earlier books. It was now decided that these workers should not only take the same oath as free goldsmiths but also pay quarterage. Furthermore it was resolved that they should be charged double the rates which had lately been introduced for assaying and marking certain small wares, and that twice the amount of diet should be taken from their large wares (8 grains per pound troy).

Nevertheless the Company was worried. Its legal position in these matters was by no means crystal clear. Was it permitted to refuse the 'assay and touch' to non-freemen? Was it allowed to take double the normal diet from freemen of other City Companies? How did the Acts of 1697 and 1700 affect its powers? Did the Act of 1700 apply to the Company as well as the newly established assay offices? Such was its concern that in 1716 legal opinion was taken on these questions at the same time as advice was sought on its right of search. The unequivocal opinion of counsel was that the Company was obliged to assay and hallmark articles brought by any person, whether a freeman or not, and whether residing in London or elsewhere. Counsel also advised that it was not entitled to discriminate against workers who were not on its roll of freemen. This opinion was disappointing in view of the efforts the Company was making to improve its finances. Notwithstanding counsel's advice, for several more years anyone who was not a free goldsmith was obliged to pay double the normal diet. According to the detailed records of the trials of the diet these workers were submitting about one third of the total weight of silver wares received.

There was, however, one encouraging aspect of the new legislation introduced in 1697. Under the Act the only exemptions from compulsory hall-marking of silver articles had been 'silver wire and such things as in respect of their smallness are not capable of receiving a mark'. This gave an opportunity to tighten up on measures to ensure that all wares liable to hallmarking were submitted to the Assay Office, particularly many small wares which had previously never been sent. And now that a charge was to be made for assaying small wares, the greater the quantity received the higher would be the income of the office. For this reason steps were taken to ensure that all makers were aware of their obligations. A notice drawn up in January 1717 and given wide publicity, stated:

> All goldsmiths, silversmiths and plateworkers, including foreigners, inhabiting the Cities of London and Westminster, the Borough of Southwark and near the same are required forthwith to enter their marks with their names and places of abode ... and to bring all their works to the Assay Office to be assayed and marked ... All such works of gold and silver which are not so assayed and marked are liable to be seized and forfeited, one half to the King and the other half to any person that will seize or sue for the same.

Incidentally, it is evident from this that the Company now took the view that gold wares as well as silver, both large and small, should be hallmarked, although there was still no statutory requirement to support it.

The new order was not well received by the Company's own trade members. For centuries they had sheltered under a form of protection by which, with few exceptions, only freemen – including latterly freemen of other City Companies – were permitted to send work for hallmarking. This virtually precluded anyone who was not so entitled from setting up in business on his own account; he could only work as a journeyman or outworker. Some makers had attempted to get round this restriction by an arrangement with someone who was registered at the Assay Office and was prepared to submit work for them, under his own maker's mark, a practice known as 'colouring'. This was certainly not approved and periodically steps were taken to stop it, usually by fining the culpable members. Petitions had already been presented to the Company by trade members in 1697 and 1703 with the object of preventing foreigners from obtaining the privilege of the 'assay and touch', and the Company had reacted favourably on both occasions. Now, not unexpectedly, there was a strong reaction from the trade members to the latest notice, which in effect permitted anyone, including aliens, to register a maker's mark and have their wares hallmarked. As a result, two further petitions were presented in February 1717, one by trade liverymen and the other by freemen working as journeymen. The petitioners pleaded that foreigners and others who had not served a seven years' apprenticeship should be denied the 'assay and touch'. The Company replied that the notice to which they were objecting had been based on counsel's opinion; if they did not like it they should themselves seek legal advice.

The petitioners duly took their own counsel's opinion which differed from that given to the Company. The advice they received was that whilst anyone outside London had the right of 'assay and touch', those who had always been excluded from it (that is non-freemen residing in London) did not become entitled to it by virtue of the new law. On the strength of this the petitioners continued to press their case and offered to underwrite the Company against any penalties resulting from legal action if it would agree to reverse its decision. At one stage they even went so far as to say they would be prepared to defray all the expense and charge of the Assay Office if the notice were withdrawn. However, the Company stood its ground and it is difficult to see how it could have acted otherwise.

Eight years later the trade members made a final attempt to achieve their objective. But the Company was by then wholly satisfied that it could not refuse to assay and mark plate wrought and submitted by non-freemen, a view that was backed by the advice it had received from various counsel including the Common Sergeant and confirmed by a report of the Attorney General.

The 1697 and 1700 Acts made it quite clear that silver articles made or sold not only in London but in any part of England had to be hallmarked. It might be expected that as a result of the new law many wares would have been sent to the London office from other parts of the country, but although this happened later the quantity submitted at this time was small. Some were of course submitted to the newly established provincial assay offices, but others still escaped hallmarking altogether.

The Standing Committee, which had been considering various suggestions for augmenting the income of the Assay Office, turned its attention in 1715 to another possible source of revenue – sizing of troy weights. This activity had lapsed; scale-makers and founders were themselves certifying the weights they supplied to the trade. Nathaniel Bowles, the former Assayer, was consulted. He said he used to size weights himself, and marking them with the lion and date letter charging 3s or 3s 6d for a 64oz set. It was one of his perquisites. However, the subject is not referred to again in the Committee's minutes, so it would appear that sizing of weights, which in earlier times had received a great deal of attention, was no longer considered a responsibility of the Company; there was no statutory authority for it. The Committee would have to look elsewhere for additional revenue.

The weight of silver submitted for hallmarking during the period in which the Britannia standard was compulsory (about 600,000oz annually) does not give an altogether true picture of the work involved. Now that the Company was taking active steps to ensure the submission of all articles capable of bearing the marks the work was becoming progressively greater. Weight for weight a disproportionate amount of effort was required in sampling and marking small wares. In 1716, shortly before he resigned, John Duck the Assayer asked if he could have an allowance for his 'extraordinary trouble' in marking small wares – he had been obliged to employ another drawer whose wages he had had to pay out of his own pocket.

Following Duck's resignation the Standing Committee recommended a major reorganization of the financial arrangements in the Assay Office and this was acted upon forthwith. In future the Assayer would not be entitled to any perquisites; the 'assay bits', for example, would become the property of the Company. In return he would be relieved of meeting the cost of materials such as charcoal and slow ashes. Furthermore, all staff would be appointed and paid by the Company, so the Assayer would no longer personally have to pay 'servants' to carry out the drawing and other tasks. A neat way of minimizing the amount of the Weigher's and Drawers' salaries was to put them on the list of recipients of the Sir Hugh Myddelton charity – a bequest for alleviating the lot of poor members of the Company!

Besides attending to the financial aspects of the Assay Office, the Standing Committee was concerned to ensure that the staff were properly carrying out their duties. For example, it was one of the responsibilities of George Garthorne (appointed Weigher in 1706) to inspect all articles received to make sure that excessive solder had not been used in their manufacture. In 1716 he was suspected of neglecting this aspect of his work and was interviewed by the Committee. His excuse was that some makers had been very angry and had threatened him for refusing to accept their work; also that he did not attend on the days on which only by-assays were supposed to be sent. It transpired that plate also was being sent on those days, so Garthorne was ordered to attend daily in future and in return his annual salary was increased to £50. As a further check, the Drawers were instructed to look for excessive solder when sampling. Garthorne was reprimanded again five years later for the same neglect and he promised to take more care. He was a gifted silversmith (see page 179) and it is not without irony that some twenty-four years earlier before becoming an officer of the Company, Garthorne had been one of the signatories of a petition complaining about the use of excessive solder by some members of the trade.

As a further measure aimed at preventing the use of unnecessary solder the Company issued a new order which applied to all workers 'within the Cities of London and Westminster or within three miles of the same'. The order stated that flagons, tankards or mugs if melted down should be not less than 5 dwt worse than standard. Similarly dressing plate, castors, punch bowls, coffee-pots and teapots should be not less than 3 dwt worse. A third category comprising cups and covers with hollow handles, mugs with round bottoms and barbers' pots were to be not less than 2 dwt worse when melted. This regulation would have been difficult to enforce in practice since it would have involved melting down a whole article to prove an offence. Nevertheless the Touchwarden, assisted by the Assayer and Weigher, was given the necessary authority to do so if any plate were suspected of being fraudulently wrought. If the results proved to be within the permitted tolerance the Company would make good the fashion (the cost of workmanship). It is recorded that one John Thomson brought some knife hafts for hallmarking which were thought to be heavily loaded with solder. On melting the resultant silver was found to be 1 oz 15 dwt worse; he was ordered to pay £20.

It had become the practice to mark large wares and small wares on alternate days. Such was the increasing volume of work that Benjamin Pyne (Senior), the Touchwarden in 1715, was awarded a gratuity of £10 for his 'extraordinary labour and pains in the Assay Office'. In theory the Touchwarden had authority over the staff but as he was present for only part of each working day, he was not in a position to exert any strict supervision, nor would he normally have had the expertise to overrule the Assayer. He was, however, by custom always a practising goldsmith – either a plateworker, refiner or someone with related experience.

ASSAY OFFICE FINANCES

In the eighteenth century, as indeed in earlier times, much value was placed on the solemn oath demanded of persons holding positions that called for absolute integrity. Ever since the appointment of Christopher Elyot in 1478, the Assayer had been required each year to take a prescribed oath before the Court of Assistants (see Appendix I). Certain members of the trade now requested that the Drawers should be similarly sworn. The Court agreed this was desirable, especially as they were now employed directly by the Company, and that moreover the Weigher should be included. As there was no precedent – the ordinances contained no form of oath for Weigher or Drawer – they were required to make voluntary affidavits before a judge or master in Chancery for the faithful discharge of their duties, using a form of words which are recorded in the minute book (see Appendix I). This practice, started in 1717, was continued for the next 150 years.

In view of the increase in workload it was agreed that there should be two assayers and that the Assay Office premises should be enlarged. Nathaniel Bowles, who had left in 1695 to take up a position at the Bank of England (see page 158), returned as Assayer in place of John Duck. At the same time Joseph Ward was engaged as Second Assayer. The re-appointment of Bowles is rather surprising, considering he was then seventy years of age, but perhaps it was felt that his experience was required even for a short time.

Joseph Ward was a colourful character, as his subsequent career was to show. He was one of two sons of John Ward who had been a warden in 1692, 94 and 96. Joseph had been apprenticed to his father in 1686 and at the time of his appointment was himself a member of the Court of Assistants. He had been in business on his own account as a private assayer and was therefore not required to take a practical test to assess his abilities. Both assayers agreed to a salary of £100 with no perquisites but Bowles, as senior, had rent-free accommodation.

The introduction of charges for marking small wares and the changes in the terms of employment of the staff resulted in a significant improvement in the finances of the Assay Office, as illustrated by the following account of receipts and payments for the year ended 29 May 1720. However, although showing a credit balance of £118 12s 2d, the cost of the Assayers' living quarters is not included, nor is there any rental charge for the premises used by the Office. It can be seen that fines for substandard wares still provided a substantial income but it was one which would virtually disappear within a few years.

	£	s	d
Debtor			
Two assayers & Weigher	250	–	–
Three drawers	78	–	–
Charcoal	58	–	–
Twelve bushels slow ashes	6	–	–
Scalemaker	2	–	–
Muffles & glasses	5	–	–
Luting furnaces	2	–	–
Aqua fortis	7	10	–
Lead	2	10	–
Workmen's deficiency*	20	–	–
Engraver (punches)	4	–	–
Candles	5	–	–
Total	440	–	–

*Compensation for diet taken from small wares.

	£	s	d
Creditor			
Small wares (charges for marking)	218	10	–
Diet silver Assay bits } Sweep	173	16	–
Coarse wares (fines for)	139	16	2
Ditto remaining in Hall which cost	26	10	–
Total	558	12	2

By the end of the seventeenth century the membership of the Company was no longer restricted to working goldsmiths since it was possible to gain admission by patrimony instead of service. If a non-trade member was elected Touchwarden, he was obliged to pay a fine in order to be excused from carrying out the duty. Sometimes two or three such members would be elected in turn, each paying his fine – a useful source of income at a time when it was

THE SEYMOUR SALT, *c.1662*.

badly needed. In 1706, for example, Jeremiah Johnson was elected Touchwarden but 'not being of the Mistery and therefore incapable of serving the office' was excused on payment of £10. Usually the fine was £30 but for some reason Johnson was let off lightly. Occasionally, instead of paying a fine the elected Touchwarden would present a piece of silverware. One such was Thomas Seymour; in 1693 he gave the Company a magnificent silver-gilt salt, which had been a present from the citizens of Portsmouth to Catherine of Braganza when she arrived in 1662 for her marriage to Charles II. This unique piece, which was seen by Samuel Pepys and described in his Diary as 'one of the neatest pieces of plate that ever I saw', is still in the possession of the Company.[16] Thomas Seymour had probably acquired it when Catherine returned to Portugal in 1692 – Seymour was a trade member and therefore liable for service as Touchwarden but it seems he was released from the obligation because of his splendid gift.

ASSAY OFFICE STAFF

Except for apprentices it was a prerequisite that candidates for any position in the Assay Office should be members of the Company. Furthermore, practical experience as a silversmith was considered essential for the posts of Weigher and Drawer, applicants for which had usually served an apprenticeship and had often worked for some years on their own account. To be able to take scrapings or cuttings that were free from contamination by small amounts of solder, drawers had to be familiar with the methods used in the manufacture of a wide variety of articles. Moreover, samples had to be removed without causing damage and this demanded a high level of skill.

Many of the pieces made by members of the staff before joining the Assay Office have survived and the names of at least some of them or their masters will be known to present-day collectors of antique silver. There were three drawers in 1716. The senior was Charles Overing, who had entered a maker's mark as a largeworker in 1697 and had thus had a number of years' experience in the trade before he was employed in the Assay Office. The Second Drawer was Overing's son Thomas, and the Third Drawer was James Dickins who had been a silver bucklemaker. John Fawdery, who succeeded Dickins, had been apprenticed to the eminent silversmith Anthony Nelme and had obtained his freedom in 1695. He also worked as a master silversmith until employed by the Company in 1722. Richard Watts, who succeeded him on his death two years later, had been apprenticed to another silversmith, Christopher Canner. Watts had registered his first mark as a largeworker in 1710 and a second (sterling) mark in 1720. But perhaps the most noteworthy member of the staff at this period was George Garthorne, the Weigher, whom we have already mentioned.

Garthorne had been first indentured to Thomas Payne and then 'turned over' to his brother Francis Garthorne. An exceedingly talented silversmith, he set up on his own after receiving his freedom in 1680. For a number of years he ran a successful business, obtaining several royal commissions, such as one from William III for a magnificent twelve-branched chandelier which is still at Hampton Court. A silver-gilt altar dish made in 1691 for Lord Lucas, Constable of the Tower, which is kept in the Jewel House and placed on the altar of Westminster Abbey during the Coronation service, is another notable piece of his. Garthorne is also credited with making the earliest surviving silver coffee pot (1681), now in the Victoria and Albert Museum, (see page 169) and a rare gold beaker (1685). He rapidly attained the status of a liveryman and was one of the seventy-four who were displaced by order of James II in 1687. With Carey Lane as his address he registered a Britannia standard maker's mark in 1697. Presumably his business subsequently suffered for in 1706 he gave up his former trade on joining the Assay Office, where he served for the next twenty-five years.

Benjamin Pyne, the son and former apprentice of a renowned silversmith, also Benjamin, was appointed in 1720 to assist in firing assays and drawing. His father, who had been Touchwarden in 1715, became Prime Warden in 1725 (see page 176). By then he had fallen on hard times and two years later he successfully applied for the position of Beadle, a post he held until he died in 1732, at the age of about seventy-seven. The son continued to work in the Assay Office until his own death in 1737.

Christopher Canner, the son of the Christopher Canner mentioned above, was engaged as a drawer in 1731. He had entered a mark as a largeworker in 1716. Charles Gibbons who had been apprenticed to Gabriel Sleath in 1724 was appointed a drawer in 1737. He died two years later and was succeeded by

HALLMARK ON A TANKARD *showing the figure of Britannia, the date letter for 1700 and the lion's head erased. The maker's mark is that of the eminent silversmith Benjamin Pyne (senior).*

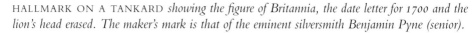

Meshac Godwin, who had been apprenticed to Humphrey Payne in 1709 and had entered a mark in 1723.

It is interesting to speculate why these and other established silversmiths should have changed their occupations to become full-time members of the Assay Office staff. Most of them were aged about forty at the time of their appointments. It may be that business was slack – we know that native crafts-men were suffering from the competition of Huguenots who had settled in England (see page 191). Or perhaps they felt that a regular income, though not a large one, was preferable to an uncertain living; a position with the Company must have carried considerable prestige and there was also the certainty that when they died the Company would not be ungenerous to a surviving widow, assuming they had completed a reasonable length of service. For the assayers there was the added attraction of a rent-free house in the Hall. All staff were obliged to relinquish completely their former trade as manufacturing silvers-miths, which would have been incompatible with working in the Assay Office; on more than one occasion they reminded the wardens of this when asking for a review of their salaries. One of them, however, had another interest; Gawen Nash, while Junior Weigher, kept a coffee house in Gutter Lane for several years before his death in 1763. When the Court was considering a successor it was decided that such an arrangement would definitely not be permitted in future. Nash had also found another – more acceptable – way of supplementing his income by acting as butler to the Company at their social functions for more than twenty-four years. On his death his two daughters were given £50 'to set them forward in any business they may attempt or to go out into the world for their future subsistence'.

We are not sure whether Joseph Marlow, who was appointed Weigher in 1731, had been a practising silversmith because there is no record of a maker's mark in his name. He was a member of the Court of Assistants and had regularly attended meetings, though he ceased to do so entirely after his new appointment. He continued as Weigher for thirty-one years, eventually becom-ing very infirm and incapable of doing the work himself. He was permitted to employ a deputy and was kept on the payroll until his death in 1762 at the age of eighty-four. Perhaps the Company felt under an obligation to a member of the Court, especially as it appears he was in some financial straits towards the end of his life. He was succeeded by Thomas Townraw who had been deputizing for him for nine years and had earlier entered three marks.

There was of course some risk in employing staff who had themselves been engaged in the manufacture of silverware. Even though they were required to cease trading on their own account, the temptation to augment their income must sometimes have been strong, especially in view of the low salaries the Company were forced to pay at this time. In 1713, Charles Overing, the Drawer was severely reprimanded by the wardens for having assisted in making some substandard tumblers; but on promising 'never to be guilty of a like offence', he was allowed to continue his employment. His son, however, was later discharged for various misdemeanours.

In this connection it has been suggested that Joseph Ward, who was appointed Second Assayer in 1716, was responsible for the manufacture of a kettle and stand bearing transposed hallmarks for the year 1720. This interesting and well-made piece is part of a set in the Company's possession. It bears the maker's mark of a Joseph Ward which was entered in 1717. But whatever other faults the Assayer may have had, he can be exonerated from this one. There was another Joseph Ward, usually referred to in the records as Joseph Ward Senior, who was a practising silversmith in St Paul's Churchyard, and there is conclusive evidence that the maker's mark on the kettle is his. Joseph Ward the Assayer never entered a mark.

TEA SET *by Joseph Ward (the silversmith not the Assayer).*

As in previous centuries, makers from time to time felt their work was being unfairly rejected by the Assayer. In July 1717 Richard Green, Gabriel Sleath, Richard Bayley, Thomas Langford and others complained that Bowles had cut (broken) plate which he should have passed and which they maintained his predecessor, John Duck, would have accepted. They pressed for an inquiry to establish if there was any mistake in the Assayers' weights or in the way in which the cupels were made. They also asked if any plate 'brought in doubt' by him could be tried by Ward, the Second Assayer. Their complaints were considered and directions given for all doubtful plate to be re-assayed alongside the trial piece.

The matter was not allowed to rest; a long and rambling petition was received by the Company in December of the following year. This stated that the quantity of plate that had been broken in two years had resulted in a loss of nearly £2000 to its makers, more than in the preceding twenty years. Other hardships were mentioned, including delays by the Assayers in repeating doubtful assays and damage caused by the drawers in sampling. A special committee appointed to consider the complaints reported that several assays had been made – 'with all the exactness and care possible' – of some of the broken plate referred to in the petition. Two candlesticks and a snuffer pan made by David Green, a tankard by John Eckford and a punch bowl by Mr Coates were all found to be 2½dwt worse, and a coffee pot, set of castors, two salvers and two salts by Richard Watts 3 dwt worse. In their formal reply to the petitioners the Company said that 'it was no severity to cut plate that is coarser than it ought to be by law and that it appeared to them that the complainants were pleading for having an allowance for silver wrought into plate, contrary to law'. The reply did confirm, however, that directions had been given that plate found to be worse was to be tried again on the same day and that drawers would be reminded to take all possible care in sampling. Manifestly, the Company was endeavouring to co-operate with the trade as far as possible, but there is a note in the records to say that the cost of the fashion of the broken plate was no more than £500, not £2000 as alleged.

That the Assayers also had their problems is evident from affidavits sworn by Ward and Bowles seven years later in connection with a case brought against officers of the Company for making illegal charges for marking small wares (see page 193). They both stated that makers frequently submitted parcels containing a mixture of standard and substandard articles. Ward said that he found 'more trouble in assaying and marking works of gold and silver by reason of the crafty artificers and subtle contrivances of the workers to deceive the assayer and impose on His Majesty's subjects'. Bowles maintained that when the culprits were detected they 'scandalised him and the Company in a most extraordinary manner, and to terrify him from doing his duty they sometimes spread abroad such threats as made him afraid to walk the streets for fear of receiving some mischief.'[17] By this time Bowles had retired but plainly he had not forgotten the hazards of his former post.

The scale of the work in the Assay Office at this period (circa 1720) can be judged from the weight of articles received. Unfortunately we have no record of the number of individual items submitted – only the total annual weight – but we do know that although small wares were increasing in quantity, large wares still accounted for the greater part of the intake. These varied in size and type, from ordinary domestic pieces such as coffee pots, jugs, plates, tankards and spoons to expensive individual commissions. An unusual piece was received in July 1724 – a 'vessel for bathing' made by Paul Crespin for the King of Portugal.[18] It weighed 6030 oz; the cost of the silver alone would have been more than £1500. The Assay Office would have been entitled to retain just over 4 oz of diet, worth about £1 – a useful boost to the day's takings.

So far little reference has been made to the hallmarking of gold wares; hitherto the numbers received had been insignificent in comparison with silver. Most gold wares would have been considered too small to bear a hallmark. They had always figured prominently in the wardens' searches, but few pieces were large enough to be described as gold 'plate'. Most articles in that category were probably made to special order and may not have been submitted for hallmarking. But in the early part of the eighteenth century receipts of gold wares started to increase. Approximately 1000 oz were submitted in the twelve months commencing May 1689 but thirty years later the weight had increased fivefold. It is recorded that in 1714 about 600 parcels containing some 2500 gold articles were submitted in the course of the year.[19] It is significant that whatever policy may have been adopted in the past, the notice issued to the London trade in 1717 clearly stated that all articles – both gold and silver – were to be assayed and hallmarked.

CHAPTER EIGHT

STERLING STANDARD RESTORED

A LL SILVER ARTICLES passed by the Assay Office between 27 March 1697 and 31 May 1720 received hallmarks denoting the Britannia standard. Experience had shown that, due to the softer nature of the alloy, such articles were slightly less serviceable than those made of sterling silver.[1] For this reason a demand arose for a return to the old standard. Sir Isaac Newton, as Master of the Mint, was not in favour and managed to delay matters for several years. But he was eventually overruled and a clause restoring the sterling standard was inserted in a Bill that was put before Parliament in 1719.

The Bill included another measure – one that was far from acceptable to the trade. In order to raise revenue the government had been considering the introduction of a duty of 6d per ounce on all newly manufactured silver articles. Members of the trade, feeling that their livelihood would be put in jeopardy, petitioned the Company to oppose it. The Company did so, but to no avail; the Plate Duty Act 1719 was duly passed.[2] In spite of its title the Act was concerned with a variety of matters, but here we are concerned with only two – the restoration of the sterling standard and the imposition of the duty on new silver wares.

Not all silversmiths were in favour of working in sterling silver; some had become accustomed to the Britannia standard and were anxious that it should continue. Their wishes in this respect at least were granted – the Britannia standard was not abolished by the new Act but retained as an alternative to sterling. The two standards have continued to this day. Under the new Act the Britannia marks (the lion's head erased and the figure of Britannia) were still to be used for the higher standard and the old marks (leopard's head and lion passant) for sterling. The Act made no reference to the style of the maker's mark, but it was assumed that for the sterling standard it would revert to the initials of the Christian and surname. Many makers accordingly registered new marks in this form.

The Act stipulated that the leopard's head and lion passant marks were to be struck on sterling silver at every assay office in England. The Company was not at all pleased; the leopard's head had been its own distinguishing mark from time immemorial. Legal opinion was taken, but it was beyond dispute that the provincial offices were required by the Act to use the mark and the Company could not stop them – it was too late to object.[3]

The leopard's head and lion passant punches had not been destroyed when the Britannia standard was introduced in 1697 because they were still required for marking gold. Nevertheless, a new set was made in 1720 when the sterling standard was restored. The number of punches in use was surprisingly small – in 1726 for example it was only twenty-two, including those for the two standards and the date letter. We know this from an account of an inspection of the Office which was carried out by the Standing Committee in that year. Marking was still carried out entirely by hand, each symbol being struck separately; it was not for another forty years that marking presses and punches with more than one symbol were used. About six new date letter punches were required annually and other replacements were necessary from time to time because of wear or breakage. The small number of new punches taken into use each year at this period is in sharp contrast to the 500 or so a century later.

After 1 June 1720, the date on which the Plate Duty Act came into force, silversmiths were able to choose between two legal standards of silver. At first the Britannia standard was still used for the majority of articles submitted for marking, but the proportion gradually diminished in favour of sterling. In the first full year after the Act took effect the weight of Britannia silver was nearly 77 per cent of the total received by the Assay Office; in the second year approximately 60 per cent; in the third year 40 per cent; but by the fourth year it had dropped to about 22 per cent and by the tenth year to only 4 per cent.

The worst fears of the makers were confirmed; in consequence of the imposition of the duty the weight of silver sent for hallmarking dropped almost immediately by about 30 per cent. The trade did not fully recover until the duty was removed thirty-six years later. In view of the reduction in work it was decided in 1721 to dispense with the services of Bowles, the senior of the two assayers. A year later, at the age of seventy-six, we find him petitioning the wardens for some allowance, saying that his daughter was much indisposed. He was awarded £15 a year – not a very handsome sum perhaps, but the Company was still not entirely free of its financial difficulties.

EXCISE OFFICERS' DIFFICULTIES

The manner in which the duty was to be collected was set out fully in the Plate Duty Act. Makers had to send to the nearest Excise Office a list of all newly manufactured and hallmarked silver wares. The Excise officers were then required to visit the workshops, weigh the articles and take account of the relevant duty. Payment had to be made within six weeks.

It soon became obvious to the Commissioners of Excise that the arrangements for collecting the duty were far from satisfactory. In an effort to track down evasion their officers sometimes requested information from the Company on the weights and other details of articles sent for hallmarking. But there would of course be no record of any articles that were not submitted. Only three years after the Act came into force the Commissioners sent a detailed report to the Company that stated:

> Workers not only defraud in the duties but also greatly impose upon the subjects by selling that for good plate which is much worse than standard, such as will not bear to be assayed at the hall, therefore is not brought thither. Propose ... Officers be empowered to seize all plate that shall be found in the hands of any trader or dealer that is polished or burnished without the hallmarks upon them which are capable of receiving the same. The Assay Office to admit of an officer of Excise there to take or keep a separate accompt of each trader's goods ... or that there be an office belonging to the Excise near the Assay Office for the accompts to be taken and that traders be obliged when they fetch their goods from the Assay Office to bring them through that excise office so as to be accompted for ... That there be a stamp to denote the charging placed on each piece capable of bearing it at the time of weighing off ...

In replying to these proposals the Company suggested that instead of a special duty mark the date letter could be surmounted by a crown or other symbol; or if a separate mark were necessary it could be struck by the Assay Office; also that the Excise authorities could be given a daily account of the quantity of plate received with the names of the owners. Alternatively, if an office were required, there was a house adjoining Goldsmiths' Hall which would be available. The Company also took the opportunity in its reply to ask if certain provisions to strengthen its own powers could be included in any amending legislation. A further suggestion, and a novel one, was that instead of a general exemption of wares which 'in respect of their smallness are not capable of receiving a mark' – which exemption was 'uncertain and occasioned many disputes' – certain specific articles weighing under 1 oz (buttons, thimbles, clasps and chains were mentioned amongst others) should be free from liability to hallmarking. These suggestions, although not adopted – at least not imme- diately – are of some interest as they reveal the direction in which the Company and the Excise authorities were thinking. In 1735 the Commis- sioners of Excise calculated that the government was being defrauded of more than one third of the amount of duty payable, and they produced yet another set of recommendations. In these they envisaged the setting up of an office where articles would be marked by the Excise authorities after payment of the duty. But these proposals too were shelved.

DUTY DODGERS

Not only were the Excise authorities worried about the evasion of duty but so also was the Company, as it resulted in much new silverware that either had no hallmarks or, worse still, bore counterfeit or transposed marks. As probably most of these articles were made to private order, their discovery was inevitably difficult. Judging by the number that have survived to the present day – particularly pieces that are unhallmarked or bear transposed marks – the wardens' concern was not without cause. Teapots, tea caddies, coffee pots, tankards, sauceboats, standing cups and similar articles made at this date and bearing hallmarks removed from other wares are nowadays often called 'duty dodgers'. They are of considerable antiquarian interest and are recognized as such in the Hallmarking Act 1973. According to the Act, if any article in this category comes into the custody or possession of an assay office, the mark must not be obliterated – the normal fate of modern forgeries – but instead struck through in such a way that it is still clearly visible. This preserves the mark and at the same time indicates that it was not applied by an assay office on the particular article in question.

Transposing hallmarks appears to have been almost openly practised after 1720. As it was not specifically classed as an offence it may well have been difficult to bring a successful prosecution under the existing law. On many of the offending pieces that have survived from this period the mark of the actual maker is struck over the earlier maker's mark or sometimes over the date letter, showing that the culprit had made no attempt to conceal his identity – in fact quite the reverse. In 1726 one Arthur Dickens complained to the wardens that his work was being unfairly rejected by the assayer and he admitted that he had in consequence resorted to transposing, which he said was widespread. Thus the motive for transposing was not always to avoid the duty, but sometimes merely to by-pass the Assay Office, either to avoid the risk of rejection or to save time and costs. Another common ruse of some makers was to strike their mark three or four times on an article to give the semblance of a hallmark and so to deceive anyone with scant knowledge of the proper symbols.

The Company was on stronger grounds where counterfeiting was concerned, as this was a serious crime, punishable by a penalty of £500.[4] In 1717 the Court had decided that four persons – Jonathan Newton, Michael Boult, John Phillips and Charles Sutton – three of whom were members of the Company, should be prosecuted for such an offence. They were arrested but the result of the case is not recorded, there being some suggestion that it may have been out of time under the Act of Grace. But it is rather strange that both Newton and Boult were elected to the livery only three months later.

The sale or offer for sale of an unhallmarked article was a less serious

A 'DUTY DODGER': *a water fountain by Peter Archambo, with a transposed hallmark (1728) removed from another ware and soldered under the foot.*

offence, but one that was not uncommon. Even the great Paul de Lamerie, in the very year he was elected to the livery (1717), was suspected of making great quantities of large plate that he was not sending to the Assay Office for hallmarking; he was duly summoned to appear before the Court of Assistants to be admonished. He had entered his first mark four years earlier and had already been appointed the King's silversmith. Fortunately for modern collectors he normally complied with the law, as the many fine pieces bearing his maker's mark and a full hallmark testify. However, some early pieces bearing a Lamerie mark may not be his own work since he was accused of 'colouring foreigners' – that is, sending articles to the Assay Office under his mark on behalf of unregistered makers – probably foreigners of Huguenot descent. With his growing reputation as a silversmith he climbed the ladder within the Company, eventually becoming a warden in 1743, 1746 and 1747. It is perhaps slightly ironic in view of his supposed early misdemeanours that in 1737 he served on the Committee appointed by the Court of Assistants to submit proposals for a new hallmarking Act.

There was indeed no excuse for liverymen to be ignorant of the Company's rules. According to standing orders they were summoned annually to hear the ordinances read out on the day before the new wardens took office. In earlier years the whole Company had usually been summoned but by the eighteenth century only the members of the Court of Assistants and the livery were

ANOTHER 'DUTY DODGER' – *a large early eighteenth-century two-handled cup has been heated to remove the foot and the separate disc bearing the hallmark (1698) is becoming detached from the body.*

Immigrant workers

The Huguenot silversmith Paul Crespin

From the fifteenth century onwards large numbers of goldsmiths, often already qualified though apprenticeship, arrived in Britain from the Continent. Some were employed by established goldsmiths and others set up in business on their own; some were even protégés of the Crown. The Goldsmiths' Company was unable to prevent them following their craft, but they ensured as far as possible that they came under its strict control.

Those coming after the middle of the sixteenth century were usually refugees from religious persecution, particularly after the Edict of Nantes (which had guaranteed Protestants in France a certain amount of freedom of worship) was revoked by Louis XIV in 1685. Foreign goldsmiths were generally resented by native craftsmen, but the skills of Paul de Lamerie, David Willaume and other Huguenots, as well as earlier immigrants, did much to raise the standard of design and workmanship in the trade. Indeed, de Lamerie (1688–1751), who was born in Holland and brought to England by his parents at the age of 11½ months, is often regarded as the greatest silversmith of his age.

required to attend. As inducement they were offered a modicum of refreshment – in 1722, for example, 60lb of biscuit cakes and 20 gallons of white wine were provided for the occasion; each member of the Court was allowed six cakes and each liveryman four.

In an endeavour to curb the spread of offences in the trade and to warn the public, notices were placed in the *Gazette* and other newspapers. One such notice in 1724 encouraged people to report any irregularities; another in 1726 warned potential purchasers against the sale of unhallmarked silver and advised them to inspect larger articles to make sure that the marks were not soldered in or counterfeit, both of which – so the notice read – were notorious frauds.

Two further ways of discouraging the transposition of hallmarks were explored. In 1730 the drawers were ordered to strike one or more of the hallmarks on every part of an article that was capable of bearing them – for example, a handle on a tankard or the foot of a coffee pot might have a small lion struck on it. A similar order had been given before but had obviously been neglected (see pages 104 and 117). Another instruction was issued a year later: the individual symbols of the hallmark were to be struck as far distant from each other as possible so that they could not be cut out together. This was not at all popular with the makers and two months later we find some of the best known silversmiths of the time, including Gabriel Sleath, John LeSage and Richard Bayley, objecting strongly. They maintained that the marks were defaced in finishing; also that when struck in this way they diminished the beauty of the plate. The practice was accordingly discontinued but there are still in existence a number of articles marked in accordance with it.

JOSEPH WARD'S MISCONDUCT

An unusual offence came to light in 1726. It concerned an attempt to avoid the hallmarking of silverware that had been made specially for export to the Tsarina of Russia, and it seems that the Assayer's conduct in the affair left much to be desired. On 31 August three members of the Court of Assistants – Messrs. Hosier, Marlow and Wollfreys – meeting in Wills' coffee house in Cornhill, were informed that there was a large quantity of unhallmarked plate at the premises of Robert Dingley, a goldsmith dealer in Bishopsgate Street.[5] The consignment consisted in all of about 20,000 oz of silver of which about 4000 oz – made by eight silversmiths of Huguenot descent – was unmarked.[6]

The Clerk, the Prime Warden, Ward (the Assayer) and Watts (the Drawer) were called to inspect the goods at the King's warehouse whence they had been transferred by the Customs. Dingley and Sir Randolf Knipe, the exporter, were also present. As the warehouse was locked, Dingley persuaded them to adjourn to a tavern in Thames Street where he tried unsuccessfully to bribe Mr Bache, the Prime Warden. Afterwards he took Ward on one side and 'discoursed' with him privately. When they eventually gained access to the warehouse Ward seized several pieces of the unhallmarked plate, although he had no instructions to do so. It appears that this action may have thwarted any further effort by the Company to pursue the matter because the report of the incident says that Knipe and Dingley seemed unconcerned, afterwards treating Ward and the Customs officer with 'French claret and great civility' at the aforesaid tavern; furthermore that 'notwithstanding the pretended seizure the plate was sent on shipboard that night'.

The affair was considered by the Court of Assistants three weeks later on 22 September. Ward, who was a member of the Court, was several times asked to withdraw from the meeting, but refused. Then on 19 October it was decided that since he had insulted the Court he should be discharged as Assayer. On 19 January 1727, it was resolved that in future if anyone serving on the Court of Assistants were elected Assayer, he should no longer remain a member. A petition from Ward was then considered and he was reinstated Assayer after he had agreed to resign from the Court.

Dingley did not escape the consequences of his offence; after a lapse of four years he was charged by the Customs and Excise authorities for exporting the unmarked plate. Ward and Watts were ordered – against their wills – to give evidence at the trial which was held at the Guildhall. The outcome is not recorded but we may assume that Dingley was fined as he subsequently endeavoured – unsuccessfully – to claim damages from the Company.

Ward's behaviour seems to have been forgiven but not forgotten. In the year following his reinstatement it was moved at a meeting of the Court of Assistants that, since he had performed his duty to the entire satisfaction of the Touchwarden and in view of his large family, his salary might be increased, but this was not granted. Three years later Ward made one of his repeated requests for an increase, saying that it had cost him several hundred pounds more than his salary 'to undergo his office which was destructive of human nature and made him many years older in constitution as well as time'. His petition met with some success; his salary was raised by £20 per annum.

UNLAWFUL CHARGES FOR HALLMARKING

To add to its anxieties about finance and the prevalence of offences in the trade, in 1724 the Company became involved in another troublesome affair; it was faced with legal action by several of its members for making unlawful charges for hallmarking small wares. Information was laid in the King's Bench against the Touchwarden (John Cuthbert), the Assayer (Joseph Ward) and the Weigher (George Garthorne). The Company immediately applied to the Lords Commissioners of the Treasury for a *nolle prosequi*, to stop the plaintiffs from proceeding with the suit. Their lordships asked for an opinion from the Attorney General, Sir Philip Yorke, who, after receiving counsel representing both sides and studying a number of affidavits, recommended that a nolle prosequi should be granted on the understanding that the Company gave an assurance that no more than the 'ancient fees' (the diet) would be taken in future.[7]

The Attorney General's report was critical of both the plaintiffs and the defendants. He said that some workers who had pretended to represent the whole trade had made an agreement with regard to certain charges, but the Company was guilty of extortion by also charging those who had not been party to it. His report continued:

> It appears to me that the prosecution was commenced by workers who are freemen of the Company, not with a real intent to redress the mischief complained of, or for any other good purpose, but in order to compel the Company to do another illegal act, that is to exclude non-freemen from the touch and assay or to take revenge on the Company for not having excluded them ... Suffering this information to be carried on by the prosecutors ... they may make use of it to influence the Company or their

officers to exclude non-freemen or possibly to show the artificers themselves undue favour in assaying their plate, either of which will be to the
detriment of the public.

He also stated:

> In case this proceeding should be stayed, those persons who never agreed to
> the new rates but have paid them by compulsion will not be without
> remedy for their money, but may maintain actions against the Company for
> all that has been taken from them above the due fees (diet).

Fortunately no one took action.

The Attorney General also intimated that if the Company continued to
make illegal charges any prosecution should be mounted by officers of the
Crown, not by means of a private case. He finally said that the Company
could 'have no relief but by application to Parliament for a new establishment
of their fees'. The *nolle prosequi* was duly granted but since the charge for
marking small wares was continued it appears that the undertaking recommended by the Attorney General – that no fees would be taken other than the
accustomed diet – was not insisted upon. Although let off the hook the
Company was faced with heavy legal costs, amounting to £151 15s.

Naturally anxious to avoid the risk of prosecution by the Crown, the
Company proceeded to draft a Parliamentary Bill to authorize a scale of
charges for hallmarking small wares, with higher rates for non-freemen. At the
same time the opportunity was taken to seek further statutory powers and to
strengthen the penalties for offences. The following proposals were included:
the right of search in London or within 20 miles by two wardens and two
members of the Court of Assistants, with the power to seize any wares not
marked; any wares found to be substandard to be broken and double their
value forfeited; transposing to carry the same penalty as counterfeiting (£500);
and a £5 penalty for not entering a maker's mark.

Steps were taken to introduce the Bill in Parliament. Francis Child, an
Alderman and past Prime Warden,[8] used his considerable influence with Sir
Robert Walpole; the Bill was passed by the House of Commons and reached a
second reading in the House of Lords in May 1726. At the Committee stage
fourteen well-known silversmiths, most of them of Huguenot descent, including Paul de Lamerie, John Le Sage, Augustine Courtauld, Lewis Cuny,
Pezé Pilleau, Peter Archambo and John Chartier, petitioned for the removal of
certain clauses, in particular the proposed power of the wardens to seize wares
from shops and workplaces. In a cross-petition the Company cited the decree
of the King's Council in 1507 which had upheld the wardens' right of search
not only in London but throughout the kingdom. Unfortunately, Parliament was
prorogued before the Bill received Royal Assent. The Company nevertheless

decided to continue the current charges for small wares – in spite of the Attorney General's report; the receipts were nearly £200 per annum and it could ill afford to lose this source of revenue. Indeed a new and extended list of charges was issued, some of the small silver wares specifically mentioned being bosses for bridles, buttons for coats, corkscrews, pistol caps, rattles, shoe clasps, teaspoons, tea strainers and toothpicks. Besides itemizing the hall-marking charges the list included a fee of one shilling for registering a maker's mark.

Recommendations for changes in the law were also made about this time by Sir Isaac Newton, who was now a great age but still in office as Master of the Mint. Amongst those of his papers preserved in the Public Record Office are several undated manuscript drafts which include the following suggestions:

(1) in all suits at law the fineness of plate shall be decided by a trial with the indented trial piece;
(2) the Touchwarden taking with him two or more of the Assistants may search in every city and deface all plate abounding with more solder than is necessary and seize all unmarked plate exposed to sale;
(3) plate melted down if 1 dwt worse shall be forfeited to the wardens of the Company and if 2 dwt worse the maker shall be .. (blank) .. ;
(4) clean plate ½ dwt worse shall be forfeited to the wardens and 1 dwt worse shall disfranchise and disable the maker;
(5) the diet shall be tried at certain times – suppose annually for the City of London and quadrennially for other cities – by the Queen's Assaymaster in the presence of .. (blank) .. and the Company shall pay the deficiency to the crown and be allowed the excess upon account.'[9]

Newton was clearly concerned that plate brought to the Mint should not be greatly below standard after melting, which might be the case if excessive solder had been used in the making; but his recommendations were not adopted. He was still Master of the Mint when he died in 1727 at the age of eighty-four.

DAILY ROUTINE IN THE ASSAY OFFICE

In June 1726 the Court again approved a set of rules for the management of the Assay Office, some of which were repetitions of earlier ones. There were no fewer than twenty-nine separate sections. Every day was to be a 'Hall Day', except Saturdays and Sundays and twenty-six other holidays which were listed. The Weigher, Fireman and Drawer were to be in the Office from seven in the morning until seven in the evening, and the Assayer was to attend from nine until six unless he had finished work sooner. By-assays received before eleven were to be ready before five in the afternoon – the Assayer to forfeit 2s 6d for 'every neglect of the same'. A number of the rules show how expenditure was to be monitored. The Touchwarden was to account in writing for all charcoal used and no tools or materials were to be bought without his authority. A record was to be kept of all payments received for hallmarking and by-assays, also of the weight of diet and the assay bits. Another section stated: 'No officer or servant shall take any box money for perquisite or reward to himself, or any other officer or servant belonging to the Office, of any person upon any pretence whatsoever in relation to their office or service'.

From surviving records we can picture fairly clearly the layout and working of the Assay Office in the 1720s. It was situated in the Hall itself, on the south side, flanked by a courtyard called Fleur-de-Luce Court, which led into Foster Lane. Between this courtyard and Carey Lane there was a row of small houses – the property of the Company – running the whole length of the street from Foster Lane to Gutter Lane. The Assayer's house was next to the Office with an entrance into Fleur-de-Luce Court (see page 125). In the Office there was a weighing room where the parcels were handed in by the senders' messengers. Here the Weigher recorded the weight of the contents of each parcel with the names of the owners; he also calculated the charges for by-assays and for marking any small wares and took the payments for them.

The Weigher was additionally responsible for paying out the weekly wages of the drawers, for the purchase of materials and everyday requirements such as charcoal, slow ashes (bone ash), lead, aqua fortis (nitric acid), parting flasks (for gold assaying), muffles, candles, paper and ink. Slow ashes, which were relatively costly, were required for cupels which were made by the Assayer or his assistant. Judging by the frequency of entries in surviving cash books for a new broom, cleanliness must have been a high priority, but perhaps the main concern was to collect the floor sweepings for recovery of the precious metals contained in them. All expenses are recorded in the books – even a payment of sixpence 'to a boy for going up the chimney'. The Weigher was also responsible for keeping an account of the amount of cash owing to the senders of small wares as compensation for the drawings taken from their work; at a later date an equivalent weight of silver was returned in lieu.

When the Weigher had completed his main task of weighing the contents of each parcel received it was his duty to oversee the drawers and to assist with the marking. After they had been weighed the articles were transferred to another room where the drawers took their samples. They used a scraping tool called a 'grusset' or 'gresshook' which is thought to have been rather a clumsy implement compared with its modern counterpart. The drawers sat at a bench similar to those used by silversmiths and jewellers to this day; it had a semi-circular cut-out fitted with a leather apron in which the drawings were collected and a horizontal peg against which the articles were held for support. The samples were wrapped in papers bearing a reference number and passed through an opening in the wall communicating with the assayers'

ENTRIES FOR NOVEMBER *1728* in the cash book of the Weigher, George Garthorne. On the left is a record of the 'by-assays' received.

rooms. The samples were assayed by the cupellation method (see page 20). Afterwards the requisite amount of diet was taken from the residues not used in the assay and put into the diet box – of course only from samples taken from articles found to be up to standard. When two assayers were employed each had his own room and worked independently of the other. Obviously, if one of them were absent the other had to cover for him, but they each kept separate diet boxes, the contents of which were assayed at the annual trial.

The Touchwarden attended for a period in the afternoon to strike (or to witness the striking of) the leopard's head (or lion's head erased) mark on all pieces that had been passed by the assayer, the drawers having already stamped them with the marks of the lion passant (or Britannia) and the date letter.[10] All marking was by means of a hammer and steel punches, each article being supported on a suitably shaped anvil which was fixed in a vice or a section of a tree-trunk. As a final check each consignment was again weighed in bulk before it was returned to the owner or his messenger. The operations themselves had changed little from those of two centuries earlier, but the whole process was necessarily becoming more streamlined in consequence of the much greater volume of work.

Good lighting was important, especially for the assayers, who had to sit at their balances for long periods and weigh small quantities of drawings to a high degree of accuracy. When the Office was enlarged later in the century it was found that the natural lighting in the assayers' closets was inadequate to such an extent that they had to work by candlelight and the Company's surveyor was given directions for 'enlightening' them. Four circular skylights were subsequently provided. Candles were one of the main items of expenditure – working after dark must have been particularly trying, although by 1730 a single oil lamp had been provided.

The daily routine was inevitably disturbed during a Trial of the Pyx or when new trial plates had to be made; as for instance in 1728 when the Company was requested to provide replacements for the depleted 22 carat gold and sterling silver plates. On this occasion they were made in the Assay Office and Joseph Ward was detailed to carry out the melting as well as the assaying, the pure metals being provided by John Blachford, an eminent refiner and a member of the special jury.[11] For the silver plate 77 oz of fine silver and 6 oz 6 dwt of pure copper (the theoretically correct weights assuming the silver to be absolutely pure) were melted together and cast into an ingot, but the assays indicated that it was slightly below standard and it was decided to remelt after adding a further quantity of fine silver. This was a departure from the procedure that had previously been adopted since 1601; from that date all trial plates had been made by exact co-mixture of the calculated weights of the constituent metals without subsequent adjustment. Modern assays of surviving portions of the 1728 plate show it to be approximately 928 parts per thousand, which is 3 parts per thousand higher than the true standard. As the plate was in use for the next hundred years the assayers were presumably working to a standard slightly above sterling during that period.

THE FIRST DEPUTY WARDEN

In 1731 the Company made an important decision concerning the management of the Assay Office which undoubtedly resulted in a great improvement in efficiency. The minutes of a meeting of the Court of Assistants in March of that year state:

> The Court taking into consideration how they might further ease the members of the Company by exempting the youngest Warden [i.e. the Touchwarden] from the great fatigue of constant attendance and officiating in the Assay Office which he is obliged to perform or pay a heavy fine to be excused therefrom, it was moved that it might be referred to the [Standing] Committee to consider how to ease the youngest Warden of the attendance of the said

office for the future, either by appointing a person to act in his stead or otherwise. If they shall be of the opinion a person should be appointed, then to consider the manner of his appointment and how he shall be paid.

The Committee met and recommended that 'a person be appointed of known reputation, credit, integrity and skill, fit to exercise the office of a Deputy to the Wardens'. Further, that members of the Court should not be disqualified but if one were appointed he should be 'subject to the orders and directions of the Court relating to the office.'

At a subsequent meeting of the Court on 26 May the Wardens nominated John Harris 'to be their deputy to attend and officiate in the assay office in their stead for the year ensuing'. The nomination was unanimously approved and the wardens were thanked for having made so good a choice of a deputy. John Harris was then required to swear an affidavit before a Master in Chancery for the due execution of his office. He was subject to re-election each year at the same time as the election of the wardens. From thenceforth the Deputy Warden was the head of the Assay Office and all staff including the Assayer were responsible to him, a management structure that has continued to the present day.

John Harris was about sixty-three years old when first elected Deputy Warden. He had been apprenticed to John Horton in 1682, becoming a liveryman in 1705 and a member of the Court of Assistants in 1724. He was one of the liverymen who in 1717 had signed the petition against allowing foreigners the 'assay and touch' and he had entered a maker's mark in the same year, with an address in Foster Lane. Although trained as a silversmith we do not know how active he had been in the trade. We do know he was a member of the jury for making the 1728 trial plates and was paid £3 3s for 'planishing and flatting' the ingots. Having served as Touchwarden (Fourth Warden) in 1729 he would have been familiar with the working of the Assay Office. The new appointment did not affect his membership of the Court nor prevent his becoming Second Warden in 1737, but he relinquished his position in the Assay Office when elected Prime Warden in 1739; he died in the following year. The fact that he had made a loan to the Company of £400 in the year he was elected to the Court shows that he was a man of some substance.

Within one month of his appointment the Deputy Warden produced a list of new equipment required in the Office – an assay balance and case, a large balance with sets of weights, a pair of shears, a file and a block with anvil for marking spoons. Eight months later he reported that two furnaces were almost burned out and not fit to be repaired any more. Several new regulations were approved, probably at his instigation, including one which said that the drawer should sample each distinct part of every large and small ware; another stated that the drawers and the Assayer's Assistant should strike the marks with great care. The Deputy Warden was not expected to carry out any of the marking himself – merely to act in a supervisory capacity, but he had to be present when any plate was marked. He was to be paid £50 per year, which seems a small reward, but at this date he was not expected to attend for the whole of the day.

THE PLATE (OFFENCES) ACT 1738

Conscious of its vulnerability in law with regard to its charges for marking small wares the Court of Assistants decided that only a new Act of Parliament would afford a satisfactory solution. The opinion of the Attorney General in 1725 – that any fees taken (other than the 4 grains per pound diet) were extortion – had since been confirmed by the Company's own counsel. A special committee was appointed to prepare another draft Bill; the four wardens and eighteen members of the Court of Assistants were chosen and they, or any five of them, were authorized to consult with 'the most eminent shopkeepers and manufacturers'. The committee met seven times between 16 December 1757 and 17 January 1738. Members attending included Nathaniel Wollfryes (Prime Warden), John Blachford, the refiner, and Nathaniel Brassey (Wardens), John Harris (Warden and Deputy Warden) and Richard Hoare,[12] together with some prominent silversmiths – Paul de Lamerie, Thomas Farren, Richard Bayley, Thomas Boulton and Humphrey Payne.

After considering the ill-fated Bill of 1726 (see page 194) and the arguments put forward at that time, the committee reluctantly decided not to include the clause empowering two wardens and two of the assistants to make searches – a clause probably opposed by Paul de Lamerie who had been one of the petitioners objecting to its earlier inclusion. There was much discussion on the question of charges for hallmarking, in particular whether those who were not freemen of the Company should pay double or half as much again as freemen. It was eventually resolved that if this discrimination were likely to jeopardize the passage of the Bill the principle of equal charges for all should be accepted. Clauses relating to penalties for infringements and a list of exempted wares were agreed; there was also a lengthy discussion as to whether a tolerance should be allowed on the standard, but this proposal was dropped. Unlike the practice in some countries no tolerance on the legal standards has ever been permitted under British law.

To assist in their deliberations the members of the committee called for accounts of the receipts and expenses of the Assay Office for the past twenty years from which it appeared that, after allowing for rent and repairs of the Office and the Assayer's house, there had been a loss of £950 17s 6d in total and that the current loss was about £100 per year. The suggested scale of marking charges would, it was hoped, put the finances of the Office on a sound basis.

Without waiting to finalize their proposals the committee decided that three of its members should seek the help of Sir Robert Walpole, First Lord of the Treasury, and that they should call on the Speaker of the House of Commons. On 19 January the draft Bill and accompanying petition to Parliament were approved by the Court of Assistants, whilst seven of their number who were considered to have best acquaintance with Members of Parliament were appointed to take such further action as they thought necessary.

The Bill was presented to the House of Commons in February 1738 and received a second reading, but owing to pressure of other business failed to make any further progress before Parliament was prorogued. It was reintroduced in the next session early in 1739. Although opposed by many gold workers who did not wish to see any change in the law, the Bill was eventually passed becoming known as The Plate (Offences) Act 1738.[13] If the Bill had passed as originally drafted it would have referred only to the Goldsmiths' Company and wares made in London or within fifty miles, but as finally enacted the statute applied to the whole of England (but not Scotland or Ireland); thus the English provincial assay offices as well as the London Office were covered by it.

The promotion of the Bill had been costly; the legal fees and other expenses amounted to £504 5s 6d, but the Company was well satisfied with its efforts and at a meeting on 22 June the members of the Court expressed their gratitude to Sir Francis Child MP and to Nathaniel Brassey for their 'trouble and pains', following this with thanks to the special committee.[14]

The Act of 1738 was the most comprehensive hallmarking legislation enacted up to that date; it covered exempted wares, charges for hallmarking, powers and duties of assay offices, makers' marks, offences and penalties. Although subsequently amended on several occasions, it remained the principal basis of hallmarking law in England until 1975. The list of wares that were exempt from hallmarking was to cause many problems for the assay offices in later years as the intended meaning of some of the items mentioned became obscure with the passage of time. The exact legal interpretation of, for example, 'jeweller's works, sleeve buttons, stock or garter clasps, sliding pencils and small or slight ornaments put to amber or other eggs or urns' was probably clear in 1738, but it was much less so two centuries later. Were cuff-links the same as sleeve buttons, for example? A new list of exempted silver wares was substituted in 1790 but it was no less difficult to interpret in the twentieth century. The original list of exemptions in so far as they applied to gold wares remained until 1975.

The new legislation established unequivocally that gold articles as well as silver were subject to compulsory hallmarking. But from the Company's point of view perhaps the most important provision in the Act was the authority to charge for marking small wares. No longer need it have any qualms about the

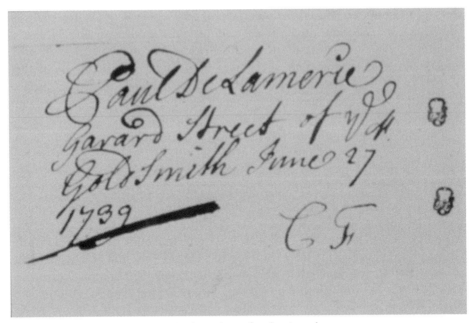

ENTRY OF PAUL DE LAMERIE *in the register of makers' marks.*

legality of demanding a fair price for its services. The itemized list of the maximum charges permitted by the Act gives us a good picture of the types of small articles that were routinely received. The gold wares listed were: buckles, snuffboxes, watchcases, watch boxes and hooks for watch-chains. The silver wares were: sword hilts, snuffboxes, spurs, watchcases, watch boxes, knife and fork hafts, buckles, tea tongs, teaspoons, tea strainers, belt buckles, belt locks, runners and pendants, orange strainers, nutmeg graters, dram cups, seals, salt cellars, clasps and buttons. The maximum charges for assay and marking gold articles varied from 5d for a buckle and 10d for a watchcase to 3s 9d for an article weighing between 30 and 50oz troy. Typical charges for marking silver wares were 3¾d per dozen for buttons and the same amount for a single snuffbox or a pair of spurs. There was also a provision for a minimum charge of 5d for any single parcel. The payment for large silver wares continued to be by way of the diet; the maximum amount which the assay offices were entitled to retain was 10 grains per pound troy, a considerable increase on the 4 grains customarily taken hitherto. It was realized when the Bill was drafted that it would not be practicable to retain sufficient diet to cover the costs when parcels contained only one or two large articles; the offices were therefore allowed to make a charge not exceeding 5d in place of the diet for parcels weighing less than 4lb troy.

   To combat evasion of the duty that was still payable on all silver liable to hallmarking, a clause was included in the Act requiring every parcel submitted to an assay office to be accompanied by a work sheet showing the name and address of the sender together with the type and quantity of articles. The weight of the parcel's contents was to be entered on the sheet by the Weigher. All such sheets had to be retained for one month and then taken to the nearest Excise Office. Also the Commissioners of Excise were authorized to appoint an officer to inspect the books of the assay offices once a month to check such entries of plate that were chargeable with duty.

A further clause in the Act gave the Wardens or Deputy Warden (or the Assayer in the provincial offices) power to refuse to assay or mark any plate which they adjudged to have too much solder or to be insufficiently advanced in workmanship – with the stipulation that such Warden or Deputy Warden (or Assayer) had to be (or have been) a working goldsmith or silversmith. Another clause provided the opportunity for anyone who thought themselves aggrieved by any order of any Warden or Deputy Warden of the Goldsmiths' Company pursuant to these powers, to appeal to the other wardens and, failing satisfaction, to the Standing Committee of the Company, and then, if still not satisfied, to the Court of Assistants, whose decision would be final. It is of interest that the Standing Committee should have had legal recognition under the Act.

The Act required all workers to register new makers' marks, consisting of the initials of their Christian and surnames but of a character or alphabet

HALLMARK *for 1739 with the maker's mark of Paul de Lamerie.*

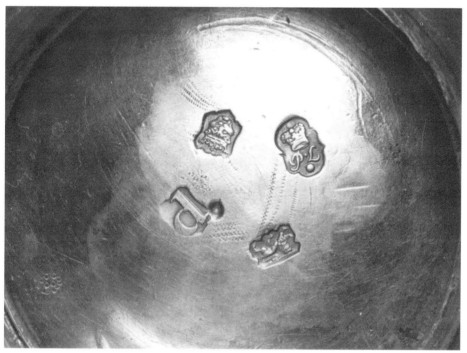

different from their former marks. Consequently, some makers have marks of three distinct designs – one entered in the period of the Britannia standard (1697 to 1720) and two subsequently.

Partly to discourage counterfeiting and partly to identify plate marked after the new Act took effect, the Company modified the design of the London hallmarks by altering the shape of the shields surrounding the leopard's head, lion passant and date letter. The changing of the date letter and election of new wardens, which at that period normally took place on 28 or 29 May, was on this occasion delayed until 6 June 1739, when it was expected the Act would come into force. In the event the Act did not receive Royal Assent until 14 June. During the six weeks between 6 June and 18 July the new letter 'd' was used but all the shields were of the old design (straight sided). The punches incorporating the new designs of the marks with scalloped shields were then taken into use. There are accordingly two variations of the date letter mark for the year 1739.

To comply with these changes twenty new punches were delivered by the Engraver, for which he was paid 10 guineas. Thomas Long, who had held the position of Engraver since 1727, felt this was an insufficient reward and he was not slow to inform the Company that the new designs of marks had occasioned him much additional work. Although his salary had already been increased eighteen months earlier from £8 to £10 per annum he reminded the Court that there were now more 'strikers of marks' and consequently the punches needed replacing more frequently. He also took the opportunity to tell the Court that he had thought of a method to render the Company's marks more difficult to counterfeit. His proposal referred to the design of an iron fly-press for marking. The press was finally perfected by his successor, Thomas Pingo (see page 208).

Another aspect of the new legislation was a revision of the penalties – for example £10 for selling an unhallmarked or substandard article (instead of its value). For counterfeiting the maximum was reduced from £500 to £100 – an inadequate deterrent as later events were to prove. And for the first time transposing hallmarks was made a specific offence, carrying the same penalty as counterfeiting. One half of any sum recovered through action in the courts was payable to the Crown and the other half to the person or persons suing.

PROSECUTION OF OFFENDERS

Within months of the passing of the Act the Company's attention was drawn to an offence committed by Dru Drury, a knife-haft maker and a member of the livery, who had caused a counterfeit punch to be made of the lion passant. He was the same Dru Drury who with others fourteen years earlier had taken proceedings against officers of the Company for making illegal charges for marking small wares. He offered to pay the penalty of £100 rather than be exposed to trial, but the Company decided that it could not accept a payment as a substitute for a public trial, reasoning:.

> it is probable a great part of the punishment of offenders, in such good circumstances as the petitioner was reputed to be, may be the exposing of their characters at public trials, and be a greater concern to them than the charge of the penalty with costs. It is, besides, hoped that no prosecution of this kind will be set on foot for the sake of the penalty, or any other motive than to redress the fraud and abuse of counterfeit marks on wrought plate, especially as the standard of plate was always deemed an honour to the nation and the great quantity of plate has now become a considerable part of the riches of the kingdom.

Accordingly, although Dru Drury had made no use of the punch, the Clerk was ordered to proceed against him. The case was heard before Lord Chief Justice Lee at the Guildhall in March 1740 and the jury imposed the statutory maximum penalty of £100 with costs.

The Act did not stem the flood of forgeries; it was even alleged that counterfeit punches could be readily purchased. The Company decided that if sufficient evidence were available prosecutions should be undertaken in any cases that came to light. But the cost of court action was high and there was no guarantee that the Company would recover the full amount. In 1743 the Clerk presented the following bill for his legal fees in connection with nine prosecutions for counterfeiting; all the defendants were working goldsmiths, seven having marks registered at the Assay Office.

> Richard Gosling £17 0s 0d
> Lewis Laroche £40 11s 4d
> Edwd. Aldridge £42 10s 3d
> John Lovett £11 0s 7d
> Chas. Jackson £4 4s 6d
> David Mouden £29 9s 10d
> James Smith £24 6s 11d
> John Volander £20 15s 1d
> Matthias Standfast £103 4s 6d

If the Company undertook a successful prosecution it was entitled to one half of the penalty with whatever costs might be awarded, but if the defendant could not pay then nothing would be received, as happened in the case of David Mouden who was committed to Bridewell with twelve months' hard labour. Laroche and Standfast were also unable to pay and were accordingly imprisoned. Nor were prosecutions always successful. For example, Edward Aldridge was acquitted, and later in 1757 the Company was forced to suffer a non-suit in a case against Thomas Swift, a knife-haft maker, the Clerk's fees for which amounted to £47 14s over and above the sum of £30 16s 8d for costs awarded to the defendant. The Company was conscientiously carrying out its duty but litigation was proving costly.

EXPANSION OF THE ASSAY OFFICE

One month before the new Act had received Royal Assent, John Harris resigned as Deputy Warden on his election as Prime Warden; he died in April of the following year. James Pugh, another member of the Court of Assistants, who had been apprenticed to John Harris nineteen years before, replaced him as Deputy Warden and continued in the post until his own death in 1753. In 1751 Pugh was elected Fourth Warden, but he nevertheless continued as Deputy Warden. As in the case of John Harris some years earlier it was a slightly odd situation, being, as it were, his own deputy!

Realizing that there would now be a greater workload in the Assay Office, it was decided that extra space should be provided and that there should again be two assayers – the senior to be responsible for the assays of large silver plate, silver watchcases, gold work and gold by-assays; the junior to carry out assays of small wares and silver by-assays. Each assayer was to retain diet from silver wares for the annual trial at the rate of 1 grain per pound (in place of the 2 grains previously taken) and to keep it in a separate box. The 10 grains allowed under the Act had also to cover the amount used for the assays. Any further surplus was to be used to recompense the makers of small wares because in this case the samples inevitably exceeded 10 grains per pound. If the surplus were insufficient they were to be paid an equivalent in cash. The Senior Assayer was to have a salary of £150 per annum with a rent-free house and the Junior Assayer £100. The Weigher was to have an assistant and another drawer was to be engaged, bringing the total complement of staff to eight, including the Deputy Warden.

Under the new arrangements Joseph Ward became Senior Assayer and Samuel Edlin was appointed Junior Assayer. Charles Alchorne was engaged as a Drawer and Gawen Nash as Assistant to the Weigher. Alchorne and Edlin, both liverymen, and Nash had all been practising silversmiths.[15] Edlin, who had latterly been working as a private assayer, was aged fifty-nine when appointed and the Court had to waive a rule made eight years earlier – that no new member of the staff was to be over the age of fifty. He is recorded as saying that he left a good business to come to the Assay Office; also that he brought an apprentice with him who was useful in attending the fires and doing any menial work in the Office. Before long Edlin was complaining that Ward was not doing his fair share of the assaying – probably due to illness. He said that he had been forced to carry out all the gold assays because Ward refused to do them, and furthermore that he had to make far more silver assays than Ward because there were twice as many parcels of small wares as there were of large. He maintained that he had made the equivalent of 1650 silver assays in fifteen days.

A solution was shortly to hand due to the death of Joseph Ward at about the age of about sixty-nine. Samuel Edlin was promoted and Joseph Shillito was engaged as Junior Assayer. Shillito had been apprenticed in 1692, so was aged about sixty. Since he was appointed without need of training he too had probably been working as a private assayer; neither he nor his master had entered marks.

Ward's widow, Ann, petitioned the Company for relief, saying that she was now in her sixtieth year, without friends and support, and that her husband had died leaving her in very poor circumstances. She added that she had been married to him for more than forty years having brought him a fortune of £1500. The Company was not unsympathetic and awarded £10 immediate relief with an annual pension of £20, on the grounds that she had been 'left in deplorable circumstances of old age, with a "paralitick" disorder, unable to help herself and destitute of any subsistence'.

Such was the increased activity in the Assay Office that the annual receipts of small wares in the first few years after the new Act came into force were running at about four times those of ten years earlier. However, the quantity of small wares diminished by about thirty per cent after 1746, and for the next few years there was insufficient work to justify two assayers. This slack period was short-lived, however, because in 1749 the charge for silver by-assays, which had been raised from 2d to 3d in 1739, was reduced to 2d again, after which the number submitted soon doubled to about forty per day.

Francis Pages, a liveryman who had been appointed a drawer in 1745, was elected Junior Assayer in the following year on the death of Edlin and the promotion of Shillito to the senior post. Pages had been apprenticed to the celebrated Huguenot silversmith David Willaume and had first entered a mark in 1729.[16] A number of his pieces made before he joined the Assay Office have survived. He soon became Senior Assayer owing to the death of Shillito in 1748, and was succeeded as Junior Assayer by William Kidney who had been apprenticed to David Willaume II. Kidney had practised in business, not only as a silversmith but also as an assayer, having been taught the necessary skill by Pages himself. He had entered marks in 1734 and 1739 and his surviving silver work shows high technical competence. One of his pieces, known as the Kidney Cup, a fine two-handled cup and cover, hallmarked in 1740, was acquired by the Goldsmiths' Company in the nineteenth century.[17] Kidney died in 1756 at the age of about forty-seven without attaining the position of Senior Assayer. Another of David Willaume II's apprentices was John Vowels who was appointed Assayer's Assistant (or Fireman) in 1750 and promoted to Junior Assayer on the death of Kidney. The vacant position of Assayer's Assistant was filled by the appointment of Richard Collins who had been apprenticed to John Payne in 1747.

SILVER-GILT CUP AND COVER, *1740, with maker's mark of William Kidney, who was appointed Junior Assayer in 1748.*

'AN ENGINE FOR MARKING'

The year 1753 saw a significant development. Thomas Long, the Company's Engraver, had at last produced two patterns of his 'engines for marking', which we would now call hand-operated fly-presses. He was asked to make one but unfortunately he died a year later. His incomplete prototype press was brought to the Standing Committee by his widow who was paid £60 for it. The prototype was further developed by Thomas Pingo, Long's successor as Engraver and in 1757 he gave a demonstration before the members of the Standing Committee, marking several buckles and spoons in their presence. The Committee immediately sanctioned its use. This was an important innovation as it meant that several symbols could now be combined in a single

TRADE CARD *of Francis Pages, who relinquished his business on appointment as a drawer in the Assay Office in 1745.*

punch. The striking of a complete hallmark in one operation resulted in greater uniformity and appreciably reduced the time involved in marking spoons and some other wares submitted in quantity. Simple hand-operated fly-presses are still used two centuries later as the best method of marking certain articles, although Pingo's original press has long since disappeared.

PENALTIES FOR COUNTERFEITING

Although the Act of 1738 had clarified the law in many respects, it soon became evident that its reduction in the maximum penalty for counterfeiting from £500 to £100 was mistaken. In December 1750 the Company received a petition signed by thirty-nine of its members, complaining of 'sundry abuses' in the trade and in particular the counterfeiting of hallmarks and avoidance of the duty.

When first introduced in 1720 the plate duty had yielded some £20,000 annually but owing to widespread evasion it had dwindled to about £8000. The Standing Committee was asked to consider a suggestion that had been put forward to remedy the situation, namely that the duty be abolished and that instead every dealer be required to take out a plate licence. In order to assess the likely total return from licence fees it was elicited from the Excise authorities that there were 465 silversmiths in the City and a further 246 in the country who had been charged with duty, and that the total number of all traders in gold or silver wares in the City, including watchmakers, toymen and pawnbrokers was 954. Gabriel Sleath and John Swift – both later to become Deputy Wardens – acting on behalf of the trade members independently estimated that there were some 4000 dealers in plate in the whole of England; from which statistics the Committee concluded that a plate licence would not yield the required revenue. It then proceeded to formulate alternative proposals as the basis for a new Parliamentary Bill in consultation with prominent members of the trade. In December 1755, after extensive deliberations it recommended provision for the striking of a special mark alongside the hallmark to show that the duty had been paid, and the introduction of much harsher penalties for counterfeiting. It was envisaged that the duty would be collected and the new mark struck at a place close to the Assay Office. The Court of Assistants appointed a special committee – the four wardens together with John Payne, Thomas Whipham, Sandilands Drinkwater, Samuel Spindler and Philip Howe – to seek the concurrence and assistance of the Lords of the Treasury.[18]

In the meantime the Government introduced legislation in 1756 which, contrary to the advice of the Company, imposed an annual duty to be paid by 'all persons and bodies corporate having in their possession silver plate in excess of one hundred ounces'.[19] Collection of this tax was predictably unsuccessful; the Act was largely ignored and it was eventually repealed in 1777.

The Company's proposals, along with those of the Commissioners of Excise, were also considered by Parliament and as a result a further Act was passed in 1757.[20] This totally abolished the duty on newly manufactured silver but required a licence costing £2 – raised to £5 a year later – to be taken out by every person trading in gold or silver wares. Under the same Act, the counterfeiting of hallmarks was made a felony punishable by death.

It was thought that the first of the above two Acts would result in a diminution of the work of the Assay Office, but the passing of the second a year later, as might be expected, had exactly the opposite effect; there was an immediate and dramatic increase in the amount of silver submitted. Within three years the total weight of large wares rapidly rose from approximately 350,000 oz per annum to 600,000 oz and small wares from about 100,000 oz to 400,000 oz, a remarkable change showing that, even allowing for evasion of hallmarking, what a restrictive effect the duty had had on the trade. Within a decade there was even further expansion, the total weight of large wares reaching figures of almost 800,000 oz in some years.

AN INCREASING WORKLOAD

James Pugh, appointed Deputy Warden in 1739, had been succeeded on his death in 1753 by Gabriel Sleath, a well-known silversmith, many of whose pieces are still in existence.[21] Sleath's appointment is surprising, considering he was seventy-nine years old, and indeed he lived for only three more years. Shortly before he died, the Court resolved that any member of the Company who had been a warden might officiate in the Assay Office when the Deputy Warden was indisposed – a measure probably thought to be necessary in view of the incumbent's age! Following Gabriel Sleath as Deputy Warden was John Swift, a younger man of about fifty-one who had entered marks both as a smallworker and a largeworker. His work as a silversmith appears mostly to have been tankards, coffee pots and teapots.[22]

The Assay Office was now exceptionally active; the work of the two assayers had more than doubled since the passing of the 1757 Act. The Deputy Warden's duties also were inevitably more arduous than in the past; in May 1758 the Court agreed that his salary of £50 'was very short of a sufficient recompense and that £100 per annum was little enough for a gentleman of skill and ability who would give all due attendance on that service' – the Company's finances were now in much better shape. In the next few years the staff was increased by the appointment of two further drawers and a book-keeper, bringing the total up to ten. This was in addition to the part-time appointment of the Clerk of the Company as Accountant in the Assay Office. John Vowells died shortly after his appointment as Junior Assayer and was succeeded by Joseph Hollowey, who had only recently completed his apprenticeship to the silversmith Thomas Whipham. Hollowey was therefore much younger than most entrants but he was presumably nevertheless already a skilled assayer.

The work of the Assay Office had increased to such an extent that it was decided to discourage the sending of by-assays by again increasing the charges – from 2d to 6d for a silver assay and from 6d to 2s for a gold assay. This had the desired effect and the numbers fell from about forty to a mere three or four per day. There were obviously private assayers who charged less for the same service.

The staff had to be continually on their guard – as they always had been – against attempts by unscrupulous silversmiths to get substandard articles accepted and hallmarked. David Mouden of Addle Street, who had been imprisoned in 1743 for non-payment of the penalty for counterfeiting, had apparently not reformed. In 1759 he sent six milk ewers for hallmarking. Some of the bodies were better and some were below standard, while the feet were 1 oz 4dwt worse. It was assumed that this was a deliberate fraud and he confessed his guilt. His work was broken and redelivered to him on the condition that he entered into a bond of £50 to cover the Company for any damages they might sustain by inadvertently marking any of his deceitful work.

Another disquieting incident that occurred in 1768 is worth recounting. William Cox, a silversmith in Little Britain, submitted a parcel of six tumblers, in the sampling of which the drawer found one to be made of copper with a silver coating.[23] It had been marked in three places with the letters IH in addition to Cox's own mark. Cox was summoned to appear before the Standing Committee. He said the tumblers belonged to Joseph Hancock and Sons of Sheffield who had asked him to submit them for hallmarking. As he had received seven tumblers altogether he had assumed an extra one had been included in error and he had only submitted six to the Assay Office. He then went back to his workshop and brought another tumbler which proved to be up to standard. It certainly seemed to have been a genuine mistake but the Clerk was asked to obtain a legal opinion with a view to a possible prosecution. Mr William Hancock was called from Sheffield to appear before the Committee. He said the silvered copper tumbler had been sent by one of his servants in error. The tumbler was broken and given to Hancock and the chairman warned him to be careful of his conduct in future – counsel had advised the Company against prosecuting. This episode is of particular interest because the tumbler was obviously an early example of Sheffield plate, the manufacture of which had been pioneered by Joseph Hancock, William's father. We shall see later that the incident was mentioned at the Parliamentary Enquiry in 1773. It served to emphasize that the officers in the Assay Office had to be constantly on the alert as the tumbler in question was indistinguishable by eye from a silver one. The Sheffield plate industry was developing rapidly and becoming a serious rival to the silver trade.

The ability to spot irregularities of this sort was expected of the Weigher and drawers; it is evident that the Court took great pains to assess the experience and credentials of applicants for all vacancies in these posts. One of five petitioners for the position of Junior Weigher following the death of Gawen Nash in 1763 was William Gould, who is well known to present-day collectors as a maker of candlesticks. He did not get beyond the preliminary consideration of the candidates. The records state 'it was observed that the said William Gould had some years ago been guilty of a fraud in concealing a quantity of copper in a silver chandelier made for the Fishmongers' Company and that the same was a fact well known to the members of the Court and therefore it was moved and seconded that the said William Gould's petition be rejected'. The chandelier, a magnificent piece, is still in the possession of the Fishmongers' Company; although it bears the mark of William Alexander, William Gould was the actual maker.

From now on there was a change in the policy for filling vacancies in the Office and – except for the most junior drawer and the post of Deputy Warden – they were filled by promotion according to seniority. A junior drawer could expect in the fullness of time to work his way up to Assayer – if he lived long enough! He might even jump a few places as happened in the case of Fendall Rushforth, who had been elected Junior Drawer in 1760. When the position of Junior Assayer became vacant in 1766 he was the only applicant; he had obviously learned how to assay, and after two days during which five members of the Court exhaustively examined his practical ability, he was appointed to the post.

John Swift, who had been Deputy Warden for ten years, died in 1766 and was succeeded by Samuel Bates, another former silversmith who had first entered a mark as a largeworker in 1728. He was fifty-nine and serving as Third Warden when appointed. The following year he became Second Warden but was excused the office of Prime Warden. He resigned as Deputy Warden in 1772 owing to age and infirmities.

REVISION OF HALLMARKING FEES

The 1738 Act had laid down the maximum charges the Company could raise for marking small wares. Any surplus money above that required to defray the expenses of the Assay Office had to be used for prosecuting offenders against the Act; and should such prosecutions not require the whole of the surplus, the marking charges had to be reduced. The Company was thus precluded by statute from making any profit from administering the Office. There were difficulties in adhering strictly to the letter of the law, not least because new types of articles came into fashion from time to time which were not specifically mentioned in the Act. In practice the Company had to use a certain amount of discretion in fixing charges for them. However, taking one year with another, it was at pains to ensure that no overall profit resulted.

The maximum permitted charges were appropriate in the climate of the 1740s, but after the repeal of the duty in 1757, when the workload of the office more than doubled, surpluses began to accumulate. Accordingly in 1761 the charges were reduced by one fifth. This proved to be insufficient and a year later they were reduced to three fifths of the maximum allowed under statute, with a further necessary reduction to two fifths of the maximum in 1765. This was held for some years, but by 1777 the expenses incurred in providing additional accommodation together with the heavy legal costs of prosecutions had reduced the surpluses of previous years and the Office was beginning to run at a loss. It was accordingly decided on an increase to three fifths of the maximum allowed under the Act – for example, silver buckles or clasps were now charged 4d per dozen, a milk ewer 1d, a sword hilt 3d and a gold snuff box 9d. Payment for marking large silver wares remained the diet, retained at the rate of 10 grains per pound troy. When issuing a printed list of the new fees, advantage was taken to include many new types of articles that had come into fashion. The list was a long one and contained a number of items that were specifically exempted from hallmarking under the 1738 Act, such as rings, sleeve buttons and thimbles. It appears therefore that some manufacturers were voluntarily submitting articles that were legally exempt, no doubt finding that the guarantee afforded by a hallmark substantially enhanced their sales value.

In 1767 the Court ordered that diet should be retained from gold wares and that it should be tried annually in the same manner as silver. A piece of standard gold of equivalent weight was given to the sender as compensation. An amount of one grain per parcel was to be placed in the diet box for the trial. From that date the reports of the annual trial show the weights of gold diet, thus enabling us to calculate the number of parcels of gold wares hallmarked. In the first full year after the order these totalled nearly two thousand.

CHAPTER NINE

PARLIAMENTARY ENQUIRY

T HE INCREASE in staff following the much greater quantity of silver articles received for hallmarking after the repeal of the duty in 1757 meant that larger accommodation was badly needed. This was eventually provided in 1772 by alterations to the rooms within the Hall together with a programme for rebuilding part of the adjacent premises. The so-called 'New' Assay Office with an entrance in Carey Lane was housed in the same part of the Hall, on the ground floor on the south side, but it was now extended to include an area on which were formerly private houses and courtyards. The old Fleur-de-Luce Court was built over and a new house facing Carey Lane was provided for the Deputy Warden as well as one for the Senior Assayer on the first floor. Apart from the evidence of their cost (£2498 17s 6d), there is further proof that the alterations were extensive, namely a surviving receipt signed by the Senior Assayer, Fendall Rushforth, for food and drink for those engaged in moving tools and fixtures out of the old Office into the new. The receipt shows expenditure of £7 2s 3d for supplying beer, bread and cheese on 28 May 1773; breakfasting eight and dinner, beer etc. for sixteen persons on 31 May; dinner, beer etc. on 1 June and dinner, beer etc. for twelve persons on an unspecified date. Moving was a thirsty business! In 1780 another of the houses in Carey Lane adjoining the Assay Office was taken over as living accommodation for the Junior Assayer.

DAVID HENNELL,
Deputy Warden 1772–86.

In 1772 Samuel Bates was succeeded as Deputy Warden by another silversmith, David Hennell, who had built up a successful business as a maker of salt cellars in one of the houses in Foster Lane adjoining the Hall. He had entered a mark of his own in 1736, the year following

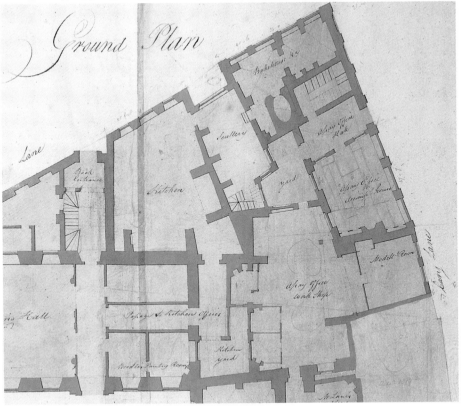

receipt of his freedom. David was first in line of eight members of the Hennell family who were practising silversmiths over a period of more than 150 years.[1] On his appointment as Deputy Warden at the age of fifty-nine, he transferred his business interests to his son Robert and moved into the rent-free house that had been built as part of the Assay Office extensions.

THE BIRMINGHAM AND SHEFFIELD ASSAY OFFICES

There must have been some disturbance of the daily routine due to the rebuilding and it came at rather an inopportune time. The Company had become involved in a concerted effort, together with the London trade, to prevent the opening of two new assay offices – in Birmingham and Sheffield. A demand had arisen for hallmarking facilities in these two towns, and largely through the persistence and influence of two eminent Birmingham industrialists, Matthew Boulton and Samuel Garbett, a Bill was introduced in Parliament in 1773 for establishing local autonomous offices. Garbett was a manufacturer of chemicals and iron ordnance as well as a refiner of gold and silver. Boulton's business encompassed a wide range of products, including silverware and plated goods. He was proprietor of the famous Soho Manufactory with some seven to eight hundred employees in the 1770s, which had a constant stream of distinguished visitors from all over Europe. He is rightly regarded as one of the outstanding figures of the industrial revolution for his role, in partnership with James Watt, in developing the use of steam power for industry. In an effort to expand the silverware side of his business and to compete with London craftsmen he had found that having to send his products to Chester – the nearest assay town – was both inconvenient and restricting. To promote the Bill he used his great influence with members of both Houses – in particular Lord Shelburne and the Earl of Dartmouth, a neighbouring landowner who was Colonial Secretary in Lord North's government. Two pairs of candlesticks ordered by Lord Shelburne, a future Prime Minister, had not been received back from the Chester Assay Office in time for Christmas and furthermore had been damaged because of bad packing – thus no doubt helping to further Boulton's cause. Manufacturers in Sheffield decided to join forces with the Birmingham promoters; they too had powerful supporters in Lord Rockingham (a past and future Prime Minister) and the Earl of Effingham.

Members of the trade in the capital, who united as 'The Goldsmiths, Silversmiths and Plateworkers of the City of London and places adjacent', feared that if the offices were established it would be injurious to their livelihood. They persuaded the Goldsmiths' Company to oppose the application. It is unlikely that the Company was worried by any foreseeable competition as

THE SECOND GOLDSMITHS' HALL *in the early 19th century, by Thomas Shepherd. Detail of a ground plan by Charles Beazley, 1802, showing the Assay Office accommodation.*

far as hallmarking was concerned; in comparison with London very little silverware was manufactured either in Birmingham or in Sheffield at that time. However, it was persuaded to do all it could to obstruct the Bill. A special Committee was convened by the Court of Assistants on 18 December 1772 and it immediately took steps to find out whether there was any evidence of irregular practices in the two towns or at the existing provincial assay offices. Richard Hughes, the Junior Assayer, was sent on a fact-finding mission to Birmingham, Sheffield, York, Newcastle and Chester with instructions to go round the shops and to buy any articles that appeared to contravene the law. He was also asked to find out whether the offices in the last three towns were operating according to the relevant statutes. His tour took nearly a month and included a visit to Boulton's factory in Birmingham. He could well have given York a miss, as when he arrived there he was told that the Assay Office had been closed for nearly a hundred years! The exercise proved abortive; although he bought several articles apparently none was found to be in breach of the hallmarking law.

Petitions from Birmingham and Sheffield were presented to the House of Commons at the beginning of February 1773 and these were followed a fortnight later by a petition drawn up by the Company and presented by the Rt. Hon. Thomas Harley MP, which alleged that the establishment of assay offices in the two towns 'would open the door to deceit and uncertainty in the standards ... and ruin the goldsmiths' trade in the kingdom'.[2] A similar petition from the London trade was presented on 25 February. Nevertheless, leave was given for the Bill to be introduced and it was read for the first time on 26 March. On 6 May, Harley presented to the House a further petition from the Company. It stated:

> ... most of the plate made in the two towns is made or stamped with dies and their chief employment is in plating or covering base metal with silver. The power of assaying and marking is too great and important a trust to be committed to persons and places where the same is likely to be abused or be prejudicial to the public. Your petitioners are apprehensive that if the said Bill should pass into law it will greatly increase the number of frauds in wrought plate and render the detection of such frauds more difficult ...

Notwithstanding the objections, however, the Bill was passed on 28 May and the two assay offices were established with their own governing bodies known as Guardians.[3] From then on the Company showed no animosity and co-operated with the new offices as far as was possible in the days of poor communications. During the next hundred years there was an enormous expansion of the trade in both Birmingham and Sheffield and consequently also of the work of their assay offices. Birmingham became particularly noted for the manufacture of jewellery and Sheffield for silver hollow-ware and flatware.

THE PARLIAMENTARY ENQUIRY OF 1773

As a result of the charges and counter-charges that had been levelled in the Commons debate, Parliament had ordered an enquiry into the manner in which the existing assay offices were conducted; it was held concurrently with the progress of the Bill. (By chance its chairman was member for the constituency in which the Soho factory lay, and a friend of Boulton.)

Representatives of the various offices were asked to explain their procedures. The Company's officers – George Fair (Clerk), David Hennell (Deputy Warden), Fendall Rushforth (Senior Assayer) and Richard Collins (Fireman and Drawer) – were called upon for this purpose. They were also requested to produce details of rejected plate and results of recent prosecutions. Peter Floyer, the Prime Warden, who happened to be the principal refiner in London, gave evidence, as did another warden, Samuel Smith.[4] The report of the Committee of Enquiry, which was presented to Parliament on the 29 April 1773, is an informative document recording the evidence of numerous witnesses.[5] Not only does it provide a detailed account of the practice at each of the assay offices but it also gives an insight into some of the problems faced

DETAIL FROM THE REPORT *of the Committee of Enquiry held in 1773, with annotations by George Fair, Clerk of the Goldsmith's Company.*

Copper Tumbler instead of a silver one to be assayed & marked.

traordinary Care in the fcraping; and that he never knew or heard of any Pattern being taken off at the Affay Office.

Mr. ALBION Cox (a Refiner at Sheffield) informed Your Committee, That he had received from Mr. Bernard Holbrook fome Affay Bits, which had been returned to him as fine Silver, from Affays made at Goldfmiths Hall; that they did not appear to him as fine Silver; and, upon fending them to a private Affay Mafter, they were reported only 14 dwt. better than Standard.

Qu. His veracity?

Possibly some Convoy-Spoons were in the same Parcel.

That fome Spoons, which had been broke at Goldfmiths Hall for being 2 dwt. worfe than Standard, were brought to the Houfe where he was an Apprentice, and fome Bits were cut from the fame, and fent to Goldfmiths Hall to be affayed again; when the Report upon that Affay was 4¼ dwt. worfe than Standard; and he has no Doubt, if a Piece of Plate of 100 Ounces was fent to Goldfmiths Hall to be affayed, that was only 11 Ounces fine, but it would have paffed before this Enquiry began—and that if a Purchafer of the fame Plate, when finifhed, fcraped a little therefrom, and fent it to Goldfmiths Hall to be affayed, that it would be reported full 4 dwt. worfe than Standard.

The Evidence of this witnefs confident with his Character.

If this is true it shews the Character of this witnefs as well as his Mafter who ought to have acquainted the Company therewith.

That about Four Years ago he many Times bought Silver of a Drawer or Scraper belonging to Goldfmiths Hall, melted into Ingots of about 17 to £.20 Value; and judged them to be Scrapings or Cuttings, from his coming at unfeafonable Hours; they being generally brought in the Evening, or betimes in the Morning; and from his concealing them in a fecret Manner; for if there were other Perfons in the Shop, he waited till they were gone; that the Witnefs never afked the Scraper any Queftions, as his Mafter by them in dealing with unscrupulous manufacturers. Furthermore it throws some light on the assayers' understanding of the cupellation method at that time. The procedures used for assaying silver were described in some detail. Stanley Alchorne, the King's Assay Master at the Mint, explained for the benefit of the members:

> If silver could be absolutely freed from all admixture of allay, without losing any atom of its substance, the art might be deemed perfect, but there will always remain some small quantity of allay, or even of the lead used in the process; and the silver itself will not pass through the operation without losing a small part of its substance, which is carried by the lead into the coppel – all of which may be proved to a demonstration by skilful chymists. The above obstacles to the perfection of assaying depend upon various circumstances; the quantity and equability of the fire, the conduct of air, the proportion and quality of the allay, the weight of lead, the substance of the coppel, and even alterations in the atmosphere, will all of them produce variations, so that the extent of these defects can never be precisely ascertained before the operation. But by long observation and real experience skilful persons may learn to counterbalance, and allow for these several accidents, so as to make good judgement of common allayed silver, within about one half pennyweight.

'Allay' in the above context refers to the base metals present in the material being assayed. Alchorne must have known of the series of papers by Matthieu Tillet published in Paris about ten years earlier, describing a series of investigations on the cupellation method which he had carried out at the request of the French Government.[6] They were the first attempt at a critical look at the method using a truly scientific approach. Chemistry was still in its infancy, however. Assayers' knowledge was therefore still largely empirical – they were ignorant, for example, of the principal chemical reaction involved in cupellation, namely oxidation of the lead and base metals. The parliamentary enquiry took place one year before Joseph Priestley's discovery of oxygen and before Antoine Lavoisier had made known the results of his experiments on combustion, which may be said to have laid the foundation of modern chemistry.

A number of accusations were levelled at the Company by witnesses attending the enquiry from Birmingham and Sheffield. It is likely they were exaggerated, but there was undoubtedly an element of truth in some of the statements. One of the main charges was that some small wares that were below the legal standard had been hallmarked in London. As evidence a number of silver items (including a castor, two buckles, two teaspoons, a pair of tea tongs, a punch ladle and two bottle tickets) were produced, as were assay reports on sample pieces which had been cut from these articles and sent to the Assay Office in London as 'private' assays. Most of them were substantially below standard. The Committee ordered that further samples should be cut from these articles and given both to Stanley Alchorne and to the Company's Assayer, Rushforth, for further assays. Their results, which are given in full in the report of the enquiry, show remarkably close agreement and indeed nearly all of them are below standard, some as much as 6 or 7 dwt in the pound troy. It does therefore seem that some substandard articles were slipping through the Assay Office net without detection.

Rushforth was asked many questions about his method of assaying. Only some of his evidence is recorded in the official report but additional transcript notes are available in the Company's archives. According to the report itself he said he would pass plate which came within 2 dwt of the standard; also that plate which was 11 oz fine would be passed as standard but never less than 11 oz. Although the minimum legal standard was 11 oz 2 dwt this does not mean he was allowing a tolerance. It is difficult to unravel some of the answers he gave to his questioners but we know that no corrections were applied by assayers to their reports to compensate for cupellation loss. Thus the true figures were about 2 dwt higher than those they recorded. According to Rushforth's evidence articles were ultimately passed or rejected with reference to a standard trial piece which was equivalent to the indented trial plate of 1728. He answered 'No' to the question 'Do you pass or report as standard any plate that is worse than the standard piece?' Therefore the 2 dwt which Rushforth said was allowed before plate was broken was to compensate for cupellation loss and no additional tolerance was permitted. This is corroborated by the evidence given at the enquiry by the Assay Master at Newcastle and in later writings by a private assayer.[7] Rushforth undoubtedly had great difficulty in explaining in an intelligible manner how assay results were reported and the members of the Committee must have been perplexed by his evidence. In any case, if he had allowed a tolerance additional to the cupellation loss there would have been a risk of the diet failing at the annual trial when assayed against the trial plate. It has often been assumed from the report of the enquiry that the Company had been allowing a tolerance on the standard but this is clearly not the case.

The report of the enquiry also sets out the evidence of witnesses with regard to frauds or attempted frauds by manufacturers and vendors of gold and silver wares. It states that Rushforth produced some watchcases, the wires of which were more than 2 oz worse and the bottoms ½ dwt better than standard. He said they had been received for hallmarking from a manufacturer in Birmingham but he admitted that he had discovered many frauds of the same nature committed in London. Both he and Hennell drew attention to the malpractice referred to as 'convoying', of which some workers in London were guilty, presumably implying that it would be even more likely to occur in the provinces. As an example, Rushforth said that several spoons of different sorts of silver, some 6dwt better and others 6dwt worse than standard had been brought to the office in one parcel by a London silversmith only a few days previously. He also mentioned the plated tumbler from Hancock and Sons of Sheffield (see page 212), but said that there had been no prosecution as it appeared to have been sent in error. William Hancock himself gave evidence at the enquiry and took the opportunity of getting a little of his own back. He insinuated that the drawers in the Assay Office were not above accepting some encouragement in the form of drink to treat his work carefully; but he admitted that his goods were never returned 'unscraped'. Although not mentioned in the report, an unofficial transcript of the evidence states that, on being further questioned, Hancock said he had conversed with the Assay Master and the scrapers, and that they had 'some punch and beer and some cold beef ... but no money was passed'; but he could not remember whether his complaint regarding damage to his work was made before or after the liquor was produced.

The main criticism levelled by witnesses at the enquiry against traders in Sheffield and Birmingham was in regard to plated wares, the so-called 'Sheffield plate', which had lately become popular due to its comparative cheapness, while appearing almost indistinguishable from sterling silver. Its manufacture was mainly confined to Sheffield and Birmingham at that time. Several London manufacturers submitted that the makers of plated wares were stamping these products with a series of marks, usually three, which it was claimed could easily be mistaken for hallmarks. There were certainly some grounds for this complaint and the report of the Committee stated that 'if the practice ... shall not be restrained, many frauds and impositions may be committed upon the public.'

Some London witnesses, however, spoke forcefully against the Company. Francis Spilsbury, a silversmith, was particularly hostile, despite the fact that he was a liveryman. One cannot help surmising he must have fallen foul of the Deputy Warden. Giving evidence at the enquiry he maintained he had been several times to Goldsmiths' Hall 'to treat the workmen with drink', thinking it to be 'of consequence to be upon good terms with the scrapers, as they have a power of showing favour in passing work'. Yet on his own admission some of his goods had been broken because they were substandard. Another London witness, John Williams, whose trade was providing castings for the London silversmiths, discredited him to some extent by revealing that Spilsbury had supplied him with 'brass clippings or cuttings coloured like silver' for making cast work – adding that he had 'refused to be further employed by the person who had made use of such practices lest it should hurt his other customers, as it was usual to cast all their work together. George Fair, Clerk of the Company, annotated his copy of the Committee's report at the relevant paragraph with the words: 'This proves Spilsbury to be a great rogue'! It may be significant that Spilsbury was subsequently favoured with an order from Matthew Boulton – to supply a furnace and other equipment for the new Birmingham Assay Office at a cost of £8 8s 2d. However, he did not continue to trade as a silversmith; on his death in 1793 *The Gentleman's Magazine* reported:

> At Hamstead aged 60, Mr Spilsbury of Soho Sq. proprietor of the anti-scorbutic drops. He was a silversmith in Noble St, Cheapside & turned quack about 25 years ago when he first kept a shop in Mount Row, Lambeth. By his second wife who survives him he has left a numerous family.[8]

Such an obituary seems to leave his reputation in some doubt.

As a result of its survey the Committee of Enquiry found that the operations at Chester and Newcastle had been conducted with fidelity and skill, but in referring to all the offices the report states that they were liable to many abuses and impositions and that some further checks and regulations were necessary. In consequence, the Act establishing the Birmingham and Sheffield offices did contain a number of regulations concerning the manner in which they were to operate, in particular with regard to their diets, which were required to be tried annually by the Mint Assay Master.

Although the Goldsmiths' Company was not directly affected by these regulations, the adverse criticism levelled against it at the enquiry prompted the wardens to take a close look at the procedures in the Assay Office. That some substandard small wares had apparently been hallmarked in error must have caused considerable embarrassment and required appropriate action to prevent a repetition. As a result of evidence given at the enquiry by Albion Cox, one of the brothers of the family firm of silversmiths and refiners in Little Britain,[9] Richard Collins, the Fireman and Drawer, was dismissed. Cox, who had recently moved to Sheffield attested that about four years previously, Collins had many times brought silver ingots for sale. He suspected they were melted scrapings or cuttings. Cox explained that he had never asked any questions because his brother, who was also his master, was generally present, adding that his brother and Collins were well known to each other, having been fellow apprentices together – surely a broad hint that there had been some collusion. Whether Collins' dismissal was entirely warranted is questionable in view of an annotation by the Clerk on his copy of the report; against other evidence of Albion Cox he has written: 'Little credit given to this witness by those who know him. He is capable of saying anything'. But clearly the suspicion was there and the Company was taking no chances, which shows the importance it attached to the trustworthiness of its staff. It was another brother, William Cox, who had been in trouble with the Assay Office five years earlier when he had submitted the base metal tumbler on behalf of William Hancock (see page 212).

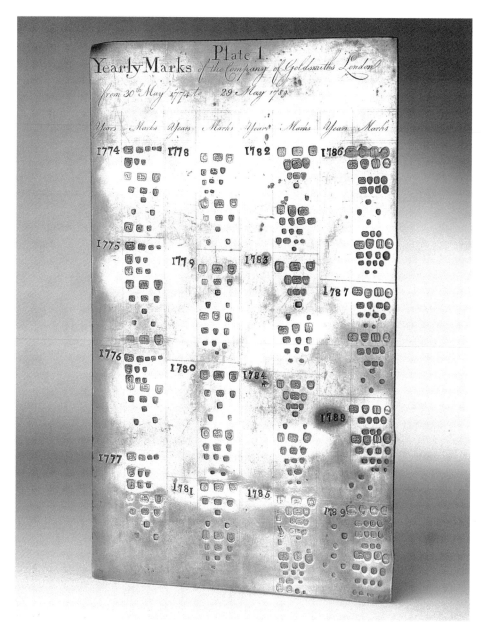

PLATE *bearing impressions of the hallmarks used between 1774 and 1789.*

Soon after the report of the enquiry had been published new record books were provided in the Assay Office, and commencing in 1773, full daily entries were made of the total weights of articles received showing separately small wares, large wares and watch cases in silver, and gold wares. It is unfortunate that no record was kept until much later (1891) of the number of items received, but the full series of books showing the weights have been preserved and give a good picture of the workload from day to day as well as from year to year during the last two centuries.

FURTHER OFFENCES

The Company agreed to meet all legal expenses incurred in objecting to the Birmingham and Sheffield Bill, which (excluding the Clerk's fees), amounted to £538 8s 11d. The Clerk was remiss in not submitting a statement of his own fees and expenses; a year later it had still not been presented and indeed no record of it can be traced. He blamed ill-health for the delay and said he wished to go to Margate to benefit from the sea water, a request that was duly granted. He was shortly replaced by Edward Reynolds, who was to be kept busy in prosecuting a succession of offenders.

One such offender was Thomas Jackson, who was tried and found guilty at the Guildhall in June 1774 for making and selling a substandard cruet frame. In 1777 the wardens received information that many small gold and silver wares, much worse than standard, were being offered for sale, and that others were not properly marked. Accordingly, sundry articles were bought in the cities of London and Westminster 'without favour or ill-will'. All the articles – such as watch chains, rings, seals and toothpick cases – were exempt from compulsory hallmarking, but were nevertheless required to be up to standard. The fifty-eight recorded assay reports show that most of the items bought were below standard and the Court of Assistants ordered that the persons who had sold them should be sued for penalties. Additional penalties were recovered in some instances because the articles did not bear a maker's mark.

Several cases of forgery came to light at this time, but although the legislation in force between 1757 and 1772 provided for the death penalty for counterfeiting a hallmark, there is no record of this being invoked. Under the Plate (Offences) Act 1772 the maximum sentence was amended to fourteen years' transportation.[10] In January 1776, John More received the full term for feloniously counterfeiting the Company's marks on a pair of base metal shoe buckles.

Some years before, in 1764, the Assay Office had been involved in an incident which is a reminder of the harshness of the penalties incurred in those days for certain other crimes, notably theft. John Jones was a young man convicted of forging an order on the Assay Office for the delivery of silverware submitted for hallmarking by one Lydia Bell, the widow of a silversmith in Fleet Street, who was carrying on the business after her husband's death. Jones was caught when endeavouring to dispose of a tankard that was in the parcel. He was tried, convicted and sentenced to death. After detention in Newgate prison for fifteen months he petitioned the Company, saying that he had been prevailed upon by Lydia Bell's apprentice to commit the crime and imploring the Company to recommend him to His Majesty's mercy out of compassion for his 'youth and sufferings and ignorance of the seriousness of his crime'. The Company did recommend accordingly and again on receiving a second petition. The outcome is not recorded. In a similar case twenty years later, in which a parcel of silver buckles had been collected from the Assay Office by means of a forged order, the offender named John Owen, who was only about twenty years of age and had served part of an apprenticeship as a silversmith, was duly hanged outside Newgate prison.[11]

The minute book of 1780 records an interesting case which arose from a report by the Junior Assayer. William Brockwell had sent to the Assay Office a parcel containing nine pairs of tea-tongs which were 5 dwt worse than standard, together with five ladles, the handles of which were 16 dwt better than standard (nearly pure silver). It was assumed that this was done with fraudulent intent, in other words it was an instance of 'convoying', a practice mentioned at the parliamentary enquiry. Brockwell was prosecuted, found guilty, fined 40s and imprisoned in Wood Street compter for one week. He was informed by the judge that 'the mildness of the sentence was on account of it being the first offence of the kind punished by indictment, but it was under the circumstances of the case clearly an offence under the Act of Parliament, and that every person in future who should be convicted of a like offence should receive a much heavier punishment'. Despite the judge's comments there have been very few instances where a prosecution has been undertaken solely for making, as opposed to offering for sale, a substandard article, although it was only in 1975 that this ceased to be an offence (see page 305).

Following the removal of the duty on new silverware in 1757 and the consequent surge in the workload of the Assay Office the staff establishment had been modestly increased. But for the next seventy-five years the number employed remained fairly constant at around eleven. In 1777 a new recruit in the position of Fifth Drawer was William Le Bas, a young silversmith who had served an apprenticeship in the trade and had entered a mark as a salt-maker on receiving his freedom six years earlier. He was to remain on the staff of the Assay Office for the next forty years, eventually becoming Senior Weigher. He would have progressed further up the ladder had he not chosen for some reason to decline the position of Junior Assayer which was offered him when it became vacant. He was twice married and had thirteen children, one of whom, James Le Bas, after serving an apprenticeship in London, started a business as a silversmith in Dublin. James' grandson Samuel was Dublin Assay Master from 1880 to 1890 and Samuel's two sons followed in turn from 1890 to 1941. Ronald Le Bas, Samuel's grandson held the same position from 1963 to 1988 and his son (also Ronald) has succeeded him.[12]

David Hennell, the Deputy Warden, died in 1785 and Fendall Rushforth, the Senior Assayer was appointed in his place. Thus for the first time the position went to one of the staff and not to a prominent but elderly member of the silversmithing trade. It was to be the pattern of promotion for the next fifty years. Rushforth had joined the office as Junior Drawer in 1760, a year after receiving his freedom, and had served in the capacity of Junior and then Senior Assayer for a total of nineteen years before this latest appointment. Those of his personal daily record books that have survived indicate a methodical and careful worker.

Rushforth's work as Senior Assayer has already been mentioned in connection with the parliamentary enquiry in 1773. Shortly after the report had been published a complaint was received from the newly established Birmingham and Sheffield Assay Offices that some small silver articles were being passed in London which would not qualify for hallmarking under their own Acts. There was no attempt to hide the facts; when sent some buckles and spoons bearing London hallmarks Rushforth assayed them and forwarded his reports to the Birmingham Office. They are recorded in its first minute book and show results between ½ and 7 dwt worse than standard. Even if these results are corrected for the usual cupellation loss it seems that some substandard articles had been submitted and passed in error. However, no more complaints of a similar nature were received from Birmingham, so we may assume that there were no grounds for any.[13] Part of the problem can be blamed on the new trial plates which Birmingham and Sheffield used as their standards – they were 1½ dwt (6.25 parts per 1000) better than sterling; the error was not discovered until 1830!

This occurrence was certainly not due to any lack of skill on Rushforth's part. Indeed his expertise in assaying was widely recognized, and perhaps unusually for those days he was prepared to impart it to others. In 1784 for instance, the Newcastle Goldsmiths' Company asked John Robertson, a partner of John Langlands, a well-known silversmith in that town, to call at Goldsmiths' Hall when next visiting London to seek information on the assaying of gold. He reported back that Rushforth had promised to send a complete apparatus for gold assaying and would 'give every assistance in his power to make you Masters of the Process'. According to the records of the Newcastle Company the apparatus cost £13 2s 6d with an additional 13s 6d for 'a salmon sent in gratitude to Mr Rushforth and its carriage to London'.[14]

THE PLATE DUTY

⟨decorative divider⟩

T HE SILVER TRADE, which had been prospering since the removal of
the duty in 1757, received a set-back in 1784 when William Pitt (the
Younger) decided to re-introduce this form of taxation as part of his
programme of fiscal reform. Surprisingly, it was not until 12 August, the day
before the Bill was due to be read a third time and likely to be passed, that the
Clerk was asked to seek an urgent conference with Mr Pitt, to persuade him
to delay further progress until the Company had time to state objections. At a
hastily convened joint meeting with trade representatives on the following day
the Clerk and Sir Thomas Hallifax – Member of Parliament for Aylesbury, a
former Prime Warden and one-time Lord Mayor – were asked to accompany
a trade delegation to the Treasury to state the Company's objections to the Bill
and to 'entreat the Chancellor of the Exchequer that if the Bill must be passed,
some clauses may be amended and added to give relief to makers and vendors
of gold and silver manufactures'.[1] Their entreaties were in vain – inevitably the
Bill was passed and duty became payable from 2nd December 1784 at the rate
of 6d per ounce for silver and 8s per ounce for gold wares.[2]

Although apparently taken off its guard when the Bill was introduced, it
seems the Company must have had an inkling of what Pitt had in mind.
Earlier in the year the Court of Assistants had unanimously resolved to offer
him the honorary freedom of the Company, but he had declined since he had
already accepted the same from the Grocers' Company, of which his father
had been a member. In the following May, however, after a general election
had confirmed his position as Prime Minister at the early age of twenty-five,
he had accepted an invitation to an extravagant dinner for fifty people at
Goldsmiths' Hall, at which 193 bottles of wine were drunk. But this hospi-
tality clearly did not influence his resolve to proceed with the re-imposition of
a duty on gold and silver wares.

The statute called for special arrangements for payment of the duty. Whereas
between 1720 and 1757 the Excise authorities had been directly responsible
for its collection, now the Company and the other assay offices were entrusted
with this task. To signify that the duty had been paid an additional mark in the

form of the reigning monarch's head in profile was to be struck alongside the other symbols of the hallmark. In return the assay offices were to receive 6d in each £1 collected.[3] They continued to provide this service for the Government for over a hundred years, until the abolition of the duty in 1890. The existing exemptions from hallmarking were retained in the new legislation, such articles being thereby also free from duty. But rather unfairly, it would seem, exempted wares were charged with duty if they were sent voluntarily for hallmarking.[4] Gold wares of the 18 carat standard (introduced in 1798) were liable to duty in the same way as those of the old standard of 22 carat. Wares of the 9, 12 or 15 carat standards (introduced in 1854) were not struck with the sovereign's head but duty was levied on them if they were submitted for hallmarking. In an attempt to protect the British watch trade against foreign competition, the government repealed the duty on both gold and silver watchcases in 1798.[5]

The duty mark on silver was at first intaglio (incised) in an oblong shield with clipped corners. It is found in this form in conjunction with the date letters 'i' and 'k' for 1784 and 1785. But after May 1786 it was in cameo (in

DETAIL OF THE PLATE *on page 224 showing impressions of the duty and duty drawback marks for the years 1785 and 1789.*

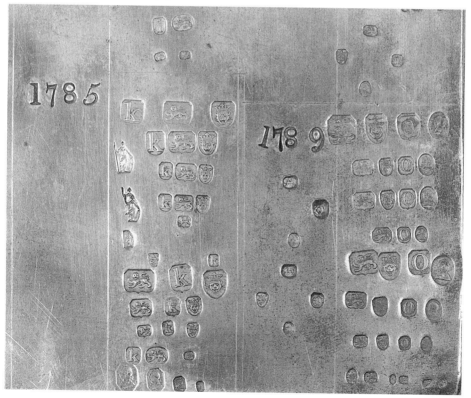

relief), thus matching the other symbols of the hallmark; at the same time the shield was changed to an oval shape. The reason for the alteration in design was probably because of the difficulty of making a composite punch incorporating the intaglio mark alongside symbols in relief. Slight variations in the outline of the shield of the duty mark are to be found in certain years when the rate of duty was changed. Thus, when the rate for silver was doubled to 1s per ounce from 6 July 1797, the mark had a slightly modified shield until the date letter was changed on 28 May 1798. This was so that the amount of duty that had been paid would be known should an article be exported and a claim for drawback be received. For the same reason, when the rate was again increased to 1s 3d per ounce from 11 October 1804, another small alteration was made to the mark. The foregoing modifications took the form of one or more cusps in the oval shield surrounding the sovereign's head. There were also three varieties of the mark used during the assay office year 1815/16 due to a change in the regulations for the refund of duty (from 14 June) and an increase in its rate to 1s 6d per ounce (from 1 September). From 29 May to 13 June the simple oval shield was used; from 14 June to 31 August the shield had a single basal cusp; and from 1 September to 29 May 1816 it had a flattened base. These simple modifications could be made without the necessity of making new punches.[6]

All punches of the duty mark were made by John Pingo, working under instructions from the Commissioners of Stamps. He had succeeded his father, Thomas (see page 204) as the Company's Engraver in 1776. The additional work gave him an opportunity to petition the Company for an increase in salary. Although some punches consisted only of the duty mark, far more were required where it was combined with other symbols on the same punch. Pingo's petition is revealing in that it shows that considerable strides had been made in using fly-presses for marking. In it he spells out the extra work involved:

> ... marks were originally on single punches which were used with a hammer; now united and made on stubbs to be used with presses the better to prevent and detect frauds ... better appearance, equal distance and depth and plate marked more expeditiously ... Additional press mark for watch-case lids which were never marked before. Double marks on single punches for tea-spoons and additional marks for a large new press for table and dessert spoons ... At another time was ordered to make a entire new set of marks in low relief for experiment consisting of upwards of 100 marks, in consequence of which all other good marks in office destroyed ... in a short time afterwards the shallow or low relief marks were thought not to make a sufficient bold appearance, therefore they were all destroyed. Then ordered to make another set of a bolder relief which were approved ... ordered to add the new duty mark to to those of the Company against 29th

May which entirely alters the form of the marks throughout. Duty mark only made on single punches before. Obliged to engrave the whole of the marks over again by uniting the duty marks with the others for to be used with presses rendering all the other good duty marks in hand useless.

This petition resulted in an addition of £20 to Pingo's annual salary. His work was to expand still further in the next few years as an increasing number of articles were marked by press. There were 240 new punches incorporating the letter 'q' delivered on 29 May 1791, and twelve months later he submitted yet another petition with 262 punches of the letter 'r'. His salary this time was increased to £120 per annum. Considering he was supplying punches to other offices as well as performing his work as Mint Engraver, he was not doing too badly. He was in some disgrace in the following year, however; when the new punches were received it was found that he had made the date letter in the form of a large Roman 'S' instead of a small 's'. As this was thought likely to cause confusion should an alphabet consisting of large Roman letters be used at any time in the future, he was ordered to modify all the punches by putting an oblique line through the centre of the 'S' – to have scrapped all the punches and made new ones would have been an impracticable task at this late juncture. After his lapse from grace it was decided that the Engraver should in future be required to take an oath each year for the due execution of his work, in line with the staff of the Assay Office.

THE DUTY DRAWBACK MARK

In his earlier petition, Pingo did not mention another mark for which punches were required – the duty drawback or exportation mark. Duty already charged on articles subsequently exported could be recovered. Provided they were brought to the Assay Office before shipment the duty was refunded and the drawback mark was struck on them. The mark consisted of an incised standing figure of Britannia (not to be confused with the Britannia standard mark, for which the figure was seated). It was found that finished articles were sometimes damaged when the mark was struck on them and it had only a

HALLMARK FOR *1785 showing, on the right, the duty mark and the duty drawback mark.*

short period of use between 2 December 1784 to 24 July 1785; pieces bearing this mark are therefore rare.[7]

The new legislation necessitated the appointment of an accountant who would be responsible for the duty money. The Clerk had for some years held the additional post of accountant in the Assay Office but on the death of Edward Reynolds in February 1785 the offices were split; Thomas Lane became Clerk and Richard Banks, who resigned from the Court, was appointed Accountant in the Assay Office, in which capacity he had to give security of £1000 because of his responsibility for the duty money. Twelve years later, on the death of Banks, the Clerk took over both posts again and this arrangement held until the duty was abolished. Another member of the staff, known as the Duty Clerk, was appointed to carry out the routine work. The money collected was paid into the Bank of England twice weekly and it was the responsibility of the Weigher to check that the correct amount had been sent by the manufacturer according to the weight of articles. In the first month after its introduction the total duty collected at the Assay Office was £565 17s 10d, of which the Company retained £14 2s 11d.

The trade inevitably suffered an initial set-back as a result of this new tax. Small wares were the main casualty, the weights submitted for hallmarking dropping by one third. The weight of large wares, however, suffered only a temporary drop of about one tenth and soon made up for the decrease in small wares. Nor did the total sales of silverware (by weight) diminish appreciably as a result of the French Revolutionary and Napoleonic wars (1793–1815). High inflation during this period affected the spending habits of the poorer classes far more than the wealthier members of society who could still afford to buy luxury goods. Even the successive increases in the rate of the duty, which were part of the government's policy for raising revenue to maintain the army and the navy, had no lasting effect on the trade. Indeed, figures for the total weights of silver received for hallmarking between May 1809 and May 1811 show a record peak that was not surpassed for another eighty-five years.

DIFFICULTIES CONCERNING EXEMPTIONS

The imposition of the duty on new silver underlined the particular significance of those sections of the Plate (Offences) Act 1738 relating to exemptions, since wares exempted from hallmarking were also free of duty. The ambiguity of the law was highlighted in a case heard in the Court of Common Pleas in 1789. A retailer at Charing Cross was prosecuted for selling an unhallmarked silver nutmeg grater (one of the articles listed as exempt). The presiding judge in his direction to the jury ruled that this article and indeed all the articles specifically listed in Section 6 of the Act were exempt only if they weighed less than 10 dwt. Hitherto it had always been assumed that this proviso had been intended by the legislators to apply only to articles that were too small to bear the marks. The case had been launched by a common informer employed by an attorney at a yearly fee to purchase articles from shopkeepers for the purpose of bringing actions against them. In view of the judge's interpretation of the law retailers were fearful of other similar actions. A petition with about fifty signatures was brought to the Company asking for assistance in an application to Parliament to amend the law so as to clarify the position regarding exemptions. The petitioners' solicitor produced a draft Bill with an entirely new list of proposed exemptions for silver.

At the same time manufacturers of gold articles and jewellery also made representations. They were anxious that the exemption for 'jeweller's works' in Section 2 of the 1738 Act should remain, but they asked if there could be two lower standards for gold – 20 and 18 carat – in addition to the current 22 carat standard; the export market, so it was said, would be greatly assisted.

After deliberation, the Court of Assistants decided to support the recommendations of the silver workers for a revision of the law on exemptions, but to oppose the introduction of lower standards of gold. It was agreed that the Company should make the application to Parliament on the basis of the silver workers' draft Bill and in this it was successful. This meant that in future there were two separate lists of exemptions, one for silver and one for gold. The new legislation – The Silver Plate Act 1790 – repealed section 6 of the 1738 Act in so far as it related to silver wares, and in its place was a provision exempting most silver articles weighing under 5 dwt.[8] There were, however, exceptions – such as teaspoons, buttons, buckles (other than shirt buckles), patch boxes, caddy ladles and bottle tickets – which were not exempted at all. Certain other specified articles – such as chains, shirt buckles and stamped medals – were exempted whatever their weight. The new Act was no doubt perfectly clear at the time it was passed, but as in the case of the 1738 Act, parts of it later gave rise to uncertainties in interpretation.

The silver trade was understandably worried by the prospect of an increase in the rate of duty which the government was proposing to introduce in 1797. In May of that year the Company was persuaded to join in a deputation to William Pitt – still both Prime Minister and Chancellor of the Exchequer – to ask for a reconsideration. Under the prevailing circumstances there was little chance of success. The Government was under enormous stress owing to the grave danger facing the country. Britain had suffered many reverses in the war against Republican France which had begun in 1793, having lost all its continental allies except Portugal. Invasion was expected at any time. In the previous month the navy had mutinied at Spithead and although discipline had been restored, it was only at the cost of a promise of better conditions and improved rates of pay. And now, only days before Pitt was due to receive the joint deputation from the Company and trade, mutiny had broken out at the Nore where the seamen were making further demands. The government's debts were mounting alarmingly. Higher taxes were inevitable and an increase in the rate of duty on silverware was just one of many measures taken. Two months later the Company decided to make its own contribution to the war effort by curtailing its entertainments and subscribing £1000 per annum in aid of the 'exigencies of the State during the continuance of hostilities'. The increased duty on silver wares (from 6d to 1s per ounce) took effect from 5 July. But although there was an initial drop in the weight of silver submitted for marking, after two years the lost ground had been fully recovered.

At the meeting with Mr Pitt in May the delegates also recommended that there should be a duty on silver-plated wares (Sheffield plate) and that such articles should be required to bear the maker's initials and the word 'plated'.[9] This was, however, turned down in spite of the prospect of additional revenue.

Walter Coles became Deputy Warden on the death of Fendall Rushforth in December 1796. He had been apprenticed to William Grundy, a largeworker; and like Rushforth he had joined the staff of the Assay Office as Junior Drawer and had progressed through the various grades. In 1804, when vacancies for two drawers arose, there were as many as twenty applicants for the posts, perhaps indicating some unemployment within the industry, although, as we have noted, the silver trade appears to have been fairly buoyant. A few years later, in 1808, some workers became a little impatient at the service they were getting from the Assay Office and the Company received a petition signed by thirty-one craftsmen asking if more staff could be engaged. Many of the names appended to this petition will be familiar to present-day collectors of antique silver as they include such well-known makers as John Eames, Peter and William Bateman, Eley and Fearn, Phipps and Robinson, Robert and Samuel Hennell. After due consideration the Company decided not to increase the number of staff. Instead, the petitioners were told that if they brought their work at the beginning of the allotted period instead of during the last few minutes this would produce the best remedy. One cannot help feeling that they had little cause for complaint considering that in normal circumstances they were able to collect their work on the same day as it was submitted.

A vacancy arose for another drawer in 1810. One of the candidates was George Miles, a cousin of John Johnson, the son of the founder of the well-known firm that later became Johnson & Sons, Assayers, of Maiden Lane. Johnson was a member of the Company, as was his father and in due course many of the future generations of his family. Miles had lost his own father at the age of about seven and Johnson had taken him into his household, arranging for him to be apprenticed to his brother, Charles Halsey Johnson, who had set up business on his own as a refiner. After two years Miles's apprenticeship was transferred to William Holmes, a silversmith. As he helped in the family firm during part of this time he also gained useful experience of assaying. On completion of his apprenticeship in 1804, and after an unsuccessful application for a post then vacant at the Assay Office, he set up as a silversmith in Clerkenwell.[10] But it seems his business was not prospering and six years later following a second application he was appointed Fourth Drawer, Johnson putting up the security that was now demanded. In 1822 Miles was promoted to Third Assayer and two years later to First or Senior Assayer, a position he held until his death in 1837. The Company had a high regard for his skill.

WATCHCASE MAKERS

Since the middle of the eighteenth century the range of articles received for hallmarking had significantly expanded, but perhaps the most notable feature of the workload was the increasing number of watchcases. Silver cases weighing a total of 98,628 oz were received in the twelve months from May 1773 to May 1774, but in the same twelve months 1804/5 this had increased to 170,592 oz. A temporary set-back for the watch trade had occurred in 1797 when William Pitt imposed a tax on the wearing of watches and the use of clocks — 10s per annum for a gold watch, 2s 6d for a silver watch and 5s for a clock.[11] As might be expected this resulted in a marked drop in the quantity of watchcases sent for hallmarking. Between the months of May and October 1796, 3,301 gold cases were marked, whereas in the same months in 1797 the number had dropped to 1,560. The corresponding figures for silver cases were 93,476 and 74,319.[12] It is hard to understand how, in practical terms, the tax could have been collected and it was in fact abolished a year later. In the meantime, however, many people had their gold or silver watchcases melted, which may indeed have benefited the trade in the long term.

In July 1797 the Prime Warden reported to the Court that he and the Clerk had attended an interview with William Pitt with regard to a petition which the government had received from the watch trade asking for an additional standard for gold. The Court expressed concern that the Company had not been sent full details of the proposal in advance and two days later an apology for this omission was received from Mr Pitt. It appeared that watchmakers, with the support of the Clockmakers' Company, were anxious that there should be a standard of 14 carat so that they would be able to compete on equal terms with the Swiss manufacturers. They pointed out that a 22 carat gold watch cost approximately twice as much to make as one of 14 carat. On this occasion the Company decided not to object in principle but suggested that the lower standard should be not less than 18 carat. The Company's advice was accepted and an additional standard of 18 carat was introduced by the Gold Plate (Standard) Act 1798.[13] Special marks — a crown and the figure 18 — were to be used, but 22 carat gold continued to bear for the time being the same standard mark as silver, namely the lion passant, until 1844 (see page

HALLMARK FOR *18-carat gold, 1798, the year in which this standard was introduced.*

252). A trial plate of the 18 carat standard was made by the Company and used at the annual trial of the diet for a number of years, but was later discarded as it was found to be slightly below the correct fineness.

In the year 1812 the activities of certain watchcase makers were the cause of particular concern. Several were using substandard silver for the wires or bezels, hoping that it would not be discovered since it was difficult for the drawers to take much sample from these parts without causing damage. A few such watchcases had passed through the Office undetected and their discovery at a later date caused much friction between the respective Companies of Goldsmiths and Clockmakers. The latter included watchmakers among its membership, some of whom had been supplied with substandard cases. The weakness in the assay procedure having been identified, steps were taken to overcome it by increasing the number of samples and by appointing William City, a skilled watchcase maker, as a drawer.[14] Nevertheless, the Company felt that it had insufficient powers to enable it to take effective action against the perpetrators of this form of deceit; the only course available was to break the offending articles, but this was considered an inadequate deterrent. The Chancellor of the Exchequer, Nicholas Vansittart, was consulted, but he was unable to help and intimated that a new Act of Parliament would be required to give the Company power to prosecute the culprits. Four years later, in 1816, the advice of the Solicitor General was sought but he was of the same opinion. In the following year the Government was again approached and promise of support was obtained. A draft Bill entitled 'For the better prevention of Frauds and Abuses in the Manufacture of Gold and Silver Wares' was prepared by the Company on behalf of the Government, but for some reason it was never presented to Parliament.

As it was suspected that these abuses might not be restricted to London, several cases were purchased from Coventry, another important watchmaking centre. Some had been hallmarked at the Chester office and others at Birmingham; they all proved to be below standard. The two offices were notified and both were co-operative, recognizing the problem. At the same time George

GOLDSMITHS' HALL,

LONDON.

WHEREAS by several Acts of Parliament, passed for preventing Frauds and Abuses in Gold and Silver Wares, and for preserving the Standards appointed for Wrought Plate, various Penalties of Fine, Forfeiture of Goods, and Imprisonment, are imposed, both against Manufacturers and Shopkeepers, making or selling any Wares inferior to the Standards required, and until the same shall have been to Hall to be marked.

The **WARDENS** of the **GOLDSMITHS' COMPANY** having received Information, that many Offences are committed in violation of existing Laws, **DO HEREBY GIVE NOTICE** to the Trade in General, **AS A CAUTION,** that they are resolved, in discharge of the Duty they owe to the Public, to proceed to the utmost for the Penalties, against every Person who shall infringe any of the Provisions of the Acts now in Force.

The Penalty is **FIFTY POUNDS,** besides Forfeiture of Goods seized, to be recovered in any of the Courts of Law, one Moiety thereof to His Majesty, and the other Moiety, with full Costs of Suit, to the Person who shall sue for the same.

By Order of the Wardens,

JOHN LANE,

JUNE 9, 1821.   CLERK TO THE COMPANY.

E. Butler, Engraver and Printer, Crooked Lane.

A TYPICAL NOTICE, *dated 1821, issued by the Goldsmiths' Company to the trade.*

Miles, now Second Drawer, visited the Birmingham Office and was shown their methods of working. It was becoming increasingly obvious that co-ordination of the practices adopted at the different offices was not only desirable but essential if an effective hallmarking system was to be maintained nationally. Since the offices were managed by separate autonomous governing bodies, meetings between their representatives would have been the most satisfactory way of ensuring this, but in the early 1800s personal contacts between the staff of the offices were extremely sporadic and only became less so when improved means of transport were available later in the century. About two years after the visit of Miles to their office, the Birmingham guardians asked the London wardens if they would receive a deputation to see 'the state and manner in which work was sent to the Hall'. Their local manufacturers had accused them of 'unnecessary vigour'. The deputation, consisting of two guardians and the Assay Master, was duly received in November 1814. Their subsequent report to colleagues in Birmingham referred to the 'handsome manner' in which they had been received by the wardens and the 'polite and friendly disposition manifested by them'. They stated that the only discernible difference between the procedures at the two offices was that base metal tangs to silver knives and forks were allowed at Birmingham and not at London, but as London permitted the slide of pencil cases to be made of base metal they recommended that their own practice should be continued.[15]

ASSESSING THE SKILLS OF THE STAFF

In 1814 it was found necessary to increase the number of assayers to three. Throughout the many volumes of the records there is abundant evidence to be found of the importance attached to the skill and integrity of the assayers. As we have seen, not all of them in the past had been temperamentally suited, but it is obvious from some of the entries in the minute books that the wardens were prepared to go to great lengths to check the qualifications and abilities of those applying for any vacancy. An entry in 1813 is typical:

> The Prime Warden, Mr Warden Brind, Mr Warden Makepeace, Mr Moore and Mr Ritherdon spend the whole day (a Saturday) in the Assay Office making the trial of the fireman (Richard Lee), the only candidate for position of Junior Assayer, and the assays not being ready to be reported until a late hour in the afternoon when they must have used candles in the office, the Committee thought it most proper to postpone further proceed-ings until the Monday morning.

Lee was duly appointed. By reason of his duties as Fireman — or Assayer's Assistant, as the post was sometimes called — he would in any case have already had considerable knowledge of assaying, but the wardens obviously wanted first-hand confirmation. George Miles was subjected to a similar tough practical examination before being appointed Third Assayer in 1822.

Indeed, the Company was concerned to assess the abilities of all staff, not only on their appointment but throughout their subsequent careers. Thus, in 1824 it was decided that there should be an annual test or 'trial' to monitor their skills in assaying and that the wardens should 'have leave to give a premium as an encouragement in their endeavours to become masters of the art'. All members of the staff were expected to learn how to assay, even if this was not their normal work. Between 1830 and 1860 the junior assayers had to take part in the trial as well as the weighers and drawers – only the senior assayers were exempt. On the appointed day the office was closed for normal work and the staff were given several specially prepared samples for determination of fineness. Their results were compared with the figures obtained by both the Senior Assayer and independent private assayers. Afterwards each examinee was given an award of between £2 and £5, depending on his seniority and the accuracy of his results. A surviving notebook kept by a member of the staff shows that in the 1870s three or four practice trials were held each year and that after the trial proper the participants partook of a fish dinner in Billingsgate. They had to wait for about a fortnight before they were summoned by the wardens to hear the results; it must have been an anxious time for them. After the first of these annual 'trials' the special committee appointed to supervise it reported 'much satisfaction in finding all of the assays exceedingly correct, all of them agreeing so nearly with each other as to induce the Committee to be fully satisfied with the result'. The trials were continued on an annual basis until 1919, but after 1900 some of the junior staff were excused.

All the individual assay results reported at these Trials of the Officers, as they were called, are recorded in detail in the minute books. As participants were given samples from the same test pieces they provide a good indication of the accuracy of the methods used as well as the competence of the staff. The results in general show excellent agreement. For silver, only seldom is the difference between the highest and lowest result more than 1 dwt and most are within ½dwt (about 2 parts per thousand), and the results for gold show a similar consistency.[16]

By 1824 the various items of equipment – balances and furnaces in particular – were superior to those used in earlier centuries, and furthermore, the cupellation method was becoming more clearly understood. Nevertheless, assaying was still treated more as an art than a science, although this attitude must have been gradually changing in view of a number of scientific publications on the subject which had appeared during the preceding thirty or so years. That the staff were at pains to improve their knowledge of the technique of assaying is well illustrated by a petition for assistance that was received by the wardens in 1821 from the widow of John Latham, the Fireman or Assayer's Assistant:

> ... For some time previous to his decease he had expended various sums of money in attending lectures on Chymistry and trying experiments in the art of assaying metals with the view (as your petitioner is persuaded) of rendering himself useful in any superior situation which he might at a future period be appointed. Which with the expenses of his late illness precluded the possibility of making any savings out of his income.

The change in attitude towards the practice of assaying was not universally shared. Even thirty-five years after Latham's death a former Prime Warden, James Garrard, giving evidence to a Select Committee of the House of Commons and replying to the question as to whether any considerable amount of chemical knowledge was required of an assayer, answered 'No, practical skill rather than chemical knowledge. A man arrives at results without knowing exactly why.' But James Garrard was not an assayer and not everyone would have agreed with his remarks. In a memorandum written for an earlier Select Committee in 1837 Robert Bingley, the King's Assay Master at the Mint, stated 'It [assaying] is from first to last a chemical operation and demands an acquaintance, both theoretically and practically, with chemistry generally.'[17]

Some two years after this pronouncement a junior member of the Assay Office staff showed that he had some scientific interest exceeding the minimum required in his immediate employment. He was Thomas Hough, who had served an apprenticeship as a silversmith before being appointed a drawer in 1835. After learning to assay he wrote to the wardens in 1839 to report that he had made a number of experiments on samples of gold alloyed with iridium; and he thanked the wardens for the encouragement they had given him.[18] Iridium was a relatively new metal (one of the platinum group) which had been discovered in 1804. Hough described the colours of the alloys and referred to a method of assaying them. This piece of research is remarkable considering his early background. But promotion was slow; he had to wait until 1863 before reaching the status of Assayer. Hough's research and the earlier endeavours of Latham demonstrate a commendable show of enthusiasm by members of the staff, who well knew that promotion was strictly a matter of 'dead men's shoes'.

COMPANY'S ENGRAVERS

In recounting the above we have moved forward about twenty years. In the interim Edward Witham had succeeded Walter Coles as Deputy Warden in 1813, followed in turn by John Barrow and Benjamin Preston, who served until 1834. Witham, Barrow and Preston had each been Senior Assayer before their final promotion. At this juncture the wardens had serious doubts about

HALLMARK FOR *1810, the punches for which were made by John Pingo. The maker's mark is that of Paul Storr.*

the wisdom of the automatic appointment of the Senior Assayer to fill the vacancy caused by the death or retirement of the Deputy Warden, which had been the established practice for the past fifty years. The next appointee, Josiah Sharp, was from outside the Office.

Further changes had occurred in 1815 with the ending of the association with the Pingo family – father and son – engravers of the punches for sixty-one years. When John Pingo resigned owing to failing eyesight his long service was duly recognized by a continued annual payment of £200, equivalent to full salary. He lived for another twelve years – probably longer than had been bargained for. Like his father he had been Mint Engraver and no doubt would have received a pension from that source as well. John Smith, who had been employed as assistant to Pingo, was now appointed Engraver to the Company.

In 1819 the Court of Assistants convened a special committee to consider the difference in the manner in which private assays were reported by the Assay Office and the Mint. The Mint reports were corrected for cupellation losses whereas it is probable the Assay Office still reported their results as found. In the event it was decided to stop receiving private assays altogether, thus ending a service that had been provided since the fifteenth century. Formerly the by-assays, as they were once called, had been a substantial part of the work of the Office and an extra source of income.

In the same year the Clerk, Thomas Lane, was asked to monitor the progress of an application to Parliament from silversmiths in Glasgow who wished to have an assay office in that city. No objection appears to have been raised by the Company and the office was established;[19] it was closed in 1964. In 1820 Thomas Lane was succeeded by his son John, who was simultaneously appointed Accountant in the Assay Office and thus responsible for collecting the duty.

The fortunes of the silver trade had declined since the exceptionally good years between 1809 to 1811 and in consequence the Assay Office was sustaining a loss of about £1000 a year – a substantial sum considering the turnover was

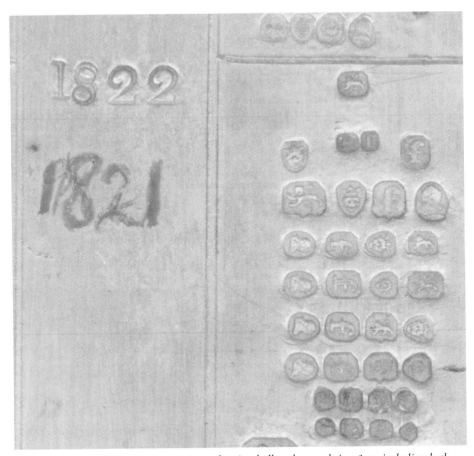

DETAIL OF AN ASSAY OFFICE PLATE *showing hallmarks struck in 1821, including both crowned and uncrowned leopards' heads.*

only about £4000. In 1820 it was decided that marking charges would have to be increased. A petition received in the same year from John Smith, the Engraver, asking for a review of his salary was not welcomed. He reminded the Court that he was now supplying nearly five hundred punches annually, and he could not resist mentioning another matter, which obviously rankled, namely that his predecessor, John Pingo, was allowed a seat at livery dinners, a privilege that had never been granted to him.

Whether or not Smith was successful in his appeal is not clear but we do know that in the following year he was instructed to produce new designs for the marks of the leopard's head and lion passant. A few trial punches were made in combination with the date letter for 1821 and used during part of the year for marking spoons. Then in May 1822 all the existing punches were destroyed and replaced by new ones incorporating the modified designs. The main change was that the crown on the leopard's head, which had been a feature of the mark since 1478, was omitted. At the same time the form of the standard mark for sterling silver was altered from a 'lion passant guardant' to a 'lion passant'; that is the head of the lion instead of turning towards the beholder was now pointing straight ahead. The records give no specific reason for re-designing the marks, but the most likely explanation is that it was to discourage counterfeiting, which was causing concern at the time.

The need to strengthen existing hallmarking legislation was still apparent and in 1828 an initiative came from the Commissioners of Stamps, whose interest stemmed from their responsibility for the duty on silver. The Commissioners had several years earlier asked the Company for a copy of the draft Bill of 1817, the contents of which they incorporated in a new measure designed to consolidate and amend the various Acts then in force. When asked for its views the Company responded by appointing a special committee, which two influential members of the trade were asked to join. One was Edmund Waller Rundell, of Rundell, Bridge and Rundell, the celebrated Royal Goldsmiths, who dominated the London trade in the early nineteenth century. The other was William, the son of Jonathan and Ann Bateman and grandson of Hester Bateman. He had taken over the flourishing business in Bunhill Row in 1814 and had just handed over to his son. The committee approved the proposed Bill with certain amendments but like many earlier ones it never reached the statute book.

However, in spite of its shortcomings the law had plenty of teeth where forgery was concerned. In 1829, John Brown of Liverpool who was prosecuted at Lancaster Assizes for counterfeiting the lion passant mark on wedding rings, was convicted and sentenced to fourteen years' transportation. A few years later the guardians of the Birmingham Assay Office mounted a successful prosecution for fraud, where the defendant had obtained money on a watch bearing forged London marks. It was agreed that the Company would pay £50 towards their legal costs which amounted to £91 10s 2d.

NEW TRIAL PLATES

By 1829 it was known that the silver trial plate then in use – made in 1728 – was slightly above the correct fineness, although of course it was still the legal standard for the Trial of the Pyx (see page 198). The Company was asked by the Treasury to provide a replacement and additionally a new gold plate. For the first time the directions included the stipulation that close contact was to be maintained with the officers of the Mint 'so as to ensure by the joint endeavours of all the most experienced persons employed in the assay of metals both at the Mint and in the employment of the Company the greatest accuracy as to the requisite degree of fineness according to the standard established by law... ' Otherwise the procedure was the same as in the past. A jury of thirteen members of the Company was appointed. Included with

George Miles of the Assay Office were three other assayers of eminence: John Johnson, the son of the founder of the company in Maiden Lane, and his own two sons George Richard and Percival Norton who had six years earlier left the firm and started his own business.[20]

As in 1728 the plates were made on a 'trial and error' basis, the ultimate proof of successful alloying being based on the results of assays. John Johnson's bill for work carried out includes an item 'For accurately preparing standard pieces from perfectly fine gold and silver for assaying the trial plates against'. It seems therefore that standard alloys were used as checks when assaying the plates.

The assays of the gold ingot after the first melting were too low, so more fine gold had to be added. When all the assayers were satisfied the jury took the silver and gold ingots to the Mint where the King's Assayer, Robert Bingley, removed samples. He later reported that the ingots were satisfactory and the jury proceeded to have them 'flatted' (rolled) and planished. After being re-assayed and found to be correct they were taken to the Mint for approval. But Bingley now reported that the two opposite ends of the silver plate did not agree in fineness. It was therefore decided that the plate should be melted with the addition of two Spanish dollars (the significance of which is obscure). Bingley also thought that there was a slight error in the gold plate, so it was decided that it too should be re-melted.

The silver ingot was still not satisfactory, so fresh metals were obtained and the whole operation repeated from scratch. The new ingots were then taken to the Mint as before. Bingley accepted the silver but would not approve the gold ingot: it was now October and the jury had begun their task in April. The gold plate was re-melted and after both ingots had been flatted it was arranged that the two resulting plates would be thoroughly tested in the Assay Office on 31 October. The whole day was devoted to making numerous assays and it was unanimously agreed that the plates were correct. Finally having been passed by the Mint assayers the gold plate was cut into twelve portions and the silver into fifteen, all of which were engraved and delivered to the Treasury in January 1830 with the jury's verdict. They were received by the Duke of Wellington in his capacity as First Lord. Portions of the plates were distributed to the Mint, the East India Company and each of the assay offices. It is of interest that samples taken from the plates were sent to the Mints in Paris and Amsterdam, whose reports confirmed they were of the correct fineness.

This account has been given in some detail as it shows the great care that was taken by the jury, as well as demonstrating the difficulty involved in producing a satisfactory trial plate of sterling silver. We shall see that, even with advancing metallurgical knowledge, similar problems were encountered when replacement plates were made in 1873 and 1900. Recent assays of a surviving portion show that the average silver content of the 1829 plate is close to sterling. The gold plate is, however, slightly below the true standard.

PERCIVAL NORTON JOHNSON, *1792–1866. This portrait (by G.J. Robertson, owned by Johnson Matthey plc) shows him reading an assay report dated 1830 and wearing a chain made from platinum he had refined.*

There is a footnote to the above. Percival Norton Johnson's charges for the work he had undertaken were considered by the jury to be too high and when he finally submitted a bill for £10 10s, he attached a covering letter addressed to the Clerk:

> Sir, I herewith send my account altered as considered best by the Jury. I cannot (after the observations made yesterday) refrain from observing (let the opinions of others be what they may) the charges I make will very badly remunerate me for the time and attention I have devoted to the business.

However, as we shall see, the slight disagreement did not deter this talented man from offering his services to the Company on many occasions in the years to come. His diverse business ventures included the management of several tin and lead mines in Cornwall, but his main achievement was undoubtedly the founding in 1822 of the firm in Hatton Garden that is now Johnson, Matthey & Company Ltd.[21] The assaying of bullion and ores was the mainstay of Johnson's new enterprise which also embraced the refining of gold, silver and platinum. In 1838 he took George Matthey as his apprentice, later making him a partner.[22] The business progressively expanded and became the principal supplier in Great Britain of precious and rare metals, with worldwide interests. Both of these brilliant men were Fellows of the Royal Society and highly respected in scientific circles. Johnson became Prime Warden in 1852, Matthey in 1872 and again in 1894. Their advice on Assay Office matters was frequently sought by the Company and freely given.

CHAPTER ELEVEN

TECHNICAL ADVANCES
1830 to 1914

T HE COMPANY had been pursuing a policy of strict economy since the
turn of the century, partly so that it could give money 'in aid of the
exigencies of the State' during the Napoleonic wars and partly because
it was determined that its charitable activities should not be diminished. The
upkeep of the Hall had been badly neglected in consequence. A building fund
was established, which by 1829 was sufficient for a new Hall to be planned on a
grand scale. The old structure was demolished but it was not until 1835 that the
new one was completed on the same site. In the meantime the Assay Office
had to move into rented accommodation close at hand in Aldermanbury. It
continued to operate smoothly in its temporary home, apart from a minor fire
which occurred one morning in July 1830 and was soon extinguished.

The new Hall was built in neo-classical style to the plans of the celebrated
architect Philip Hardwick, who was the Company's surveyor. It was officially
opened on 15 July 1835 at a special dinner attended by many distinguished
guests, including the Duke of Wellington and Sir Robert Peel. The building,
which now covered an area of about half an acre, was extravagantly praised by
the guest speakers. Before the rooms allocated to the Assay Office at the rear
of the Hall were occupied, opportunity was taken to replace some of the old
equipment such as marking presses and associated tools at a cost of £476. A
suggestion that gas should be installed, 'given the inconvenience arising from
the use of oil and candles' was approved; the cost of laying down gas pipes in
the Assay Office came to only £6. Gas was not yet used for the assay furnaces,
which continued to be fired with charcoal and later with coke.

Living accommodation for the Clerk, the Deputy Warden and two assayers
was provided in the new Hall. Most of the working population of London
still dwelt at or close to their place of employment although this was
beginning to change with the advent of the railways. An interesting reflection
on the unhealthy living conditions in London at this time is a decision of the

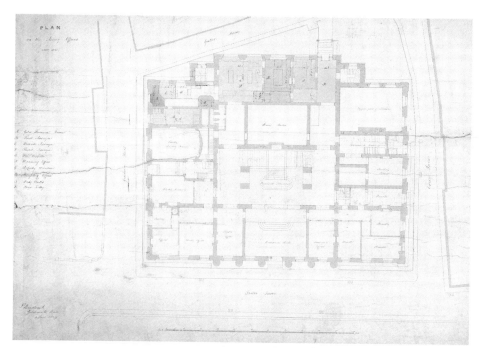

wardens, made several years after the opening of the Hall, to allow the two senior assayers – then Jeremiah Fuller[1] and William City – to vacate their official accommodation and reside out of town. They had complained of their 'altered state of health' since occupying their present residences, which they attributed to the confined state of their rooms and want of regular exercise. At a meeting in April 1840 the wardens recommended 'their special wishes be complied with and an allowance of £50 made to each.' The minute continues:

> In justification the wardens beg to remind the Court how highly important it is to the regular discharge of the duties of the assayers that not only should their health have the greatest care but that their minds should come to business free from anxiety and as much as possible capable of resisting the bad effects of the fumes of the Assay Office. They regret that such is not the case at present with Mr Fuller whose constitution is already much impaired … Mr City who is advancing in years and of nervous habit and whose health is also much affected from similar causes would be equally benefited by a change.

Fuller took up residence in Islington and on receipt of a doctor's letter saying that the walk to work would 'lend greatly to keep him in good health', the Company agreed that the arrangement should be permanent. William City, however, did not take advantage of the offer.

REGULATIONS FOR THE ASSAY OFFICE

The wardens felt that with the building of the new Hall it was an opportune time to review the way in which the Assay Office was managed. A thorough enquiry was instituted; every member of the staff was re-appraised and a comprehensive list of rules comprising twenty-two paragraphs was issued. These referred to the duties of the staff, hours of work, directions about sampling and other matters; many were repetitions of former regulations but they are of interest as they provide a good indication of the modus operandi of the Office.

Manufacturers had to bring their work between eight and nine o'clock in the morning and three furnaces had to be prepared ready for the assays. Samples were to be passed to the assayers under a number without divulging the name of the sender. New instructions included one which debarred strangers or visitors from entering the Assay Office on any pretext whatever. The Deputy Warden was made personally responsible for the safekeeping of the punches and for ensuring they were perfect and free from dirt. He was also required to see that the presses were properly set and in good order. The continued efficiency of the Office was considered to be of paramount importance.

WATERCOLOUR PERSPECTIVE *of the third Goldsmiths' Hall c.1830 and (above) a ground plan of the building, c.1840. The Assay Office is shaded.*

JOSIAH SHARP, *Deputy Warden 1834–79.*

At the same time the wardens made recommendations for the retirement of Benjamin Preston the Deputy Warden who was now at an advanced age after forty-two years' service in the Assay Office. They suggested his replacement should be someone from outside the Office, preferably aged between 25 and 45. Although having great respect for the skill of George Miles, the Senior Assayer, who under normal circumstances would have been next in line, they decided not to appoint him. In any case his health may not have been good as he died two years later. In May 1834 four candidates were examined for their knowledge of accounts and their familiarity with the methods used in the manufacture of silverware; experience of the silversmithing trade was still considered an essential requirement. The candidate chosen was Josiah Sharp, Superintendent of the Art Department at the firm of Rundell, Bridge & Rundell, the Royal Goldsmiths. He was by far the youngest man to have held the post and he served for the next forty-five years. Other members of the staff were also still recruited exclusively from the trade – in 1835, for example, there were vacancies for two drawers; of the ten candidates interviewed four were plateworkers and six watchcase makers, all between the ages of twenty-three and thirty.

The total number of staff in that year remained at eleven. This does not include the Engraver, John Smith, who although holding an official position was employed on a part-time basis only. His eyesight was failing and the wardens were not at all satisfied with his work. Present-day collectors of antique silver may have noticed the poor designs of the marks of the leopard's head and lion passant at this period. Smith had blotted his copybook in 1833 when he made exactly the same mistake as his predecessor forty years earlier. When the newly elected wardens examined the punches which he handed to them on the day they took office in May of that year, they found that the date letter was a capital 'S', not a lower case 's' as it should have been. There was no time to remedy the mistake. The wardens felt that Smith should be replaced and soon afterwards they approached William Wyon, Engraver at the Mint; but after receiving a long and earnest appeal from Smith they relented and he was allowed to remain in the post. Six years later, however, the wardens commissioned both men to make a sample punch of the duty mark (head of Queen Victoria). On comparing the impressions they found Wyon's to be

HALLMARK FOR 1839, *the punches for which were made by John Smith, Engraver 1815–39.*

HALLMARK FOR 1840. *The greatly improved punches for these marks were made by William Wyon, Engraver 1839–51.*

much the better. He was duly appointed the Company's Engraver, Smith being awarded a generous pension.

Wyon was indeed a great artist but he had the advantage of the use of a new piece of equipment, known as a reducing machine, which had been bought by the Mint from a firm in Paris and had been used by him in cutting the master dies for the first Victorian coinage. Operating on the pantograph principle, it allowed the use of a large model which was reduced down to the size required. In making the punch for the duty mark Wyon may well have taken advantage of the model he had used for the coinage since the profiled head of the young Queen Victoria is similar on both. He also re-designed the leopard's head and lion passant marks, greatly improving them. The Company was well pleased with his work and he continued as Engraver until his death in 1851 when he was succeeded by his son, Leonard Charles Wyon.[2]

THE 1842 AND 1844 ACTS

In 1842 representatives of the Manufacturing Silversmiths' Society met the Company to express their apprehension about an anticipated reduction in the import duties on gold and silver wares.[3] There was no provision in law for the hallmarking of imported articles and the British manufacturers feared unfair competition from a flood of foreign goods of inferior standard. The Government was sympathetic and a clause in the Customs Act 1842 made imported wares – both silver and gold – liable to assay and hallmarking and subject to the same standards as wares made in the United Kingdom.[4] The marks were to be identical to those already in use except that the 'maker's mark' became that of the importer. The same exemptions were to apply as for British wares with an additional category, namely foreign articles of an ornamental kind made before 1800.[5]

We have seen that several attempts to strengthen the hallmarking law in the first half of the century had failed but the year 1844 saw the introduction of important new legislation which was based on a draft Bill prepared by the Company and submitted to the government. The Gold and Silver Wares Act 1844 was mainly concerned with offences and the penalties for infringements.[6] Under its provisions forgery and transposition of hallmarks still carried a maximum penalty of fourteen years' transportation. However, the Act extended the law by defining several additional offences, for example changing the character of a hallmarked article or adding to it without the consent of an Assay Office. Possibly the main intention was to ensure that the appropriate duty was paid if substantial additions of silver were made to an article or if its character were materially changed. But the eventual effect was to prove of considerable benefit to members of the buying public, especially purchasers of antique silver, since it made a dealer liable to penalties if he sold a hallmarked article which had been altered without the sanction of an assay office. Anyone wishing to alter a hallmarked article had not only to obtain permission, but also had to submit it to an assay office after the alteration. Providing the character was not changed and the addition or additions were not greater than one third of the weight of the original article, only the addition(s) had to be assayed and hallmarked. In this case the old hallmark could remain and duty would only have to be paid in respect of the weight of the addition(s). On the other hand, should the addition(s) be greater than one third of the weight of the article, or if the character of the article were changed the whole article had to be re-hallmarked and duty paid on its total weight. If, for example, a coffee pot had been made by refashioning a hallmarked tankard, it was to be treated by the Assay Office as if it were a new ware. In this way the integrity of old hallmarks was preserved.

Following a suggestion by the Birmingham Assay Office opportunity was also

HALLMARK ON STAFF *for the office of Gold Stick, for five hundred years a ceremonial post of the sovereign's guard, showing the 'sun in splendour' mark, signifying 22 carat gold.*

taken to bring the marks for 22 carat gold into line with those prescribed for 18 carat. Previously, the standard mark for 22 carat articles had been identical to that used on silver – the lion passant. According to the Act the standard was now to be identified by a crown and the figure '22' – a sensible change and one which was long overdue. Since 29 May 1816 the Assay Office had been striking an extra unofficial mark, a 'sun in splendour', on some 22 carat articles to differentiate them from silver-gilt wares. It was now no longer necessary.

Earlier statutes made the Company liable to penalties if substandard articles were hallmarked, but the 1844 Act went further in stating that if any assayer or other employee hallmarked an article of base metal he could, on information made to a Justice of the Peace by an officer of Stamp Duties, be dismissed and barred from employment at any assay office. Since base metal was defined in the act as any metal other than gold or silver of one of the legal standards, the offences could apply even if the article was only slightly below the minimum standard. According to the original Bill the provincial offices were to be subject to the surveillance of the Goldsmiths' Company as regards such offences but predictably they were not slow to object to this intrusion.[7] William Gladstone, who as President of the Board of Trade had introduced the Bill, was at first not disposed to give way, but in the end the power was given to the

Commissioners of Stamps and Taxes. Thus all assay offices were placed on an equal footing.

Apart from the sections dealing with forgery, which were repealed by the Forgery Act 1913, and the amending of the penalty of transportation to one of imprisonment (in 1864), the whole of the 1844 Act remained in force until 1975. It was not, however, by any means a comprehensive revision of the hallmarking law; most of the old legislation, with its many anomalies, was unaltered.

THE PRIDEAUX FAMILY

Five years later the Company faced a potential threat to its own authority. In 1849 a Royal Commission was appointed to advise on the constitution and administration of the Mint, which thirty-nine years earlier had moved out of the Tower to purpose-built premises on an adjacent site. In the course of a thorough enquiry, a suggestion was made that the London Assay Office should also be moved to the Mint building. Evidence was taken from William Bateman (Warden), John Lane (Clerk) and Josiah Sharp (Deputy Warden), who between them gave a detailed description of the hallmarking system. William Bateman stated that when the Hall had been re-built it had been decided that it should be at the centre of the trade. (By the time the Royal Commission was held many craftsmen had in fact established their workshops in Clerkenwell, but this was still reasonably close to the Hall.) The Commissioners accepted the view that to transfer the Assay Office to the Mint would seriously inconvenience the trade and in their final report recommended no change either in the location or the administration of the Assay Office.[8]

In 1851 the Clerk, John Lane, died and his place was taken by Walter Prideaux, who had assisted him for many years in his practice as a solicitor. Three subsequent generations of the Prideaux family, all eldest sons named Walter, held the position. They rendered distinguished service to the Company over a period spanning 123 years.[9] In addition to their many responsibilities as Clerk, they were frequently called upon as the Company's solicitors to advise on the legal aspects of hallmarking and to initiate proceedings against offenders. Sir Walter Sherburne Prideaux, Clerk from 1882 to 1919, was influential in obtaining a number of amendments to the hallmarking laws, including the provisions in the Revenue Act 1883 which made the Customs authorities responsible for ensuring that all gold and silver wares imported for sale in this country were sent to an assay office. Assistance with the framing of legislation for marking watchcases was another of his concerns. He also frequently reminded the wardens of the necessity of ensuring that adequate facilities were made available so that the Company could fulfil its hallmarking obligations – especially at a time of increased workloads. Much of the credit is due to him for the successful outcome of two important legal cases which will be referred to later – Goldsmiths' Company v Wyatt and Fabergé v Goldsmiths' Company – as well as for satisfactory results in a number of prosecutions for serious hallmarking offences.

NEW STANDARDS FOR GOLD

In 1846 the Company was asked by the Committee of the Privy Council for Trade to give an opinion on petitions which had been received from watch and watchcase makers in Birmingham and Coventry requesting a lower minimum standard for gold articles. The petitioners had stated that their trade with the United States was confined to watch movements only, because they were not permitted to supply cases of a lower standard than 18 carat as desired by their customers. The French and Swiss – the main competitors of the British – were not restricted in this way. The Company consulted the London watch and watchcase makers who were strongly opposed to the proposal, maintaining that the watch trade was 'in as flourishing state as has been known for some years' and suggesting that if a lower standard were to be permitted the hallmarks should be restricted to the Birmingham and Chester Offices.

No immediate action was taken by the government; but four years later the Council for Trade received a further petition from the Coventry makers, which was followed this time by powerful lobbying by watchmakers from Liverpool, the other important provincial centre for the industry, with extensive overseas markets. The members of the London watch trade again objected, on the grounds that any lowering of the standard would be detrimental to the high prestige throughout the world, not only of the British watch trade but also of the London hallmark. However, they now shifted their ground slightly by saying that should a lower standard be permitted they would not wish to be precluded from using it. The Company naturally supported the London trade but the government nevertheless agreed to meet the request of the provincial watchmakers. The resulting Gold and Silver Wares Act 1854, made it lawful for Her Majesty to authorize lower standards for gold (down to 8 carats) by Order in Council.[10] Such an Order, passed in December of the same year, provided for additional standards of 15, 12 and 9 carat.

Although it was watchmakers who had pressed for the change, the new legal standards were not confined solely to watchcases – they applied to all gold wares. In the long run this resulted in the operation of Gresham's Law – wares of the lower standards driving out the higher. At first, few items under 18 carat were submitted for hallmarking: in the twelve months May 1855 to May 1856 the total weight of articles of the three lower standards was only 4032 oz, compared with 39,692 oz of 18 and 22 carat, or 9 per cent of the total. Even forty years later this figure had increased to only 11 per cent, but by 1912 it had risen to 56 per cent, and by 1975 over 80 per cent by weight of all gold wares submitted were of the 9 carat standard.

According to the Order in Council of 1854, wares of the new standards were to be marked with the carat number and its decimal equivalent – eg 9 carat was hallmarked '9' and '.375'. The crown mark was reserved for 18 and 22 carat, although its use was eventually extended to all standards by the Hallmarking Act 1973. The introduction of the three additional standards naturally complicated the work of the Assay Office to some extent, in that many more punches were required and separate diets had to be kept for the annual trial. But since the silver trade was not unduly buoyant at the time it was not necessary to employ extra staff.

The Act of 1854 contained another provision, not related to the standard. When the Birmingham and Sheffield Assay Offices were established in 1773 they were each given a monopoly to assay all plate made within a radius of twenty miles. The Glasgow and Edinburgh Offices enjoyed a similar monopoly but in their case extending to the whole of Scotland. This did not suit all manufacturers and when the Coventry watchcase makers petitioned for a lowering of the standard for gold they also asked for a change in the law so that they could submit work to the London Assay Office. As might be expected, the Company intimated that it was not averse to this proposal and in consequence Section 2 of the Act enabled all workers and dealers to register their marks at any assay office or offices of their choice.

PROVINCIAL ASSAY OFFICES

For several years members of the London trade had been drawing the Company's attention to the supposed inefficiency of some of the other assay offices. At that time there were offices in Birmingham, Sheffield, Chester, Exeter, Newcastle, York, Edinburgh, Glasgow and Dublin.[11] Although their workloads were comparatively small, the London manufacturers nevertheless thought that laxity at some of them was affecting their own trade. A number of silver watchcases which had been marked at Chester between 1841 and 1846 were sent to the Company. The wires were found to be well below standard and a report was sent to the Commissioners of Stamps who instituted proceedings against the Chester Assay Office. But as there was no witness to corroborate the assay results, the charge was withdrawn.

Another petition was received by the Company in November 1849, this time from London spoon and fork manufacturers, suggesting that the provincial offices should be closed. On this occasion the Company forwarded the petition to the Treasury. The Chancellor of the Exchequer, after receiving yet further complaints from the London trade, responded by ordering a tour of inspection of the English provincial and Scottish offices by William Garnett, the Inspector-General of Stamps and Taxes. This took place in 1851 and Garnett was accompanied unofficially by the Prime Warden, James Garrard, a former partner in the family firm which had been appointed Royal Goldsmiths some twenty years earlier, and Percival Norton Johnson, who was serving as Third Warden. All three formed an unfavourable impression of some of the English offices, particularly Exeter, Newcastle and York, but were complimentary about those at Birmingham and Sheffield. Garrard and Johnson expressed the view that all the provincial offices in England except Birmingham and Sheffield should be closed and that the work at Glasgow should be transferred to Edinburgh. They also recommended that Goldsmiths' Hall in London should be considered the 'parent' Hall and that the Company should have some connection with or control over the Birmingham and Sheffield offices.

Nothing was done until 1855 when the Treasury was again approached on the matter, this time by the Commissioners of Inland Revenue. As a result, in June of that year a Bill to abolish the assay offices at York, Exeter, Chester and Newcastle was introduced in the House of Commons. In support of the Bill the report of William Garnett was submitted to the House, as were the petition from the London spoon and fork manufacturers together with relevant extracts from the memorandum of Garrard and Johnson. But the provincial assay offices concerned had not been consulted; as soon as they had been alerted they were quick to protest. Their delegations were favourably received by the Chancellor of the Exchequer and the Bill was subsequently withdrawn. However, the York office closed within five years through lack of work, followed by Newcastle and Exeter later in the century. Chester survived until 1962 and Glasgow finally ceased to operate two years after that.

Notwithstanding the withdrawal of the Bill, in the following year (1856) a Select Committee of the House of Commons was appointed to enquire into the operation of all the assay offices in the United Kingdom. Evidence was taken from a large number of witnesses. They included William Garnett, James Garrard, Walter Prideaux (the Clerk), Josiah Sharp (the Deputy Warden) and Jeremiah Fuller (the Senior Assayer). Evidence was produced to show that substandard wares had been hallmarked at both the Chester and Exeter offices. The proceedings of the Committee were published in full and they include many searching questions put to the representatives of both the provincial offices and the Company.[12] A minority of the members of the Committee thought that hallmarking was unnecessary but most of the witnesses appearing for the trade strongly supported it. In its final report the Select Committee did not suggest any drastic change in the system but stated:

Your Committee find that those offices in which a larger amount of assaying is performed are conducted in a satisfactory manner; while the smaller offices are, generally speaking, in an inefficient condition ... ' The report also contained the following passage: 'Your Committee are of the opinion that the practice of assaying (hallmarking) is calculated to afford protection to the public against fraud, and ought to be maintained ... strongly recommend that the several Statutes by which the assay offices are now governed should be repealed, with a view to removing the anomalies and confusion of the existing law by consolidating into one Statute all the provisions requisite ...

A draft Bill in line with this proposal was prepared in the following year by the Commissioners of Inland Revenue but it was never laid before Parliament; more than a hundred years were to elapse before the Committee's recommendation was put into effect.

The Select Committee also recommended that under a new statute there should be provision to open new offices if required and to close any office where the amount of work was insufficient to support it, or where the work was inadequately performed. Much of the evidence given to the Committee related to the activities of the provincial offices, but there were, however, some interesting observations about a new method of assaying silver which had been developed in France some sixteen years earlier.

THE GAY-LUSSAC METHOD

A truly scientific investigation into the fire-assay (cupellation) method for silver had been carried out in the years 1760–63. The results were published in the *Mémoires de l'Académie des Sciences* in a series of papers by Matthieu Tillet, who, in collaboration with J. Hellot, had undertaken this research at the request of the French government. They confirmed that silver is lost during cupellation and that small amounts of lead and copper are retained in the silver bead. They also showed that certain factors could influence these errors, such as furnace temperature and condition of the cupels. In spite of its inherent disadvantages, however, no attempt was made to find an alternative to the fire-assay method until 1830. In that year the French government, being concerned about possible financial losses in the minting of silver coinage due to uncertainties in the results of assays, set up a Royal Commission to consider the matter. The Commission confirmed that fire-assaying gave results which were appreciably lower than the true values and recommended the adoption of an entirely novel method, specially devised for the purpose by the brilliant chemist Joseph Louis Gay-Lussac, who had been working closely with the Paris Assay Office.[13] His procedure was based on a relatively new technique – volumetric analysis. It was often referred to as the 'wet' or 'humid' mode. A weighed portion of the sample was dissolved in nitric acid and a standard solution of sodium chloride added from a burette until precipitation of silver chloride was complete. The 'end-point' was reached when no further precipitation occurred on subsequent addition. The fineness of the sample was calculated from the volume added. The sodium chloride solution was standardized by titration against fine silver in the same manner.[14] In the method as originally published a sample weight of 2 g was specified, but satisfactory results can be obtained using much smaller amounts.

The Gay-Lussac method was widely adopted in France. In Britain, however, it was not at first accepted, assayers preferring the time-honoured procedure with which they no doubt felt more at home. At the Parliamentary Enquiry held in 1856 a Frenchman, Frederick Claudet, who had been practising as a private assayer in London for five years, gave his opinion on the benefits of the wet method, but others, including the Assay Master at the Mint, affirmed that the fire-assay was superior. The new method was eventually adopted at the London Mint in 1900.

Although not taking advantage of the Gay-Lussac method for many years the Company was well aware of its possibilities from the time it was published in France. In 1835 Percival Johnson accompanied by George Miles, the Senior Assayer, visited the Paris Assay Office (Bureau de Garantie) and the French Mint to see the process in operation.[15] They came to the conclusion that it would be too slow for routine assaying at the Hall, but Johnson recommended to the wardens that it would be desirable to purchase the necessary equipment as it might prove useful in cases of dispute. His suggestion appears not to have been taken up until 1884 when the apparatus was installed. The cupellation procedure, however, continued to be used for routine assays until 1922 when it was superseded by the Gay-Lussac method, which in the meantime had been considerably enhanced by the use of a special type of pipette made to the design of J.S. Stas, a distinguished Belgian chemist.

In order to achieve high accuracy it had become routine practice by the middle of the nineteenth century to include with every batch of silver assays a sample – known as a check or proof – taken from a trial piece of exactly sterling standard. When a trial piece had been expended samples from its replacement were sent for verification to the two principal trade assayers – Johnson & Matthey and Johnson & Sons – as well as to the Mint. Two other private assayers were also called upon from time to time for the same purpose – Frederick Claudet and W. H. Makins. For further confirmation of the correctness of the trial piece, samples were sometimes submitted to the Paris Mint, where the volumetric method was used, with results reported in parts per thousand. Incidentally, the millesimal system was not officially adopted by the Company until 1904, after which date it was generally recognized by the trade; for internal use, however, it had been increasingly used in the Assay Office for some years.

By the middle of the nineteenth century, due to improvements in the design of furnaces and the routine use of check assays, the cupellation or fire-assay procedure in the hands of a skilled assayer was probably almost as accurate as the new volumetric method. However, the latter technique had the great advantage that it was less empirical and less dependent on the level of skill of the operator. It should be emphasized that we are referring only to the assaying of silver. Gold was, and still is to this day, assayed by the traditional procedure. For this metal the cupellation method is extremely accurate; there is indeed no better one known.

NEW STAFF

In 1859 the Court felt that the staff of the Assay Office needed strengthening and Percival Johnson was asked if he could suggest someone with experience in assaying. Seven years earlier, Johnson & Matthey had been appointed Assayers to the Bank of England. Four such appointments had been made following the discovery of goldfields in Australia, the products of which had to come to England for refining.[16] As a result of the appointment Johnson & Matthey had been obliged to expand their own assay facilities. At the same time, their equipment had been modernized under George Matthey's direction. We may be sure therefore that their establishment was conducted with great efficiency. Now Johnson recommended the wardens to appoint Henry Matthey, a cousin of George Matthey, to assist the Senior Assayer at the Hall. Henry Matthey,

GEORGE MATTHEY, *1825–1913. Matthey joined P.N. Johnson as an apprentice at the age of thirteen. He became an influential member of Goldsmiths' Company and served as Prime Warden in 1872 and 1894.*

WILLIAM ROBINSON, *Deputy Warden 1879–97.*

who was then aged thirty, had been working as an assayer at Johnson & Matthey for some years and no doubt his arrival at the Assay Office ensured that advantage was taken of the latest improvements in technique and equipment.[17]

In the same year (1859) it was agreed that the staff should be further strengthened by the appointment of an assistant for the Deputy Warden. The successful candidate, William Robinson, aged twenty-eight, was thoroughly acquainted with the manufacture of gold and silver plate, having served an apprenticeship and worked in the manufactory of Messrs Garrard, where his father was employed for thirty-four years. As Sharp was permitted to reside away from the Hall owing to his poor health Robinson took over his accommodation – but if Robinson thought he would soon succeed Sharp he was to be disappointed as he had to wait another twenty years! He eventually became Deputy Warden in 1879.

Owing to illness, the two senior assayers – Fuller (aged sixty-six) and William Smith (aged sixty-nine) – were retired on full salary in 1863. Henry Matthey was promoted to Head Assayer and Percival Johnson, now living in Devon, again came to the help of the Company by providing an assistant for him. He recommended the appointment of Benjamin Charles Staples, who had been employed by Johnson & Matthey in Hatton Garden for twenty-three years and was then head of their assay department. Staples no doubt provided a further beneficial injection of expertise from outside the Office, although his appointment by the Company may have been resented by some of the existing staff, since it would have adversely affected their promotion prospects. He had compiled a book of assayers' tables for converting assay reports from the traditional 'better or worse' system to the millesimal notation. The tables were subsequently published by Johnson, Matthey & Co. in 1865 and were highly valued. Staples died in 1872 and Henry Matthey in 1878.

George Matthey, by then head of the firm, was elected a member of the Court of Assistants in 1865. He was subsequently asked for advice concerning the Assay Office on numerous occasions. The verification of new trial plates was carried out under his supervision in 1873 and again in 1900; he was also for many years chairman of the committee for the Trial of the Diet, even as late as 1910, when eighty-five years old. In another sphere, it was due largely to his influence that the Company in 1908 resolved to endow a Readership in Metallurgy at the University of Cambridge – a decision that was to have beneficial consequences for the Assay Office. Dr Charles Thomas Heycock, the first Reader, was elected to the Court of the Company in 1913 and became Prime Warden in 1922.[18] Heycock's achievements as a pioneer in the field of non-ferrous physical metallurgy were many, but it is not so well known that in 1902 he applied for the vacant post of Chemist and Assayer (King's Assay Master) at the Royal Mint. To improve his chances of obtaining the position George Matthey arranged for him to spend some time in his firm's assay laboratory. He did not in fact obtain the post but returned to Cambridge to resume his researches on alloy systems in collaboration with F.H. Neville, which led to significant advances in the science of metallurgy. On his admittance to the Goldsmiths' Company, Heycock not unnaturally became interested in the work of the Assay Office and was able to offer much helpful technical advice over a long period, particularly in connection with the verification of new trial plates in 1925.

THE COINAGE ACT, 1870

The second half of the nineteenth century witnessed a number of changes in the administration of the Royal Mint. In 1870 a single consolidating statute replaced the complex legislation and traditional practices under which it had operated for many years.[19] The Coinage Act of that year recognized the importance of an independent test of sample coins and included a provision for a Trial of the Pyx to be held annually at Goldsmiths' Hall. The procedure – which is still followed today – retained its ceremonial flavour; the Queen's Remembrancer administered the oath to the jury and on completion of the Trial received the verdicts in the presence of the Chancellor of the Exchequer who attended in his capacity as ex-officio Master of the Mint. By 1870 the number of coins to be tested had become so great that it was not possible to complete the Trial in one day; so after they had been counted and weighed a period of several weeks was allowed for assaying them. This meant that the Assay Office did not have to close for normal work during the Trial as in former times.

The Coinage Act called for the provision of new trial plates, which on this occasion were made at the Mint by the Chemist and Assayer, W. C. Roberts (later Sir William Roberts-Austen). The Company was entrusted with their verification and a jury was accordingly appointed to undertake this task: the certificate appended to its verdict bears the signatures of both George and Henry Matthey.

After a lengthy research programme at the Mint, Roberts concluded that it was not possible to produce a plate of sterling silver that was completely homogeneous in composition.[20] He eventually resorted to the expedient of preparing a very large plate from a casting of 1000 oz. He then assayed samples taken from different parts and for the final plate he selected a smaller portion showing the best results. The preparation of the 22 carat gold plate presented fewer problems. Roberts also made subsidiary plates of fine silver and fine gold, recommending their use in place of the sterling and 22 carat plates for testing the coinage at the Trial of the Pyx. However, his advice was not accepted by the Treasury.

In 1899, Sir William Roberts-Austen, by this time an eminent and highly respected scientist and one of the pioneers of modern metallurgy (holding the post of Professor of Metallurgy at the Royal School of Mines in addition to Chemist and Assayer at the Mint), was again asked to make new plates, whereupon he resumed his former researches. His conclusions were the same as before; after no less than thirty-one attempts to cast a satisfactory sterling silver plate, he adopted an identical method to the one he had used twenty-nine years earlier.[21] However, he utilized new and improved techniques involving

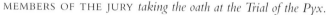

MEMBERS OF THE JURY *taking the oath at the Trial of the Pyx.*

electrolytic refining for the fine gold and fine silver plates which he made at the same time as those of sterling silver and 22 carat gold. The general responsibility for the plates had been transferred from the Treasury to the Board of Trade but, as before, the Company was asked to verify them.[22] Thirteen samples were removed from both the fine and standard gold plates, twenty-five from the fine silver plate and twenty-three from the standard (sterling) silver plate. The samples were divided between F.W. Harrold and George Pite (the two Senior Assayers) and George Matthey. When submitting the verdict the Company suggested the use of the fine gold and fine silver plates at the Trial of the Pyx in preference to the standard plates. This advice, which had first been given by Roberts-Austen nearly thirty years earlier, was not accepted until 1920 and then only for silver, not for gold.

EDWARD WATHERSTON'S CAMPAIGN

To return to hallmarking: in the 1870s the government received a number of representations from members of the trade pleading for repeal of the duty on gold and silverware. A tireless and vociferous propagandist in this cause was a liveryman of the Company, Edward J. Watherston, who was a director of a firm of retail jewellers, Brogden and Watherston of Pall Mall. He was reputed to have written over a thousand letters on the subject to various newspapers and journals. He did not confine himself to canvassing for repeal of the duty but devoted an immense energy, which can only be described as an obsession, in a campaign for the abolition of compulsory hallmarking and for the substitution of a voluntary system. Watherston's father was a member of the Court of Assistants but was never elected a warden, possibly because of his son's activities. In 1877 Watherston (the son) read a paper in which he propounded his views at a meeting of the Social Science Congress at Aberdeen, and in February 1878 he accompanied a delegation of London, Liverpool and Coventry watchmakers to the President of the Board of Trade to support a motion in the House of Commons for a committee of enquiry on hallmarking. The watchmakers were only concerned about the practice of passing off foreign watches as British-made on the strength of the hallmark, but Watherston took the opportunity to deliver a speech highly critical of the Company and its constitution, which received national newspaper coverage. For the next sixteen years he never ceased in his crusade for the abolition of compulsory hallmarking, causing the Company much aggravation.

There were other mutterings, in particular from watchmakers, about some aspects of the hallmarking statutes. In response to these and Watherston's activities the government appointed a Parliamentary Select Committee in 1878. Watherston was, of course, one of the witnesses examined. James Garrard, who had appeared before the previous Enquiry in 1856, gave evidence, as did Walter (later Sir Walter) Sherburne Prideaux, and William

Robinson. Although Watherston had some support in his plea for voluntary hallmarking, there were far more witnesses who were strongly in favour of its continuance as a compulsory system and in May 1879 the Committee recommended accordingly. In the words of its report:

> ... in this country the system has existed substantially in its present form since the reign of Edward I. Without speculating on its origin, and while making due allowances for its defects, it is established that it has resulted in the creation and maintenance of a high standard of excellence for all British assayed wares, which has not only raised the reputation of British work-manship at home and abroad, but has also created a large amount of private wealth readily convertible by reason of the guarantees of value which the hall-marks afford. As far as can be ascertained, most British manufacturers and by far the largest number of the dealers cling to the maintenance of the system with marked tenacity. The public do not complain of it. It also appears that foreign watch-cases are sent to this country to be hall-marked in yearly increasing numbers. Nor should the antiquarian aspect of the question be altogether disregarded. At any rate this should prevail to the extent of throwing the burthen of proof on those who propose the abolition of a system which has existed for 500 years. Your Committee do not consider that a voluntary or optional system of hall-marking would be satisfactory.[23]

The Committee made the following additional recommendations:

(i) That 'considering the importance of promoting silver as an article of manufacture' the plate duty should be abolished 'whenever the condition of the nation's revenue will permit'.

(ii) That all foreign watchcases assayed in this country should be impressed with an additional distinctive mark.

(iii) That the standards of gold below 18 carat should be discontinued.

(iv) That all the assay offices should be placed under the direct supervision of the Mint.

It was several years before the government took action on the first two recommendations and the last two were wholly disregarded.

In spite of the Committee's recommendations Watherston persisted in his dual campaign, delivering another paper at the Social Science Congress in Edinburgh in 1880, writing innumerable letters to the press and contributing articles for publication in the trade journals. But he had the support of only a small minority. In 1881 a letter purporting to represent the views of nearly every member of the trade was sent to Mr Gladstone (then Prime Minister and Chancellor of the Exchequer); it stated that the abolition of the present system would be viewed with the greatest possible alarm. In the following year

Wilfred Cripps, the author of *Old English Plate*, in a lecture to the Royal Society of Arts also strongly advocated its continuation. And in 1883 the Gold and Silver Trades section of the London Chamber of Commerce wrote to the Chancellor of the Exchequer pressing for repeal of the duty but retention of compulsory hallmarking. Nevertheless in 1884, a motion, no doubt engineered by Watherston, to abolish both the duty and compulsory hallmarking was introduced in the Commons during the debate on the Revenue Bill. In reply, the Chancellor of the Exchequer pledged to repeal the duty, although not immediately, and the motion was withdrawn.

Protests also came from another quarter. The government of India was pressing for a repeal of the duty on imports of silverware into Britain. Furthermore, since most Indian silverware was below sterling it was at the same time asking for a dispensation on the standard. Watherston and his supporters welcomed this new development and made great play of the fact that some imported pieces had been spoiled by the process of assay. After consulting the assay offices, the government responded by including in the Revenue Act 1884 a clause exempting from assay any articles which in the opinion of the Commissioners of Customs could be properly described as 'hand-chased, inlaid, bronzed or filigree work of oriental pattern'.[24] But this apparently did not satisfy the authorities in India, who maintained in a despatch dated 9 February 1888 that: ' ... the present system is maintained solely in the interests of the (Goldsmiths') Company and those whom it represents'. On receipt from the Chancellor of the Exchequer of a copy of this despatch, the Clerk, Walter Sherburne Prideaux, replied with a terse memorandum in which he said:

(1) the allowance to the Company for collection of plate duty never paid for the actual cost.

(2) Instead of the Company deriving benefit from the system of hall-marking, the reverse was the case, last year for instance the loss exceeded £1000 which had to be made good out of the private funds of the Company.

(3) The Company had at no time opposed the abolition of plate duty.

The duty on all gold and silverware was finally repealed from 1 May 1890.[25] Watherston, however, continued to press for the abolition of compulsory hallmarking, lobbying anyone he thought might be in a position to exert some influence. He propounded his views in an address at a meeting of the Royal Society of Arts in January 1891.[26] The discussion which followed showed that some of his audience supported him, but no doubt he had arranged for them to be present. In his lecture Watherston returned to a favourite theme, that the methods used at the assay offices were outdated and damaging. He now suggested that they should be replaced by touchstone testing, endeavouring to convince his listeners that the latter technique was of modern origin! F. W. Harrold, the Company's Senior Assayer, lost no time in preparing a counter-paper for the wardens; he clearly and convincingly set out the disadvantages and relative lack of accuracy of the touchstone method, particularly when used for silver or for gold of a standard below 14 carat. Watherston doggedly continued to pursue his objective for several more years without success; an article in the *Watchmaker and Jeweller* in May 1894 was the final effort of his lengthy campaign.

VARYING TRENDS

By the middle of the nineteenth century the manufacture of silverware had appreciably declined. In the early 1800s some 800,000oz of large and 400,000oz of small silver wares (excluding watchcases) were received on average at the Assay Office each year. But by the 1850s these figures had dropped to about 500,000oz and 250,000oz respectively. The silver trade was clearly in the doldrums and remained there until almost the end of the century. One reason was the invention of electro-plating and the consequent development of the trade in cheaper silver-plated wares, which had become fully established by 1850. There was, however, a welcome change in the fortunes of the real silver trade from 1890 onwards. The weight of silver wares received at the Assay Office more than doubled in the next ten years, largely due no doubt to the abolition of the duty. The effect was similar to that following the comparable decision by the government in 1757 (see page 211).

After 1891 records were kept of the number of articles received in addition to their weight. In that year 118,000 large silver wares and 800,000 small wares and watchcases were processed. By 1900 the numbers had risen to approximately 250,000 and 2,800,000 respectively (see Appendix III). In the next decade the numbers of small wares continued to rise dramatically, reaching about 4.5 million annually by 1910. Manufacturers were sending great quantities of small lightweight articles, such as mounts (for pipes, walking sticks and umbrellas) and corners for pocket books. Since most articles under 5dwt were exempt from compulsory hallmarking, the presence of a hallmark was obviously a good selling point. The assay offices deliberately encouraged the practice by reducing the charges for these articles to 3d per dozen items.

The decline in the receipts of silver in the mid-nineteenth century was counterbalanced by an upsurge in the quantity of gold articles submitted. In the early 1800s an average of about 4000 parcels of gold wares were handled annually; by the mid-1870s this figure had risen to about 15,000. Over the same period the weight of gold wares increased from approximately 20,000oz annually to nearly 100,000oz. Towards the end of the century it had contracted to about 50,000oz, but by the outbreak of the First World War it had increased again to around 100,000oz – almost 500,000 articles, of which over half were watchcases. However, by this time Birmingham had become the main centre of jewellery manufacture and consequently the assay office there was receiving a considerably greater quantity of gold wares.

The significant rise in the receipts of gold wares can be partly attributed to two changes in the law. The first was the Act of 1854 and the subsequent Order in Council of the same year introducing 15, 12 and 9 carat standards, resulting in a slow but definite trend towards gold wares of the lower standards, particularly 9 carat, for reasons of cost (see page 255). By 1912, for example, the total weight of 9 carat watchcases received annually was approximately 31,000 oz compared with 21,000 oz of 18 carat cases. The remaining standards were used to a much lesser extent. This trend continued unabated in the following years except for a resurgence in the popularity of 22 carat for wedding rings after 1916.

The second relevant legislation was the Wedding Rings Act 1855.[27] Previously all gold rings had been exempt from compulsory hallmarking, but according to this Act wedding rings were specifically required to be marked. It may well be that the Exchequer was eager to lay its hands on the duty which these articles would thus attract.

IMPORTED WARES

Watchcases, which since 1798 had been free from duty, accounted for a substantial part of the work of the Assay Office. Between 1800 and 1886 an average of 6000 parcels of silver cases were received annually, in amounts varying between 100,000 and 250,000 oz each year. Many gold watchcases were also received but the quantities are not recorded. In the eighteenth and early nineteenth centuries Britain had a watch industry that was second to none in the world, but its dominance gradually diminished and eventually Switzerland took the lead. By the 1880s large numbers of watchcases were being sent from Switzerland to London for hallmarking. They were received in an unpolished state and after assaying and marking they were returned abroad for finishing. Then after being fitted with Swiss movements they were re-exported to Britain and frequently sold as British watches. Home manufacturers not unnaturally considered this to be a misleading practice, injurious to their business and their reputation. The hallmarks struck on imported and British wares were almost identical, the only difference being an additional letter 'F', signifying foreign origin.[28]

The Select Committee had recommended that since the letter 'F' resembled existing marks there should be a further distinctive mark for foreign watch-cases, but no immediate action had been taken. In 1887, however, in an endeavour to protect the British watch trade, the government did make such provision by way of the Merchandise Marks Act of that year and a subsequent Order in Council.[29] This Order stipulated that anyone sending watchcases for hallmarking had to make a statutory declaration before an officer of the assay office or a Justice of the Peace, stating the country of origin; also, all imported watchcases had to be stamped 'foreign'. Submissions of foreign cases soon fell dramatically, but the importation of finished watches was not greatly affected. Rather strangely, the Customs authorities did not consider foreign watchcases to be liable for hallmarking if they had movements incorporated at the time they entered the country; they did not therefore insist that the importers should send them to an assay office. The Company disagreed with this view and in 1904 the Board of Customs consulted the law officers of the Crown who upheld the Company's opinion that the cases were not exempt. Nevertheless, the Customs were reluctant to alter their practice without a judicial decision. The Board accordingly asked the Company if it would undertake a test prosecution. The Company agreed and legal proceedings were instituted in November 1906 against a shopkeeper and importer named William Wyatt for selling unhallmarked foreign watches.

The judgment in Goldsmiths' Company v Wyatt went against the Company in the lower court but was reversed in the Court of Appeal. As a result there was an immediate flood of unfinished foreign watchcases at the Assay Office – the number of silver cases received in the twelve months to May 1908 was approximately 200,000 compared with a mere 3000 for the corresponding period 1906 to 1907. By 1912 the amount had increased to around 700,000 cases, reaching a peak in 1918 with more than 1.25 million cases. There was also a spectacular increase in the quantity of gold watchcases, jumping from approximately 4700 cases in the twelve months May 1906 to May 1907 to 78,500 in the following year and to almost 255,000 in 1912/13. Then owing to an import duty on gold watches the figures showed a sharp decline. Nearly all the watchcases received between 1908 and 1918 were of Swiss manufacture.

Not only watchcases but all imported gold and silver wares had been the subject of new legislation in 1883. According to the Revenue Act of that year the customs authorities had been made responsible for ensuring that on entering the country all imported gold or silver articles liable to hallmarking (except those for private use) were sent to an assay office under bond; and under the same Act there was a further provision that any such articles found to be below the minimum standard could be returned abroad as an alternative to being broken.[30]

Foreign watchcases were subject to special marking after 1887, but some years later it was recognized that further measures were desirable to ensure that not only watchcases but all imported gold and silver wares could be easily identified. Accordingly, in 1904 special standard and assay office marks were prescribed for all articles of foreign origin submitted for hallmarking, the letter 'F' being discontinued.[31] For such wares the lion passant, Britannia and crown symbols were replaced by decimal figures – for example .925 for sterling silver, .750 for

18 carat gold. The special assay office mark for London was a 'Phoebus' but in 1906 this was altered to 'the sign of the constellation Leo'.[32] After 1907 watchcases no longer had to be marked 'foreign'.

As already mentioned, the duty on gold and silverware was abolished in 1890, thus relieving the Company of the task of collection and of stamping the mark of the sovereign's head. Before the repeal took effect, the Board of Inland Revenue had been carefully considering how to mount a difficult operation – the rebate of the duty for items which had not been sold by the effective date. The help of the Company was requested and it was readily granted. A notice was sent by the Revenue authorities to each of 15,400 licensed dealers requesting details of unsold articles. The number of items qualifying for repayment was large: claims in respect of 1,257,894 oz of silver were received, mostly from London dealers. The claimants had to send the goods to one of several centres where they were checked and the repayments made. The centre for London was at Goldsmiths' Hall and the staff of the Assay Office worked arduously for a fortnight, often from 7 o'clock in the morning until 9 o'clock at night, checking and recording the weights of each parcel in the presence of Revenue officers. The Clerk, Walter Sherburne Prideaux, as Accountant of the Duty Money supervised the work throughout. The operation was successfully concluded and effusive letters of thanks were received from the Treasury and the Board of Inland Revenue. In further recognition of his services, the Clerk shortly afterwards received the honour of a knighthood.

EXPANSION AND MODERNIZATION

There had been little change in the staff establishment of the Assay Office between the last quarter of the eighteenth century and the middle of the nineteenth, except for an additional assayer in 1828. However, the substantial increase in receipts of gold wares after 1850 and silver after 1890, necessitated a larger workforce and more extensive premises. In 1850 the staff numbered twelve and by 1874 sixteen, which included five assayers, two weighers and seven drawers; but by 1906 there were seven assayers and a total staff of forty. By 1914 the total number employed was eighty including nine assayers.

Josiah Sharp died in 1879 after forty-five years in office and was succeeded as Deputy Warden by his assistant William Robinson. He in turn was followed in 1897 by his son Herbert, who had been engaged as assistant to his father in 1889. Another son, Sydney, was appointed Assistant Assayer in 1887, becoming Head Assayer in 1919. Since the death of Henry Matthey in 1878 the post of Head Assayer (or First Gold Assayer as it was then usually called) had been held by Henry Pizey, then by Frederick William Harrold from 1887 and George Pite from 1906.

It was not many years after the opening of the new Hall that the space provided for the Assay Office proved to be inadequate. In 1847 three distin-

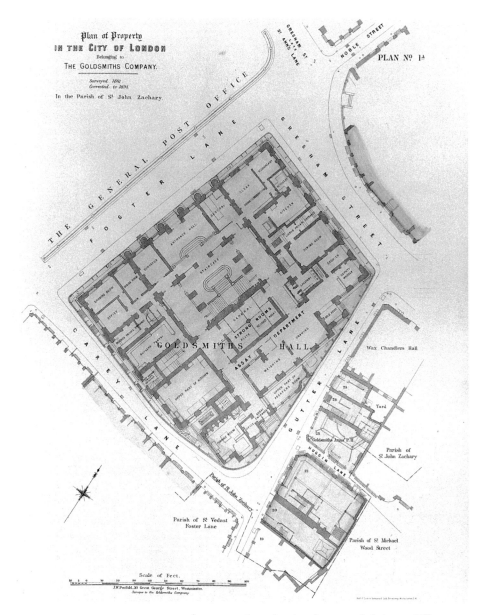

Plan of Property
IN THE CITY OF LONDON
Belonging to
THE GOLDSMITHS COMPANY.

Surveyed 1819.
Corrected to 1894.

In the Parish of St John Zachary.

PLAN Nº 1ᴬ

GRESHAM ST
St ANNS LANE
NOBLE STREET

THE GENERAL POST OFFICE

FOSTER LANE

GRESHAM STREET

GOLDSMITHS HALL

STRONG ROOMS
DEPARTMENT
ASSAY

CAREY LANE

GUTTER LANE

HUGGIN LANE

Wax Chandlers Hall

Yard

Goldsmiths Arms P.H.

Parish of
St John Zachary

Parish of St John Zachary

Parish of St Vedast
Foster Lane

Parish of St Michael
Wood Street

Scale of Feet.

J.W.Penfold, 30 Great George Street, Westminster.
Surveyor to the Goldsmiths Company

GROUND PLAN OF GOLDSMITHS' HALL, *1894, showing the expanded Assay Office (compare with the plan on page 248).*

guished members of the Court (William Bateman, Jonathan Hayne and Percival Norton Johnson) were asked to consider suggestions for enlarging it.[33] As a result of their recommendations, a substantial extension was built on vacant land at the south-east corner of the Hall which served as a fire-room (furnace-room) for the next 120 years.

Another small extension on the east side of the Hall was completed in 1872. But though the accommodation was sufficient in the short term, by 1900 more was needed. There was clearly no room for further expansion in the

Hall itself. Fortunately, however, the Company owned the freehold of a building on the east side of Gutter Lane at the corner of Huggin Lane, exactly opposite that part of the Hall in which the Assay Office was housed.[24] Arrangements were made to take possession of all floors and the City Corporation was persuaded to permit the construction of a subway under Gutter Lane, thus effectively linking the two parts of the Assay Office. Lift hoists were installed in both buildings to aid the flow of work. Parcels of work were received in the Hall itself and transferred via the lifts and subway to the new building for sampling and marking, then returned to the Hall for delivery. The new arrangements were in operation by October 1902.

A few years later even more space was needed to accommodate the additional staff taken on to cope with the sudden flood of foreign watchcases resulting from the Goldsmiths' Company v Wyatt judgement in 1907. Again the Company was fortunate in holding the freehold of premises next to the building in Gutter Lane which had already been taken over. They were on lease for an eighty-year term but an underlease was negotiated and the rooms were interlinked with those in the adjacent building.

In the meantime there had been a number of advances in assaying techniques. In 1897 new cupellation furnaces were installed using gas in place of coke. Those fuelled by coke had been in use for about fifty years, being

ASSAY OFFICE FIRE-ROOM *(furnace room) c.1890. Coke furnaces were still being used. In the foreground is the apparatus used for the parting process in the assay of gold, see page 295.*

WEIGHING SAMPLES *on an Oertling assay balance.*

WARES *awaiting hallmarking at the Assay Office, c.1890.*

themselves replacements of types which for centuries had been dependent on charcoal. The Fletcher gas furnaces offered considerable advantages, rapidly reaching working temperature and providing an even heat throughout the muffle; they were also cleaner in operation.

Improved assay balances became available, notably from the firm of L. Oertling, which was established in London in 1847. Oertling balances, which incorporated steel (later agate) knife-edges and agate planes for beam and pan suspension – replacing the old hook and swan-neck pattern – were used for the next hundred years. The accuracy of assay balances was further enhanced by the introduction of the rider system, whereby the beam was engraved with scale divisions on which a small wire weight was placed. These changes in the construction of assay balances ran parallel to similar developments in the design of chemical balances, the latter being an essential requirement in the rapidly expanding field of analytical chemistry. In 1898 new and better bullion balances were purchased for bulk weighing – the Deputy Warden had been much impressed by one which he had seen on a visit to the Birmingham Assay Office.

The Assay Office was thus taking full advantage of the rapid progress that was taking place in the fields of chemistry and metallurgy. Its close association with the Royal Mint and with bullion dealers such as Johnson Matthey, combined with the active help of prominent scientists who were members of the Court – for instance Percival Norton Johnson, George Matthey and later Sir Frederick Abel, C. T. Heycock and Sir William Jackson Pope – were naturally important factors.[35]

That not all assay offices had kept up with modern developments, however, is clear from comments in the report of a special small committee appointed by the Board of Trade in 1887 to consider the hallmarking of foreign watch-cases. The committee's membership included the Clerk of the Company, the Head of the Standards Department of the Board of Trade and the redoubtable W. C. Roberts-Austen of the Royal Mint. Besides their main recommendations they gave a general description of the process of assaying and hallmarking, including the following passage:

> … and reports of the Deputy Master of the Mint issued annually since 1870 have given prominence to the necessity for the use of trial plates and have resulted in the almost universal adoption in mints of a uniform method of manipulation. In the assay offices, on the other hand, practice is far from uniform and with regard to this point we find that while in London, Birmingham and Sheffield accurate balances and modern appliances have been adopted, in other offices less accurate and even primitive methods of treatment have been retained. In certain offices the results are not systematically controlled by 'check assays', the balances closely resemble those

described and figured by an early metallurgical writer Biringuccio in 1540 and the balances are hardly more delicate than those of which illustrations were given by Lazarus Ercker in 1580 ...

In fact these criticisms were a little late as the Exeter, Newcastle and York offices had already closed by the date of the report. Although not mentioned anywhere by name, Roberts-Austen was undoubtedly the main protagonist of yet another proposal to put all the assay offices under the control of the Mint, a move successfully countered by the Clerk.

MARKING METHODS

Whilst improvements had been made in the techniques of assaying at the London, Birmingham and Sheffield offices, drawing (sampling) was still carried out in much the same manner as in the past. Owing to the variety of the articles received it was inevitably a manual operation requiring considerable dexterity. If anything even greater skill and experience were necessary than formerly because of the delicate nature of many of the small items. However, some new and better methods had been introduced for marking. Although larger pieces were still marked by hand, fly-presses were used on a much wider scale than hitherto for small wares, especially if sent in quantity. But with the submission of ever-increasing numbers of mounts for umbrellas, corners for note-cases and similar items, it was realized that some form of mechanized marking would be of great benefit. Thus in the early 1900s some specially designed reciprocating presses, powered by electricity, were installed. These proved to be remarkably versatile and are still used for marking many types of article.

An essential feature of the marking operation is the provision of suitably shaped tools or beds for supporting the articles. This became of particular concern with the receipt of many small and fragile items for which specially contoured beds were required. The Assay Office is expected to be able to mark any piece submitted and naturally no wasters are permitted; moreover, it is often necessary to provide a new tool at short notice as manufacturers are not slow to complain if there is any delay. With the increase in the volume and scope of the work it was decided that the Assay Office should have its own toolmaker and in 1910 a suitably qualified man – William Gregory – was engaged and remained as an indispensable member of the staff for forty-three years. He and his successors have also been responsible for general maintenance of the presses and other equipment.

The arrangements for the manufacture of the hallmarking punches were reviewed in 1914 as the Company's Engraver, John H. Pinches (the son of John Pinches who had taken over from Leonard Wyon in 1891) was shortly to retire. New punches were required in greater number and variety than ever.

For centuries they had been supplied by the Engraver working either at his own premises or at the Mint, but it was now decided that it would be preferable if they were made in the Assay Office. Two highly skilled men were engaged – Arthur Clinch and Alfred Cole – who were initially supervised and paid by John H. Pinches. In 1918 they were taken on to the Assay Office staff and successfully ran the punch department until the outbreak of the Second World War. Soon after their appointment they produced new designs of the leopard's head and the lion passant to coincide with a new cycle of date letters commencing in May 1916. The design of the leopard's head was still further improved in 1923. Subsequently the crown mark used on the higher standards of gold and the Britannia marks for silver were also modified. Each new master punch was made from a large model by means of a reducing machine similar to those used for making new coinage dies at the Mint; the detail and clarity of the resultant hallmarks bear testimony to the punchmakers' expertise.

Marking charges had been kept remarkably constant since the beginning of the nineteenth century but changes in prevailing fashions had brought new types of article in their wake, such as picture frames, napkin rings, cigarette cases and trophies. A new schedule of charges was issued in 1891. Apart from a revised list of articles, the time-honoured practice of retaining diet from larger silver wares in lieu of monetary payment was replaced by a charge at a rate of ¼d per ounce. A small quantity of diet was, however, still retained from each parcel for the annual trial.

PROSECUTIONS FOR HALLMARKING OFFENCES

Throughout the nineteenth century many offences against the hallmarking laws were brought to the notice of the Company, some serious, some less so. All were investigated and action taken where appropriate.

A case brought by the Company in 1849 against two dealers in Bath attracted considerable local attention. Horatio Warren and Samuel Fuller were charged with felony – having in their possession without lawful excuse an apostle spoon of recent manufacture bearing a hallmark (for 1774) transposed from another spoon or possibly a skewer and knowing the same to have been transposed. They were further charged with offering for sale a number of unhallmarked articles. It was alleged that the silversmith who had made the spoon was in their employ. The case was heard before Lord Denman at Taunton Assizes and an eminent leading counsel, Mr Cockburn, who later became Lord Chief Justice, was briefed by the Company. The courtroom was crowded with members of the public.

The trial is of particular interest as it illustrates some of the difficulties associated with prosecutions under the hallmarking laws then in force. Acting on information received, Thomas Hough, the Weigher (later Senior Silver

Assayer) had been sent to Bath to the shop of the defendants where he purchased eleven unhallmarked silver articles. On another visit a week later he bought another thirty-four articles. On a third visit he procured a search warrant and seized about a hundred articles. Hough, who was the principal witness for the prosecution, was subjected to a long and searching cross-examination by defending counsel, but answered all questions satisfactorily. He stated that he had assayed the apostle spoon – the subject of the most serious charge – and had found parts below standard, explaining that although he was not the Assayer, competence in assaying was expected also of the Weigher. He said that he had served an apprenticeship as a silversmith and was thus able to describe how the spoon would have been made had it been genuine.[36]

In his summing up the judge said the question was whether the defendants had made a transposition as alleged by the prosecution or whether they had merely made an addition (ie the bowl and finial) – a lesser offence with which they had not been charged. He himself thought the former to be the case but he qualified this by saying that he was much perplexed by certain sections of the relevant Act of Parliament (The Gold and Silver Wares Act 1844). The jury, perhaps not surprisingly in view of the judge's remarks on the law, acquitted the defendants on the charge of transposition but found them guilty on the other charges of selling forty-five unhallmarked silver articles.

The defendants did not escape too lightly; in addition to having to pay penalties of £450 for the lesser offences they had spent one month in prison before being granted bail. But the outcome was disappointing for the Company. Its legal expenses were heavy – £732 3s 4d after deducting costs allowed by the court. It was only entitled to one half of the penalties; an attempt to persuade the Treasury to grant the full amount met with no success. An interesting facet of the case is that it was alleged by the prosecution that the objective of the defendants was not only to defraud in the payment of duty but to pass off a modern spoon as an old one. In his opening address Mr Cockburn stated: 'I need hardly say such persons who are fond of old plate in preference to new, will from the circumstances of its antiquity pay a higher price for it.' This was to become a common motive for transposing or counterfeiting hallmarks.

Other offenders were brought to trial. At the Central Criminal Court in 1876 David L. Gooch, who had a shop in Oxford Street, was sentenced to six months' hard labour for uttering base metal wares (a ewer and a coffee pot) bearing transposed hallmarks. The articles had been purchased by Thomas Harman, one of the drawers (later Senior Silver Assayer), following information received by the Company. An electroplate worker called Brown, who carried out the actual transpositions for Gooch, gave evidence for the prosecution but nevertheless received a two-month sentence. A chaser named Price, who worked for Brown, stated that he had seen the articles being made and that the mark (1744) on the bottom of the coffee pot had been cut out of a silver salt cellar whilst the mark (1747) on the ewer was from a half-pint cup. Thus besides being fraudulently described as silver, the articles were falsely represented as antique. In his report of the case to the Standing Committee the Clerk said: 'I hear from well-informed sources that the effect of these prosecutions upon the trade has been of a most marked and satisfactory character.' As it transpired his words were premature.

To counterfeit or transpose a hallmark or to utter or possess an article bearing a counterfeit or transposed mark with guilty knowledge, were felonies under Section 2 of the Gold and Silver Wares Act 1844, and punishable by a maximum term of fourteen years' penal servitude (transportation having been abolished in 1864). However, it was often difficult to obtain evidence of sufficient strength to persuade a jury to convict on charges carrying such a severe penalty. In many of the cases that were investigated counsel advised that it would be safer to rely on Section 3 of the same Act which applied to dealers only and which enabled the Company to sue for penalties of £10 for each offence of possessing or selling a ware bearing a counterfeit or transposed hallmark without lawful excuse – proof of guilty knowledge not being necessary.

Naturally it would have been preferable, although less lucrative for the Company, had it been able to take legal proceedings on one of the more serious charges. To this end the Company in 1880 circulated a notice offering a reward of £500 in return for information leading to a conviction for counterfeiting or transposing. In the following year, one James Davis came forward with evidence which led to charges being brought against William Cantle and Walter Roberts for forging 18 carat hallmarks on rings. But the jury were not impressed by Davis, the defending counsel making great play of the suggestion that he was interested only in the reward. Furthermore, the judge took a totally unexpected view of the case. He dwelt at length on the fact that makers of electroplate could use marks which might be taken by the public to be genuine hallmarks, and said that so long as the law allowed this, he would be against conviction not only in the present case but in any similar prosecution brought by the Goldsmiths' Company. The defendants were found not guilty. The Clerk reporting later to the Court of Assistants said that in his opinion it was a perfectly clear case of forgery and he could not help feeling that there had been a great miscarriage of justice. However, within the next eight years there were two successful prosecutions for uttering silver-gilt watchcases bearing forged gold hallmarks, resulting in terms of five and six years' penal servitude.

Later in 1898 it came to the knowledge of the Company that spurious silverware was being sold by Reuben Lyon, a retailer with a shop at 125, Holborn. A search warrant was obtained and Herbert Robinson (the Deputy

Warden) with James Field (the Second Silver Assayer), Henry Adams (one of the weighers) and a detective inspector of the City of London Police spent five hours searching the premises. Two cab-loads of articles – coffee pots, ewers, jugs, cups and other items – were seized. Most bore counterfeit hallmarks of the George III period and were manifestly of recent manufacture. The Company tried hard to discover the original source of supply but without success. Again acting on counsel's advice and relying on Section 3 of the 1844 Act, penalties of £3090 were recovered from Lyon in respect of 309 pieces.

The Company received some criticism for the way it had acted in this case. The proceedings had been reported in the national press but Lyon's name had not been disclosed. Some bona fide members of the trade felt that their businesses were likely to be discredited as a result of this omission and were quick to write to the newspapers. In reply the Clerk pointed out that under the existing law the Company had no power to publish the identity of a wrongdoer. The magazine *Truth* eventually uncovered Lyon's name and carried a series of features critical of the Company. At the instigation of the newly formed National Retail Jewellers' Association, Sir Stafford Northcote, MP for Exeter and a vice-president of the Association, raised the matter in the House of Commons, asking the Home Secretary if he would amend the law so as to transfer to the Director of Public Prosecutions the duty of dealing with persons charged with 'tampering with the hallmark'. But the reply on behalf of the Minister was that he saw no reason for finding fault with the way the Goldsmiths' Company carried out its statutory powers. Nevertheless the Company was unhappy about the adverse publicity it had received, however unjustified it may have been. The wardens were keen to take further measures in regard to the undoubted prevalence of serious offences against the hall-marking Acts. They were particularly concerned that nothing had come to light which gave any clue as to the source of the forgeries. Fortunately it was not long before the evidence they were looking for came into their possession.

THE TWINAM TRIAL

Facts now emerged from earlier cases that pointed to a journeyman silver-smith, Charles Twinam, as a possible source of spurious articles. The break came in March 1899 when a man called at the Hall and showed some articles bearing forged marks which he had obtained from Twinam. The informant said that if the Company cared to give him an unmarked piece he could probably get Twinam to strike forged marks on it. The offer was eagerly taken up and conclusive proof that Twinam was a forger was thereby provided. A carefully planned operation for searching his house in Holloway, involving twelve police officers aided by the Deputy Warden, revealed nearly a hundred counterfeit punches, some of which corresponded with marks found on items in the Lyon case. In addition there were almost a thousand articles, a number

A COUNTERFEIT HALLMARK — *one of the Twinam forgeries.*

of them bearing counterfeit hallmarks. Twinam was tried at the Central Criminal Court and found guilty; James Garrard and John Pinches (the Company's Engraver) were witnesses for the prosecution, as were the Deputy Warden and two other officers in the Assay Office.

Mr Justice Grantham sentenced Twinam to five years' penal servitude and directed that the plate with forged marks be delivered to the Goldsmiths' Company to be melted and sold to defray the costs of the prosecution. The Company subsequently produced a printed booklet with illustrations of the marks on these articles and on the illicit pieces seized from Lyon, sending copies to some 600 dealers for their information.[37]

There is no doubt that the Twinam trial, which received wide publicity, served as a warning to would-be transgressors. The action taken by the Company had the desired effect; few offences of a like nature came to notice during the next forty years. There were, however, several cases of forgery which were not concerned with the faking of antique silver. For instance, in 1903 Solomon Solomons and George Curtis were sentenced at the Central Criminal Court to three years' penal servitude and Alfred Gould to three months' hard labour for uttering base metal chains bearing forged 18 carat hallmarks. And in 1907 Henry Carpenter, an undischarged bankrupt, was found guilty at the same court for forging hallmarks on 1461 silver mounts for umbrellas and walking sticks. The mounts were in fact up to standard but he was nevertheless sentenced to nine months' hard labour. One case that was concerned with the passing of fake antiques was heard in 1933; Charles Isaac Fileman was sentenced to six months' imprisonment for selling silver pepper pots, cream jugs and other articles with counterfeit marks of the early eighteenth century.

Another type of offence was prevalent at the end of the nineteenth century — that of adding to a hallmarked article or altering its character without permission and without sending it to an assay office for further marking.

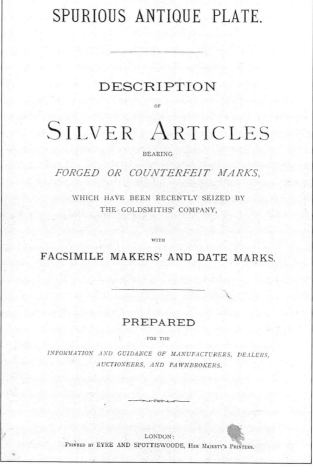

TITLE PAGE *of a booklet containing illustrations of counterfeit hallmarks found on articles seized from Lyon and Twinam.*

SPURIOUS ANTIQUE PLATE.

DESCRIPTION

OF

SILVER ARTICLES

BEARING

FORGED OR COUNTERFEIT MARKS,

WHICH HAVE BEEN RECENTLY SEIZED BY
THE GOLDSMITHS' COMPANY,

WITH

FACSIMILE MAKERS' AND DATE MARKS.

PREPARED

FOR THE

*INFORMATION AND GUIDANCE OF MANUFACTURERS, DEALERS,
AUCTIONEERS, AND PAWNBROKERS.*

LONDON:
PRINTED BY EYRE AND SPOTTISWOODE, HER MAJESTY'S PRINTERS.

Often the work was carried out by a silversmith with no fraudulent intent, merely to satisfy a customer who wished to have a privately owned piece brought into line with current fashion. In other instances, however, the intent was clearly not so innocent. The legacy of these infringements and the more serious offences of Twinam and others is still felt to this day when spurious pieces come to light after reposing in private collections for nearly a century.

FABERGÉ V GOLDSMITHS' COMPANY

In 1910 the Company was involved in an important civil case – important because, like the Wyatt case three years earlier (see page 269), it resulted in a ruling on one aspect of the hallmarking law which hitherto had not been entirely clear. The plaintiff was Carl Fabergé, the celebrated Russian jeweller, who had a London office to which artefacts for sale in this country were consigned. The Goldsmiths' Company was the defendant. A parcel of imported enamelled goods, which included silver matchboxes, letter clips and a gold cigarette case, had been sent by the Customs authorities to the Assay Office, in accordance with the provisions of the Revenue Act 1883. The plaintiff claimed exemption from hallmarking on the grounds that the articles were enamels – not gold or silver plate – and did not therefore come within the relevant statutes; alternatively that the enamel was within the meaning of the expression 'jewels or other stones' used in sections 2 and 6 of the Plate (Offences) Act 1738. 'Jeweller's works, that is to say, any gold or silver wherein any jewels or other stones are or shall be set' were exempt under the first of these sections and certain gold articles that could not be marked without damage were exempt under the second. Mr Justice Parker, however, was of the opinion that all the items were clearly articles of gold or silver, and that they did not cease to be so because they were used as the basis for enamel work; nor could it be held that the gold or silver foundation on which enamels are worked is gold or silver in which they are 'set' within the meaning of the statute. He ruled that the articles were therefore liable to compulsory hallmarking. He stated that the question of damage did not arise because there was no reason why the items should not be sent for marking before they were enamelled, in the same way as foreign watchcases were normally submitted before finishing and polishing.

Although the decision clarified the law in one important respect it raised doubts about another – namely the meaning of 'jeweller's works' in this context. It had always been taken to mean that stone-set jewellery was exempt from hallmarking. The Company continued to adhere to this interpretation for some forty years after the Fabergé case; but then, as the result of further legal opinion, it was accepted that the exemption only applied to the actual settings in which stones were mounted and not to the article as a whole. This illustrates the difficulty the assay offices often experienced in having to operate within the framework of an outdated Act of Parliament.

CHAPTER TWELVE

RECENT YEARS
1914 to 1973

IN THE EARLY PART OF 1914 the eighty members of the Assay Office staff were exceptionally busy, the workload having reached a peak of approximately six million articles per annum. But following the outbreak of war in August there was an immediate decline. On 3 September the Clerk reported to the Court of Assistants that there was likely to be a loss to the Company of not less than £1000 per month. Twenty members of the staff were serving the country, either in the Territorial Army or in some other similar capacity, and eighteen others were special constables. But in spite of the expected financial losses it was decided that the appointments of all who volunteered for the

GOLDSMITHS' HALL *in 1913, a watercolour by Herbert Finn.*

TOOLROOM AND PUNCHMAKING DEPARTMENT *in the Assay Office building in Gutter Lane, c.1920.*

Forces would be kept open and that their wages and salaries would be continued at their present rates, subject to a reduction in respect of remuneration from other sources. Despite many of the staff being absent on active service the Office continued to operate normally, and as events turned out, the gold and silverware trade soon picked up. Although between August 1914 and November 1918 the average receipts of large silverware were less than half the immediate pre-war figures the quantity of small lightweight silver articles hardly changed. During the first month of the war an unusual consignment was received for urgent hallmarking – twelve silver passes for the use of 'special officers of high rank at the Front'. And the number of silver watchcases submitted was even greater than before; between 1915 and 1917 the annual average was about one million, almost all from Switzerland. Also, remarkably, the number of gold articles progressively increased following a temporary decline on the outbreak of hostilities. In each of the years leading up to the war about 200,000 gold wares (excluding watchcases) were received, but in the twelve months May 1916 to May 1917 this had risen to nearly 400,000, a high proportion of them being 22 carat wedding rings. After an initial drop the number of gold watchcases submitted also rose but fell again from about a quarter of a million in 1915 to a mere 5498 in 1917/18 due to the imposition of an import duty.

For a short period following the Armistice there was a boom in all branches of the trade. The numbers of gold wares continued to rise, reaching a maximum in the year 1919/20 during which nearly 700,000 articles (excluding watchcases) were marked (see Appendix III). In the same year over half a million gold watchcases were submitted as a result of the lifting of the import duty. The trade in large silverware, which had been severely curtailed during the war, recovered to some extent. But after 1920 the figures showed a pronounced decline for both large and small silver wares; by 1923 they were only about half those of the immediate post-war years. Receipts of gold wares also dropped but to a lesser degree, the quantities being still almost double the pre-war figures. The world financial crisis of the early 1930s hit the trade however, and the Assay Office suffered with it – both gold and silver were affected. Compared with three years earlier the total weight of silver wares received in 1932/3 had fallen by thirty-seven per cent and their number by more than fifty per cent. Receipts of gold wares likewise decreased by approximately fifty per cent both in number and weight. There was a slight improvement after 1934, in line with the generally brighter economic climate.

Watchcases were always treated as a special category at the assay offices because of the various regulations concerning them. The annual receipts fluctuated considerably. After a record number of 1,343,834 silver cases in the year May 1918 to May 1919 there followed a steady decline; in 1934/5 only 36,832 were submitted. Receipts of gold watchcases also diminished; in 1924/5 for example there were 555,308 but in the following year the number had dropped to 371,813, and by 1933/4 to only 60,281. Wrist watches had largely replaced the old pocket type and the cases were increasingly made of base metal. Another factor contributing to the decrease was that the Glasgow Assay Office was charging considerably less for marking watchcases than were the English offices and it was thereby attracting the bulk of the importations. In spite of entreaties from south of the border the Glasgow office was not prepared to bring its prices into line and the Company reluctantly decided that it would have to reduce its own charges.

STAFF CHANGES

The 1914–18 war had sadly taken its toll; four members of the Assay Office staff were killed in action and others wounded. In the short-lived post-war boom there had been some hasty recruitment of new staff, but due to the general decline in the trade which followed, the Company found itself in the position of having an over-staffed establishment, and in consequence suffering heavy financial losses. It was hesitant to dispense with any of the staff, but by

1924 this became inevitable; the numbers were reduced from seventy-six to fifty-eight and at the same time part of the Gutter Lane premises were vacated. Then in 1933 the situation had to be reviewed again; the staff was further reduced to a total of forty-two and it remained at approximately this level until the outbreak of the Second World War. In the inter-war years the Company was forced to subsidize the Assay Office substantially from its corporate income – not the first time that it had been in this position.

Following the decline in the workload a committee met in 1937 to review the organization and working of the Office. It was not disbanded on completion of its task and continued to meet at intervals as the Assay Office Committee. Between 1939 and 1946 the Prime Warden usually took the chair but then Robert Salmon Hutton, former Goldsmiths' Professor of Metallurgy at Cambridge, became permanent chairman, serving until 1965. He was succeeded by Lord Runciman, who resigned in 1973 on his election as the first chairman of the Hallmarking Council (see page 306), the vacancy being filled by the appointment of Ian Threlfall QC.

As regards the permanent staff of the Company: the Clerk, Sir Walter Sherburne Prideaux, had retired in 1919 and was followed by his son Walter Treverbian Prideaux. There was a break in the Prideaux succession in 1939 when George Hughes became Clerk but it was continued again in 1953 when Walter Arbuthnot Prideaux (son of Walter Treverbian) was appointed. He retired in 1975.

Herbert Robinson, the Deputy Warden, retired in 1925 and was succeeded by Arthur Bishop, his assistant. Bishop was followed in 1931 by Charles Hobday, who had joined the staff in 1899 as an assayer. He retired in 1937 and Horace Lindsey, his assistant, who had been employed in the Office for many years in a clerical and administrative capacity, became Deputy Warden. The post of First Gold Assayer was filled in 1919 by the promotion of Sydney Robinson, the brother of Herbert Robinson. He was succeeded by Hugh Gamlen eight years later. By this time the number of assayers had been reduced from a maximum of ten in 1915 to a mere five. Gamlen's successors were Sidney Haydon, Henry Ingrey and David Dalladay. (see Appendix 11b)

The Deputy Warden (Arthur Bishop) and the two Senior Assayers (Sydney Robinson and Charles Hobday) were members of a special committee appointed by the Company in 1926 to verify two new trial plates – 22 carat and fine gold – which had been made by the Mint on instructions from the Board of Trade. The committee included two eminent metallurgists, C.T. Heycock of Cambridge University and H.C.H. Carpenter, Professor of Metallurgy at Imperial College. It was decided that the assays should be carried out in comparison with a sample of fine gold of the highest possible purity. For this purpose a special refining technique was developed jointly by Heycock and Hobday, the former working in the metallurgical laboratories at

Cambridge and the latter at the Assay Office. They used their process to purify samples of gold from India, South Africa, British Guiana and Australia. The new 22 carat trial plate was deemed to be satisfactory but the mean result of a number of individual assays of the new fine gold plate showed it to be fractionally below the purest sample of gold produced by Heycock and Hobday – 999.96 against 1000. The Assay Master at the Mint, Sir Thomas Kirke Rose, agreed with these findings. The fine gold plate was therefore not taken into use and in 1929 the Mint submitted a replacement. However, the 22 carat plate of 1926 is still the legal standard against which gold coins are assayed at the Trial of the Pyx, the fine gold plate being used merely as an additional check.

After the turn of the century another precious metal, platinum, became popular for certain types of gem-set jewellery, such as rings and brooches, and to a lesser extent for wedding rings and watchcases. There was a feeling in the trade that as platinum was more costly than gold, such articles should be subject to hallmarking, or at least to a minimum standard. A draft Bill was prepared by the trade associations in 1924 and the Company was asked for comments. These were favourable but only on the understanding that compulsory hallmarking was envisaged. This proposal was discussed by the assay offices on several occasions during the next twenty-five years but little progress was made. There would indeed have been practical difficulties in the absence of any known method of assay that was both sufficiently rapid and accurate. However, by the time enabling legislation was passed in 1973 this obstacle had been surmounted.

14 CARAT GOLD STANDARD

Matters such as the foregoing naturally called for close co-operation between all the offices. There were well-established lines of communication through correspondence, mainly on questions of interpretation of the law, but before 1918 there had been no formal meetings. The first conference attended by representatives of all offices took place in that year specifically to discuss means of protecting British hallmarks from imitation in foreign countries. As a result the various symbols were registered as 'trade marks'. Seven further meetings on this and other matters of mutual interest were held between 1919 and 1923.

There were several occasions in the 1930s on which a joint decision was required by all six assay offices. For example the trade had been considering the desirability of a change in the legal standards for gold. The 12 and 15 carat standards had never been popular with the public; 14 carat gold on the other hand was much in demand for jewellery on the Continent and was recognised as a legal standard in many countries. In 1932 the Company was approached for its views on a proposal to replace the 12 and 15 carat standards by one of 14 carat. To assess the general opinion, representatives from the trade and the other assay offices were invited to a meeting at the Hall; more than 300 attended and the Prime Warden took the chair. It became clear at this meeting that the trade was almost unanimously in favour of the proposal and the assay offices accordingly supported it. It was put into effect by Order in Council in the same year, with the result that there were now four legal standards for gold – 22, 18, 14 and 9 carat.[1]

In spite of the original enthusiasm of the trade, however, the 14 carat standard has not been used to any extent in this country except for the manufacture of nibs for fountain-pens. In an attempt to attract more work the assay offices decided to find out whether it would be possible to strike a full hallmark on a pen-nib without causing damage. A very small composite punch was produced – another challenge for the Company's punchmakers – and marking proved to be a practicable proposition. But the fountain-pen manufacturers were not in favour and were even prepared if necessary to put forward a Bill specifically exempting gold pen-nibs from hallmarking. The matter was not resolved and with the advent of the war it was shelved. The production of gold nibs subsequently declined with the invention of the ball-point pen.

In an endeavour to boost the sales of silver, the trade associations approached the assay offices in 1933 to ask if they would be prepared to strike a special mark to commemorate the forthcoming Silver Jubilee of King George V and Queen Mary. This was a departure from traditional practice in the sense that it would be a voluntary mark, struck only at the request of the manufacturer, and not therefore, strictly speaking, an official hallmark. The assay offices nevertheless agreed to the proposal and, after obtaining royal

HALLMARK *for 1934 with the Jubilee mark.*

assent, struck the mark – the heads of the two sovereigns in profile – on silver wares only. Although the Jubilee year was 1935 the mark was first used on 11 February 1934 and appears with the date letters for 1933, 1934 and 1935.

THE ANTIQUE PLATE COMMITTEE

Although many facets of the hallmarking system were of common interest to all the offices, one in particular was mainly the concern of the London Office. Silver articles purporting to be antique but suspected of contravening the law were frequently received from both dealers and members of the public; most were the legacy of past offences, such as counterfeiting, transposing or illegal alterations. The Deputy Warden often had to call upon the advice of specialists to determine the genuineness or otherwise of such pieces. This was not entirely satisfactory and it was felt that it would be preferable to set up a permanent committee which could meet at regular intervals to advise the Company with regard to any suspect articles submitted for an opinion. Such a committee, consisting of the some of the foremost experts in the field of British antique silver, was accordingly appointed and met for the first time in December 1939: it became known as The Antique Plate Committee. When an article was found on examination not to comply with the law the committee recommended how it could be regularized. This was usually effected by re-marking – provided, of course, it was up to the minimum legal standard. An auxiliary panel of advisers was also appointed, the members of which were asked to inform the Assay Office if any offending articles came to their notice so that appropriate action could be taken. The committee operated, and continues to operate, in close co-operation with auction houses and has undoubtedly served not only to protect the consumer but also to maintain the high reputation of the British antique silver trade. Between the date of its formation and 1975 the Antique Plate Committee examined more than 20,000 items.

THE WAR YEARS: 1939–45

In the late 1930s war clouds were gathering again, and when hostilities commenced in September 1939 it was soon apparent that the effect on the work of the Assay Office would be far greater than was the case in 1914–18. In the twelve months May 1938 to May 1939, approximately 1,590,000 silver wares and 462,000 gold wares were received, but in the same months of 1940 to 1941 the quantities had dropped to approximately 246,000 and 262,000 respectively. The decline continued throughout the war (see Appendix III). Gold wedding rings accounted for a high proportion of the receipts during these years; at first they were mainly 22 carat – the most popular standard for wedding rings – but in 1942 a Government order restricted their manufacture to 9 carat. Their weight and price were also controlled and the assay offices were required to strike a special 'utility' mark (two intersecting circles) alongside the hallmark. The only other gold articles received in significant quantities at this time were watchcases and lockets, which were also restricted to 9 carat by government regulation.

In the latter half of 1940 central London became the focus of enemy air-raids. The gas supply soon became severely curtailed and this in turn caused problems with the gold assaying. Fortunately the wardens had foreseen that it might be necessary to vacate the Assay Office premises in the event of air-raid damage. In the first month of the war Blanford Lodge, a large private house in Reigate, had been rented and equipment installed. The gold assaying was transferred there in September 1940 under the direction of Sidney Haydon, the Second Assayer, but all other departments remained in the City for the time being. Night raids intensified in the following months. In November the Deputy Warden reported that equipment and tools in the Assay Office building in Gutter Lane had been badly damaged by water from the hoses of the fire services. The structure itself had been saved but it was destined not to survive for much longer; it was in an area that was the centre of enemy activity night after night. Like nearby St Paul's the Hall itself managed to escape by virtue of the prompt action of fire-watchers who were able to extinguish incendiary bombs as they fell on the roof, but nearly all the surrounding buildings were either badly damaged or reduced to ruins.

The worst night was 29/30th December 1940 and is best described in the words of Mr Dawe, the Company's carpenter, who was in charge of the fire-watchers. His report to the wardens reads:

> On Sunday 29th December at 6.35 pm the alert sounded and at once went to the roof and found the whole city around us was alight with flares. Got down to shelter and found all hands ready and on the alert, then we started. Was not long before fires were burning all round, the fire bombs kept dropping in all directions until the Hall was surrounded with fires – only west side free from danger … At 5.30 (am) I cried off, danger to Hall seemed over and all watchers dead beat with their efforts. Wish to bring to your notice the great help all these men were, stuck to their post through 11 hours of fire, including 6 hours of severe bombing and taking great risks … 3 women we must not forget: Mrs Dawe, Mrs Cooke and Mrs Wilson [wives of the watchers] … When the Assay [the Gutter lane building] caught fire, at once shut the iron doors [at the entrance to the tunnel connecting it to the Hall] and kept it from spreading to this side.

This was the night the Guildhall and many other city buildings were partially or completely destroyed.

The staff arriving for work the next morning found the Hall almost unscathed but their building in Gutter Lane burnt to the ground. This was the fourth time in its history the Assay Office had been ravaged by fire; on three occasions the premises were destroyed. The staff were able to extricate a few pieces of equipment from the rubble and ashes, including the reducing machine which, remarkably enough, although badly damaged was found to be repairable. There were also sufficient parts remaining from about twenty power presses to make three serviceable ones, which incidentally are still in daily use after almost sixty years – the original presses had been purchased in the early years of the century! One of the most serious losses apart from the building was the large collection of marking tools which had been built up over many years. Most of the staff were transferred to Reigate on 2 January 1941. From then on work was handed in at the Hall, taken to Reigate by road and returned after completion of the drawing, assaying and marking.

In April 1941 the Hall received a direct hit from a high-explosive bomb which destroyed the south-east corner of the building, but the remaining two-thirds of Hardwick's solid structure stood defiant. Gradually the air-raids subsided. In September it was decided that it would be safe to carry out the whole of the work of the Assay Office in the Hall; with the great reduction in

REAR VIEW *of part of Goldsmiths' Hall in 1950. The one-storey buildings in the foreground are on the site of the Assay Office building which was destroyed by air attack on the night of 29/30 December 1940. At the left-hand corner of the Hall is the single-storey extension built in 1847 to house the Assay Office fire-room.*

the workload sufficient accommodation was available in the part that was still standing. By November all the staff had left Reigate but the premises were retained in case of further air-raid damage to the Hall. With the arrival of the V1 bombs and the V2 rockets in 1944 it seemed likely they might be needed again, but in the event it was not necessary to evacuate a second time. In spite of the condition of the Hall the work continued as usual for the duration of the war. As in 1914/18 even the annual Trial of the Pyx was held without once being missed.

The two senior members of the punch department had reached retiring age in 1941 and were not replaced. Other arrangements were made for the supply of punches. One of the last tasks entrusted to Arthur Clinch, who with his colleague Alfred Cole had rendered valuable service for twenty-seven years, was to mend the damaged reducing machine and to remove the master dies to another part of the country for safekeeping. Most of the other staff were on war service. In 1941 sixteen were still working but by the end of the war there were only eleven.

Soon after the cessation of hostilities such rooms as were available in the Hall were suitably refurbished with benches, presses and other equipment and for a few years the space was adequate. But nobody could foresee the enormous extent to which the trade in gold wares would expand in the next twenty-five years. Immediately following the end of the war there was a slight boom in the silver trade – as in 1918 – but it lasted for less than two years. The industry was burdened by the imposition of a crippling 100 per cent purchase tax, the effect of which is clearly reflected in the hallmarking figures – 411,802 silver articles received by the Assay Office in the year 1946/7 dropping to 195,891 in 1952/3.

TECHNICAL INNOVATIONS

The number of staff in 1946 stood at twenty-five, most of them elderly. Although they were highly proficient in their particular skills which they had learned over many years, the Company decided that if the Assay Office was to keep abreast of new technical developments it was desirable to engage someone from outside the Office with scientific qualifications. A younger man (the writer) with experience of modern methods of chemical analysis was accordingly recruited and was shortly afterwards appointed Assistant Deputy Warden; he succeeded Horace Lindsey as Deputy Warden in 1953.

Many improvements and innovations were introduced in the next two decades. One major change was the employment of women for the first time – for assaying in 1950 and marking in 1953. Their performance proved so satisfactory for the precision work involved, that with the increase in personnel that was soon to become necessary, recruitment of both sexes resulted in a staff establishment of which about half were women.

There had been no formal apprenticeship training in the Assay Office for some two hundred years. This is strange considering that the Company still continued to bind apprentices to its trade members, a custom which had remained virtually unchanged throughout the centuries, apart from a reduction in the period of service from seven to five years. However, in view of a predictable future shortage of trained staff in the Office it was decided to resume the former practice and after 1956 apprentices were indentured to the Deputy Warden from time to time. The majority continued to follow careers in the Assay Office and became valuable members of the staff.

During the war years there had inevitably been little technical advancement in the Office and this, coupled with a severe loss of equipment and working space, meant that many matters needed attention. The Assay Department was strengthened in 1955 by a scientifically qualified recruit, David Dalladay, who later became Superintendent Assayer and eventually Assistant Deputy Warden; and in 1960 by the appointment of Paul Johnson who succeeded Dalladay as Superintendent Assayer in 1974. The assay procedures were thoroughly investigated and their accuracy improved; the Gay-Lussac method, for example, was enhanced by the use of a potentiometric end-point, thereby

WOMEN *were first employed in the Assay Office in the 1950s. The reciprocating presses shown here were introduced at the turn of the twentieth century.*

WEIGHING COINS *in bulk at the Trial of the Pyx.*

enabling consistent results to be obtained by less experienced personnel. New and better balances were purchased, the simple free-swinging assay balances hitherto used being replaced by up-to-date types incorporating air-damping and projected scale reading. These were later replaced in turn by electronic balances.

ASSAY OF PLATINUM

In 1953 a programme of research into suitable methods for assaying platinum was initiated in consultation with the principal suppliers – Johnson Matthey & Co., Mond Nickel Co. (later International Nickel), Baker Platinum (later Engelhard Industries) and The Sheffield Smelting Company. Since the classical methods of determining platinum were too time-consuming for routine use several modern analytical techniques were explored, including emission spectrography, UV spectrophotometry and X-ray fluorescence. Eventually, however, a method called atomic absorption proved to be the most suitable for the purpose and was adopted when hallmarking of platinum was introduced in

1975. Although less accurate than the procedures for gold and silver it had the advantage that only a small sample (10mg) was required, a distinct advantage for the reason that platinum is mainly used in the manufacture of delicate pieces of jewellery.

In parallel with the above investigations a method was developed for dating silver articles using spectrographic analysis, which proved to be of great assistance to the Antique Plate Committee in examining suspect articles. At the same time the scope of the assay department was broadened by the testing on request of various products such as gold-plated and silver-plated articles. Special assays (the old by-assays which had been discontinued in 1819) were again undertaken on behalf of any person or firm wishing to submit samples and this service was extended to include metals of the platinum group in addition to gold and silver. Miscellaneous investigatory work in the precious metal field was also undertaken on behalf of organizations such as the British Standards Institution, the Victoria & Albert and British Museums and Weights and Measures Authorities.

No history of the Assay Office would be complete without recording the debt owed to the many eminent scientists who have been members of the Court of Assistants since the middle of the last century. Some have already been mentioned; another was Sir Harold Hartley, scientist and industralist.

APPARATUS MADE OF PLATINUM *used for the nitric acid parting operation in the assay of gold. The apparatus was supplied by Johnson Matthey & Company in the nineteenthth century and the dishes, but not the covers, are still in daily use.*

One who took a great interest in the Office in the 1950s was Sir Henry Tizard, best known for his leading role in the establishment of the radar installations which formed a vital link in Britain's defences in the last war. Other scientists who later served on the Assay Office Committee were Sir Owen Wansborough-Jones, Sir Alan Wilson, Sir Robert Honeycombe and Professor E. T. Hall. Not only scientists but, as we have seen, eminent men in many walks of life have rendered equally valuable assistance. A notable stalwart who served continuously between 1940 and 1970 was George Matthey, Chairman of Johnson Matthey & Company and grandson of the first George Matthey who had given such great support at an earlier date.

THE STONE COMMITTEE

Although the Assay Office was taking advantage of modern developments in the technical field, it had long had to work in accordance with laws which were badly in need of revision and consolidation. The regulations were contained in more than thirty statutes and Orders in Council, the earliest dating from 1423. A positive attempt to identify the worst of the anomalies and to suggest appropriate changes in the law was taken in 1954 with the first of a number of joint meetings of representatives of all the offices with their legal advisers. One might say it was history repeating itself, but whereas in the past the Company had largely acted independently, now all the assay offices co-operated. After much discussion, agreed proposals were forwarded to the Board of Trade in 1955. In response the government appointed a Departmental Committee under the chairmanship of Sir Leonard Stone, Vice-Chancellor of the Duchy of Lancaster, to examine the state of the law and to recommend what revision was desirable. The Stone Committee met on fifty separate occasions, taking evidence from many people. The result was a long and in parts rather complex report, which was presented to Parliament in March 1959.[2] The assay offices were not in favour of some of the recommendations, but they were of course fully in agreement with the conclusion that hallmarking should continue as a compulsory system – in the words of the report:

> The worth and prestige of British Hallmarks on modern gold and silver carries the guarantee of a standard of fineness, which is respected not only in the home market but also overseas. In our opinion control over the manufacture and sale of articles wrought from gold and silver is essential, if the public is to be protected from fraud.

Another of the recommendations with which the assay offices were in full accord was that there should be a co-ordinating committee. The offices decided to set up such a committee on a formal basis without waiting for any new legislation: it was known as the Joint Committee of Assay Offices of

Great Britain and continues to meet regularly, as does its technical sub-committee. The government, however, took no immediate steps to implement any of the recommendations in the report.

In the meantime the assay offices were obliged to deal with infringements according to the law as it existed. The most frequently encountered offence in the years immediately after 1945 was that of selling an unhallmarked or substandard article. According to the relevant statutes one half of the prescribed penalty could be recovered by a 'common informer' taking action in a court of law, the other half going to the Crown. The Company was normally prepared to accept a 'mitigated penalty' which, if paid, avoided the necessity of court proceedings. However, it was unable to adopt this procedure after the passing of the Common Informers Act 1951.[3] According to that Act, a common informer could no longer recover penalties for his own use; all relevant statutes were amended so that a fine of £100 on summary conviction was substituted for the former forfeiture or penalty. But since the Gold and Silver Wares Act 1844 was not affected the assay offices were still entitled to sue for penalties for some offences, such as making an illegal addition to a hallmarked ware or possessing a ware bearing counterfeit or transposed marks.

A COUNTERFEIT HALLMARK *purporting to be 1774, with the maker's mark of Hester Bateman. This mark was struck on a tankard, one of a number of pieces sold by a silversmith, George Jones of Sheffield.*

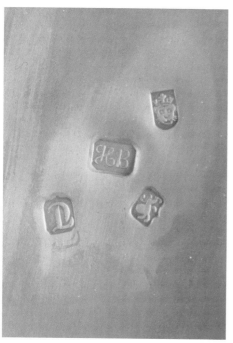

In the next two decades a number of prosecutions were mounted by the Company for the sale of unhall-marked or substandard wares. However, in view of the unsatisfactory state of the law, it often refrained from resorting to court action provided the offences were clearly unpremeditated and provided acceptable assurances of future compliance with the regulations were received. Instances of counterfeiting were few at this period, but one came to light in 1971 when the attention of the Assay Office was drawn to a number of pieces of modern manufacture, bearing forgeries of eighteenth-century hallmarks. These had been sold as genuine antiques to unsuspecting dealers and private owners. The culprit, George Jones – a silversmith in Sheffield – was traced, and a police raid, in which the Deputy Warden and the Sheffield Assay Master assisted, uncovered a number of false punches on his premises. Successful proceedings by the Director of Public Prosecutions resulted in a two-year prison sentence for the offender. At about the same time it came to the notice of the Office that fake eighteenth-century silver wares – candlesticks, tureens, dishes – bearing counterfeit British hallmarks, were being offered for sale in Italy. After several items had been purchased as evidence, personal representations were made to the Italian authorities by the Deputy Warden, and no further sales were reported.

In the post-war period the Assay Office was frequently asked to assist in prosecutions not directly concerned with hallmarking: for instance to provide expert witnesses in criminal proceedings concerned with the illegal importation of gold watches and bullion, or in cases involving misdescriptions of plated wares. Such prosecutions were normally mounted by either HM Customs, the Board of Trade or local Weights and Measures Authorities.

Co-operation in the drafting of standards for electroplated wares is a further example of a wider recognition of the Assay Office as an authority in precious metal analysis. Active participation on committees concerned with the preparation of standard specifications for gold and silver plating by the British Standards Institution and the International Standards Organization was combined with experimental work in formulating test methods.

The future of the Trial of the Pyx was in some doubt following the replacement of the silver coinage by cupro-nickel in 1947. Although the trial would naturally have less significance than hitherto, the government nevertheless decided that since it provided an independent check on the work of the Mint at no cost to the public purse, the ancient practice should be continued and cupro-nickel coins should be included. New trial plates of pure copper and pure nickel were verified in time for the Trial of the Pyx in 1948. Thenceforth, silver coins were restricted to Maundy money and special commemorative issues. The production of gold coins had ceased in 1917, but in 1951 a number of sovereigns were again minted. Although these were not for circulation as currency in the United Kingdom, samples were nevertheless submitted at the Trial of the Pyx. Gold coins were again included in the Trial in 1958 and in subsequent years.

THE CORONATION MARK

On the accession of Queen Elizabeth II the assay offices were asked by the trade if they would strike a special mark to commemorate her coronation. In view of the success of the earlier Jubilee mark, it was felt that this might boost the diminishing sales of silver. The mark, consisting of a specially designed crowned head of the Queen, received royal approval, and at the request of the manufacturer it was struck alongside the hallmark on both gold and silver

THE PLASTER MODEL *for the Coronation Mark, 1953–4.*

wares during 1953 and 1954. The sales of silverware certainly increased at this time, due possibly to the attraction of the coronation mark but also because the crippling purchase tax had been reduced by the government (the weight of silver received at the Assay Office in the year May 1953 to May 1954 was nearly 30 per cent up on the previous year). The quantity of gold wares was also beginning to rise, nearly half a million being received in the year 1955/6; small gold items, such as brooches, bracelets and pendants, the manufacture of which had previously been mainly centred in Birmingham, were now also being made in London on an extensive scale.

A steady increase in the receipts of silver was maintained for the next ten years; by 1966 they had reached more than half a million articles per annum. More spectacular was the rise was in the quantity of gold wares, their total weight increasing from an annual figure of approximately 80,000 oz in 1955 to 600,000 oz by 1968 or 4 million items. This was primarily a result of a boom in the jewellery trade, but a contributory factor was that active measures were being taken by the assay offices to ensure that all articles capable of bearing a hallmark were being sent by manufacturers. It had been demonstrated that many small articles, such as gold charms, which had not normally been submitted in the past could be satisfactorily hallmarked and were therefore not exempt.

The phenomenal increase in the workload created some problems; not only was it necessary to appoint and train additional staff, but also to extend the accommodation. The total number employed in the Assay Office had risen from twenty-five in 1953 to ninety-seven in 1966. Due to improvements in methods, a staff of only nine was adequate for the work in the assay department, but the personnel of the other sections of the Office had been substantially augmented. Fortunately, more accommodation was available in the Hall itself. A number of additional rooms had been created as a result of the rebuilding of the south-east corner after the war. These were at first occupied by the newly established Design and Research Centre for the Gold and Silverware Industries, but after operating for thirteen years it moved from the Hall and the Assay Office was able to expand into the vacant area. When in due course this proved to be inadequate it was found possible to build over part of the existing roof, thereby providing a large area of working space.

DRAWING (SAMPLING) AND HAND MARKING *silver in the Assay Office, c.1960.*

The upward trend in the workload was temporarily halted in 1968. In April of that year an increase in the rate of purchase tax on fine jewellery resulted in an almost immediate reduction in the receipts of gold articles (see Appendix III). The decrease for silver was slightly less, probably because there was a lower rate of tax on many silver articles. But the weight and number of silver wares started to pick up again in 1970 and gold wares followed suit in 1971. Then, in March 1972, the lowering of purchase tax on most gold articles from 45 per cent to 25 per cent resulted in a record 5.5 million items of gold and more than 1.5 million of silver being hallmarked. Silver jewellery became fashionable at this period and by 1975, when purchase tax had been replaced by value added tax (VAT), approximately 3 million silver articles were received per annum, mainly brooches, pendants and bracelets. After July 1972 the assay offices abandoned the use of troy ounces in favour of grams for recording weights and calculating charges – the pound troy and the pennyweight had already ceased to be legal units of weight.

INTERNATIONAL HALLMARKING CONVENTION

The proportion of foreign wares to the total receipts had shown a progressive increase since the end of the war, especially after 1959 when licensing restrictions were lifted by the government. In the past, imports had usually been sent for hallmarking in an unpolished condition and returned abroad for finishing. But foreign jewellery was now frequently received at the Assay Office in a completed state, calling for exceptional skill on the part of the drawers and markers. Importers were not prepared to accept the high cost of transport and the delay involved in returning the goods to the overseas manufacturer for finishing, especially in view of the complex customs formalities that existed until 1975. Consignments were received from many countries, in particular from Switzerland (watchcases), Germany (jewellery) and Denmark (domestic silverware). Later Italy became the principal source of imported gold jewellery, consisting mainly of chain bracelets and necklets. By 1962 foreign wares accounted for about 6 per cent of the total number received. The rejection rate was considerably higher than for British wares, since many came from countries without the strict control of a national hallmarking system.

It was evident in view of the increase in both imports and exports that some form of internationally recognized hallmark would be of great benefit to all parties and when such a proposal was put forward within the European Free Trade Association (EFTA) it was enthusiastically supported by the British assay offices. In the late 1960s the Deputy Warden and the Birmingham Assay Master took part in a series of meetings in Geneva at which the technical provisions of a Hallmarking Convention were discussed and finally agreed between the EFTA countries – Austria, Finland, Norway, Portugal, Sweden, Switzerland and the United Kingdom. The representatives felt, however, that the Convention should not be restricted to EFTA countries and its terms were accordingly drafted so that it was truly international in character. In November 1972 the Convention on the Control of Articles of Precious Metals was signed in Vienna. It came into effect in June 1975, Britain ratifying in the following year. Several countries outside EFTA subsequently joined.

Under the Convention special marks were authorized which, if applied at an approved assay office in one participating country, would be automatically accepted in the other countries as equivalent to their own hallmarks without further assay or marking – provided the marks denoted a standard that was legally recognized in the importing country.

The full Convention mark consists of a series of symbols – a sponsor's mark (ie, the maker's mark), a common control mark, an assay office mark and a fineness mark. The common control mark depicts a balance with figures showing the standard, the nature of the metal (gold, silver or platinum) being distinguished by the shape of the surrounding shield. Assay methods specified in the Convention are the same as those used at the British assay offices. The Convention also provides for regular meetings of a Standing Committee, of which the Deputy Warden was the first Chairman.

Co-operation between European countries had already been stimulated at the first International Hallmarking Conference held at Goldsmiths' Hall in 1965 under the auspices of the four British assay offices. Representatives from fourteen countries attended and one of the main items on the agenda was the possibility of introducing an international hallmarking system. Tentative proposals were put forward and there is no doubt that the cordial relations and mutual understanding which followed these broad discussions eased the path towards the creation of the Convention which was signed some years later in 1972. Subsequent successful conferences were held at the Hall at intervals of five years and they provided a useful forum for the exchange of views on technical and other matters.

NEW HALLMARKING ACT

In the meantime the assay offices kept up the momentum of pressure for revision of the hallmarking laws. In 1969, after receiving several delegations, the Board of Trade had at last indicated the government's intention to revise the legislation. It soon became evident, however, that it was seriously considering the abolition of compulsory hallmarking and in its place relying

HALLMARKS ON GOLD WARES: *(i) 18 carat gold hallmark for 1985. (ii) 9 carat gold hallmark for imported wares, 1988. (iii) A convention hallmark for 9 carat gold.*

on the Trade Descriptions Act 1968 for consumer protection in the precious metal field. The offices put up a convincing case for continuing the time-honoured system. They received strong support from the trade and from organizations representing the buying public. Eventually, in January 1970 the Parliamentary Secretary of the Board of Trade (Gwyneth Dunwoody) announced that the government was satisfied that reform of the law should be based on compulsory hallmarking of gold, silver and platinum wares, with limited exemptions.

Detailed proposals for a complete revision of the law were now discussed and generally agreed between the assay offices, the various trade organizations and the Board of Trade. However, it seemed unlikely that the government would be able to find the necessary parliamentary time for introducing new legislation for several years. In March 1970 a Private Member's Bill aimed at a limited revision of the law had failed to get a second reading. Fortunately, two and a half years later when the opportunity again arose to introduce comprehensive legislation by means of a Private Member's Bill, the government indicated that on this occasion it would support the measure. The Bill, introduced and ably guided through its stages in the House of Commons by Jerry (later Sir Jerry) Wiggin, Member of Parliament for Weston-super-Mare, received royal assent on 25 July 1973. All the old statutes were repealed and the whole of the relevant legislation incorporated in a single measure – the Hallmarking Act 1973.[4]

In February 1975 Peter Jenkins became Clerk of the Company on the retirement of Walter Prideaux, the last of the four members of the family to hold the position in successive generations.

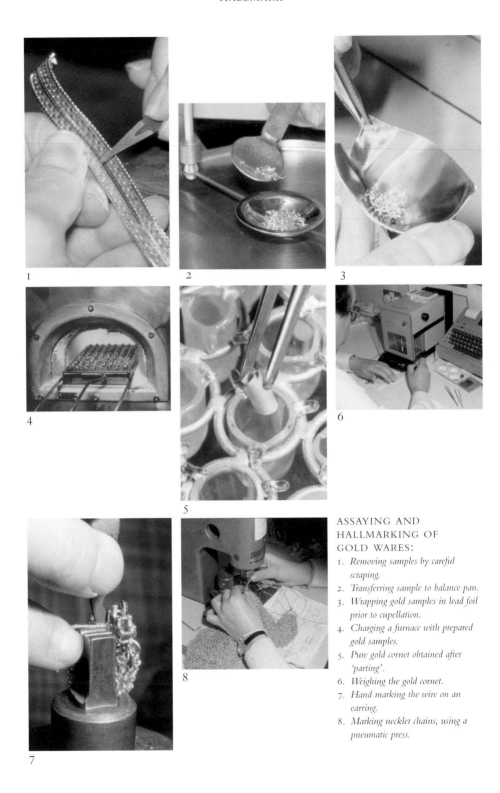

ASSAYING AND
HALLMARKING OF
GOLD WARES:

1. *Removing samples by careful scraping.*
2. *Transferring sample to balance pan.*
3. *Wrapping gold samples in lead foil prior to cupellation.*
4. *Charging a furnace with prepared gold samples.*
5. *Pure gold cornet obtained after 'parting'.*
6. *Weighing the gold cornet.*
7. *Hand marking the wire on an earring.*
8. *Marking necklet chains, using a pneumatic press.*

CHAPTER THIRTEEN

THE HALLMARKING ACT
AND AFTER

T HE HALLMARKING ACT 1973 took effect from 1 January 1975. The former complicated lists of exemptions, which had caused so many problems of interpretation for the assay offices, were replaced by a well-defined list including '*inter alia*' gold articles under one gram, silver articles under 7.78 grams[1] and platinum articles under half a gram. Articles intended for export, whatever their weight, were also now exempted. Exempted wares can, however, still be submitted voluntarily for hallmarking.

There was a significant departure from the previous legislation concerning the offence of selling an unhallmarked article. Section 1 (1) of the Act states that, subject to the permitted exemptions:

> ... any person who, in the course of a trade or business (a) applies to an unhallmarked article a description indicating that it is wholly or partly made of gold, silver or platinum, or (b) supplies, or offers to supply, an unhallmarked article to which such a description is applied, shall be guilty of an offence.

Under the previous law the offence was not related to the description applied to the article – if an article was gold, for example, and it was not exempt, to sell it unhallmarked was illegal, regardless of how it was described. This alteration in the law, although not wholly in line with the recommendations of the assay offices, was introduced at the express request of the government so that the new legislation would be in line with the Trade Descriptions Act 1968. Furthermore, as the law now stands, it is no longer an offence to *make* a precious metal article which is below the minimum standard, but such an article – whether exempt from hallmarking or not – must not be *described* as gold, silver or platinum in the course of trade.

As regards the hallmarks themselves, the new Act provided for a maker's mark (now called sponsor's mark), standard mark, assay office mark and date letter as before. There were, however, some modifications. The leopard's head replaced the lion's head erased, which was formerly used as the London Assay Office mark on Britannia silver. The crown mark was now to be struck on British gold wares of all standards, not merely the two highest; and the carat figure and/or decimal equivalent were replaced by the figure for the millesimal fineness. Otherwise the London marks were not altered by the Act – the time-honoured leopard's head, first used in 1300, remained as the assay office mark for British wares and the sign of the constellation Leo for foreign imports. The same date letter became common to all offices and changed on 1 January each year. Platinum was brought within the hallmarking system for the first time, with a single standard of 950 parts per thousand and a distinguishing mark of an orb (on British wares) alongside the sponsor's mark, assay office mark and date letter.

Another section of the Act was concerned with makers' or sponsors' marks. For many years the term 'maker's mark' had been misleading since it was often the mark of a retailer, not the actual maker of the article. After 31 December 1975 all existing makers' marks ceased to be authorized and as had happened on a number of occasions in the past, individuals or firms wishing to continue to submit to an assay office had to re-register their marks, which could be of the same design as before.

Under the Act a new body called the British Hallmarking Council was created, with powers to regulate the charges for hallmarking and to exercise a general supervision of the assay offices. The Council has sixteen to nineteen

APPARATUS *used for assaying platinum by atomic absorption*

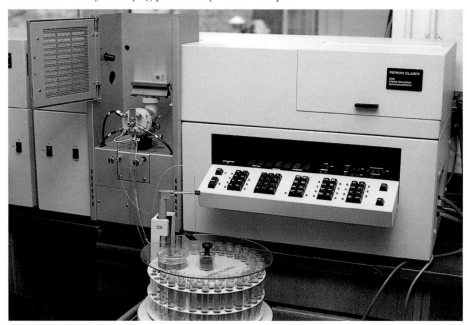

THE SECOND PLATINUM *article to be hallmarked in London – a cup donated by Johnson Matthey Ltd to the Goldsmiths' Company. The first piece to be marked was a medal awarded by the Institute of Metals to Professor Hutton, a former Chairman of the Assay Office Committee.*

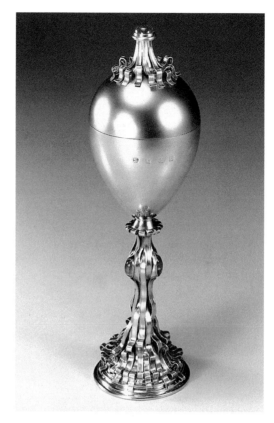

HALLMARKING *the above platinum cup on 2 January 1975 by W. D. Brown and P. T. Santall in the Livery Hall of the Goldsmiths' Company, in the presence of about 300 invited guests.*

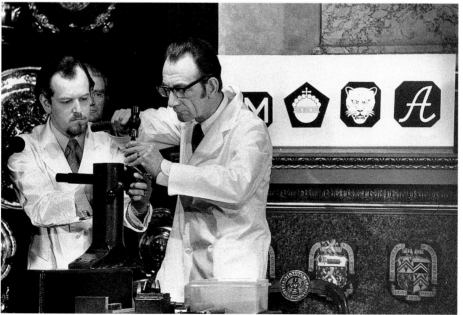

members, six of whom are appointed by the assay offices and ten – including representatives of manufacturers, retailers and consumers – by the government. The first Chairman, who held office for nine years, was Lord Runciman, a member of the Court of Assistants of the Company and a past Prime Warden. The Joint Committee of the Assay Offices established in 1960 was not dissolved and continues to meet regularly, working closely with the Council.

The Act also provided for an inspection of the assay departments at the four offices by the Assay Master of the Royal Mint, who is required once in every fourteen months to present a report to the Hallmarking Council on the accuracy of the methods in use. With this independent check the former Trial of the Diet was discontinued.

An important section of the Act covered enforcement. In England, Scotland and Wales this became primarily the responsibility of Weights and Measures Authorities or Trading Standards Departments, but the assay offices and the Hallmarking Council may also institute proceedings. This arrangement has worked well, as Trading Standards Departments are widely spread throughout the country. Officers of Trading Standards authorities and the assay offices have been given statutory powers to enter business premises for the purpose of ascertaining whether any offence has been committed, to inspect goods and to make seizures, thus restoring to some extent the powers formerly exercised by the wardens under the Company's charters. Members of the Assay Office staff routinely assist Trading Standards officers and give evidence in prosecutions as expert witnesses.

Counterfeiting and transposing hallmarks are classified as serious offences under the Act, carrying a maximum penalty of ten years' imprisonment. Altering or adding to a hallmarked article without the permission of an assay office is also an offence, as is the sale of an article which bears counterfeit or transposed marks or which has been the subject of an illegal alteration or addition. Thus the Company is able to maintain its role in monitoring sales of antique silver and examining suspect pieces with the help of its advisory body – the Antique Plate Committee.

SILVER JUBILEE MARK, 1977

Not unexpectedly, the Assay Office, in common with the other offices, was faced with an immediate increase in the workload in the early months of 1975 following the commencement of the new Act. In particular, gem-set gold rings, which were exempt under the previous Acts, were received in quantity, many of them being old stock and already set with stones. A increase in the rate of VAT on precious metal articles from 8 to 25 per cent from 1 May of the same year put a brake on the trade. The net effect was that the level of gold wares received at the London Assay Office remained at about 5.5 million items

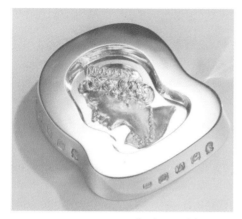

PLASTER MODEL *specially designed by Leslie Durbin for the Silver Jubilee mark in 1977, and a paperweight incorporating the same design that was presented to HM the Queen by the United Kingdom assay offices in the same year.*

per annum and silver at 3 million. However, when the rate of VAT was reduced to 12½ per cent half way through 1976, the trade experienced a totally unforeseen and unprecedented boom. By 1978 receipts of gold articles had risen to some 10.5 million per annum and silver to 4 million, creating a temporary problem for the Office until extra staff could be recruited and trained. At this time about half the total number of articles submitted to the four assay offices were hallmarked in London, where the staff now totalled more than two hundred. The number of platinum articles submitted since the Hallmarking Act came into force has not been large, fluctuating between 4,000 and 24,000 per annum.

A further impetus to the sales of silverware was provided by the Silver Jubilee of Her Majesty the Queen in 1977, during which year the assay offices struck a special mark on silver articles weighing more than 15 grams. The mark (the crowned head of the Queen in profile) was designed by Leslie Durbin, the talented and well-known silversmith, a liveryman of the Company. At the same time there was a pronounced rise in the receipts of foreign wares – mainly gold chain necklets from Italy – reaching nearly 2 million items per annum at the London Office.

With the accommodation in the Hall becoming increasingly inadequate it was fortuitous that, as was the case some sixty years earlier, the leases of a conveniently situated property owned by the Company were about to expire.

The building, known as 11/12 Foster Lane – later named Elyot House – was on the same side of the road as the Hall but separated from it by Carey Lane.[2] In 1975 the Assay Department was transferred to these premises from the third floor of the Hall and was later joined by the accounts section and the department responsible for the drawing and marking of imported wares.

A cause for celebration by the Company was the 500th anniversary, on 17 December 1978, of the appointment of Christopher Elyot, the first Assayer. It was commemorated by a prestigious exhibition at Goldsmiths' Hall illustrating five centuries of hallmarking – appropriately entitled 'Touching Gold and Silver'. It attracted over 18,000 visitors.

There was no cause for celebration, however, when a general recession in the national economy in the early 1980s was inevitably reflected in the fortunes of the gold and silver trades. The effect was exacerbated by escalating prices of the raw materials, especially silver. Between January 1978 and January 1980 the price of silver rose from approximately £2.50 an ounce to over £17, due largely to the speculative activities of the Hunt brothers in the USA, who endeavoured to gain control of the world's silver markets. Although the price soon dropped again the trade did not recover from the damage it had suffered. In a similar period there was a fourfold increase in the price of gold. Except for craft pieces made to special order, receipts of larger silver wares, such as tea sets and salvers, once the mainstay of the work of the Office, almost ceased. By 1983 the total number of articles received annually at the London Office had dropped by nearly 40 per cent from the peak of 1978 and remained fairly static between 8.5 and 9 million for the rest of the decade. Then, disappointingly, a further and more severe recession in the early 1990s resulted in another set-back for the trade and consequently for the assay offices.

In spite of the recessions foreign imports continued to rise. Whereas in 1976 they accounted for only 6 per cent of all wares hallmarked at the four assay offices, by 1996 the figure was nearly 40 per cent. London's share, however, progressively diminished, due in part to a vigorous marketing policy adopted by the Sheffield Assay Office which had formerly dealt almost solely with locally made silver hollow-ware and flatware. This trade in Sheffield had become practically extinct but the assay office there was able to take advantage of the great influx of gold necklet chains from Italy by offering not only attractive discounts on hallmarking charges but also a rapid service which the other offices, with their heavy workloads in the late 1970s, found difficult to match. More than 70 per cent of all imports were hallmarked in London in 1976 but only 14 per cent in 1996.

Owing to this loss, coupled with a relocation of much of the manufacture of mass-produced jewellery from London to the Birmingham area, the London Office was left with a greatly reduced share of the hallmarking market. By 1993 it was receiving annually about 4 million gold wares and 1 million silver, about one fifth of the total submitted to all the offices. The London Office suffered a further disadvantage in that it had to deal with an undue proportion of parcels containing only one or a few items which are not as cost effective to process as larger parcels of mass-produced articles.

After thirty-six years service in the Assay Office John Forbes retired as Deputy Warden in 1983 and was succeeded by Frank Bennett, a Cambridge PhD who was recruited from the chemical industry. His retirement followed in 1989 and his successor, David Evans, is a qualified metallurgist with long experience in the precious metal trade. Robin Buchanan-Dunlop had succeeded Peter Jenkins as Clerk in the previous year. All were in turn faced with the difficulties arising from the reduction in the workload of the Office. A number of organizational improvements were insufficient in themselves and, in common with many industries the Company was reluctantly forced to accept that redundancies were inevitable. By 1997 the number of staff had been reduced to fifty-five. Elyot House was vacated in 1994 and a new assay laboratory installed on the third floor of the Hall in the same location as the one in service some twenty-five years earlier. With the whole operation again

THE TRIAL OF THE PYX, *1982, attended by HM Queen Elizabeth II.*

under one roof greater efficiency was achieved. This was particularly relevant in the changed circumstances as the assay offices were now aggressively competing for business. Of significance in this context were a number of technical innovations such as computerization of part of the gold and silver assay procedures. First introduced in 1974, the computer proved of great benefit in streamlining many of the Assay Office operations. Other more recent developments include laser marking of delicate hollow articles and the use of x-ray fluorescence analysis, which can be carried out without the necessity of sampling. The latter technique has proved useful as a preliminary test but has not replaced the traditional assay methods which have greater accuracy.

The work of the Company's Antique Plate Committee has continued. Additionally, regular seminars have been organized to help auctioneers and members of the antique silver trade to identify articles that contravene the law.

The Company has continued to fulfil its traditional responsibility for the annual Trial of the Pyx. In 1982 Her Majesty Queen Elizabeth II attended, the occasion being the 700th anniversary of the first known writ summoning a trial. It was the first time the sovereign had been present since James I and his son Prince Henry attended in 1611.

In 1984 a new trial plate of pure zinc was required as a standard for the determination of this metal in the £1 nickel-brass coins which had been introduced for general circulation. Special commemorative issues of both gold and silver coins have been authorized from time to time and samples have always been included in the Trial in addition to the current coinage.

For more than sixty years coins made by the Royal Mint for the New Zealand currency have also been submitted at the Trial and in 1991 the introduction of one and two dollar coins made of an alloy containing aluminium necessitated the preparation of a trial plate of this metal.

THE INTERNATIONAL FIELD

Reference has already been made to the International Hallmarking Convention. This was strengthened by the accession of Ireland, Denmark and the Czech Republic, and also by the ratification by former EFTA countries Portugal and Norway. The chairmanship of its Standing Committee, which was held by John Forbes until his retirement in 1983, passed to his successor, Frank Bennett, between 1990 and 1995.

Shortly after Britain had joined the European Union – then known as the EEC – the Commission in Brussels issued a draft directive on hallmarking. Although similar in principle to the International Hallmarking Convention it was inferior in many respects and was strongly opposed by the British assay offices and the government. There were a number of weaknesses such as inadequate provision for enforcement. It was ultimately withdrawn, but in 1993 in an attempt to harmonize the marking of precious metal articles

FLY PRESSES *are still used for marking many types of gold wares.*

throughout the Community the Commission produced a fresh draft directive. This turned out to be radically different from its predecessor. It was even less acceptable to the United Kingdom since it provided for a sponsor's mark and a European mark plus a millesimal fineness mark, which could either be struck by the manufacturer (or by whoever was responsible for placing the article on the market, for example an importer) or by an independent assay office. In the former case the marks would merely signify the manufacturer's own guarantee. A country would have the option to adopt either of these alternatives, or indeed both, but would be forced to accept the marks of any of the other member states irrespective of the method chosen by them. At one stage, as the government's stance appeared equivocal, a delegation from the Company led by the Prime Warden, Lord Tombs, called on Lord Ferrers, the then Minister for Consumer Affairs. Happily, although supported by some member countries, no vote was taken when the draft directive was submitted to the Council of Ministers in March 1995, due in part to the robust stance adopted by Lord Ferrers. Its acceptance would have dealt a near mortal blow to the British hallmarking system.

Running concurrently with the above were several other developments in the international field. In 1991 the London Office, acting on behalf of the British Hallmarking Council, was instrumental in founding the Association of European Assay Offices. It has held the Secretariat from the beginning and the Goldsmiths' Company hosted the inaugural meeting. The Association has been singularly successful in establishing technical co-operation between members. Almost every European country has joined and several outside Europe have been accorded observer status. The main aim of the new Association was to provide a means of communication with the European Commission as well as complementing the work of the Standing Committee of the Convention and relevant International and European Standards Committees. The London Office has also been represented on a number of committees concerned with the drafting of standards for jewellery products – British (BSI), International (ISO) and European (CEN).

THE FUTURE

The future of hallmarking in the United Kingdom is at present uncertain since the draft directive has not yet (1999) been withdrawn. However, two legal cases have to some extent strengthened the prospects for its continuance. In 1991 a German manufacturer cited the Secretary of State for Trade and Industry, the British Hallmarking Council and the Goldsmiths' Company in a case brought before the British High Court. The German firm contended that the London Assay Office's insistence on hallmarking a consignment of imported gold clasps bearing the manufacturer's own mark was contrary to EC law; salt was rubbed into the wound when the consignment was found not to be up to the 18 carat standard. This action was in fact dropped because of a judgment by the European Court of Justice in another case. The European Court had been asked for an interpretation of the Treaty of Rome in relation to proceedings in a Dutch court in which a retailer in the Netherlands was being prosecuted for selling foreign jewellery not bearing a Dutch national hallmark.[3] The ruling, known as the Houtwipper judgment[4] effectively means that a member state of the European Union can require imported articles to be hallmarked but is obliged to accept as an alternative to its own hallmark the national marks of other member states providing they have independent hallmarking systems and the marks convey the same information and are intelligible to the consumer. It is ultimately a matter for the national court of the importing country to determine whether the information conveyed by the marks is equivalent. A further effect of the decision is that a member state cannot require articles imported from another member state to bear a date letter or any indication of their date of manufacture.

In order to comply with the Houtwipper judgment the Hallmarking Act was amended by Statutory Order which took effect on 1 January 1999.[5] Under this Order the crown, lion passant, Britannia and orb are no longer mandatory symbols. For silver and platinum the standard will now be shown by figures denoting the millesimal fineness – for instance '925' for sterling silver. The date letter is also no longer mandatory. However, at the request of the person or firm submitting an article the assay offices may strike the former symbols and/or date letter in addition to the mandatory marks.

The same Statutory Order stipulates that the marks identifying the assay office are to be the same for imported as for British wares. Thus the leopard's head will be used in place of the 'sign of the constellation Leo' on imported wares hallmarked at the London Assay Office.

The Order also authorizes additional legal standards – 990 and 999 parts per thousand for gold, 800 and 999 for silver, and 850, 900 and 999 for platinum.

A special millennium mark (see below), will be struck by the assay offices on articles hallmarked during the years 1999 and 2000. Hopefully this will signal the continuance of hallmarking and not its abandonment because of opposition from a few unsympathetic European countries.

As a final footnote it is worth recording that in the past forty years the Assay Office has provided technical assistance to the governments of no less than twelve non-European countries wishing either to introduce hallmarking or to improve their existing procedures. This serves to emphasize that in the field of precious metals, the British system of consumer protection which has stood the test of centuries is held in high regard throughout the world.

Seven hundred years have passed since hallmarking was introduced under the statute of Edward I and the Goldsmiths' Company is still fulfilling its time-honoured role. In his foreword to the catalogue of the exhibition in 1978 commemorating the five hundredth anniversary of the appointment of the Company's first permanent Assayer,[6] the Prime Warden, Ian Threlfall QC wrote:

Few systems devised by man have been found continuously useful over so extended a period and it is rare for any secular activity to be carried on almost without interruption on the same site for 500 years. Moreover, it is a legitimate source of pride in achievement that the Company should have been entrusted throughout with the conduct of an operation so important to the public and to the trade which it represents.

The oath of the assayer (1478)

Y E SHALL SWEAR that ye shall be faithful and true to the king and his heirs kings and true ye shall be in the office of Common Assayer for the craft of goldsmiths. And ye shall true assays make of all such gold and silver as shall be brought unto you to assay. And also ye shall melt all parcels of gold and silver delivered unto you truly and indifferently without any deceit to the least waste in hurting of the party as ye can, nor none avail take to the hurting of any person that the owner or bringer in of any such gold or silver. And ye shall no gold or silver admit to be touched, wrought nor sold under the goodness ordained by a statute made in the time of our sovereign lord king Edward the fourth (in) the 17th year of his noble reign. And ye shall all such stuff as ye receive of gold and silver safely keep it and truly remember it in writing. And also at all times convenient when ye shall be required duly and truly deliver it again. And truly make account thereof without favour or affection, hate or evil will showing to any party. And if any person bring any jewel wrought of old to you to make assay of and be touched, if it be not able (up to standard) then it to be delivered to him again at the first time. And if the same person or any other for him bring the same stuff the second time to be assayed and touched, then ye shall do waiting to (inform) the Wardens so that the same stuff may be corrected by the Wardens before it be delivered again to the party. And if any person of the said Craft would imagine or practise any untruth to deceive the said Wardens or you, ye shall anon warn the Wardens thereof as ye know it, so that they may ordain a remedy therefor as the case shall require. And if any person of the said Craft will melt his own gold or silver himself at his own aventure (risk) and then bring it to you unwrought to make assay, ye shall make assay thereof justly and truly. And if it be good and able so to mark it without anything taking. And if it be not able ye to melt it if the party will thereto bring in sufficient gold to make the worse gold good and sufficient silver to make the worse silver good according to the statute aforesaid. And he to bear no cost of the melting and making good, but only the waste thereto belonging. And ye shall none assay make upon gear new wrought without it be marked with the mark of the owner or of the maker. And also gold that shall be brought to you to cement ye shall cement it to the profit of the owner with the least waste that ye can or may, without any cost of the owner save the waste remaining in the cement. And moreover in all other things that ye shall deal or do for the fellowship and every member thereof ye shall do it justly and truly to your power without any deceit. So God you help and holydom and by this book.

(A shortened version of the oath was used in later years.)

Oath of the drawer (1726)

Richard Watts, Citizen and Goldsmith of London swears that he will be faithful and true to our Sovereign Lord King George and will as long as he shall continue as a Drawer of gold and silver plate to be brought to Goldsmiths' Hall to be assayed and touched, well and faithfully behave himself in the said office, and at all times carefully Draw and Mark the said plate according to the best of his Skill and Judgement, and no avail or profit to himself take to the hurt or hindrance of any person who is owner or bringer in of such plate, and that he will at all times carefully view and examine the said wares that they be not charged with unnecessary solder to the best of his skill and knowledge without favour or affection, hatred or evil shown to any person, and if any person shall practise any fraud to deceive the Company he shall forthwith give notice thereof to the Wardens and Assayer of the said Company or some of them. The secrets of the said Company not being hurtful and prejudicial to the King and Government he shall not discover and the profit and Interest of the said Company so far as he lawfully may he shall and will at all times readily promote and advance to his power. 15th March 1726

Deputy Wardens

with dates of appointment

1731 John Harris	1824 Benjamin Preston
1739 James Pugh	1834 Josiah Sharp
1753 Gabriel Sleath	1879 William Robinson
1756 John Swift	1897 Herbert W. Robinson
1766 Samuel Bates	1925 Arthur D. Bishop
1772 David Hennell	1931 Charles Hobday
1786 Fendall Rushforth	1937 Horace E. Lindsey
1797 Walter Coles	1953 John S. Forbes
1813 Edward Witham	1983 Frank W. Bennett
1818 John Barrow	1989 David W. Evans

Assayers

Head Assayer if more than one employed, with dates of appointment

1478 Christopher Elyot	1748 Francis Pages
1492(?) William Preston	1772 Fendall Rushforth
1498 John Jonys	1785 Walter Coles
1525 Edmund Lee	1796 John Marriott
1546 Oswald Lye	1804 Richard Bratton
1559 Richard Rogers	1812 Edward Witham
1567 Thomas Keeling	1813 John Barrow
1586? William Dymocke	1818 Richard Lee
Humphrey Scott	1822 Benjamin Preston
1600 William Dymocke	1824 George Miles
1617 Thomas Dymocke	1837 Jeremiah Fuller
1619 John Reynolds	1863 Henry Matthey
1629 Alexander Jackson	1878 Henry Pizey
1664 John Brattle	1887 Frederick W. Harrold
1669 Peter Trovell	1906 George Pite
1686 Nathaniel Bowles	1919 Sidney C. Robinson
1695 John Duck	1928 Hugh Gamlen
1716 Nathaniel Bowles	1948 Sidney F. Haydon
1721 Joseph Ward	1953 Henry R. Ingrey
1739 Samuel Edlin	1961 David B. Dalladay
1746 Joseph Shillito	1974 Paul V.A. Johnson

Annual Weights and Numbers
of Articles handled
at the London Assay Office

The following graphs show the annual weights and numbers of articles received or hallmarked at the London Assay Office. The figures prior to 1773 refer to articles actually hallmarked. Subsequent figures are from statistics relating to total articles received. Up to 1993 the figures span two calendar years – thus 1770 signifies the period 29th May 1770 to 28th May 1771. The figures are necessarily approximate since the Company's 'year' was not always exactly twelve months.

The weights of gold articles received between 1951 and 1953 have been omitted; to have included them would have given a false picture as a number of heavy items, which were essentially a form of bullion, were submitted for hallmarking during these years.

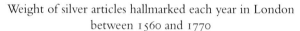

Weight of silver articles hallmarked each year in London
between 1560 and 1770

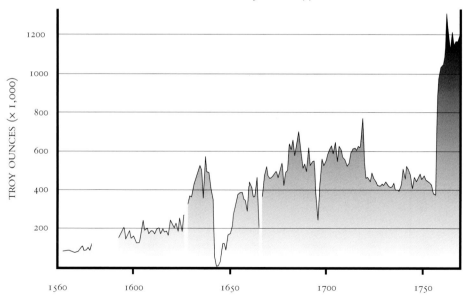

Weight of silver articles received annually at the London Assay Office between 1770 and 1995

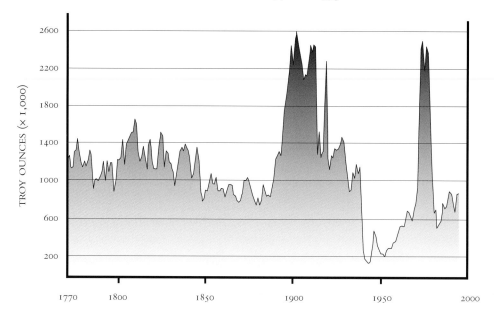

Number of gold articles received annually for hallmarking at the London Assay Office between 1891 and 1996

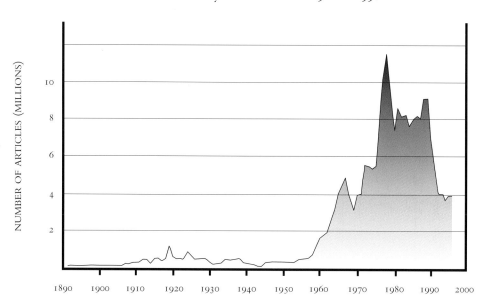

Weight of Gold articles received annually at the London Assay Office between 1773 and 1995

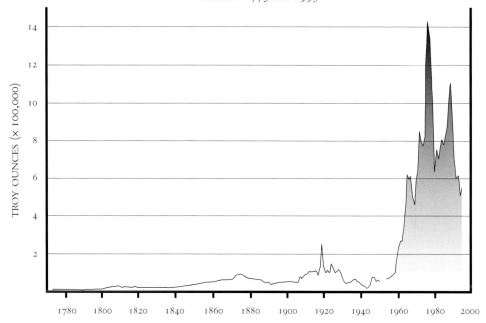

Number of silver articles received annually for hallmarking at the London Assay Office between 1891 and 1996

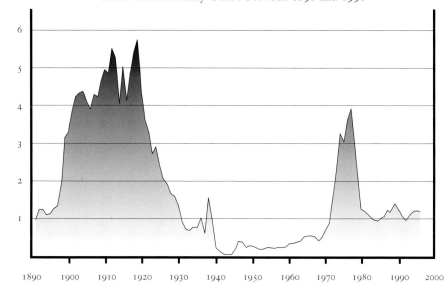

London hallmarks for silver

1478			1498	🛡	𝖆	1518	👑	𝕬	
1479	🦁	𝕭	1499		𝖇	1519	🦁	𝕭	
1480	🦁	𝕮	1500		𝖈	1520	🦁	𝕮	
1481	🦁	𝕯	1501		𝖉	1521		𝕯	
1482			1502			1522		𝕰	
1483			1503		𝖋	1523		𝕱	
1484			1504		𝖌	1524		𝕲	
1485			1505			1525		𝖍	
1486			1506	🛡	𝖎	1526			
1487			1507		𝖐	1527		𝕶	
1488		𝕷	1508	🛡	𝖑	1528		𝕷	
1489		𝖒	1509	🦁	𝖒	1529		𝕸	
1490		𝖓	1510		𝖓	1530		𝕹	
1491		𝕺	1511		𝖔	1531	🦁	𝕺	
1492			1512		𝖕	1532		𝕻	
1493		𝕼	1513	🦁	𝖖	1533		𝕼	
1494		𝕽	1514		𝖗	1534		𝕽	
1495		𝕾	1515	🦁	𝖘	1535		𝕾	
1496	🦁	𝕿	1516		𝖙	1536		𝕿	
1497			1517		𝖚	1537		𝖁	

1538		A			1559		b		1580		C	
1539		B			1560 – 6th Jan. 1561	C		1581		D	
1540		C			1561 7th Jan. – May	C		1582		E	
1541		D			1561 June onwards	D		1583		F	
1542		E			1562		E		1584		G	
1543		F			1563		F		1585		H	
1544		G			1564		G		1586		I	
1545		H			1565		h		1587		K	
1546		I			1566		i		1588		L	
1547		K			1567		KK		1589		M	
1548		L			1568		l		1590		N	
1549		M			1569		m		1591		O	
1550		N			1570		n		1592		P	
1551		O			1571		o		1593		Q	
		O			1572		p		1594		R	
1552		P			1573		q		1595		S	
1553		Q			1574		r		1596		T	
1554		R			1575		s		1597		V	
1555		S			1576		t		1598		T	
1556		T			1577		u		1599		B	
1557		V			1578		A		1600		U	
1558		a			1579		B					

1601	1623	1645
1602	1624	1646
1603	1625	1647
1604	1626	1648
1605	1627	1649
1606	1628	1650
1607	1629	1651
1608	1630	1652
1609	1631	1653
1610	1632	1654
1611	1633	1655
1612	1634	1656
1613	1635	1657
1614	1636	1658
1615	1637	1659
1616	1638	1660
1617	1639	1661
1618	1640	1662
1619	1641	1663
1620	1642	1664
1621	1643	1665
1622	1644	1666

Year			
1667			
1668			
1669			
1670			
1671			
1672			
1673			
1674			
1675			
1676			
1677			
1678			
1679			
1680			
1681			
1682			
1683			
1684			
1685			
1686			
1687			
1688			

Year			
1689			
1690			
1691			
1692			
1693			
1694			
1695	– 19th May 1696		
1696	– 27th Mar. 1697		
1697	27th Mar. – 28th May		
1697			
1698			
1699			
1700			
1701			
1702			
1703			
1704			
1705			
1706			
1707			
1708			
1709			

Year			
1710			
1711			
1712			
1713			
1714			
1715			
1716		A	
1717		B	
1718		C	
1719		D	
1720		E	
1721		F	
1722		G	
1723		H	
1724		I	
1725		K	
1726		L	
1727		M	
1728		N	
1729		O	
1730		P	
1731		Q	

1732	🛡	R	🦁	1753	👹	I	🦁	1775	👹	a	🦁
1733		S		1754		t		1776	👹	a	🦁
1734		T		1755		U		1777		b	
1735		V		1756	👹	A	🦁	1778		c	
1736	🛡	a	🦁	1757		B		1779		d	
1737		b		1758		C		1780		e	
1738		c		1759		D		1781		f	
1739		d		1760		E		1782		g	
	👹	d	🦁	1761		F		1783		h	
1740		e		1762		G		1784 Up to 30th Nov.		i	
1741		f		1763		H		1784 1st Dec. onwards		i	👤
1742		g		1764		I		1785		k	
1743		h		1765		K		1786		l	👤
1744		i		1766		L		1787		m	
1745		k		1767		m		1788		n	
1746		l		1768		N		1789		o	
1747		m		1769		O		1790		p	
1748		n		1770		P		1791		q	
1749		o		1771		Q		1792		r	
1750		p		1772		R		1793		s	
1751		q		1773		S		1794		t	
1752		r		1774		T		1795		u	

Year				
1796		A		
1797 Up to 5th July		B		
1797 6th July 1797 – 28th May 1798		B		
1798		C		
1799		D		
1800		E		
1801		F		
1802		G		
1803		H		
1804 Up to 10th Oct.		I		
1804 11th Oct. – 28th May 1805		I		
1805		K		
1806		L		
1807		M		
1808		N		
1809		O		
1810		P		
1811		Q		
1812		R		
1813		S		
1814		T		
1815 Up to 13th June		U		

Year				
1815 14th June – 31st Aug.		U		
1815 1st Sep. – 28 May 1816				
1816		a		
1817		b		
1818		c		
1819		d		
1820		e		
1821		f		
		f		
1822		g		
1823		h		
1824		i		
1825		k		
1826		l		
1827		m		
1828		n		
1829		o		
1830		p		
1831		q		
1832		r		
1833		s		
1834		t		

1835					1856				
1836					1857				
1837 29th May – 20th June					1858				
1837 21st June – 28th May 1838					1859				
1838					1860				
1839					1861				
1840					1862				
1841					1863				
1842					1864				
1843					1865				
1844					1866				
1845					1867				
1846					1868				
1847					1869				
1848					1870				
1849					1871				
1850					1872				
1851					1873				
1852					1874				
1853					1875				
1854					1876				
1855					1877				

Year					Year			
1878	🐻	C	🦁	👤	1899	🐻	d	🦁
1879		D			1900		e	
1880		E			1901		f	
1881		F			1902		g	
1882		G			1903		h	
1883		H			1904		i	
1884		I			1905		k	
1885		K			1906		l	
1886		L			1907		m	
1887		M			1908		n	
1888		N			1909		o	
1889 – 1st May 1890		O		👤	1910		p	
1890 2nd May 1890 – 28th May 1890		O			1911		q	
1890 June onwards		P			1912		r	
1891		Q			1913		s	
1892		R			1914		t	
1893		S			1915		u	
1894		T			1916	🐻	a	🦁
1895		U			1917		b	
1896	🐻	a	🦁		1918		c	
1897		b			1919		d	
1898		c			1920		e	

1921	🦁	**f**	🦁	1943	🦁	**H**	🦁	1965	🦁	**k**	🦁
1922		**g**		1944		**I**		1966		**l**	
1923	🦁	**h**	🦁	1945		**K**		1967		**m**	
1924		**i**		1946		**L**		1968		**n**	
1925		**k**		1947		**M**		1969		**o**	
1926		**l**		1948		**N**		1970		**p**	
1927		**m**		1949		**O**		1971		**q**	
1928		**n**		1950		**P**		1972		**r**	
1929		**o**		1951		**Q**		1973		**s**	
1930		**p**		1952		**R**		1974 Up to 31st Dec.		**t**	
1931		**q**		1953		**S**		1975	🦁	**A**	🦁
1932		**r**		1954		**T**		1976		**B**	
1933		**s**		1955		**U**		1977		**C**	
1934		**t**		1956	🦁	**a**	🦁	1978		**D**	
1935		**u**		1957		**b**		1979		**E**	
1936	🦁	**A**	🦁	1958		**c**		1980		**F**	
1937		**B**		1959		**d**		1981		**G**	
1938		**C**		1960		**e**		1982		**H**	
1939		**D**		1961		**f**		1983		**J**	
1940		**E**		1962		**g**		1984		**K**	
1941		**F**		1963		**h**		1985		**L**	
1942		**G**		1964		**i**		1986		**M**	

1987	[leopard head]	N	[lion]
1988		O	
1989		P	
1990		Q	
1991		R	
1992		S	
1993		T	
1994		U	
1995		V	
1996		W	
1997		X	
1998		Y	
1999		Z	

Reproduced from Ian Pickford's *Pocket Edition of Jackson's hallmarks* by kind permission of the Antique Collectors' Club.

Notes

ABBREVIATIONS

BM	British Museum.
BM, Add. Mss.	British Museum, Additional Manuscripts.
Cal.	Calendar.
Challis, Tudor Coinage	C.E. Challis, *The Tudor Coinage*, Manchester, 1978.
Craig, Mint	Sir John Craig, *The Mint*, Cambridge, 1953.
GL	Guildhall Library.
Grimwade, London Goldsmiths	Arthur G. Grimwade, *London Goldsmiths, 1697-1837, Their Marks & Lives*, London, 3rd. ed. 1990.
PCC	Register of Wills proved in the Prerogative Court of Canterbury.
PRO	Public Record Office.
Reddaway & Walker	T.F. Reddaway and Lorna History E.M. Walker, *The Early History of the Goldsmiths' Company, 1327-1509*, London, 1975.
Reddaway, Goldsmiths' Row	T.F. Reddaway, 'Elizabethan London - Goldsmiths' Row, Cheapside, 1558-1645', The *Guildhall Miscellany*, Vol.II, 3.
Watson, Trial Plates	J.H. Watson, *Ancient Trial Plates*, HMSO, London, 1962.

CHAPTER ONE

1. Pipe Roll 26 Henry II (Pipe Roll Society, vol.xxix, p.153).
2. The derivation of the word 'sterling' is obscure. A number of possibilities are discussed in detail by P. Grierson in *Anglo-Saxon Coins*, Studies presented to F.M. Stenton, London, 1961, pp.266–283.
3. Cal. Close Rolls 1237–42, p.85; 22 Henry III. According to the OED, a mark or marc is a denomination of weight formerly employed (chiefly for gold and silver) throughout W. Europe, its actual weight varying considerably but usually regarded as equivalent to 8 ounces.
4. 28 Edw.I. c.20. This statute was not repealed until 1856.
5. Reddaway and Walker, *Early History*, pp.222–4
6. 9 Edw.III. c.1.
7. 37 Edw.III. c.7.
8. Reddaway and Walker, op cit., pp.45–6.
9. Reddaway and Walker, op. cit., pp.68 ff.
10. A. Oddy, 'Assaying in Antiquity', *Gold Bulletin*, 1983, 16, (2), pp.52–9.
11. A handwritten tract dated 1507, by Thomas Aunsham, gives details of the cupellation assay for both gold and silver. BM, Harleian Mss., 38 fo.237 ff. Early printed descriptions of the cupellation method of assay are to be found in the following sixteenth-century treatises:
    (i) *Probierbuchlein auff Golt Silber Kupfer . . .* First printed circa. 1520. Translated by A.G. Sisco and C.S. Smith as *Bergwerk und Probierbuchlein*, New York, 1949.
    (ii) *Vannoccio Biringguccio, De la Pirotechnia*. First edition, Venice, 1540. Translated by C.S. Smith and M.T. Gnudi, New York, 1942.
    (iii) Georgius Agricola, *De Re Metallica*. First edition, Basel, 1556. Translated by H.C. and L.H. Hoover, London, 1912.
    (iv) Lazarus Ercker, *Allerfurnemisten Mineralischen Erzt und Berckwerken ...* , First edition Prague, 1574. Translated as *Lazarus Ercker's Treatise on Ores and Assaying* by A.G. Sisco and C.S. Smith, Chicago, 1951. This contains the best account of the cupellation method of assay and instructions for the touchstone test.
12. Tract dated 1507 by Thomas Aunsham – See note 11.
13. H.G. (Hannibal Gamon), *The Goldsmythes Storehouse*, handwritten, 1604, Chap.7, fo.4.

14. Reddaway and Walker, op. cit., pp.181–2.
15. Since the Company was not empowered under its original charter to own property the building was purchased by a consortium of nineteen goldsmiths. Ownership was conveyed to the Company after its incorporation in 1393. Reddaway and Walker, op. cit., pp.28–30.
16. Cal. Close Rolls 1247–51, pp.107–8.
17. PRO, E101/302/13.
18. Watson, *Trial Plates*, pp.8–9.
19. Two centuries later this practice had apparently lapsed; a Royal Proclamation in 1627 attempted to revive it by decreeing that for every sale of goldsmiths' work the charge for the gold or silver should be rated separately from the charge for the fashion and that 'a note or ticket' showing the same should be given to any buyer demanding it. PRO, MINT 1/1, p.106.
20. The wardens seem to have exercised the right to send offenders to prison without the aid of mayoral authority soon after the Company's charter had been extended and strengthened by letters patent of Edward IV in 1462, but they were specifically granted this power by the subsequent charter of 1505.
21. 2 Henry VI. c.17.
22. 17 Edw.IV. c.1
23. In referring to this statute William Badcock in his *A New Touchstone for Gold and Silver Wares*, p.33 defines 'harness' as follows: '... harness (in said Statute) is included all kinds of Furniture for defence of Man and Horses against the Enemy, as Swords, Buckles for Belts, Girdles and such like; and also all other manner of wearing Instruments for War ...' However the word 'harness' was probably intended to indicate a ware in a more general sense. (Reddaway and Walker, op. cit., p.243, note 4). This vagueness is unfortunate since it renders it uncertain exactly how widely the law was meant to apply.

CHAPTER TWO
1. BM Harleian Mss., 38 fo.237 ff.
2. For biographical notes on Adys, Brice, Coote and Palmer see Reddaway and Walker, op. cit., pp.275, 285–8, 292, 301.
3. Originally the maker's mark had to be added alongside the mark of the leopard's head after the article had been assayed, but by this time (1478) it was required to be struck by the maker before sending to the Assay Office.
4. J. Thuile, *L'Orfèvrerie en Languedoc*, I, pp.57–62.
5. Sir Bartholemew Read had been Prime Warden in 1500 when Elyot was Second Warden, and in common with Elyot was a former apprentice of Sir Hugh Bryce.
6. Will: Commissary Court of London. GL, Ms. 9171/8 fo.15. 31.
7. The other applicants were Matthew Hobard and William Preston, hoping to be re-appointed.
8. The fee payable to the Company by a master on taking an apprentice was fixed at 20s in 1400 and remained at this figure until it was limited to 2s 6d by a statute of Henry VIII in 1531. The apprentice was entitled to the freedom on completion of his service provided he had reached the age of either twenty-one or twenty-four; he had to pay a fee of 2s when sworn and at some periods he was also required to produce a 'masterpiece' to prove his competence.
9. Will: Commissary Court of London. GL, 9171/10 fo.75

CHAPTER THREE
1. Reddaway and Walker, *Early History*, p.196.
2. Ibid., p.221.
3. G.E.P. How and J.P. How, *Silver Spoons and Pre–Elizabethan Hallmarks on English Plate*, privately printed, 1957, Vol III, p.17
4. 2 Henry VI. c.17.
5. This ordinance is found at the end of the Company's first book of ordinances. The year in which it was passed is uncertain – Reddaway says circa 1483. A later version in the Second Book is dated 1513. Reddaway & Walker, op. cit., p.168.
6. Phillipa Glanville, 'Robert Amadas, Goldsmith', Proceedings of the Silver Society, 1984, Vol.III, No.5, p.106.

7. In 1529 Robert Cowper and two colleagues caused much trouble by pursuing a legal battle on behalf of members below the rank of liveryman for a greater share in running the Company and for a change in the method of electing the wardens. He was dismissed from the Company but probably re-instated.

8. PRO, E101/302/18; Watson, Trial Plates, p.14–5.

9. PRO, E101/303/2.

10. James Gairdner, *Letters & Papers Foreign & Domestic of the Reign of Henry VIII*, Vol.VII No.1601/11, p.597; BM, Harleian Mss., 4222, fo.16.

11. Owen Draper is mentioned in 1536 as serving as a bowman, one of twelve 'men at arms on horseback' which the Company was forced to provide out of a total of 250 demanded from the City by the King. In 1543 he was imprisoned for debt.

12. Will: Commissary Court of London. GL, Ms. 9171/11, fo.189.

13. In the list of assessments for the subsidy granted to Henry VIII in 1540 Oswald Lye's name appears alongside others known to have been working in Goldsmiths' Row, Cheapside. He was taxed on goods valued at £30. GL, Ms.132; PRO, E179/144/120.
    From the entries in the Company's minute book it would appear that Lye took over from Edmund Lee sometime between May and August 1545.

14. Portions of two trial plates, one of silver and one of gold, dated 1542(?) and 1543 are still in existence; they correspond to the standard of the debased coinage minted in those years, but there is no record of who was responsible for making them: Watson, *Trial Plates*, pp.16–7,48–9.

15. From the evidence of his will (PCC Coode 11) Matthew Dale, a member of the Haberdashers' Company who died in 1550, was a prosperous businessman with a dwelling-house and adjoining warehouse in Milk Street. As no goldsmiths are mentioned in the will, either as friends or relations, it would seem unlikely that he had any experience of assaying.

16. Thomas Stanley was appointed Assay Master of the Mint in 1545, Controller in 1552 and served as Under-Treasurer from 1561 to 1571, during which time he was responsible for the great recoinage of Elizabeth I. He was Prime Warden of the Company in 1565.

17. GL, Ms. 132; PRO E179/144/120; Reddaway, *Goldsmiths' Row*, p.204. Both Langley and Harryson later served as Prime Warden. Langley was elected Lord Mayor in 1576 and knighted in 1577; Harryson became an alderman.

18. Reddaway, *Goldsmiths' Row*, p. 205.

19. In the previous January he had been the recipient of a royal pardon from Queen Elizabeth in the first year of her reign. His name appears on a long list of persons pardoned for all treasons, felonies and other offences but we do not know his particular transgression. Cal. of Patent Rolls, 1558–60, p.172.

CHAPTER FOUR

1. BM, Add. Mss., 18759, fo.69; PRO, E101/307/1; Cal. of Patent Rolls 1555–7, p.369; ibid., 1557–8, pp.194–5; ibid., 1558–60, pp.68–70. 'Allay' is used here according to its original meaning, ie base metal (mixed with gold or silver).

2. PRO, E159/342.

3. BM, Lansdowne Mss., 48/4. This document was written by Henry Sutton in 1586. In it he says "I was one of the jurors in anno. 1561 (actually 1560) when our indented piece of silver of 11oz 2dwt out of the fire was exactly tried ...' The document lists the members of the jury including Sir Martin Rowes, Richard Rogers, John Langley, John Harryson, Robert Wygge and John Gardener.

4. The trials were later transferred from the Star Chamber to the Exchequer at Westminster. Between 1842 and 1871 the assaying was carried out in the Assay Office at Goldsmiths' Hall and the remainder of the trial held at the Exchequer. Since 1871 the entire proceedings have taken place at the Hall.

5. H.G., *The Goldsmythes Storehouse*, op. cit. Chap.18, fo.140.

6. For a more detailed account of the appointment of Richard Rogers as Assay Master at the Mint and other controversies between Stanley and the Company, see Challis, *Tudor Coinage*, p.131.

7. Reddaway, *Goldsmiths' Row*, p.184.

8. Will: Commissary Court of London. GL, Ms. 9171/16, fos.398–402.

9. GL, Ms. 2859, fo.9.

10. Parish registers, St Mary Woolnoth.

11. *Goldsmiths' Row*, p.203.

12. Gardener had also been a member, under Sir Martin Bowes of the jury chosen to make the trial plate for the 1560 trial of the Pyx.

13. R.D. Connor, *The Weights & Measures of England*, London, 1987, pp. 241–2. (The Company's minute book for the period 1579–92 is missing).

14. P.L. Hughes & J.F. Larkin, *Tudor Royal Proclamations*, Vol.II, New Haven & London, 1964–9, p.543.

15. BM, Lansdowne Mss., 52/12.

16. 18 Eliz.I. c.15.

17. Historical Manuscripts Commission, 8th Report, p.65.

18. Challis, *Tudor Coinage*, p.137.

19. PRO, E101/304/17.

20. PRO, E101/304/18, fo.58

21. PRO, E101/304/9; BM, Lansdowne Mss., 37/63 & 47/51.

22. BM, Lansdowne Mss., 47/60.

23. Ibid., 47/51 & 37/63.

24. Ibid., 37/58.

25. Keeling also said he disagreed with a decision by the Mint Assayer and others to reduce the weight of lead used in the cupellation process, as this gave rise to incorrect results. This no doubt referred to a trial carried out at Goldsmiths' Hall in the previous year in order to determine the optimum proportion for the silver assay. A copy of a report of this trial, in which four experienced assayers took part in the presence of two wardens, has survived. Those taking part were Keeling, Ralph Barton, William Williams (Mint Assay Master), John Brode (gold finer) and Thomas Robinson (gold finer). Also present were Robert Brandon and Christopher Wase (wardens) and Thomas Taylor (a member of the Court of Assistants). PRO, E101/304/18, fo.10.

26. The meeting took place during the period of the missing minute book but a record of it was borrowed by the Company from the Mint forty years later and a copy retained.

27. PRO, E351/2030

28. Watson, *Trial Plates*, pp.52–5, 58–61.

29. BM, Lansdowne Mss., 34/56.

30. There are several Exchequer documents in the Public Record Office recording the results of assays which were carried out on these three trial pieces in 1583 by Keeling, Brode, Robinson, Lawrence Johnson and Denys Gray. The indented trial plate of 1560 is the only one of the three of which a portion still survives. PRO, E101/304/18, fos.24, 30–5.

31. BM, Lansdowne Mss., 47/62.

32. Ibid., 47/52.

33. Ibid., 47/48.

34. Ibid., 48/1,2.

35. Ibid., 48/3.

36. Ibid., 48/4.

37. BM, Lansdowne Mss., 48/5.

38. Ibid., 48/22.

39. BM, Lansdowne Mss., 48/6. Some coins minted when Lonyson was Master Worker were also included. Flynte had intimated that Martin's coins were no better than Lonyson's in spite of Martin having charged Lonyson with working below standard. Whilst not conclusive because of the small number of coins tested, the results show Lonyson's to be marginally lower in fineness than Martin's.

40. BM, Lansdowne Mss., 47/58. The Company's records also mention a controversy between Flynte and Henry Cowley in July 1577, at the time Cowley was in the process of taking Keeling to law for rejecting his plate. Because Flynte and Cowley would not make their complaints to the wardens, the Court of Assistants committed both of them to the compter for misbehaviour in the Assay Office.

41. PRO, SP12/90.

42. BM, Lansdowne Mss., 48/8 & 48/9.
43. Ibid., 48/10.
44. Ibid., 48/12.
45. Will: PCC Drury 79.
46. Will: PCC Lyon 20.
47. Richard Martin (Sir Richard's son) was Prime Warden in 1596.
48. *Dictionary of National Biography*, pp.1175–6; BM, Add. Mss., 18759, fo.69.
49. George Chandler, *Four Centuries of Banking*, Vol I, London, 1954, p.
50. Craig, Mint, p.129.

CHAPTER FIVE

1. The minutes record in full the names of the offenders with the results of the assays and fines imposed – except those for Stourbridge Fair, the report for which, as the Clerk frankly admitted, was lost!
2. In spite of the events in 1599, Cawdwell held the office of Touchwarden (Fourth Warden) twenty two years later. He died in 1625 leaving £10 to the Company. See Timothy Arthur Kent, *London Silver Spoonmakers 1500–1697*, The Silver Society, London 1981, pp.21–4.
3. Sir John Fortescue had been appointed in Mary's reign to superintend the studies of the future Queen Elizabeth. He succeeded Sir Walter Mildmay as Chancellor of the Exchequer in 1589 and retained the post for the remainder of Elizabeth's reign as one of her principal advisers.
4. BM, Add. Mss., 10113, fo.362.
5. J.S. Forbes and D.B. Dalladay, 'Metallic Impurities in the Silver Coinage Trial Plates', *J. Inst. of Metals*, 1958/9, Vol.87, pp.55–8.
6. Craig, *Mint*, p.144.
7. William Ward was an ex-apprentice of Christopher Wase.
8. William Dymock, his wife and son were all buried at St John Zachary. He had been churchwarden in 1601–2 and again in 1612 and had held the office of Constable of the parish.
9. According to Sir Charles Jackson there are two variants of the date letter for 1619 and he suggests that the design was changed with the appointment of Reynolds, the new Assayer. Sir Charles Jackson, *English Goldsmiths and their Marks*, London, 1905 (reprinted 1949), p.66. Thomas Lawrence was serving as Weigher in the Assay Office.
10. Cal. of State Papers, Domestic, 1603–10, p.560; ibid. Addenda 1580–1625, p.520; ibid. 1611–8, p.479.
11. The reference by the special committee to 18 E:1 is obviously an error; perhaps the statute 28 Edward I c.20 was intended. But that statute contains no reference to marking of gold articles, only to their standard. On the other hand, if 18 Eliz. c.15 was meant, neither does that statute make any mention of the hallmarking of gold wares. In any case there is no record that the committee's recommendation was approved by the Court of Assistants – so it is probable there was no change of policy.
12. These pieces are illustrated in *Touching Gold and Silver*, Catalogue of an Exhibition at Goldsmiths' Hall, Susan M. Hare, 1978, p.42.
13. Horace Stewart, *History of the Worshipful Company of Gold & Silver Wyre-Drawers*, London, 1891, pp.123–4.
14. Elizabeth Glover, *The Gold & Silver Wyre Drawers*, London, 1979, p.10.
15. Craig, *Mint*, p.144.
16. Horace Stewart, op. cit., pp.57 ff.
17. A complete set of thirteen apostle spoons by Benjamin Yates (hallmarked 1626) is in the collection of the Goldsmiths' Company. For further information on Edward Holle and Benjamin Yates, see Timothy Arthur Kent, *London Silver Spoonmakers 1500–1697*, The Silver Society, London, 1981, p.29–31.
18. Edward Rolfe had made notes of the various meetings, including the procedure for making the Company's new trial piece, and subsequently offered them to the Company. The Company had felt it essential to keep a complete record of the whole episode, if only for its own safety, and transcribed Rolfe's notes in full into the minute book.
19. Hugh Myddelton had been apprenticed to Thomas Hartopp of Goldsmiths' Row and was a

member of the jury for making the new trial plates in 1604. He served as Prime Warden in 1610 and 1624 and was knighted in 1622.

20. John Wollaston, who occupied a large house in Foster Lane opposite the Hall, was appointed to the lucrative post of Melter at the Mint in 1625. He was Touchwarden in 1635, Prime Warden in 1639, knighted in 1641 and became Lord Mayor in 1643. William Gibbs, an ex-apprentice of Robert Jenner, was a successful refiner in his master's former premises in Foster Lane. He served as Prime Warden in 1643 and Sheriff in 1644. Simon Owen gave evidence on behalf of Holle at the hearing at the Guildhall in February 1629 (see p.). He was elected Touchwarden in 1631. As well as trading as a refiner he appears to have been responsible for making a number of basins and ewers. See Susan M. Hare, *Touching Gold and Silver*, op. cit., p.53.

21. The complainants were: Edward Holle, Benjamin Yates, Thomas Francis, Alexander Jackson, Daniel Carey, Edward Ragsall, Walter Shute, Robert Jygges, Henry Blakemore, Richard Thorniworke, William Sankey and Hugh Blackhurst. All except Blackhurst were included in the seventeen who had petitioned the Lord Mayor four months earlier.

22. Acts of the Privy Council, May 1629 to May 1630, 1043, p.330.

23. Ruding, *Annals of the Coinage of Great Britain*, op. cit. Vol.I, p.409.

24. Ibid. p.40; They were also published in *A New Touchstone for Gold and Silver Wares*, London, 1679.

25. Cal. of State Papers, 1633–4, pp. 359–361. By Royal Proclamation Sir Thomas Aylesbury, one of the Masters of the Court of Requests, was granted the monopoly of supplying sets of weights which were sold to the public for checking gold coins. PRO, MINT 1/1, pp.111 ff.

26. Acts of the Privy Council, 1630–1, p.385.

27. Cal. of State Papers, Domestic, 1631–3, p.302; PRO, SP16/215/10.

28. If, as is probable, he was the Richard Cooke who was apprenticed to John Dodson in 1589 he would have been some sixty-three years old in 1640 but he continued as Weigher until his death in 1652.

CHAPTER SIX

1. The trial held in 1649 was similarly conducted. The Lord Chancellor and Lords of the Council resumed their supervision after the Restoration. There were seventy trials between 1657 and 1870, after which date they have been held annually.

2. Backwell and Meynell were wealthy goldsmith-bankers. Backwell, who had been apprenticed to Thomas Vyner in 1635, was in business at The Grasshopper in Lombard Street, formerly occupied by Sir Thomas Gresham. He managed to survive when Charles II stopped payment from the Exchequer in 1672, but suffered bankruptcy ten years later; he died in the following year. He had been Prime Warden in 1660, and MP for Wendover in 1673 and 1679–1681; he is frequently mentioned in the diary of Samuel Pepys. Meynell was Prime Warden in 1661.

3. Bollen and Rutty were also signatories of the petitions complaining of foreigners working in the trade. But Rutty later fell from grace in 1669 when he submitted under his own mark a parcel of plate which included a chafing dish made by Henry Welch – a foreigner.

4. Will: PCC Penn 177.

5. Will: PCC Noel 139.

6. Cal. of State Papers, Domestic, 1661–62, Vol.XLIV, p.137.

7. Cal. of Treasury Books, Vol.I, 1660–7, p.4.

8. Cal. of State Papers, Domestic, 1661–62, Vol.XLIV, p.137.

9. PRO, MINT 1/4, 59; Cal. of State Papers, Domestic, 1664–5, Vol.CXXVI, p.474. Shortly after Brattle's appointment the King acceded to a petition from Charles Gifford to be admitted to the position of Assay Master at the Mint. The petition states 'notwithstanding the allegation that he (Gifford) is unfit for it, being a gentleman not a tradesman. The place was formerly held by a gentleman who had a deputy'. The appointment was clearly a sinecure and Brattle was still responsible for the work itself. Cal. of State Papers, Domestic, 1664–65, Vol. CXXVI, pp.491–2, 503.

10. Cal. of Treasury Books, Vol II, 1667–8, p.418.

11. Alan J. Nathanson, *Thomas Simon, his life and work, 1618–1665*, London, 1975.

12. Ambrose Heal, *The London Goldsmiths 1200–1800*, Cambridge, 1935, p.143.

13. Cal. of Treasury Books Vol.II, 1667–8, pp.45, 418, 510; ibid., Vol.III, Part I, 1669–72, pp.1, 21, 25.

14. See Thomas Long, *Dr Walker's Account of the Author of Eikon Basilike*, London 1693, pp.25, 29; also Edward Almack, *A Bibliography of the King's Book or Eikon Basilike*, London 1896, p.89.

15. Cal. of Treasury Books, Vol.VIII, Part II, 1685–9, p.739.

16. Thomas Spratt, *The History of the Royal Society*, 1677; facsimile edited by Jackson I. Cope and Harold Whitmore Jones, St Louis and London, 1959, p.228; Thomas Birch, *The History of the Royal Society*, Vol. I, London, 1756–7.

17. Cal. of Treasury Books, Vol.VIII, Part II, 1685–9, p.1917.

18. Newton Papers, PRO, MINT 19/1, fos. 95, 98–102.

19. The notices issued by the Company in February 1676 and January 1678 are recorded in *A New Touchstone for Gold and Silver Wares*, pp.133–5. see also note 23, Chapter one. .

20. William Badcock was Senior Warden of the Longbowstringmakers' Company in 1670. He received the freedom of the Goldsmiths' Company by redemption in 1688.

21. George Jeffreys had been elected Common Sergeant of the City of London in 1671 and Recorder in 1677. He became Lord Chief Justice in 1683 and Lord Chancellor in 1685.

22. W. Tovey, *A Trial of Gold and Silver*, London, 1678.

23. Sir John Shorter had been Prime Warden and Sheriff in the same year. Being a Dissenter he was removed as an alderman when the City surrendered its charter to Charles II in 1683 but was restored by James II who approved his election as Lord Mayor in 1687. He died in August 1688 as the result of a fall from his horse on the occasion of the opening of Bartholomew Fair. His granddaughter was married to Sir Robert Walpole.

24. Thomas Loveday held the lease of the substantial premises in Foster Lane. The building, which had been left to the Company by Robert Jenner in 1651, was destroyed in the Great Fire and subsequently rebuilt. As Loveday died in 1681 he did not progress higher than Fourth Warden. Nathaniel Bowles, a future Assayer, was one of his apprentices. See also note 2, Chapter thirteen.

25. W.B., *A New Touchstone* . . . , op. cit., pp.26–8.

26. Peter (later Sir Peter) Floyer was apprenticed to Thomas Loveday (see note 24). Together with John Loveday, Thomas' nephew, he took over his former master's business in Foster Lane in the premises left to the Company by Robert Jenner. He was elected Prime Warden in 1701 and Sheriff in the same year, but died in office in January 1702.

27. Bowles position at the Bank was for buying gold and silver. His salary was £180. Court Minutes of the Bank of England.

28. John Culme, 'The goose in a dotted circle', The Jaime Ortiz-Patino Collection, Sotheby's catalogue, New York, May 1992.

CHAPTER SEVEN

1. 6 & 7 William and Mary. c.17.

2. 7 & 8 William III. c.19.

3. 8 & 9 William III. c.7.

4. 7 & 8 William III c.18.

5. 8 & 9 William III. c.8.

6. Registrations entered between 1697 and 1837 are reproduced in *London Goldsmiths 1697–1837* by Arthur G. Grimwade, London, 1976, and those entered between 1838 and 1914 in *The Directory of Gold and Silversmiths, Jewellers and Allied Traders*, Vols I & II, by John Culme, Woodbridge, 1987.

7. The Plate Assay Act 1700 (12 & 13 William III. c.4.)

8. 1 Anne c.3.

9. The Act stated that all goldsmiths, silversmiths and plateworkers in places that had no assay office had to register a maker's mark at one of the offices in another town and submit their wares to that office. It was presumably considered by the Company's counsel that it would be illogical if the Company were obliged to accept wares for assay and marking from provincial goldsmiths but at the same time were to deny the same facility to some local workers. However, this legal opinion was not received until 1717 and in the meantime the Company continued – with a few exceptions – to refuse the 'assay and touch' to anyone who was not a freeman of a City Company.

10. Watson, *Trial Plates*, pp.98–9

11. In 1889 the Chester Goldsmiths' Company voluntarily decided that in future the diet of its office would be sent annually to the Mint to be tried with those of the Birmingham and Sheffield Offices.

12. John Cartlitch had been apprenticed to Peter Floyer in 1681. He had been on the jury for the making of the Britannia silver trial plate in 1697.

13. Newton Papers, PRO, MINT 19/2, fo.516.

14. There were two Classis lotteries, one in 1711 (20,000 tickets) and the other in 1712 (18,000 tickets): C. L'Estrange Ewen, *Lotteries & Sweepstakes*, 1932.

15. There were two reasons why some makers were members of other City Companies and not the Goldsmiths' Company: either they had obtained their freedom by patrimony through a father who was not in the trade of a goldsmith or they had been apprenticed to a working goldsmith who had himself obtained the freedom of another Company.

16. See J.B. Carrington and G.R. Hughes, *The Plate of the Worshipful Company of Goldsmiths*, Oxford, 1926, pp.41–43.

17. PRO, T1/253.

18. R.W. Symonds, 'English Furniture in Portugal', *The Connoisseur*, June 1940, p.235.

19. Records of the number of articles received were not normally kept; this was an isolated instance.

CHAPTER EIGHT

1. Although Britannia silver is softer than sterling many articles made between 1697 and 1720 such as coffee pots and tankards are still in perfect condition after nearly three hundred years.

2. 6 George I. c.11.

3. The leopard's head mark was discontinued at Exeter in 1777 and at Chester in 1838, but it was used at Newcastle and York until they closed later in the nineteenth century.

4. The £500 penalty for counterfeiting had been laid down by the Act of 1700.

5. Charles Hosier, Prime Warden in 1730, by his good advice helped more than anyone to improve the Company's financial circumstances. It seems he was not in the trade as he was excused serving as touchwarden in 1725 on payment of a fine of £10. There were three members of the Court of Assistants with the surname Marlowe. This one was probably not the Joseph Marlowe who was appointed Weigher in 1731. Nathaniel Woolfryes was Prime Warden in 1738 and a member of the special committee appointed to frame new hallmarking legislation in that year.

6. The makers of the unmarked plate were Joseph Barbutt, Abraham Buteux, Nicholas Clausen, Augustine Courtauld, Paul de Lamerie, Simon Pantin, Pez Pilleau and Isaac Ribouleau.

7. PRO, T1/253. Sir Philip Yorke was appointed Lord Chancellor in 1737 and created Earl Hardwicke in 1754. He was one of the greatest of all English judges.

8. Francis (later Sir Francis) Child had been Prime Warden in 1723. He was Lord Mayor in 1731 and MP for Middlesex from 1721 until his death in 1740. His father (also Sir Francis), who had established the banking firm Child & Co., had been Prime Warden in 1691 and Lord Mayor in 1698.

9. PRO, MINT 19/2, fos.510–1.

10. This seems to have been the usual practice, although in 1726 it was recorded that the punches of the leopard's head, Britannia and date letter were delivered to the Touchwarden to be kept in his custody and only used in his presence, whereas those of the lion passant and lion's head erased were given to the Assayer to be used by him 'for the forwarding of work'.

11. John Blachford, a former apprentice of John Cartlich (see note), traded as a refiner in Aldermanbury. He was Prime Warden in 1744 and Lord Mayor in 1750. He presented a painting to the Company in 1752 entitled 'Benn's Club' by Thomas Hudson, which shows him with five other aldermen at his country residence in the Isle of Wight. They were all Jacobite sympathisers at the time of the 1745 rebellion and had temporarily moved away from London for safety.

12. Richard (later Sir Richard) Hoare was a grandson of Sir Richard Hoare, the founder of Hoare's

Bank and was a partner in the firm in Fleet Street. He became Prime Warden in 1740 and Lord Mayor in 1745. He died in 1754 at the age of forty-five.

13. 12 George II. c.26.

14. See note 8, Chapter 8.

15. Charles Alchorne entered a mark as a largeworker in 1729 with an address in Foster Lane. Gawen Nash entered four marks at different times between 1724 and 1739, with addresses in Gutter Lane, Wood Street and Carey Lane. Samuel Edlin of Foster Lane entered marks in 1704 and 1720.

16. David Willaume, who was born in Metz, was one of the first of the Huguenot goldsmiths to settle in England after the Revocation of the Edict of Nantes, and one of the most outstanding. He was made a freeman of the Company by order of the Court of Aldermen in 1694 and became a member of the Court of Assistants in 1725. For further biographical details see Grimwade, *London Goldsmiths*, pp.703–4.

17. See Carrington and Hughes, *The Plate of the Worshipful Company of Goldsmiths*, op. cit., p.93.

18. John Payne was the son of Humphrey Payne who had died in 1751 after serving three years as a warden. John, who was Prime Warden in 1765, was married to the daughter of the Clerk, John Banks. Thomas Whipham, who had been apprenticed to Thomas Farren in 1728, first entered a mark in 1737. He established a partnership with Charles Wright in Ave Maria Lane in 1757: this firm continued under Wright's apprentice Edward Barnard and is still in existence trading as Edward Barnard & Sons. Thomas Whipham was Prime Warden in 1771. The name of Sandilands Drinkwater is well known to collectors of wine labels (bottle tickets); he was Prime Warden in 1761. Samuel Spindler was a refiner in Gutter Lane who supplied precious metal to the trade at large; he served as Prime Warden in 1765.

19. 29 George II. c.14.

20. 31 George II. c.32.

21. For biographical details of Gabriel Sleath see Margaret Grimshaw, *The Society of Silver Collectors*, Proceedings 1972–4, Vol II, 8, p.141–2.

22. Grimwade, *London Goldsmiths*, p.675.

23. William Cox was one of four brothers who traded as silversmiths and refiners in Little Britain. The eldest was Robert Albion (or Albin) Cox, an ex-apprentice of Humphrey Payne and his son John (see note 198). A third brother named Albion Cox moved to Sheffield in about 1770 and gave evidence (unfavourable to the Goldsmiths' Company) at the Parliamentary Enquiry in 1773. The fourth, called Edward, was apprenticed to his elder brother William. William's son, another Robert Albion Cox, who received his freedom by patrimony, became an Alderman and was Prime Warden in 1818. By then the family enterprise had become the foremost firm of refiners in London, trading as Cox and Merle – William Merle, who was Prime Warden in 1811, being a former apprentice of the first Robert Albion Cox.

CHAPTER NINE

1. P. Hennell, 'The Hennells Identified', *The Connoisseur*, December 1955, Vol. 136, p.260.

2. The Hon. Thomas Harley was Prime Warden in 1762 and Lord Mayor in 1767. He was an MP for London from 1761 to 1774 and for Herefordshire from 1776 to 1802. Originally a wine merchant, he later became a banker.

3. The Plate Assay (Sheffield and Birmingham) Act 1772 (13 George III. c.52).

4. This Peter Floyer was probably a great-nephew of Sir Peter Floyer (see page 000). There was also another connection: he was apprenticed in 1731 to John Foxall, the son of Matthew Foxall, Clerk of the Company from 1689 to 1712. John Foxall in turn had been apprenticed to John Cartlich, whose master had been Sir Peter Floyer. Foxall continued to trade in the same premises in Oat Lane after Cartlich's death in 1726 and was followed by Peter Floyer (the younger), who moved a few doors away to Love Lane in about 1760. In 1775 the business became Floyer and Price, which name appears in London trade directories until circa 1785.

5. Report from the Committee appointed to enquire into the Manner of Conducting the Several Assay Offices in London, York, Exeter, Bristol, Chester, Norwich and Newcastle upon Tyne, printed 1773. (In fact there was no assay office operating at York, Bristol or Norwich at this date).

6. W. J. Aldridge, *The Goldsmiths' Repository*, London, 1789, p.31. The author, himself an assayer, states that it was the normal practice in his profession to report results of silver assays without applying any correction although it was known there was a loss of 1 or 2dwt in the cupellation process. He explains that this was the reason why articles which assayed at 2dwt below the standard were passed at Goldsmiths' Hall.

7. Grimwade, *London Goldsmiths*, p.667.

8. Matthieu Tillet, Mèn. Acad. Roy. Sciences, Paris, 1760, pp.361–379; ibid., 1762, pp.10–16; ibid., 1763, pp.38–64; J. Hellot, M. Tillet & P.J. Maquer, ibid. pp.1–14 (1763).

9. Albion Cox, who was in his early twenties, became one of the original Guardians of the Sheffield Assay Office in 1773 but left the town in the following year. Twenty years later he died in America where he had been first assayer of the Philadelphia Mint. (Geo. G. Evans, *Illustrated History of the US Mint*, p.117). See also note 23, Chapter eight.

10. 13 George III. c.59.

11. A gruesome account of the hanging was reported in *The Leeds Mercury* on 11 January 1785, an extract of which is reproduced by Sir Walter Sherburne Prideaux, in *Memorials of the Goldsmiths' Company*, Vol.II, p.278.

12. Information supplied by Capt. R. Le Bas, Dublin Assay Master 1963–88.

13. Guardians' Minute Book, Birmingham Assay Office, Vol.I, pp.22–46, 51.

14. Margaret A.V. Gill, *A Directory of Newcastle Goldsmiths*, 1980, p.30

CHAPTER TEN

1. Sir Thomas Hallifax was one of the original partners of Glyn's (later Glyn Mills) Bank in Lombard Street and senior partner after the death of Sir Richard Glyn.

2. Geo. III. c.53.

3. In 1849 the percentage of the total duty allowed to the Company was reduced from 2.5 per cent to 1 per cent.

4. This was later changed by Section 3 of the Gold and Silver Wares Act 1854 (17 & 18 Vict. c.96) which allowed exempted gold wares to be submitted voluntarily for hallmarking without attracting liability for duty.

5. The Act was 38 Geo. III. c.24.

6. For a comprehensive description of the variations in the shield of the duty mark, see Anthony B.L. Dove, 'Some New Light on Plate Duty and its Marks', *Antique Collecting*, September 1984, Vol.19 No.4, p.39–42. (There is an abridged version in *Jackson's Silver and Gold Marks*, ed. Ian Pickford, Woodbridge, 1989).

7. The Act by which the mark was discontinued was 25 Geo. III. c.64.

8. Geo. III. c.31.

9. The Act of 1773 establishing assay offices in Birmingham and Sheffield prohibited makers from striking any marks on plated wares. This provision was, however, repealed by the Plate Assay (Sheffield) Act 1784 (24 Geo. III. c.20), which allowed them to use a mark consisting of their name in full followed by a device which was not an imitation of a hallmark. All such marks had to be registered at the Sheffield Assay Office.

10. It is on record that in 1809 George Miles made two platinum boilers for the distinguished chemist William Hyde Wollaston, who had discovered how to fabricate platinum on a practical scale and was promoting the commercial use of platinum vessels in the manufacture of sulphuric acid. John Johnson probably acted as an intermediary since he provided the platinum. Donald McDonald and Leslie B. Hunt, *A History of Platinum and its Allied Metals*, London 1982, pp.165–167.

11. 37 Geo. III. c.108.

12. S.E. Atkins & W.H. Overall, *Some Account of the Worshipful Company of Clockmakers*, 1881, privately printed, p.269–271.

13. 38 Geo. III. c.69.

14. William City, aged about thirty at the time of his appointment, had been apprenticed in 1795 to Thomas Richards of Bridgewater Square as a 'gold and silver worker of watch cases'.

15. Guardians' Minute Book, Birmingham Assay Office, Vol.I, pp.168–70.

16. From 1888 all figures are given in decimal notation to one part in ten thousand.
17. Report from the Select Committee on the Royal Mint, printed by Order of the House of Commons, 1837, Appendix No.4.
18. Letter dated 2 January 1839. Lane papers, GL, Ms.11460.
19. The Act establishing the Glasgow Assay Office was 59 Geo. III. c.28.
20. Johnson & Sons were tenants of the Haberdashers' Company at 6 and 7 Maiden Lane (now Gresham Street), roughly on the east corner of Staining Lane and therefore very close to Goldsmiths' Hall. George Richard Johnson was only twenty–two in 1829 but took over the running of the firm on the death of his father two years later.
21. Donald McDonald, *Percival Norton Johnson*, Johnson Matthey & Co. Ltd., 1951, p.27–28.
22. Ibid., p.129.

CHAPTER ELEVEN

1. Jeremiah Fuller was apprenticed to a plateworker, James Shallis. He received his freedom in 1820 and was appointed drawer in 1822. He became Third Assayer in 1830 and First or Senior Assayer in 1837 after the death of George Miles, a post he held until he retired in 1863.
2. Members of the Wyon family were predominant in the field of coinage and medal design throughout most of the nineteenth century, William Wyon in particular being responsible for many outstanding examples. Thomas Wyon, William's father, was Chief Engraver at the Mint until 1817, after which William continued as Second Engraver although acting in effect as Chief.
3. The representatives were Robert Garrard, Edward Barnard junior, James Samuel Hunt and Charles Reiley.
   Robert Garrard was the son of the first Robert, the founder of the firm of Garrard & Co. His younger brother James, who was formerly in partnership with him, was closely concerned with Assay Office matters. The firm Edward Barnard & Sons is still in existence (see note 18, Chapter eight). John Samuel Hunt was a partner in the firm Storr & Mortimer, trading as Mortimer & Hunt after Paul Storr's retirement in 1838 and as Hunt & Roskell after Mortimer's retirement in 1843. The firm was sold to J.W. Benson in 1889 and is now one of the Mappin & Webb group of companies. Charles Reiley was a silversmith in Carey Lane who, in partnership first with his mother and then George Storer, made fine quality snuff boxes and other small wares.
4. 5 & 6 Vict. c.47, Sections 59 and 60.
5. The Customs (Amendment) Act 1842 (5 & 6 Vict. c.56), Section 6.
6. 7 & 8 Vict. c.22. There is a reference to the earlier Bill in Lane Papers, GL, Ms. 11460.
7. Gill, *A Directory of Newcastle Goldsmiths*, op. cit. p.33; Guardians' Minute Book, Birmingham Assay Office, Vol.II, pp.137–9.
8. Report of the Commissioners appointed to inquire into the Constitution, Management and Expense of the Royal Mint, printed by order of the House of Commons, HMSO, 1849.
9. They held the position of Clerk of the Company for the whole of the 123 years except from 1939 to 1953 during which period W.A. Prideaux was Assistant Clerk.
10. 17 & 18 Vict. c.96.
11. The York Assay Office closed in 1716 but reopened circa 1776.
12. Report from the Select Committee on Silver and Gold Wares, printed by order of the House of Commons, May 1856.
13. Commission des Monnaies – Ordonnances Royales du Juin 1830, Tarif, *Instruction et Rapports sur le Nouveau Mode d'Essai des Espèces et Matières d'Argent*, Paris, 1830.
14. J.L. Gay-Lussac, *Instruction sur l'Essai des Matières d'Argent par la Voie Humide*, La Commission des Monnaies et Médailles, Paris 1832.
15. Letter dated 5 October 1833 from P.N. Johnson to John Lane: GL, Lane Papers, Ms. 11460.
16. McDonald, *Percival Norton Johnson*, op. cit., p.136–137. The title was conferred on Johnson & Matthey, George Richard Johnson, F. Claudet (who was associated with the firm N.M. Rothschild) and Dr W.H. Makins (a forerunner of the firm D.C. Griffiths).
17. Ibid., p.78.
18. For a short biography of Heycock, see L.B. Hunt, *The Metallurgist and Materials Technologist*, July 1980, pp.392–394.
19. 33 & 34 Vict. c.10.

20. Fourth Annual Report Royal Mint, 1873, p.42.

21. Thirtieth Annual Report Royal Mint, 1899, p.67.

22. A member of the jury appointed to verify the plates on this occasion was Sir Frederick Abel FRS, who had been Prime Warden in 1895. He was War Department Chemist from 1854 to 1888, an authority on explosives and co-inventor (with James Dewar) of cordite in 1889.

23. Report from the Select Committee on Gold and Silver (Hall Marking) together with the proceedings of the Committee, Minutes of Evidence and Appendix, 1879.

24. 47 & 48 Vict. c.62, Section 4.

25. The Customs and Inland Revenue Act 1890 (53 & 54 Vict. c.8).

26. Journal of the Royal Society of Arts, 30 Jan. 1891.

27. 18 & 19 Vict. c.60.

28. The letter 'F' for foreign wares was introduced by the Customs Amendment Act 1867, Section 24; (30 & 31 Vict. c.82).

29. 50 & 51 Vict. c.28, Section 8 (1).

30. 46 & 47 Vict. c.55, Section 10.

31. The Hallmarking of Foreign Plate Act 1904 (4 Edw. VII. c.6); S.R.& O. 1904/1660.

32. S.R.& O. 1906/386.

33. Jonathan Hayne, Prime Warden in 1843, was a silversmith with a flourishing business in Clerkenwell.

34. Huggin Lane no longer exists; it was built on after the 1939–45 war.

35. Sir William Jackson Pope FRS was a professor of Chemistry at Cambridge University from 1908 to 1939. He was Prime Warden in 1928. (C.T. Heycock see pages 261 and 286. Sir Frederick Abel see note 22,Chapter eleven).

36. Thomas Hough was apprenticed in 1827 to Jonathan Hayne (note 33). He received his freedom in 1835, the same year as he was appointed drawer in the Assay Office.

37. For a detailed account of both cases see P.V.A. Johnson, 'The Lyon and Twinam Forgeries', *Proceedings of the Silver Society*, 1979–81, pp.25–35.

CHAPTER TWELVE

1. The Gold Wares (Standard of Fineness) Order, 1932 (S.R.& O. 1932/654).

2. Report of the Departmental Committee on Hallmarking, Cmnd. 663, HMSO, London, 1959.

3. 14 & 15 Geo.VI. c.39.

4. 1973. c.43.

CHAPTER THIRTEEN

1. The Hallmarking Act 1973 originally stipulated an exemption weight of 5g for silver articles but this was amended to 7.78g before the Act came into force. 7.78g is equivalent to 5dwt, which was the exemption weight under the former legislation.

2. The premises on the south corner of Foster Lane and Carey Lane had been acquired by the Goldsmiths' Company in 1900 and were demolished in 1998 for redevelopment. They were directly in front of the site of the large house once belonging to the refiner Robert Jenner, which the Company had inherited from him in 1651. This house and its outbuildings, which were burnt down in the Great Fire and rebuilt, were occupied by a succession of refiners following Jenner – William Gibbs, Joseph Archer, Thomas Loveday, Sir Peter Floyer, John Loveday, John Cartlich, William Cartlich, James Hayward & Henry Allcraft, James Baston & Philip Sheppard. The house and workshops were then leased in 1779 to the silversmith Robert Hennell, the son of David Hennell who was Deputy Warden from 1772 to 1786. They were demolished some time in the nineteenth century.

3. Referral to the European Court of Justice by Arrondissements–rechtbank, Zutphen for a ruling in criminal proceedings against L.N.B. Houtwipper.

4. Delivered on 15 September 1994. (Case C293/93).

5. S.I. 1998 No.2978

6. Susan M. Hare, *Touching Gold and Silver*, op. cit., p.5.

Glossary

ASSAY. A test carried out in order to determine the precious metal content (fineness) of gold, silver or platinum, or an alloy of one of these metals.

ASSAY AND TOUCH. The assaying and hallmarking of a gold or silver article. 'To dismiss from the assay and touch' meant to deny a member of the Company the right to submit articles for hallmarking.

ASSAY BITS or ASSAY PIECES. The 'buttons' of pure silver remaining after the cupellation assay.

ASSAY OFFICE MARK. One of the symbols of a hallmark denoting the Assay Office at which an article was tested and marked.

BASE METAL. Any metal other than a precious metal. The precious metals recognised under the Hallmarking Act 1973 are gold, silver and platinum.

BRITANNIA SILVER. Silver containing a minimum of 11 ounces 10 pennyweights of pure silver in the pound troy or 958.4 parts per thousand. It was the sole standard for silverware from 1697 to 1720 and since then it has remained an additional standard to sterling. Not to be confused with Britannia metal which is an alloy of tin and lead.

BY-ASSAYS. Samples, usually taken from ingots, which were submitted to the Assay Office for a report on their gold or silver content. In former times makers regularly sent such samples to make sure their raw material was up to standard. Sometimes called 'private assays'.

CEMENTATION. An early method of refining or assaying gold.

COARSE WARES. Articles below the minimum legal standard of fineness.

COLOURING. A member of the Company was guilty of colouring if he submitted an article for hallmarking on behalf of a non-member, having first struck his own maker's mark on it. At one time this practice was contrary to the ordinances of the Company and offenders were fined.

CONVOYS. Articles of a fineness well above the minimum standard, which an unscrupulous maker included in a parcel containing substandard articles in the hope that the latter would be unsuspectingly passed by the Assayer.

COURT OF ASSISTANTS. The governing body of the Company, consisting originally of members who had served as wardens, but later including other senior members.

CUPEL. A small cup made of bone ash (or at a later date magnesium oxide) and used in the cupellation assay of gold or silver (qv). The bone ash (also called slow ashes) was moistened and shaped into the required form by compressing in a special mould.

CUPELLATION. A process whereby the base metals are removed from a gold or silver alloy, leaving a residue of the pure precious metal. It is used in both refining and assaying. In the latter context the weighed sample is wrapped in lead foil and transferred to a small cup or cupel (qv) in a heated muffle furnace. The base metals are oxidised and absorbed into the cupel leaving the gold and silver unaffected.

DATE LETTER. One of the symbols of a hallmark taking the form of a letter of the alphabet with a surrounding shield. First introduced by the Goldsmiths' Company in 1478 to identify the assayer and touchwarden responsible for assaying and marking an article. The date letter is now changed on 1st January each year but before 1975 on a day in May (or sometimes in June or July) when the wardens took office. It ceased to be a mandatory symbol after 1st January 1999.

DIET. (Supposedly from the Latin 'dies' meaning 'a day'). The sample removed from articles submitted to the Assay Office, or more usually that part of the sample (in the form of scrapings or cuttings) which was retained by the Company – partly to compensate for the work involved in hallmarking and partly for the purpose of the 'Trial of the Diet' (qv).

DOUBTFUL PLATE. An article or article found to be below standard on a first assay. At least one further assay is always carried out before an article is rejected.

DRAWING. The process of taking samples (usually by scraping) from articles of gold or silver for the purpose of assay. The samples so removed were called 'drawings' and the person who carried out the operation a 'drawer'. Samples could sometimes be taken in the form of 'cuttings'.

ENGRAVER. In the context of the Assay Office, the title of the person appointed by the Company to make the hallmarking punches.

FINENESS. The proportion of pure gold, silver or platinum in an alloy of one of these metals. 'Fine gold' or 'fine silver' means pure gold or pure silver respectively.

FINER. A finer (refiner) was a member of a branch of the trade which specialised in producing pure precious metals from scrap or other sources. The finers supplied working goldsmiths and sometimes also the Mint, with either the pure metal or an alloy of the correct legal standard – such as sterling silver. In the early days the finers had their own association but were bound to observe the ordinances of the Company, many of them being full members of it.

FIRE-ASSAY METHOD. A method of assaying gold or silver involving cupellation (qv).

GATES or GETTS. Now usually called 'sprues'. Small projections on articles or parts of articles which have been made by casting. They result from the channels through which the molten metal enters the mould and are frequently left on an article when it is sent for hallmarking so that the 'drawer' can take a sample without any risk of causing damage.

GOLDSMITH. The word originally referred to a worker or craftsman in gold or silver – as in 'working goldsmith'. Also used to denote a member of the Goldsmiths' Company.

HALLMARK. A mark (or series of marks) struck at one of the authorised assay offices to show that a gold, silver or platinum article has been assayed and is not less than the indicated standard of fineness. Literally a mark struck at Goldsmiths' Hall.

LARGEWORKER. A maker of such articles as gold or silver drinking vessels, dishes or candlesticks.

LIVERY. The Livery or liverymen are those senior members of a City Company whose status is between that of the Freemen and the Court of Assistants. At one time they were entitled to wear special clothing – hence the name.

MAKER'S MARK. Introduced by statute in 1363. Originally took the form of a device but later the initials of the maker or firm were used. Between 1697 and 1720 when the Britannia standard was compulsory the maker's mark had to consist of the first two letters of his surname. It is now known as the 'sponsor's mark' because it is the registered mark of the person or firm responsible for submitting the article to the assay office and not necessarily that of the actual maker. All sponsors' marks have to be registered at an assay office and records are kept of each individual punch.

PARTING. An operation in the fire-assay method for gold, whereby the the pure gold is separated from silver in the bead resulting from cupellation. This is achieved by treating the flattened bead with boiling nitric acid (aqua fortis).

PLATE. 'Plate', 'silver plate' and 'gold plate' are general terms to denote articles of silver or gold. They are sometimes incorrectly used to describe silver-plated (EPNS) or gold-plated articles; but 'Sheffield Plate' is a correct description for articles made from sheet formed by rolling a bar of copper in contact with a thinner bar of silver.

PLATEWORKER. See LARGEWORKER,

PRECIOUS METAL. Gold, silver and platinum are defined as precious metals under the Hallmarking Act 1973.

PRIME WARDEN. The first or senior warden of the Goldsmiths' Company, but called 'Master' in most other City Livery Companies.

PRIVATE ASSAYS. See BY-ASSAYS.

PUNCH or PUNCHEON. A steel die used for striking a hallmark or other mark – either by hand or press.

QUARTERAGE. A quarterly payment imposed on its members by a City Livery Company.

RENTER. A member of the Company responsible for collecting the rents of its properties and for overseeing repairs. Formerly two liverymen of standing were elected renters each year but the post is now abolished.

SAD ASSAY. An assay carried out on a solid sample (as opposed to scrapings).

SMALLWORKER. A maker of small gold or silver articles such as buttons, buckles, brooches or snuff-boxes.

SOLDER. The metal alloy used for joining separately fabricated parts of an article. In the case of silver, the solder must necessarily have a lower fineness than the parts themselves – hence the necessity for regulations to prohibit excessive use. A typical solder for sterling silver wares contains approximately two thirds fine silver and one third base metal.

SPONSOR'S MARK. See MAKER'S MARK.

STANDARD MARK. A symbol or symbols showing the standard of fineness of a gold, silver or platinum article; eg a lion passant to denote the sterling standard.

STERLING. The standard adopted from early times for both silver coinage and silverware, namely 11 ounces 2 pennyweights of pure silver in one pound troy or 925 parts per thousand. The derivation of the word is obscure.

TOUCH. The word was formerly used in more than one sense. It could refer to a standard of fineness or it could mean an official mark, especially a hallmark; but if used as a verb ('to touch') it meant to strike a hallmark on an article. 'A touch assay' signified a test carried out by the touchstone method. See also ASSAY AND TOUCH.

TOUCHSTONE. A hard black stone used in one method of testing gold and silver articles. Also refers to the method itself, as in 'the touchstone test'.

TOUCH-NEEDLES. Alloys of gold or silver of known composition, usually in the form of small strips or 'needles' used in the touchstone test.

TOUCHWARDEN. The Junior or Fourth Warden, whose responsibility it was to attend in the Assay Office every working day to strike the mark of the leopard's head on articles passed by the Assayer and to maintain a general supervision of the work of the office. The Fourth Warden was relieved of these duties after the appointment of the first Deputy Warden in 1731 and the title 'Touchwarden' was then no longer used.

TRANSPOSING. The fraudulent act of cutting a hallmark out of one article and incorporating it in another one, either of silver or base metal.

TRIAL OF THE DIET. A periodic assay of the accumulated portions of diet (qv), the purpose of which was to confirm the accuracy of the work of the Assayer. The trial was carried out at least annually by a Committee of members of the Court of Assistants.

TRIAL PLATE or TRIAL PIECE. An ingot or sheet of gold or silver of an exact legal standard (or more recently of fine gold or silver), samples from which are used as controls when assaying. Those used for the assay of the coinage – for example at the Trial of the Pyx – are variously described in old records as 'the King's trial piece', 'the indented piece' or 'the standard in His Majesty's Treasury', but here they are referred to throughout as 'trial plates' to differentiate them from the similar 'trial pieces' which were used by the Assay Office when assaying articles submitted for hallmarking. Trial plates of pure copper and pure nickel are now used at the Trial of the Pyx for the assay of cupronickel coins and one of pure zinc for nickel- brass coins.

TRIAL OF THE PYX. An examination by a jury to ascertain that the coins made by the Royal Mint are of the proper weight and composition (nowadays also diameter) required by law. Since 1560 the jury has been composed entirely of members of the Goldsmiths' Company.

TROY WEIGHT. A system of weights comprising grains, pennyweights (dwt), ounces (oz) and pounds, formerly used as the sole basis for recording the weight of precious metals and precious metal articles.. There were 24 grains to one pennyweight, 20 pennyweights to one troy ounce and 12 ounces to one troy pound. The prices of gold and silver bullion are still quoted per troy ounce but the other troy weight denominations are no longer legal measures. The troy ounce and troy pound are not identical to the avoirdupois ounce and pound. (1 oz troy = 1.09714 oz avoirdupois).

WEIGHER. A member of the staff of the Assay Office charged with the duty of weighing the contents of parcels of articles submitted for hallmarking and of re-weighing them after they have been marked. In the past he often had other duties, such as examining articles to see that they did not contain excessive solder and supervising the 'drawers'. After 1716 when charges were introduced for marking small wares, the Weigher was also responsible for collecting the payments and keeping accounts.

WET or HUMID METHOD (of Assay). An accurate method of assaying silver devised in 1830 by the French chemist Joseph-Louis Gay-Lussac. It was superior in some respects to the fire-assay method and was eventually adopted by the Royal Mint and later by the Assay Office. It is often referred to as the 'Gay-Lussac method'.

WORKMAN, WORKER or WORKING GOLDSMITH. The word normally used in the Company's minute books to denote a maker of either gold or silver wares.

WORSE or BETTER (Wo or Br). Used in expressing the fineness of a gold or silver alloy or article by reference to a particular standard. Before the adoption of the millesimal system the result of a silver assay was customarily expressed as so many ounces and pennyweights in the pound troy 'better' or 'worse' than the sterling standard.

Bibliography

The following list contains sources – other than the records of the Goldsmiths' Company – which have been of assistance in writing this book.

Acts of the Privy Council, 1629–30, 1630–1.

AGRICOLA, GEORGIUS, *De Re Metallica*, Basel, 1556. Translated by H.C. and L.H. Hoover, London, 1912.

ALDRIDGE, W.J., *The Goldsmiths' Repository*, London, 1789.

ALMACK, EDWARD, *A Bibliography of the King's Book or Eikon Basilike*, London, 1896.

ATKINS, S.E., AND OVERALL, W.H., *Some Account of the Worshipful Company of Clockmakers*, privately printed, 1881.

BEAVEN, A.B., *The Aldermen of the City of London*, 2 vols., 1908–13.

BIRCH, THOMAS, *The History of the Royal Society*, Vol.I, London, 1756–7

BIRINGGUCCIO, VANNICCIO, *De la Pirotechnia*. First edition, Venice, 1540. Translated by C.S. Smith and M.T. Gnudi, New York, 1942.

Board of Trade Working Party Reports, Jewellery & Silverware, HMSO, London, 1946.

Calendar of Patent Rolls.

Calendar of State Papers, Domestic.

Calendar of Treasury Books.

CARRINGTON, J.B., and HUGHES, G.R., *The Plate of the Worshipful Company of Goldsmiths*, Oxford, 1926.

CHAFFERS, WILLIAM, *Hallmarks on Gold and Silver Plate*, London, 1875.

CHALLIS, C.E., *The Tudor Coinage*, Manchester, 1978.

CHALLIS, C.E., editor, *A New History of the Royal Mint*, Cambridge, 1992

CHANDLER, GEORGE, *Four Centuries of Banking*, London, 1954.

Commission des Monnaies – Ordonnances Royales du Juin 1830, Tarif, instruction et Rapports sur le Nouveau Mode d'Essai des Éspèces et Matières d'Argent, Paris, 1830.

CONNOR, R.D., *The Weights & Measures of England*, London, 1987.

CRAIG, SIR JOHN, *The Mint*, Cambridge, 1953.

CRAMER, J.A., AND MORTIMER, *Elements of the Art of Assaying Metals*, 1764.

CULME, JOHN, 'The goose in a dotted circle', The Jaime Ortiz-Patino Collection, Catalogue, Sotheby's, New York, May 1992.

CULME, JOHN, *The Directory of Gold and Silversmiths, Jewellers and Allied Traders*, 2 vols., Woodbridge, 1987.

DALE, T.C., *Inhabitants of London in 1638*, London, 1931.

Dictionary of National Biography.

DOVE, ANTHONY B.L., 'Some New Light on Plate Duty and its Marks', *Antique Collecting*, Vol. 19, No.4, 1984.

ERCKER, LAZARUS, *Allerfurnemisten Mineralischen Erzt und Berckwerken . . .* , First edition Prague, 1574. Translated as *Lazarus Ercker's Treatise on Ores and Assaying* by A.G. Sisco and C.S. Smith, Chicago, 1951.

EVANS, GEO.G., *Illustrated History of the U.S. Mint.*

EWEN, C.L'ESTRANGE, *Lotteries and Sweepstakes*, 1932.

Exchequer etc. documents, various, PRO.

FORBES, J.S. and DALLADAY, D.B., 'Metallic Impurities in the Silver Coinage Trial Plates', *J. Institute of Metals*, Vol.87, 1958/9.

GAIRDNER, JAMES, *Letters and Papers Foreign & Domestic of the Reign of Henry VIII*, Vol.VII.

GAY-LUSSAC, J.L., *Instruction sur l'Essai des Matières d'Argent par la Voie Humide*, La Commission des Monnaies et Medailles, Paris, 1832.

GILL, MARGARET A.V., *A Directory of Newcastle Goldsmiths*, 1980.

GLANVILLE, PHILLIPA, 'Robert Amadas, Goldsmith', *Proceedings of the Silver Society*, 1984, Vol.III, No.5.

GLOVER, ELIZABETH, *The Gold and Silver Wyre Drawers*, London, 1979.

GRIERSON, P., *Anglo-Saxon Coins, Studies presented to F.M. Stenton*, London, 1961.

GRIMSHAW, MARGARET, *The Society of Silver Collectors, Proceedings 1972–4*, Vol II, 8.

GRIMWADE, ARTHUR G., *London Goldsmiths 1697–1837, Their Marks & Lives*, London, 1976.

H.G. (HANNIBAL GAMON), *The Goldsmythes Storehowse*, handwritten, 1604.

HARE, SUSAN M., *Touching Gold and Silver*, Catalogue of exhib. at Goldsmiths' Hall, 1978.

HEAL, SIR AMBROSE, *The London Goldsmiths, 1200–1800*, 1935.

HELLOT, J., TILLET, M., and MAQUER, P.J., *Mém. Acad. Roy. Sciences*, Paris, 1763.

HENNELL, P., 'The Hennells Identified', *The Connoisseur*, Dec. 1955.

HENNELL, PERCY, 'The Hennells – a Continuity of Craftsmanship', *The Connoisseur*, Feb. 1973.

HENNELL, PERCY, 'Hennell Silver Salt Cellars, 1736–1876', Hennell, 1986.

Historical Manuscripts Commission, 8th Report.

HOW, G.E.P., and HOW, J.P., Silver Spoons and Pre-Elizabethan Hall-Marks on English Plate, Privately printed, 1957.

HUGHES, P.L., and LARKIN, J.F., *Tudor Royal Proclamations*, Newhaven & London, 1964–9

HUNT, L.B., *The Metallurgist and Materials Technologist*, July 1980, pp.392–394.

JACKSON, SIR CHARLES, *English Goldsmiths and their Marks*, 1905 (reprinted 1949).

JOHNSON, P.V.A., 'The Lyon and Twynam Forgeries', *Proceedings of the Silver Society*, 1979–81.

KENT, TIMOTHY ARTHUR, *London Silver Spoonmakers 1500–1697*, London 1981.

Lansdowne Mss., BM.

Harleian Mss., BM.

LONG, THOMAS, *Dr. Walker's Account of the Author of Eikon Basilike*, London 1693.

MARTIN, J. BIDDULPH, *The Grasshopper in Lombard Street*, London, 1892.

MCDONALD, DONALD, *Percival Norton Johnson*, Johnson Matthey & Co. Ltd., 1951.

MCDONALD, DONALD, and HUNT, LESLIE B., *A History of Platinum and its Allied Metals*, London, 1982.

MCMURRAY, WM., *A City Church Chronicle*, 1914.

MCMURRAY, WM., *The Records of Two City Churches*, 1925.

NATHANSON, ALAN J., *Thomas Simon, his life and work, 1618–1665*, London, 1975.

ODDY, A., 'Assaying in Antiquity', *Gold Bulletin*, 1983, 16, (2).

PICKFORD, IAN, editor, *Jackson's Silver & Gold Marks*, Woodbridge, 1989.

PRIDEAUX, SIR WALTER SHERBURNE, *Memorials of the Goldsmiths' Company*.

Probierbuchlein auff Golt Silber Kupfer . . . First printed circa. 1520. Translated by A.G. Sisco and C.S. Smith in *Bergwerk und Probierbuchlein*, New York, 1949.

REDDAWAY, T.F., 'Elizabethan London – Goldsmiths' Row in Cheapside, 1558–1645', *Goldsmiths' Miscellany*, Vol ii, No.5, 1963.

REDDAWAY, T.F., and WALKER, LORNA T.M., *The Early History of the Goldsmiths' Company, 1327–1509*, London, 1975.

Report from the Select Committee on the Royal Mint, Printed by Order of the House of Commons, 1837.

Report from the Committee appointed to enquire into the Manner of Conducting the

Several Assay Offices in London, York, Exeter, Bristol, Chester, Norwich and Newcastle upon Tyne, printed 1773.

Report of the Departmental Committee on Hallmarking, Cmnd.663, HMSO, London, 1959.

Report of the Commissioners appointed to inquire into the Constitution, Management and Expense of the Royal Mint, printed by order of the House of Commons, HMSO, 1849.

Report from the Select Committee on Silver and Gold Wares, printed by order of the House of Commons, May 1856.

Report from the Select Committee on Gold and Silver (Hall Marking) together with the proceedings of the Committee, Minutes of Evidence and Appendix, 1879.

Royal Mint records, MINT1 and MINT19, PRO.

Royal Mint, Fourth Annual Report, 1873.

Royal Mint, Thirtieth Annual Report, 1899.

RUDING, R., *Annals of the Coinage of Great Britain*, 3 vols., 1840.

SPRATT, THOMAS, *The History of the Royal Society*, 1677.

STEWART, HORACE, *History of the Worshipful Company of Gold and Silver Wyre-Drawers*, London, 1891.

SYMONDS, R.W., 'English Furniture in Portugal', *The Connoisseur*, June 1940,

THUILE, J., *L'Orfèvrerie en Languedoc*, Vol I, Montpellier, 1966–8.

TILLET, MATTIEU, *Mém. Acad. Roy. Sciences*, Paris, 1760; ibid., 1762; ibid., 1763.

TOVEY, W., *A Trial of Gold and Silver*, London, 1678.

W.B., *A New Touchstone for Gold and Silver Wares*, London, 1679.

WATSON, J.H., *Ancient Trial Plates*, HMSO, London, 1962.

Wills, Commissary Court of London, GL.

Wills, Prerogative Court of Canterbury, PRO.

Photographic acknowledgements

The publishers wish to thank those who have kindly allowed reproduction of photographs. The sources of the photographs are as follows:

page 16   Phillips Fine Art Auctioneers
     20   Trustees of the British Museum
     25   The Folger Shakespeare Library
     27, 30, 69 Society of Antiquaries of London
     41   St Mary's Church, Nettlecombe, Somerset
     54   Trustees of the British Museum
     58, 140 Guildhall Library, Corporation of London
     73   Trustees of the British Museum
     84   The Royal Mint
     94   Guildhall Library, Corporation of London
     103   The Board of Trustees of the Victoria & Albert Museum
     112   Private Collection
     117   St Mary's Church, Fetcham, Surrey
     130   The Royal Mint
     146   The National Portrait Gallery
     149   The National Portrait Gallery
     157   © 1999, Sotheby's, Inc.
     165   The Royal Mint
     169   The Board of Trustees of the Victoria & Albert Museum
     191   The Board of Trustees of the Victoria & Albert Museum
     209   Trustees of the British Museum
     215   Hennell Ltd and Frazer & Haws Ltd
     245   Johnson Matthey plc
     260   Johnson Matthey plc
     263   United Press International (UK) Ltd
     294   Keystone Press Agency Ltd
     309   The Royal Collection © Her Majesty The Queen
     313   Keystone Press Agency Ltd

Index

Page numbers in italic refer to illustrations.